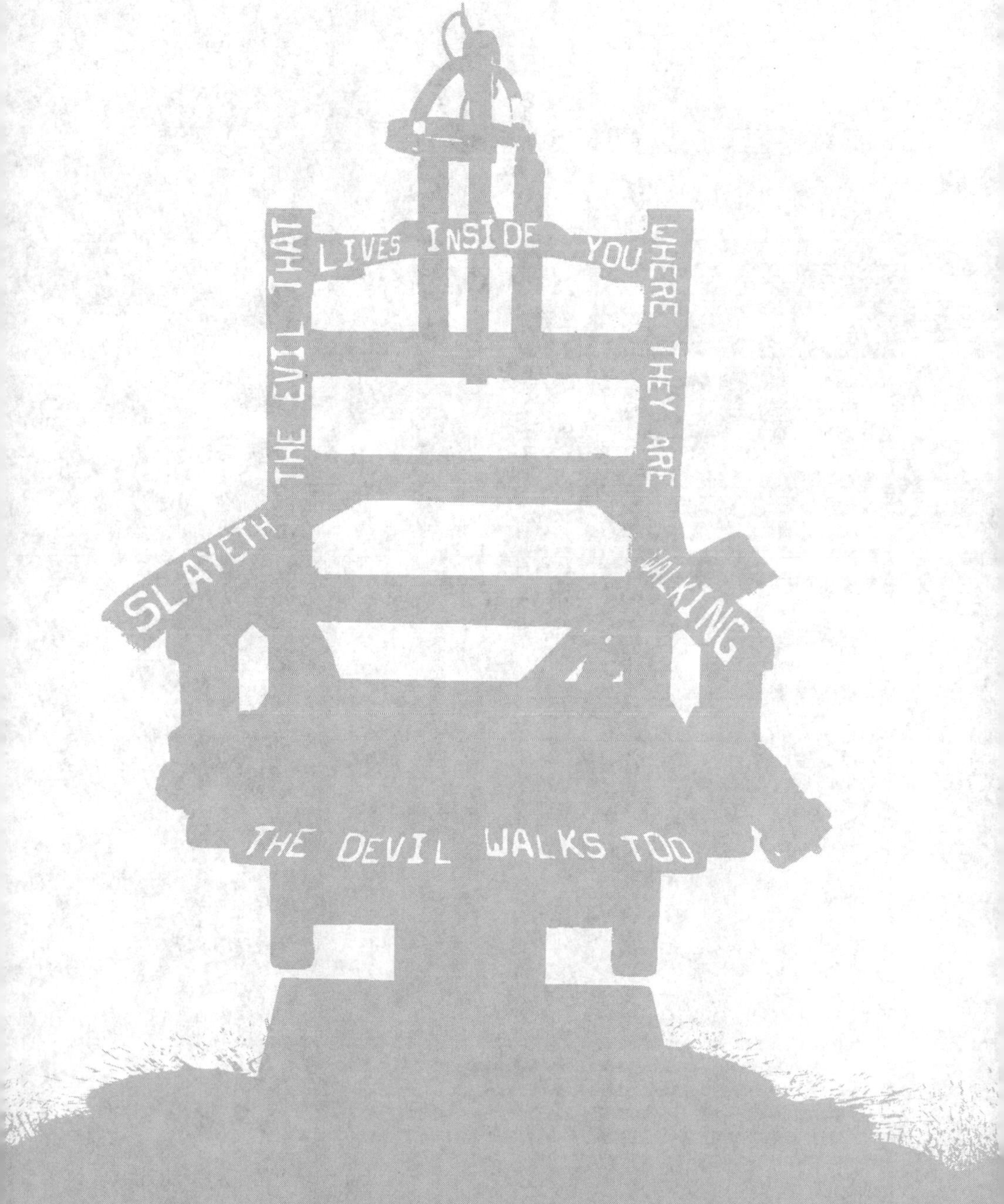
SLAYETH THE EVIL THAT
LIVES INSIDE YOU
WHERE THEY ARE WALKING
THE DEVIL WALKS TOO

ALTERNA COMICS
ALTERNACOMICS.COM

PETER SIMETI
PRESIDENT AND PUBLISHER

FUBAR PRESS
FUBARPRESS.COM

JEFF McCOMSEY
PRESIDENT AND PUBLISHER

JEFF McCLELLAND
STORY EDITOR

THE CHAIR
2016 FIRST PRINTING
THIRD EDITION
9781934985519
Published by Alterna Comics, Inc.

PETER SIMETI

WRITER/DIGITAL INKING/LETTERS/COVER

KEVIN CHRISTENSEN

PENCILS/PLOT CONTRIBUTOR ON ACT SIX

ERIN KOHUT

EDITOR

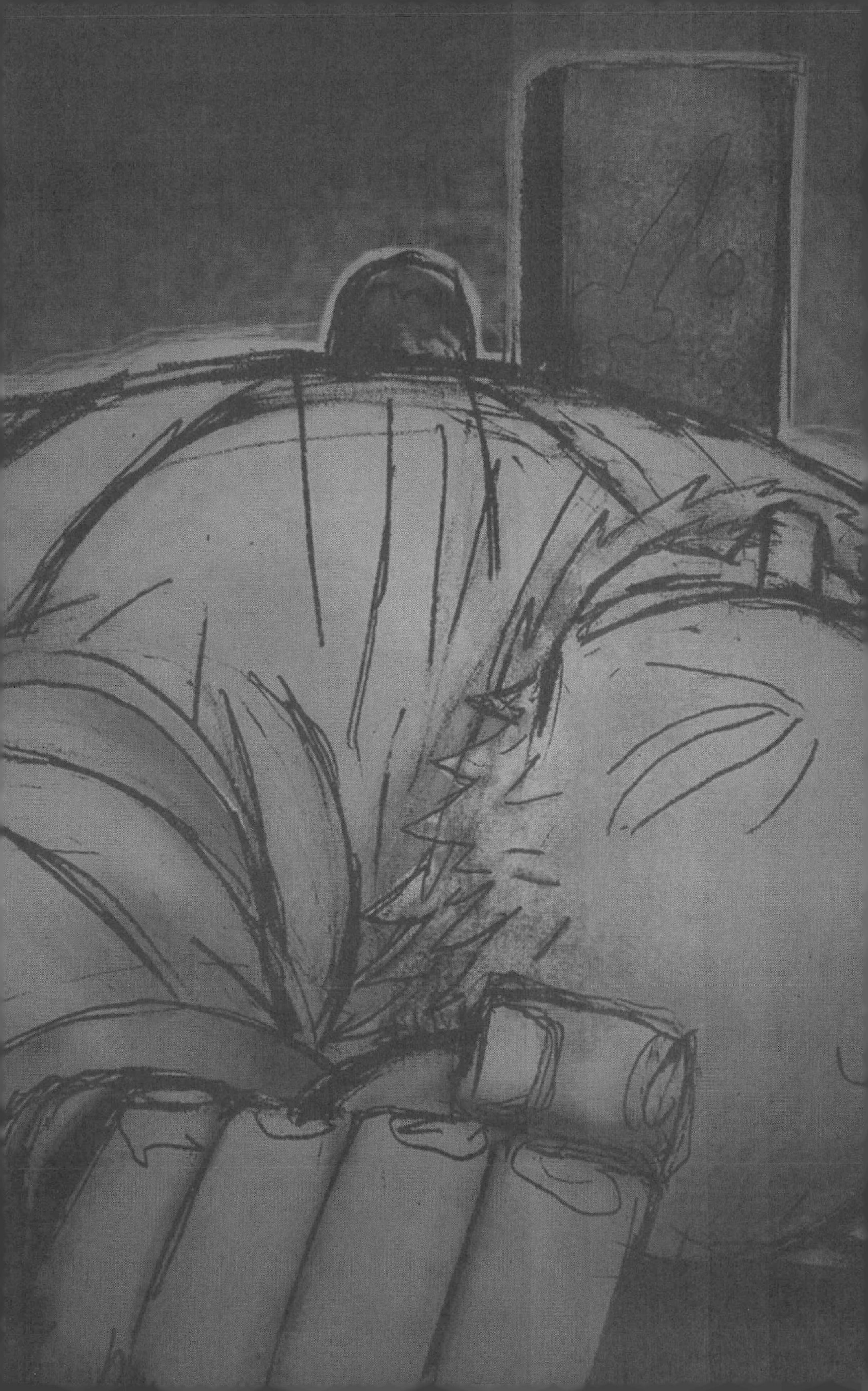

THE CHAIR

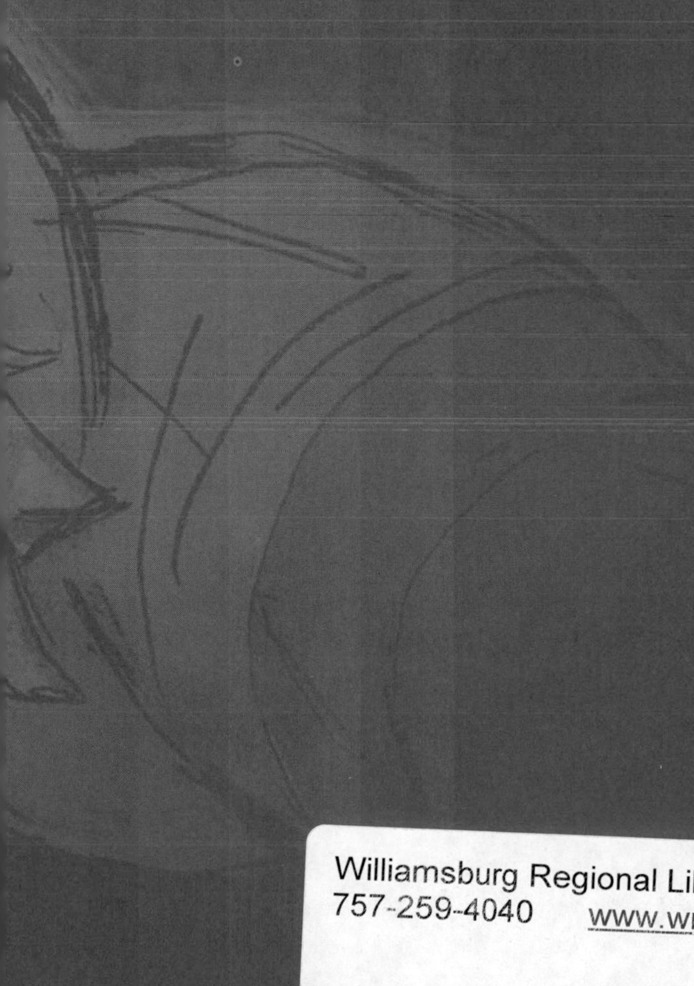

RICHARD SULLIVAN IS AN INNOCENT MAN STRUGGLING TO ESCAPE HIS FATE ON DEATH ROW...

WITNESSING THE BRUTAL KILLINGS OF HIS FELLOW INMATES AT THE HANDS OF THE PRISON'S SADISTIC WARDEN AND HIS CREW OF PSYCHOTIC GUARDS, SULLIVAN BEGINS TO REALIZE THAT HIS DAYS ARE QUICKLY BEING NUMBERED.

MATCHING THE UNSPEAKABLE BRUTALITY OCCURRING IN THE PRISON, SULLIVAN IS PUSHED TO THE BRINK OF MADNESS. WITH HIS OWN HORRIFYING PAST COMING TO THE FOREFRONT, SULLIVAN BEGINS A LONG DESCENT INTO DARKNESS...

ON DEATH ROW, THE ONLY MONSTER IS MAN

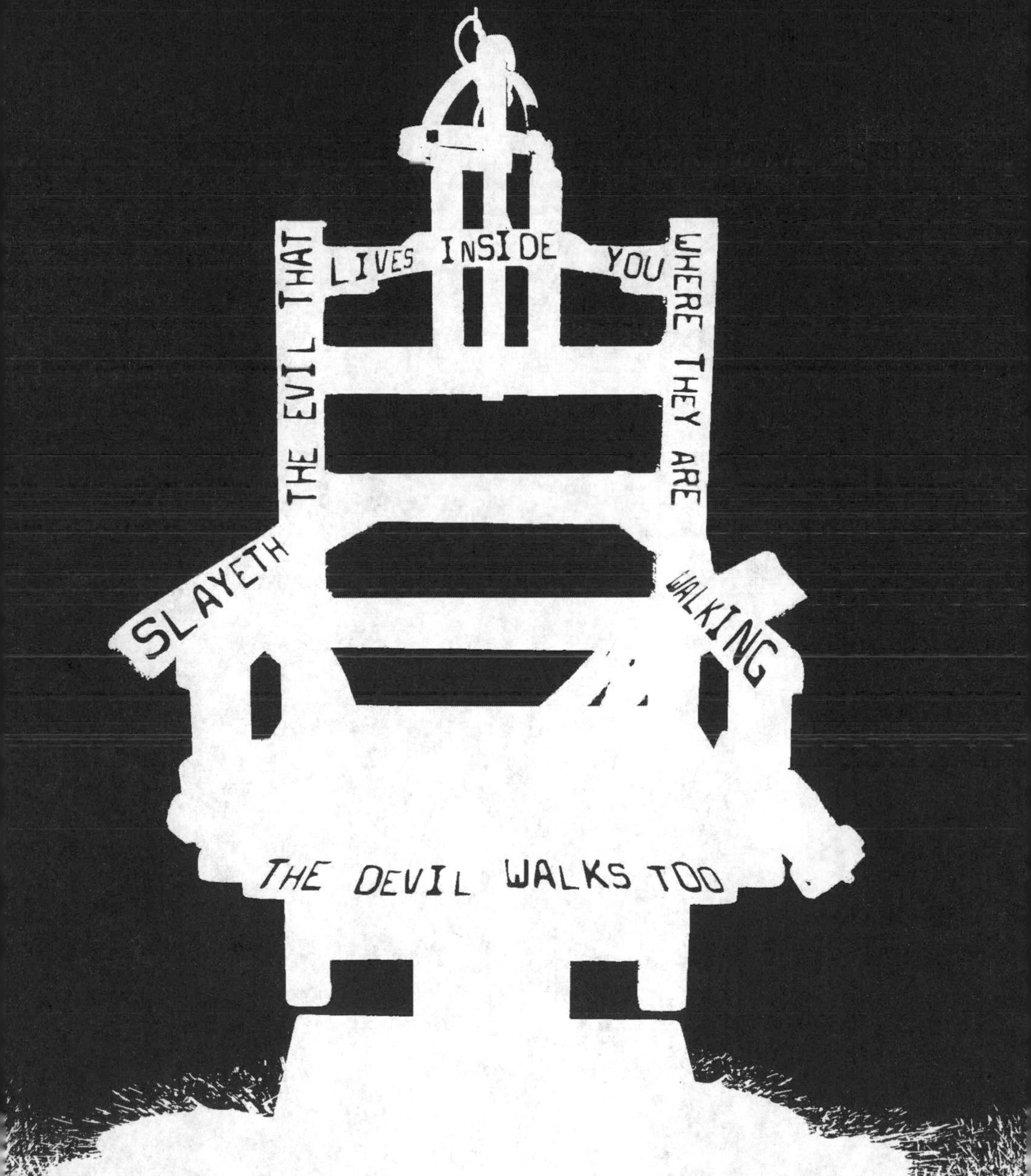
SLAYETH THE EVIL THAT LIVES INSIDE YOU WHERE THEY ARE WALKING
THE DEVIL WALKS TOO

ACT ONE: 12 COUNTS

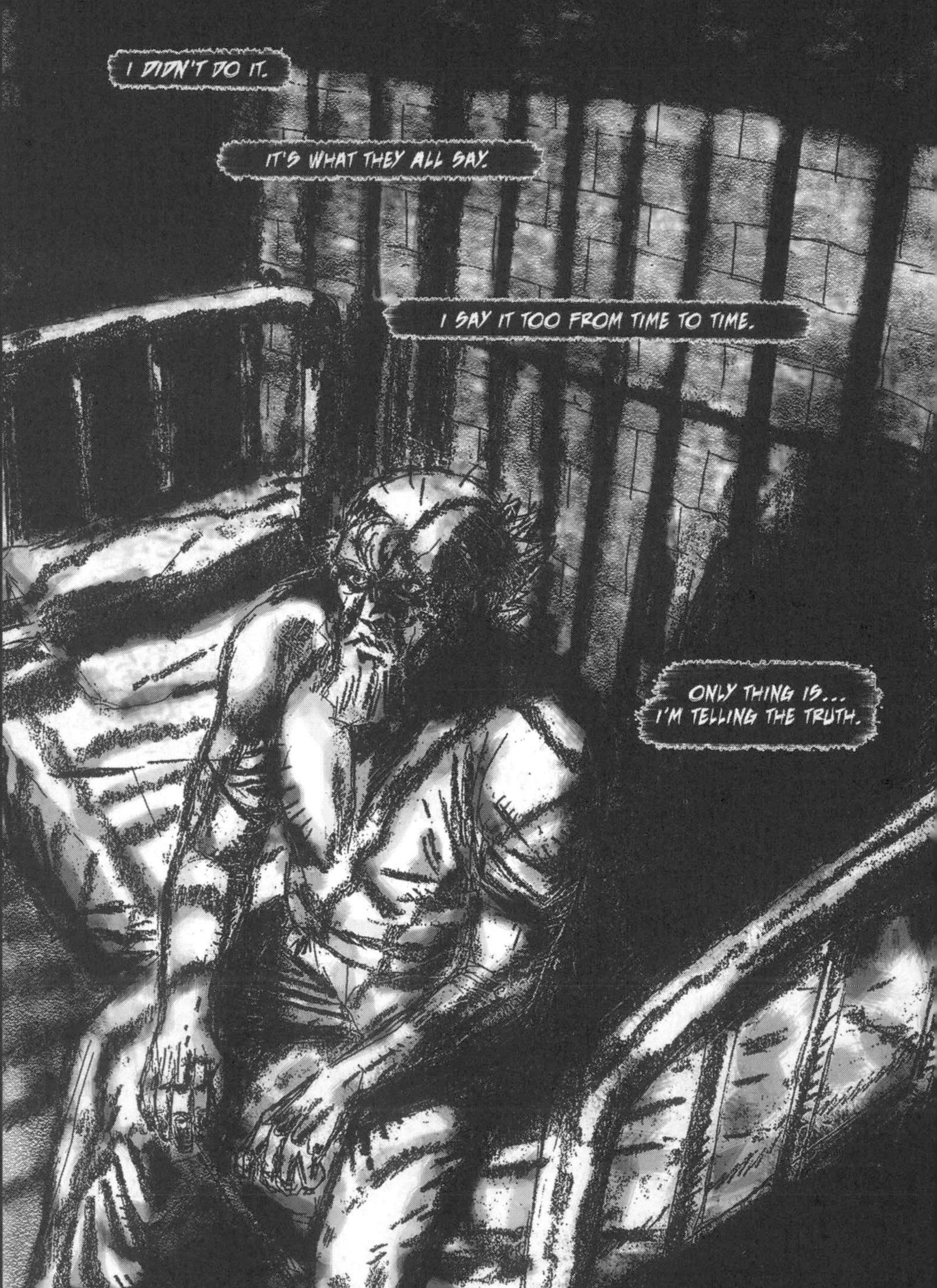
I DIDN'T DO IT.
IT'S WHAT THEY ALL SAY.
I SAY IT TOO FROM TIME TO TIME.
ONLY THING IS... I'M TELLING THE TRUTH.

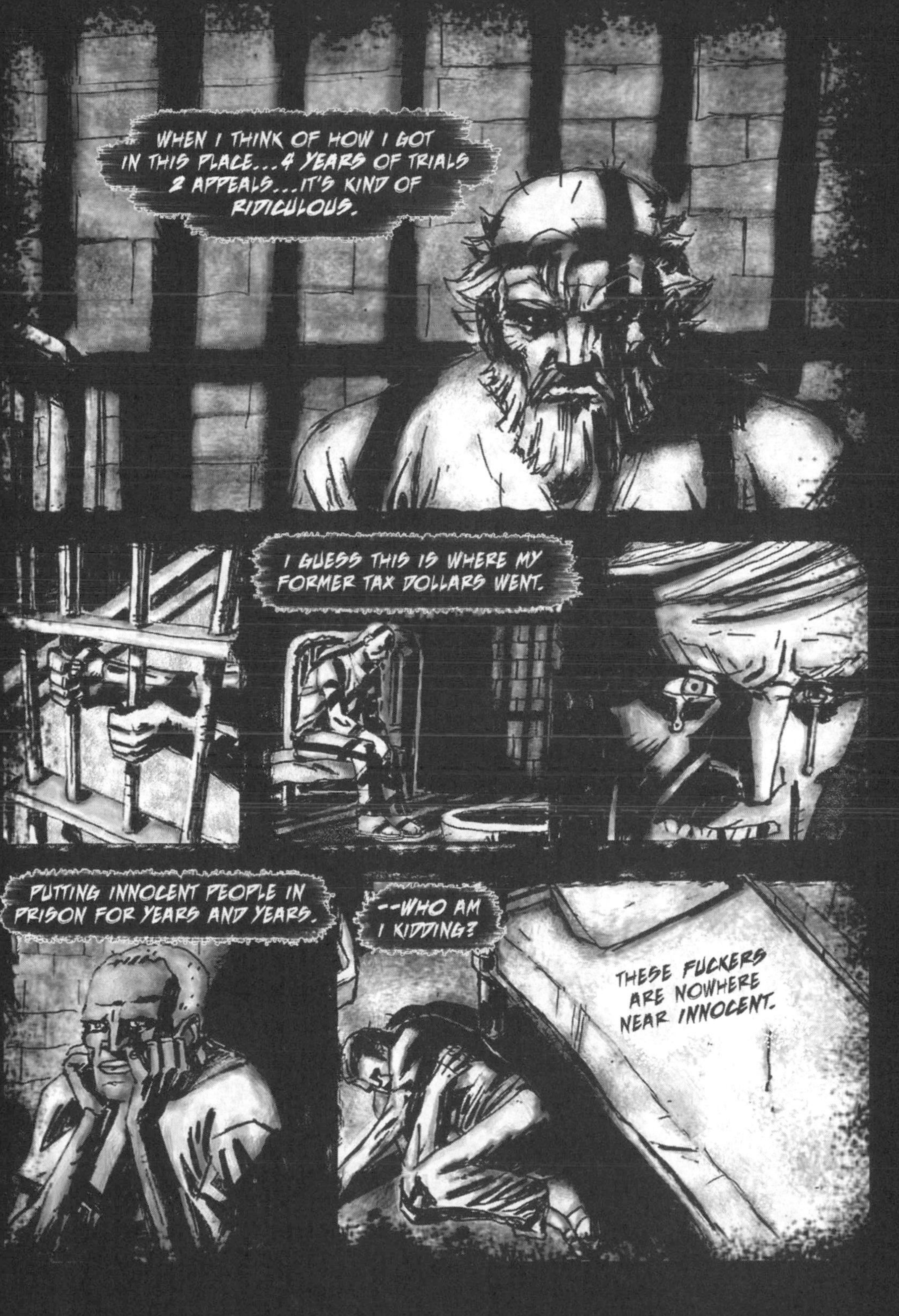
WHEN I THINK OF HOW I GOT IN THIS PLACE...4 YEARS OF TRIALS 2 APPEALS...IT'S KIND OF RIDICULOUS.
I GUESS THIS IS WHERE MY FORMER TAX DOLLARS WENT.
PUTTING INNOCENT PEOPLE IN PRISON FOR YEARS AND YEARS.
--WHO AM I KIDDING?
THESE FUCKERS ARE NOWHERE NEAR INNOCENT.

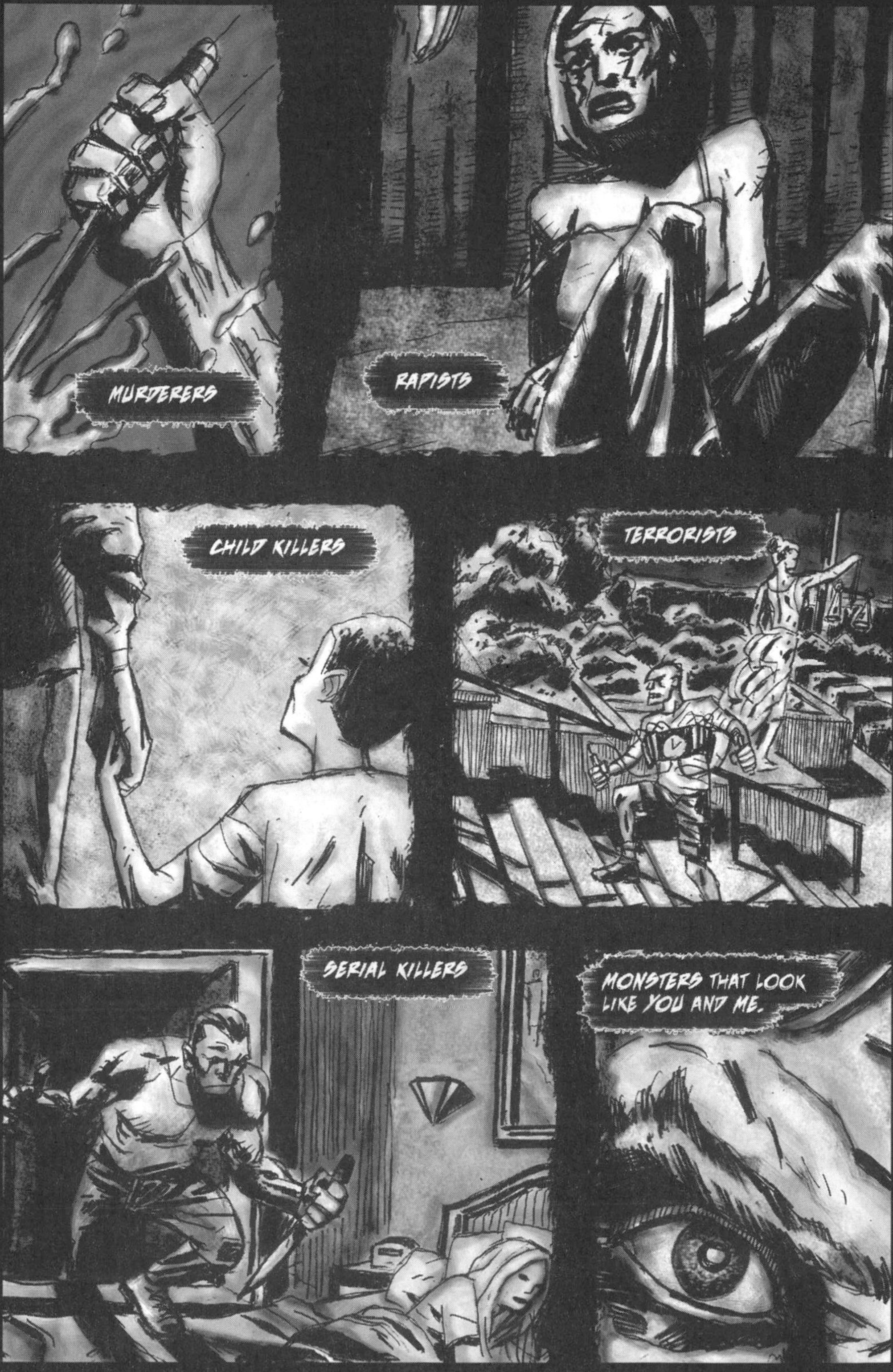
MURDERERS
RAPISTS
CHILD KILLERS
TERRORISTS
SERIAL KILLERS
MONSTERS THAT LOOK LIKE YOU AND ME.

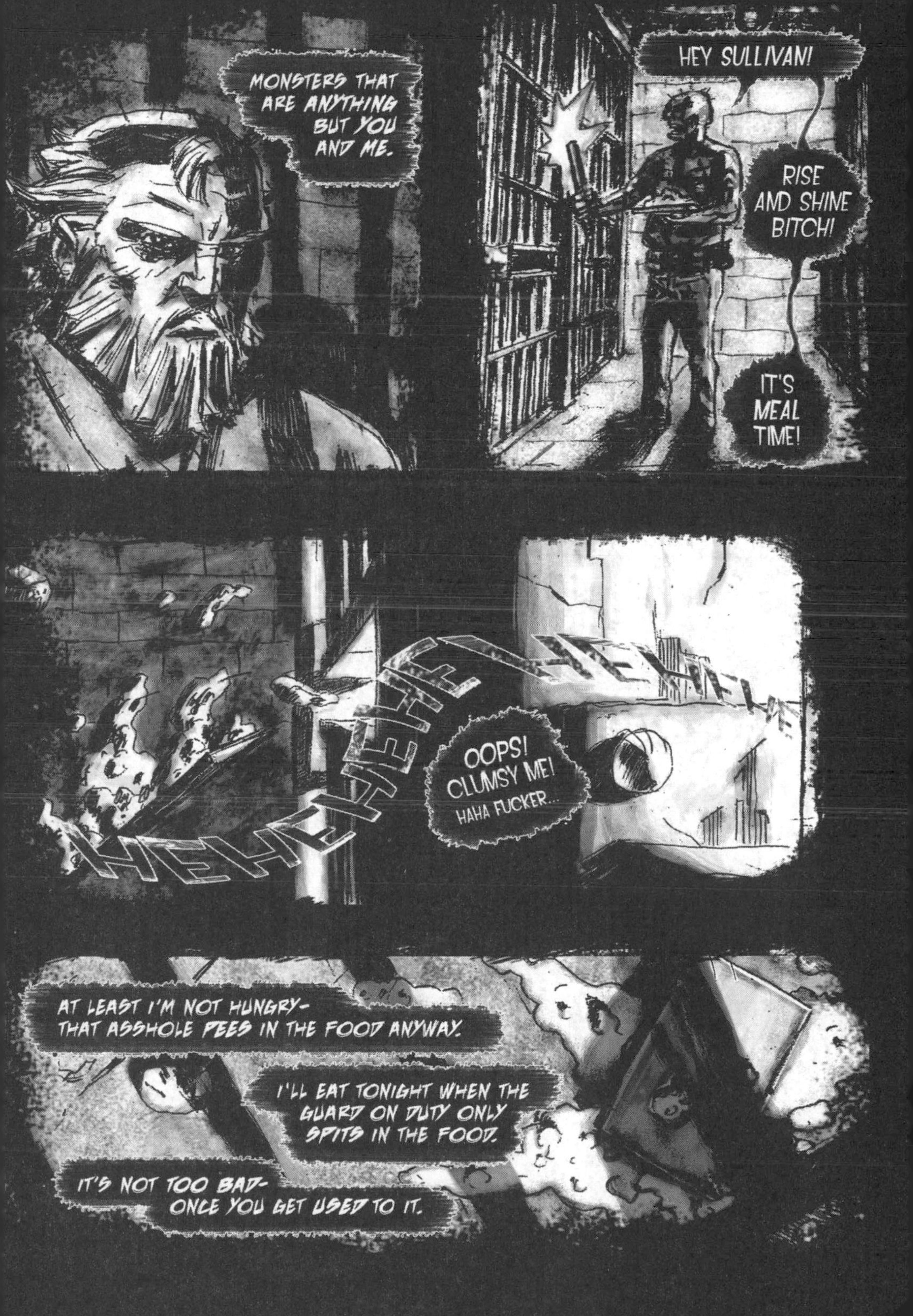
MONSTERS THAT ARE ANYTHING BUT YOU AND ME.
HEY SULLIVAN!
RISE AND SHINE BITCH!
IT'S MEAL TIME!
HEHEHEHEHE
HEHEHE
OOPS! CLUMSY ME! HAHA FUCKER...
AT LEAST I'M NOT HUNGRY- THAT ASSHOLE PEES IN THE FOOD ANYWAY.
I'LL EAT TONIGHT WHEN THE GUARD ON DUTY ONLY SPITS IN THE FOOD.
IT'S NOT TOO BAD- ONCE YOU GET USED TO IT.

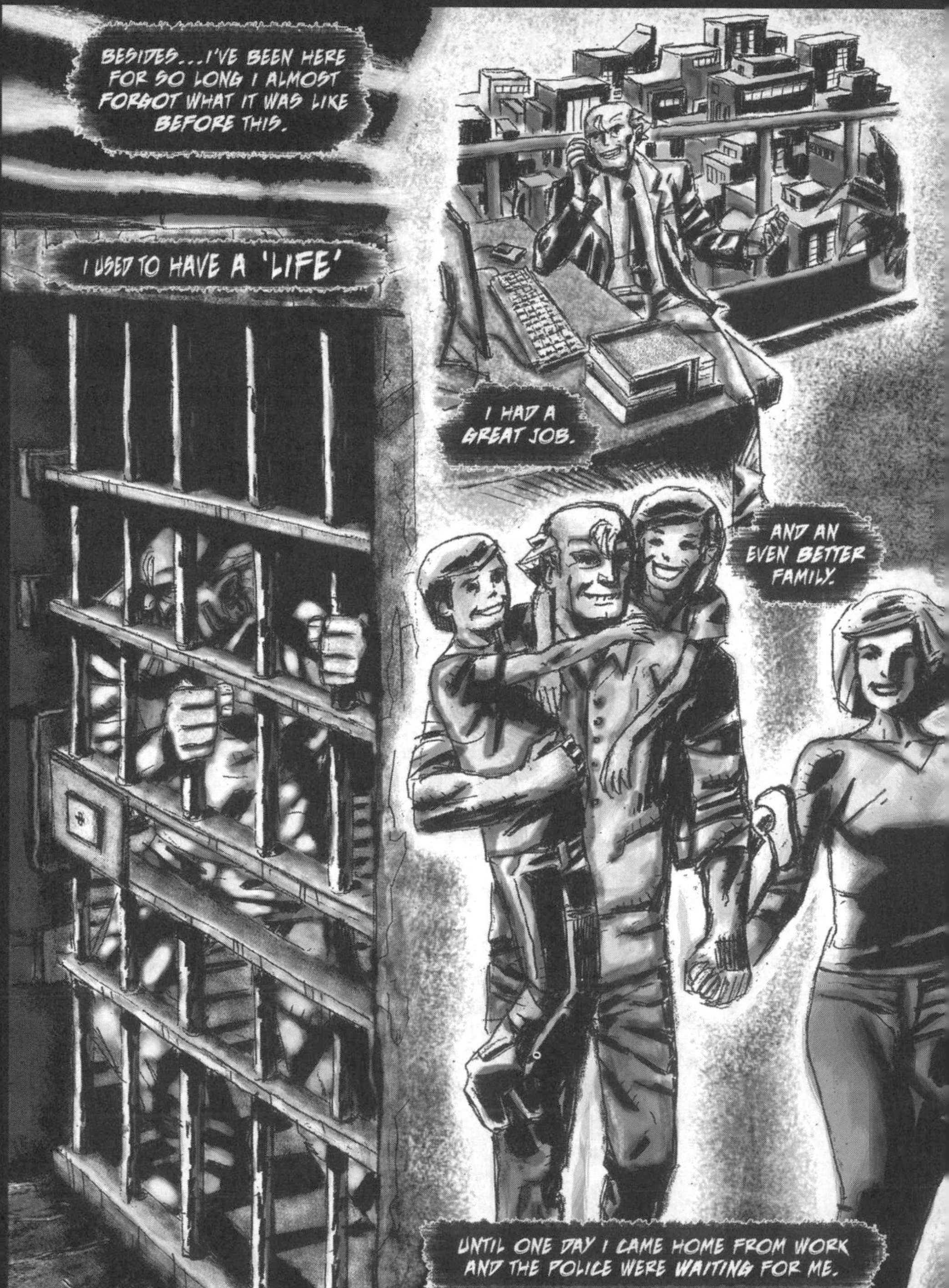
BESIDES...I'VE BEEN HERE FOR SO LONG I ALMOST FORGOT WHAT IT WAS LIKE BEFORE THIS.
I USED TO HAVE A 'LIFE'
I HAD A GREAT JOB.
AND AN EVEN BETTER FAMILY.
UNTIL ONE DAY I CAME HOME FROM WORK AND THE POLICE WERE WAITING FOR ME.

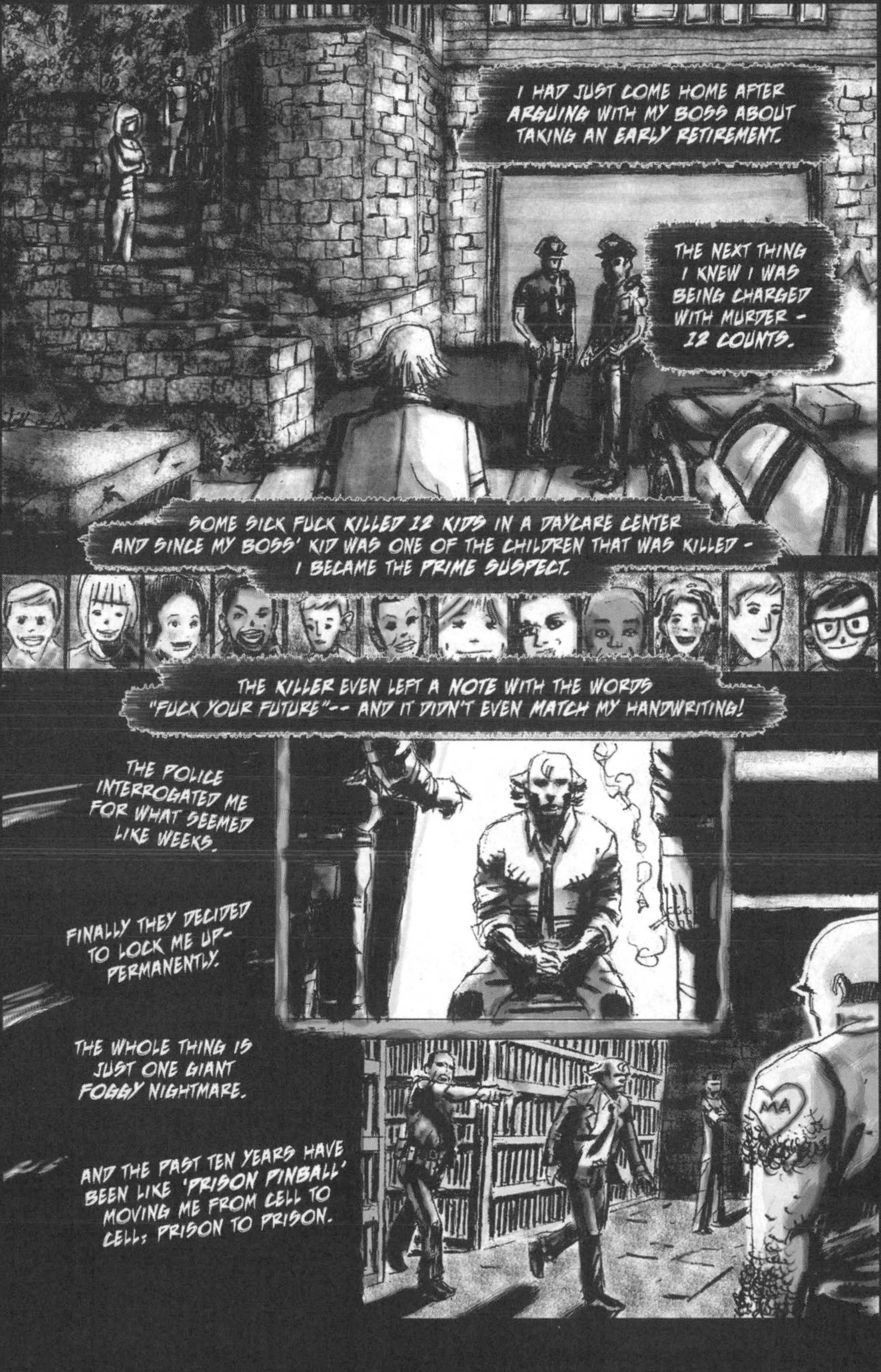

I HAD JUST COME HOME AFTER ARGUING WITH MY BOSS ABOUT TAKING AN EARLY RETIREMENT.
THE NEXT THING I KNEW I WAS BEING CHARGED WITH MURDER - 12 COUNTS.
SOME SICK FUCK KILLED 12 KIDS IN A DAYCARE CENTER AND SINCE MY BOSS' KID WAS ONE OF THE CHILDREN THAT WAS KILLED - I BECAME THE PRIME SUSPECT.
THE KILLER EVEN LEFT A NOTE WITH THE WORDS "FUCK YOUR FUTURE"-- AND IT DIDN'T EVEN MATCH MY HANDWRITING!
THE POLICE INTERROGATED ME FOR WHAT SEEMED LIKE WEEKS.
FINALLY THEY DECIDED TO LOCK ME UP- PERMANENTLY.
THE WHOLE THING IS JUST ONE GIANT FOGGY NIGHTMARE.
AND THE PAST TEN YEARS HAVE BEEN LIKE 'PRISON PINBALL' MOVING ME FROM CELL TO CELL; PRISON TO PRISON.
MA

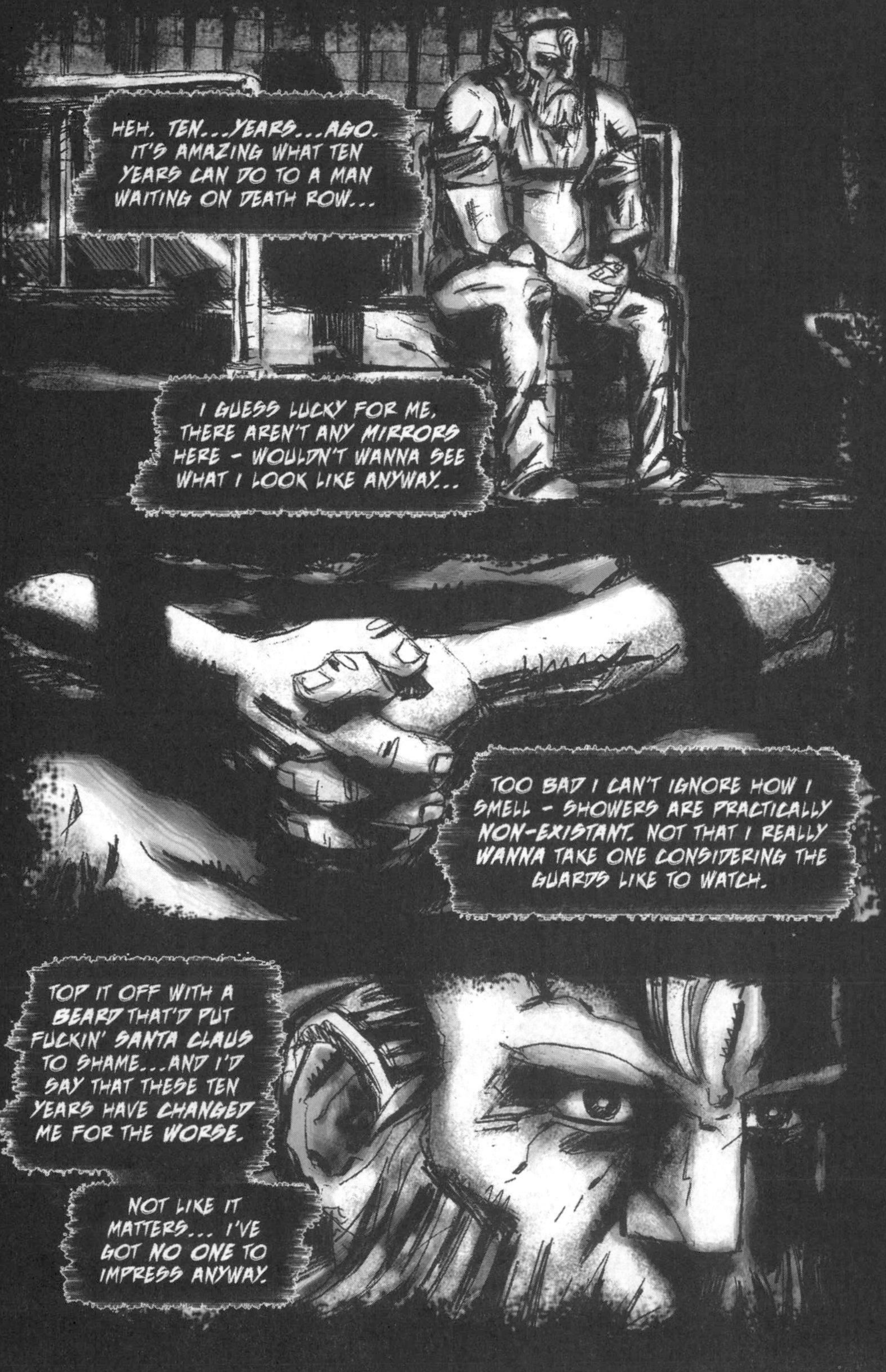
HEH. TEN...YEARS...AGO. IT'S AMAZING WHAT TEN YEARS CAN DO TO A MAN WAITING ON DEATH ROW...
I GUESS LUCKY FOR ME, THERE AREN'T ANY MIRRORS HERE - WOULDN'T WANNA SEE WHAT I LOOK LIKE ANYWAY...
TOO BAD I CAN'T IGNORE HOW I SMELL - SHOWERS ARE PRACTICALLY NON-EXISTANT. NOT THAT I REALLY WANNA TAKE ONE CONSIDERING THE GUARDS LIKE TO WATCH.
TOP IT OFF WITH A BEARD THAT'D PUT FUCKIN' SANTA CLAUS TO SHAME...AND I'D SAY THAT THESE TEN YEARS HAVE CHANGED ME FOR THE WORSE.
NOT LIKE IT MATTERS... I'VE GOT NO ONE TO IMPRESS ANYWAY.

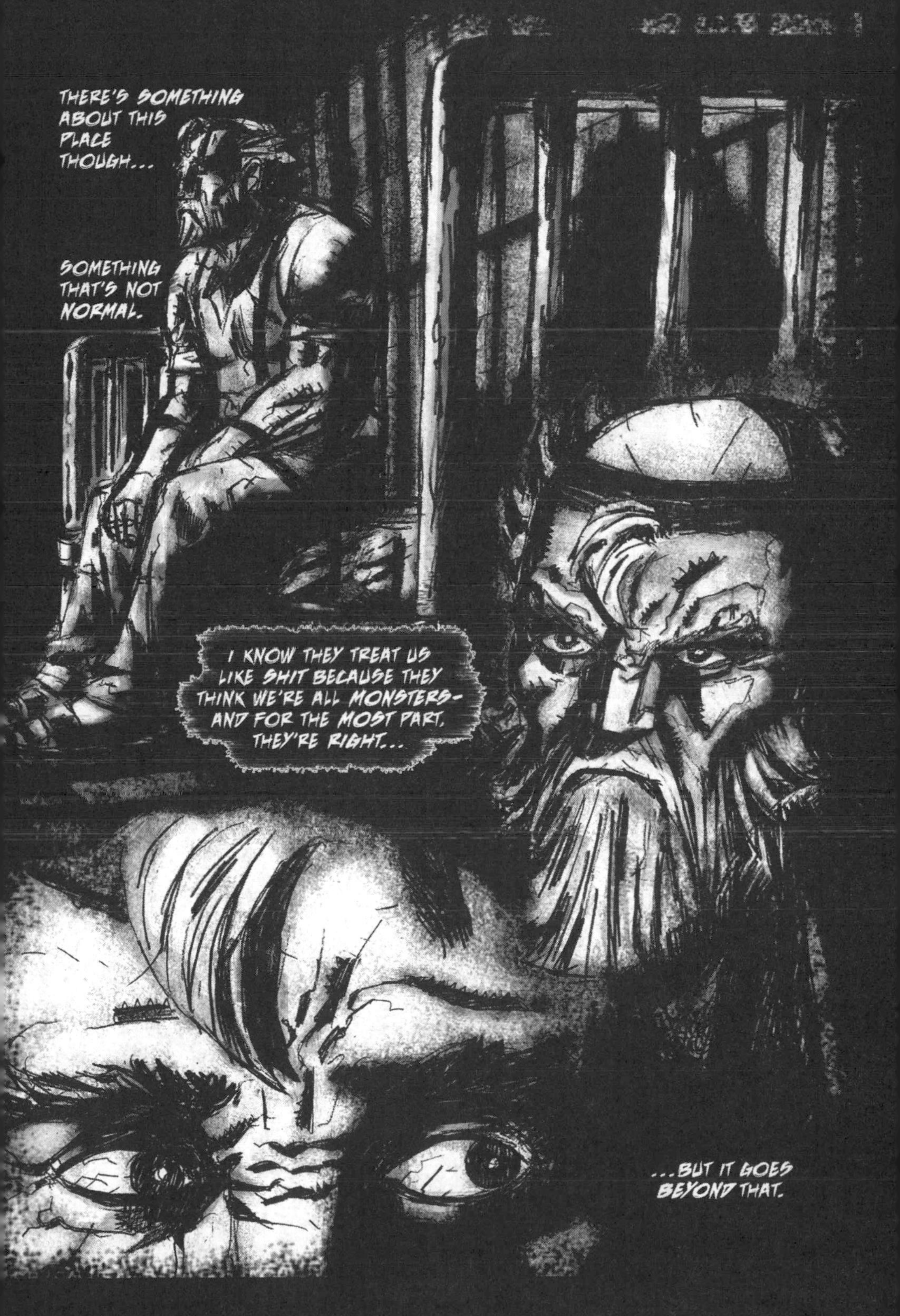
THERE'S SOMETHING ABOUT THIS PLACE THOUGH...
SOMETHING THAT'S NOT NORMAL.
I KNOW THEY TREAT US LIKE SHIT BECAUSE THEY THINK WE'RE ALL MONSTERS- AND FOR THE MOST PART, THEY'RE RIGHT...
...BUT IT GOES BEYOND THAT.

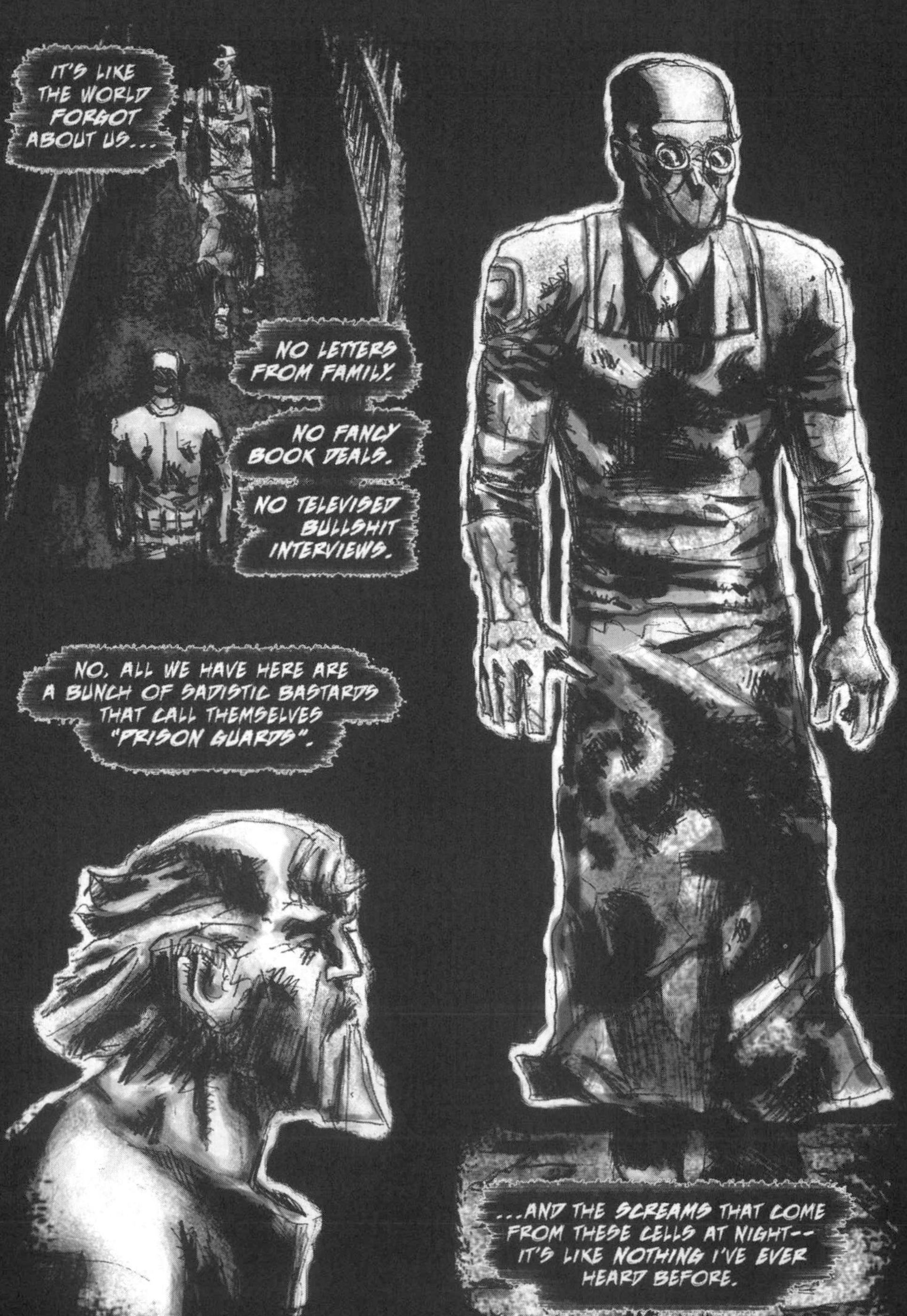
IT'S LIKE THE WORLD FORGOT ABOUT US...
NO LETTERS FROM FAMILY.
NO FANCY BOOK DEALS.
NO TELEVISED BULLSHIT INTERVIEWS.
NO, ALL WE HAVE HERE ARE A BUNCH OF SADISTIC BASTARDS THAT CALL THEMSELVES "PRISON GUARDS".
...AND THE SCREAMS THAT COME FROM THESE CELLS AT NIGHT--IT'S LIKE NOTHING I'VE EVER HEARD BEFORE.

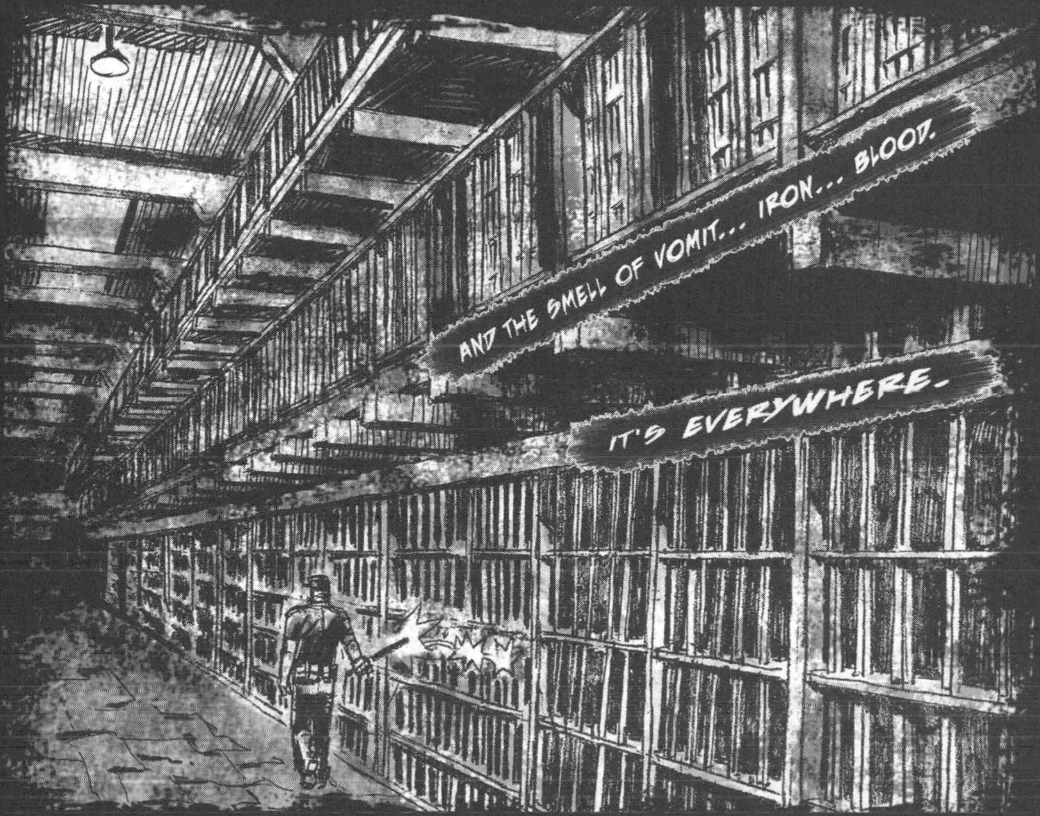
AND THE SMELL OF VOMIT... IRON... BLOOD.
IT'S EVERYWHERE.

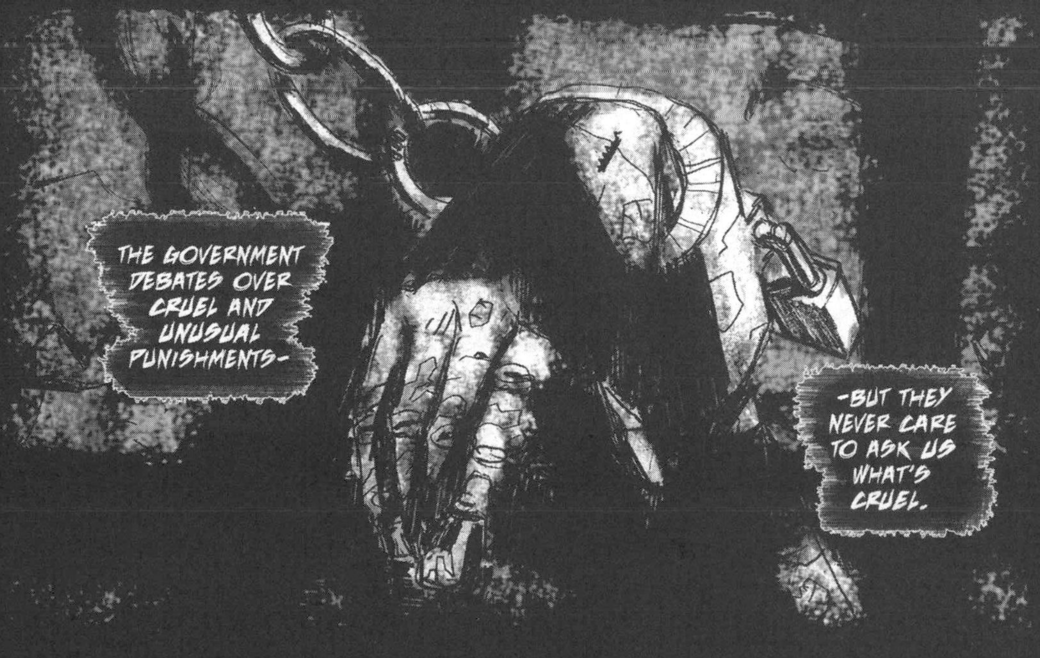
THE GOVERNMENT DEBATES OVER CRUEL AND UNUSUAL PUNISHMENTS-
-BUT THEY NEVER CARE TO ASK US WHAT'S CRUEL.

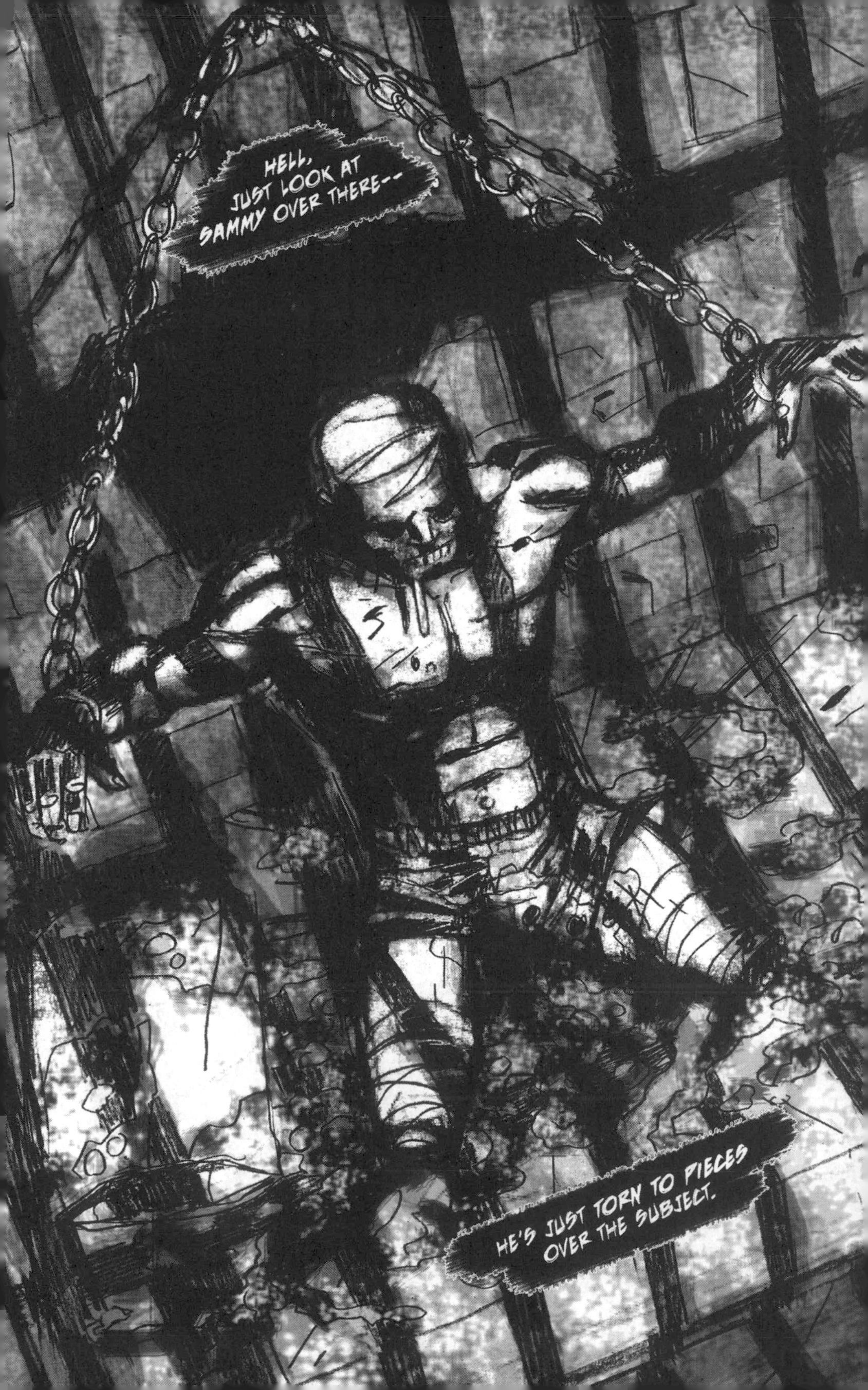
HELL, JUST LOOK AT SAMMY OVER THERE--
HE'S JUST TORN TO PIECES OVER THE SUBJECT.

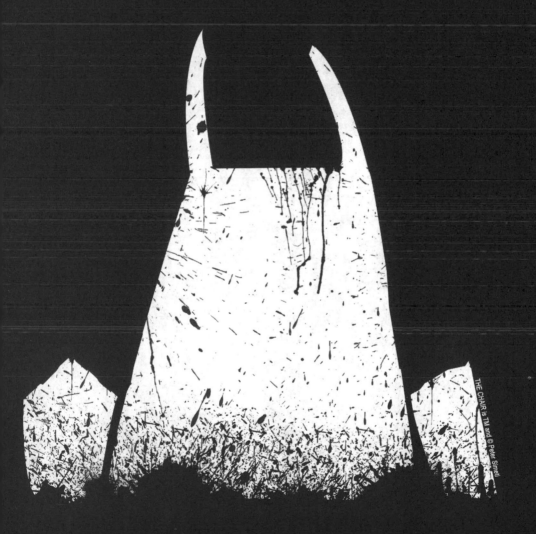

ACT TWO: PILE OF BONES

WELL, WHAT HAVE WE GOT HERE, SAMMY?
LOOKS LIKE YOU'VE BEEN MAKING A MESS!

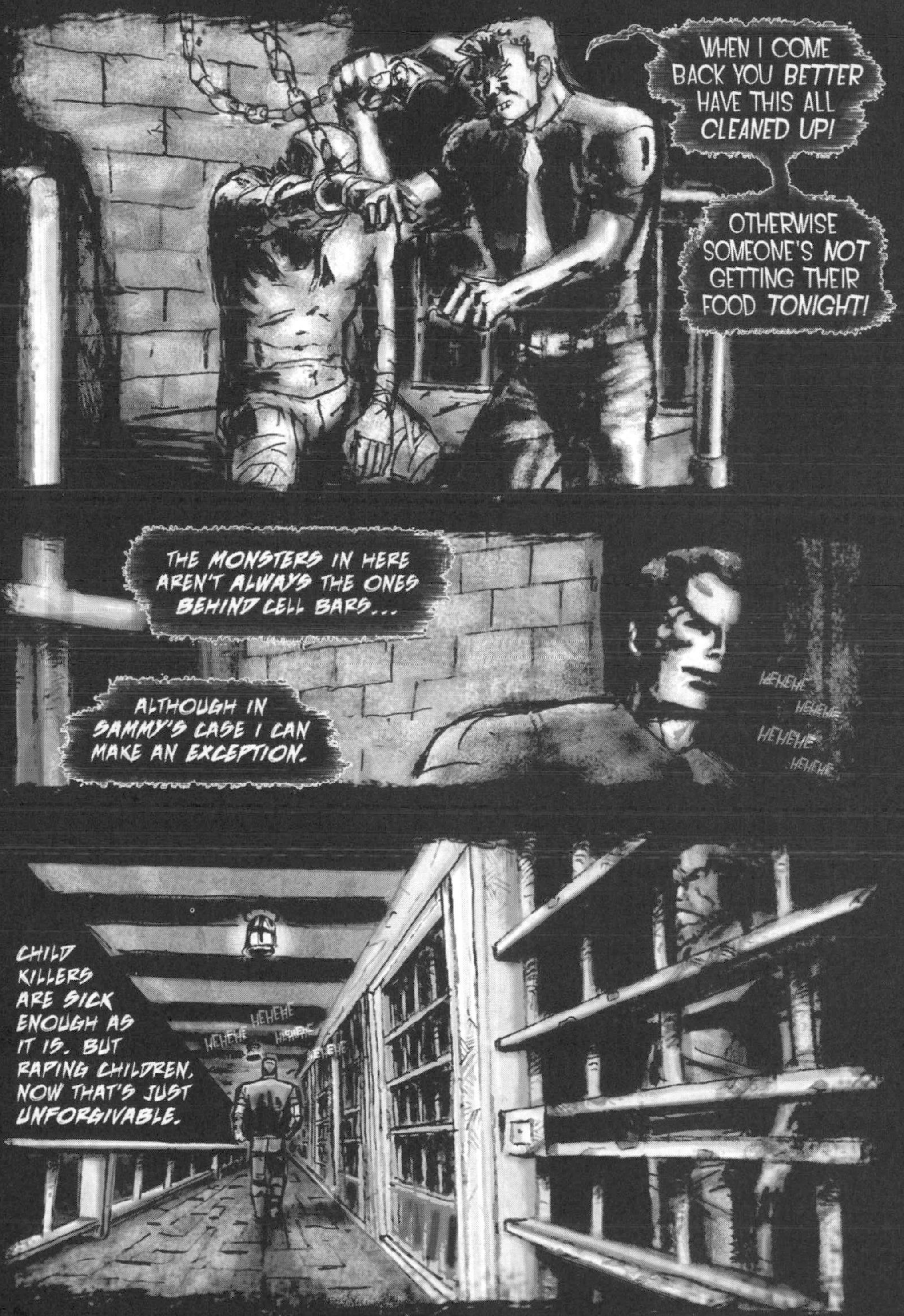

WHEN I COME BACK YOU BETTER HAVE THIS ALL CLEANED UP!
OTHERWISE SOMEONE'S NOT GETTING THEIR FOOD TONIGHT!
THE MONSTERS IN HERE AREN'T ALWAYS THE ONES BEHIND CELL BARS...
ALTHOUGH IN SAMMY'S CASE I CAN MAKE AN EXCEPTION.
HEHEHE
HEHEHE
HEHEHE
HEHEHE
CHILD KILLERS ARE SICK ENOUGH AS IT IS. BUT RAPING CHILDREN, NOW THAT'S JUST UNFORGIVABLE.
HEHEHE
HEHEHE

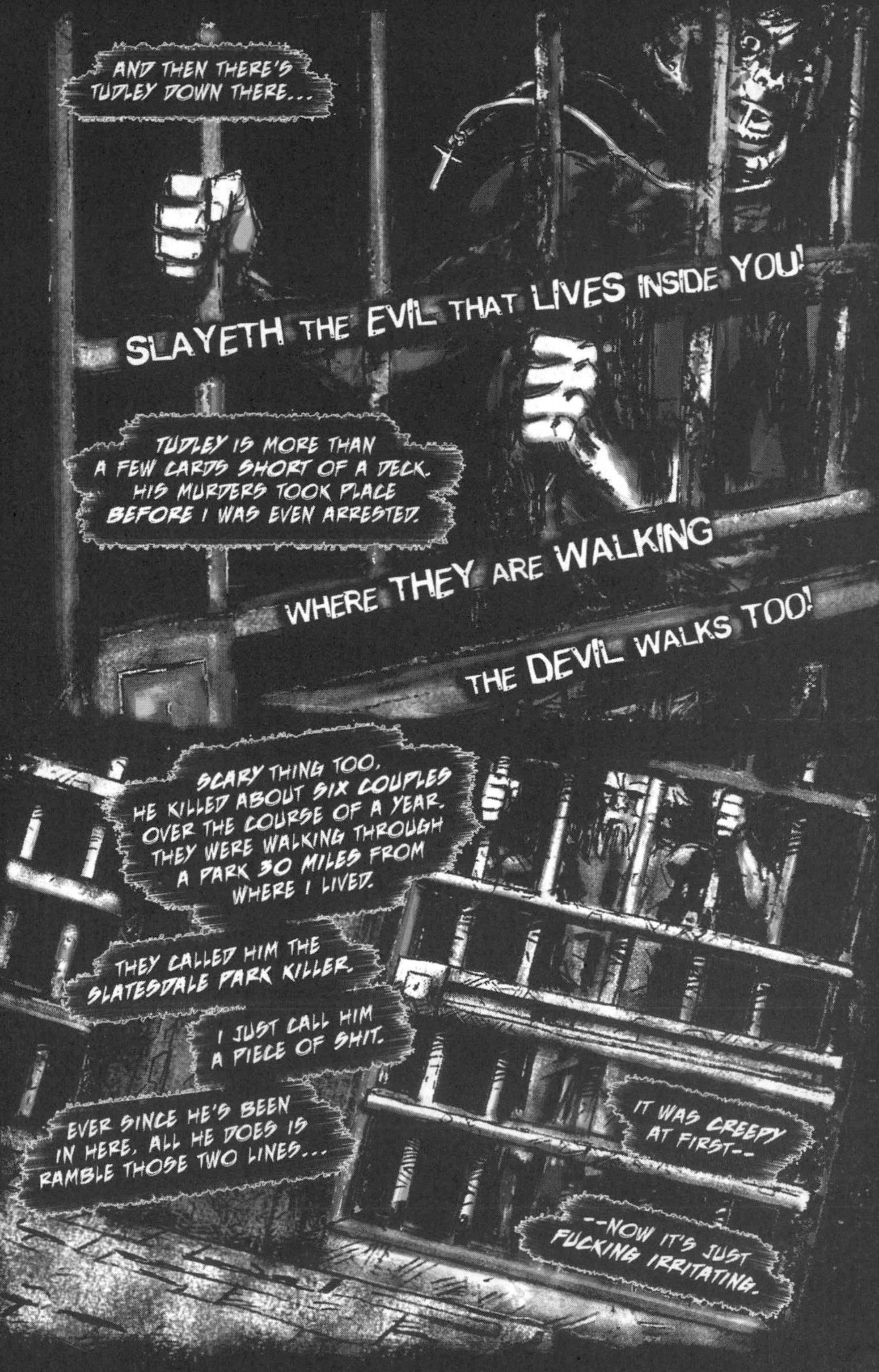
AND THEN THERE'S TUDLEY DOWN THERE...
SLAYETH THE EVIL THAT LIVES INSIDE YOU!
TUDLEY IS MORE THAN A FEW CARDS SHORT OF A DECK. HIS MURDERS TOOK PLACE BEFORE I WAS EVEN ARRESTED.
WHERE THEY ARE WALKING
THE DEVIL WALKS TOO!
SCARY THING TOO, HE KILLED ABOUT SIX COUPLES OVER THE COURSE OF A YEAR. THEY WERE WALKING THROUGH A PARK 30 MILES FROM WHERE I LIVED.
THEY CALLED HIM THE SLATESDALE PARK KILLER.
I JUST CALL HIM A PIECE OF SHIT.
EVER SINCE HE'S BEEN IN HERE, ALL HE DOES IS RAMBLE THOSE TWO LINES...
IT WAS CREEPY AT FIRST--
--NOW IT'S JUST FUCKING IRRITATING.

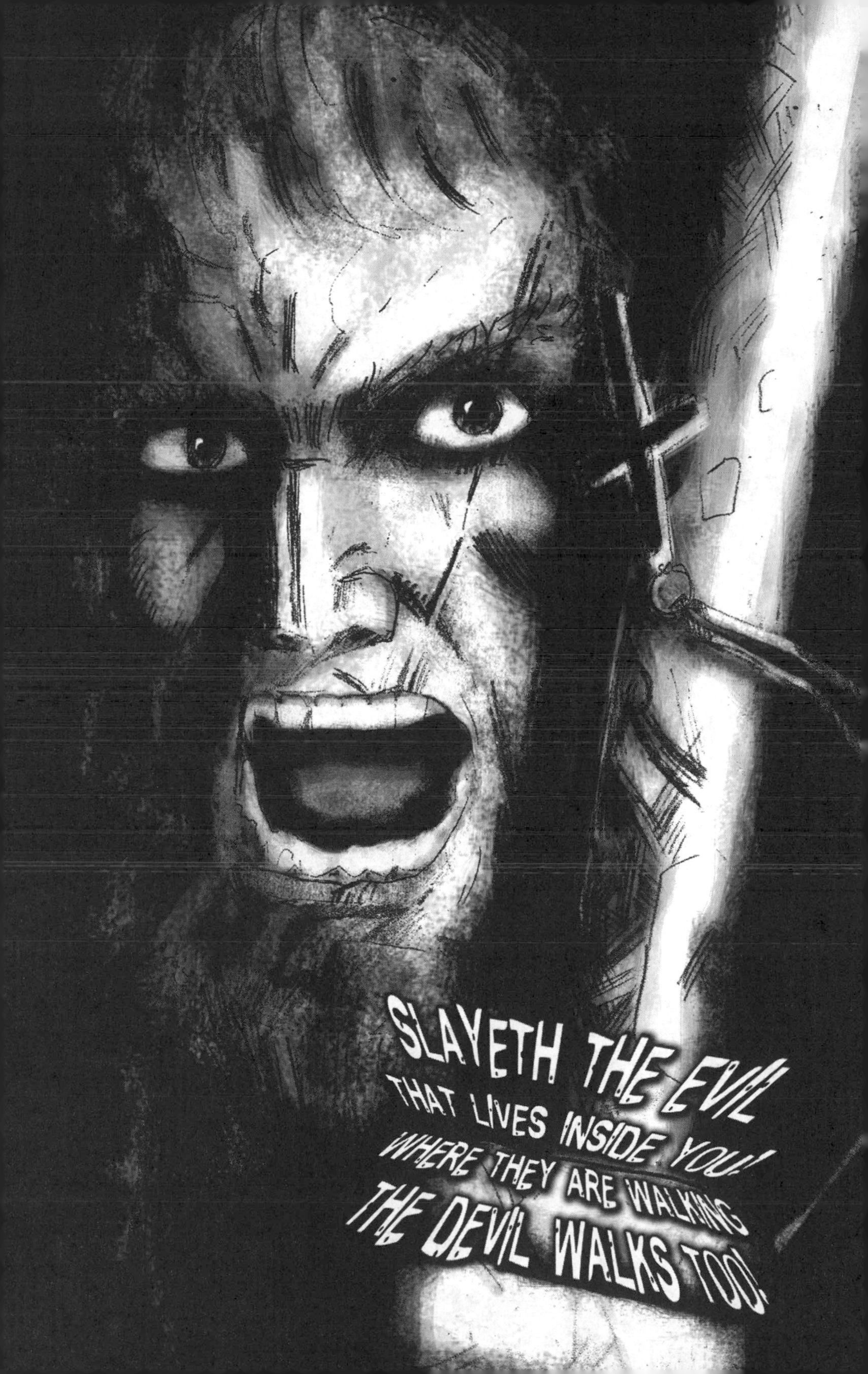
SLAYETH THE EVIL
THAT LIVES INSIDE YOU!
WHERE THEY ARE WALKING
THE DEVIL WALKS TOO!

IT'S TIME AGAIN TO STRETCH THOSE LEGS GENTLEMEN!
GET TO KNOW EACH OTHER A LITTLE BETTER!
ONCE A WEEK THEY LET US WALK AROUND FOR FIFTEEN MINUTES
TALK TO THE OTHER INMATES...
DO WHATEVER WE WANT.
IT'S WEIRD TO ME THOUGH- I MEAN AREN'T WE ALL SUPPOSED TO BE "DANGEROUS COLD-BLOODED PSYCHOPATHS"?
THEY DON'T EVEN CHAIN US UP OR HANDCUFF US. WE JUST GET TO WALK AROUND. FREE AS A JAILBIRD.
SOMETIMES FIGHTS BREAK OUT, BUT IT'S USUALLY NOTHING THE ELECTRIFIED FLOORS AND CELL BARS CAN'T HANDLE.

HEY BONES! HOW'S IT GOING?
EH NOT SO GOOD SULLY... I HAVEN'T EATEN IN FOUR DAYS.
YOU KNOW THAT GUARD RIGHT?
THE ONE THAT PEES IN THE FOOD?
YEAH...WELL LATELY THAT'S NOT ALL I'M GETTING IN MINE IF YA KNOW WHAT I MEAN...
AH MAN...I'M SORRY JIMMY. YOU KNOW IF I COULD HELP I WOULD. IN FACT YOU'RE THE ONLY PERSON I'D HELP AROUND HERE.
HEY, I STILL HAVE FOOD IN MY CELL IF YOU WANT IT.
YOU LOOK LIKE YOU COULD USE IT MORE THAN ME ANYWAY.
AH, THANKS SULLY! I REALLY APPRECIATE IT!
NO PROBLEM. BESIDES, YOU DON'T ALWAYS HAVE TO LIVE UP TO THAT "BONES" NICKNAME OF YOURS! HEH!

BONES IS IN HERE BECAUSE HE DISOBEYED ORDERS IN COMBAT. HE REFUSED TO KILL THE CHILDREN OF THE "ENEMY".
THE MILITARY WOULD LATER BLAME HIM FOR THE DEATHS OF HIS FELLOW TROOPS AT THE HANDS OF A SUICIDE BOMBER--
--THE SUICIDE BOMBER WAS A KID.
THE ARMY COURT MARTIALED HIM AND HE WAS SENTENCED TO DEATH FOR INSUBORDINATION AND COWARDICE.
JIMMY NEVER BOTHERED FIGHTING THE SENTENCE THOUGH...HE WAS RACKED WITH GUILT OVER THE DEATHS HE CAUSED.
SEEMS LIKE WE BOTH GOT THE SHORT END OF THE STICK..

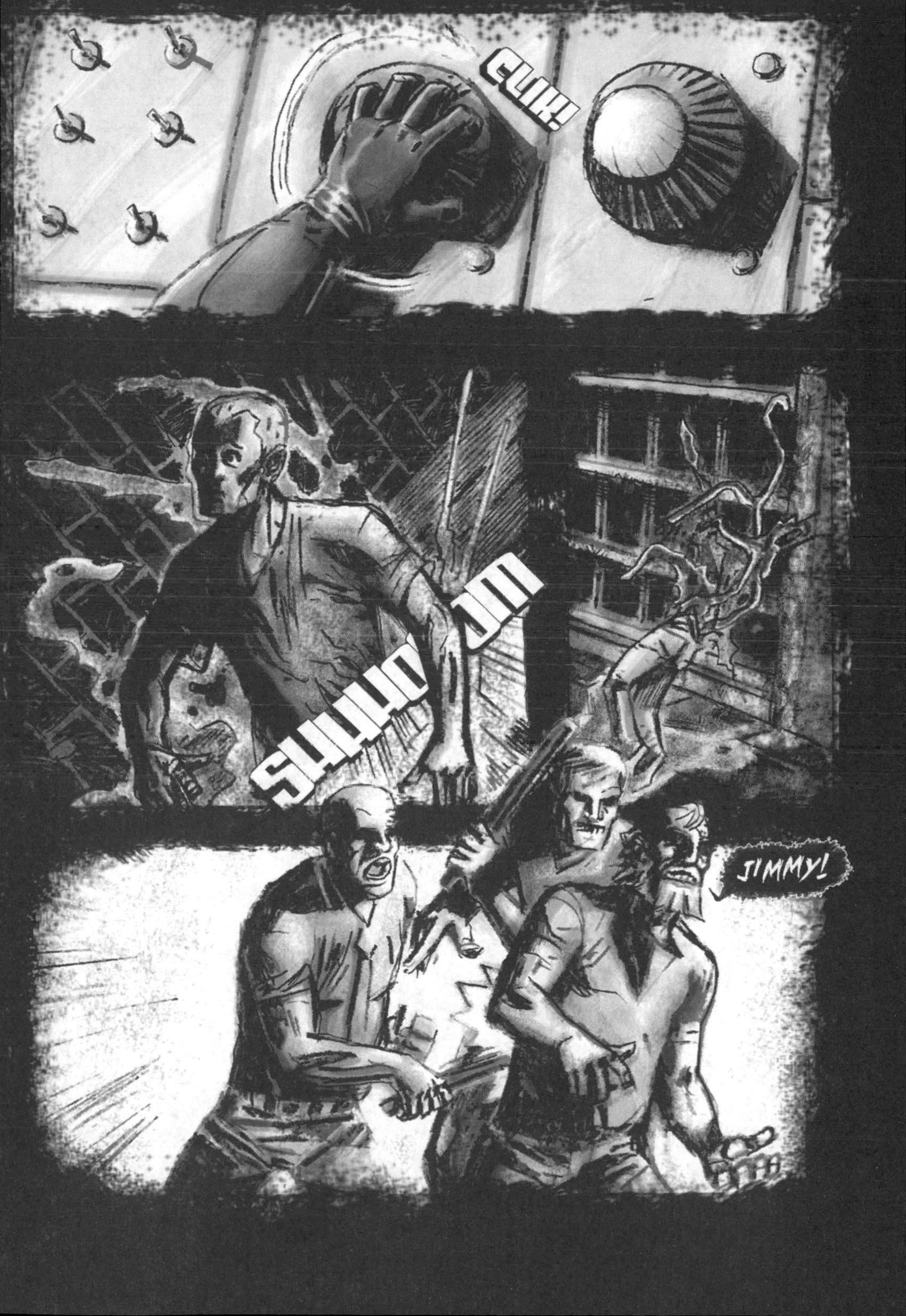
CLIK!
SHHOOM
JIMMY!

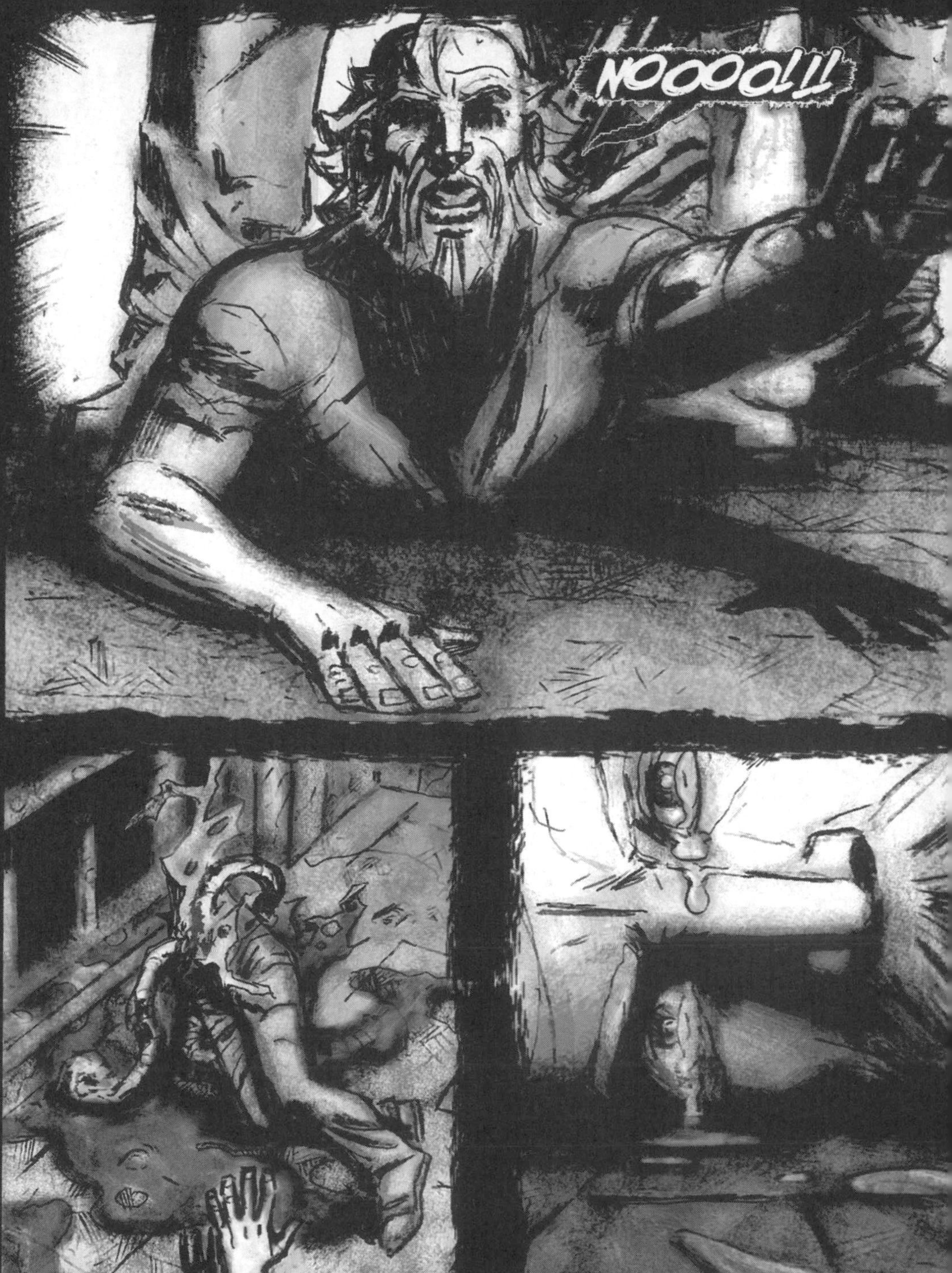
NOOOO!!!

YOU KILLED HIM!

HE WAS A GOOD PERSON—

—AND YOU FUCKERS KILLED HIM!

QUIET DOWN YOU WORTHLESS TURD—

—YOUR "FRIEND" WAS JUST AN ACCIDENT.

BESIDES, MR. SULLIVAN, YOU'RE NOT HERE TO LIVE, YOU'RE HERE TO DIE.

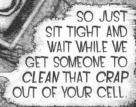

SO JUST SIT TIGHT AND WAIT WHILE WE GET SOMEONE TO CLEAN THAT CRAP OUT OF YOUR CELL.

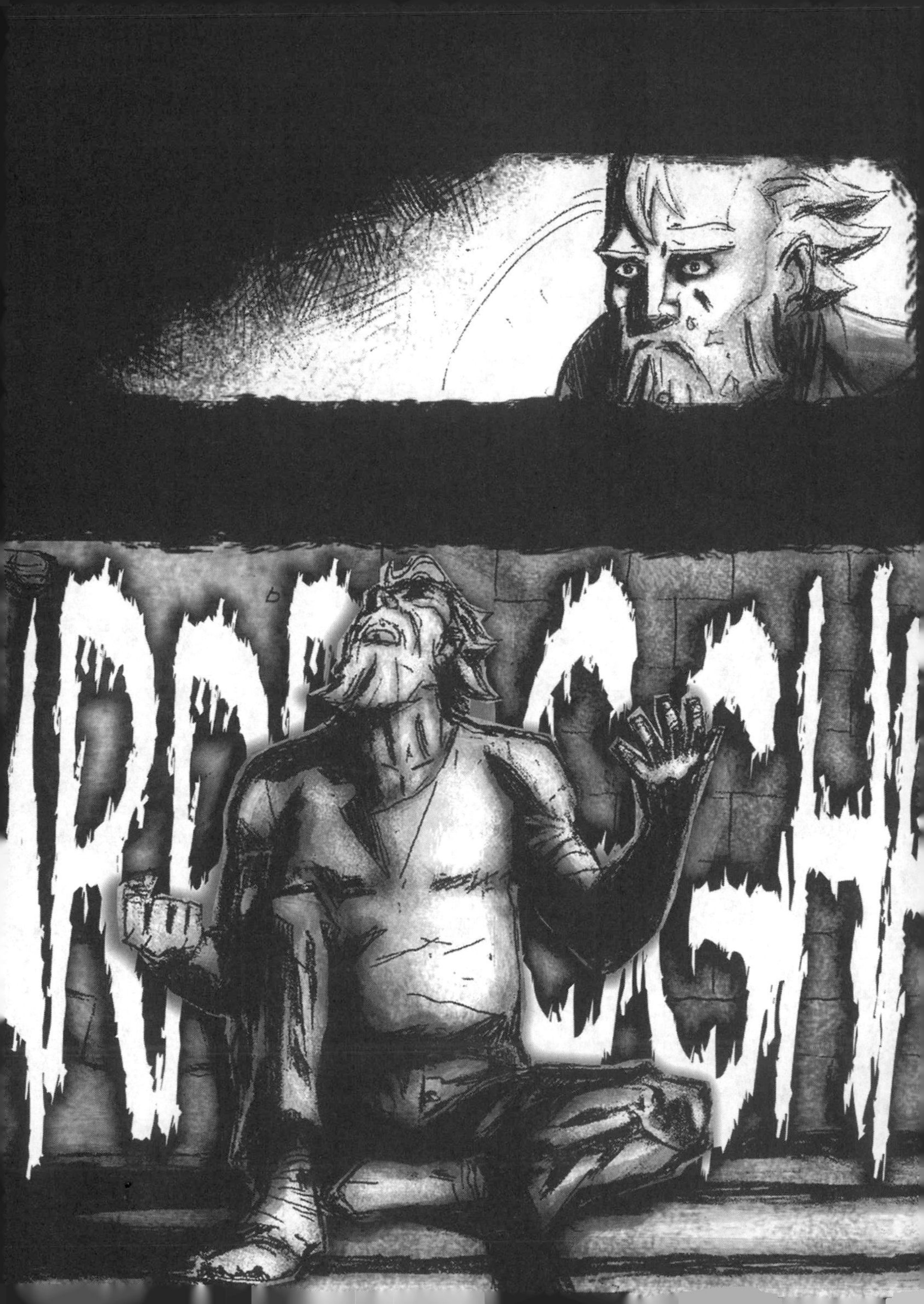

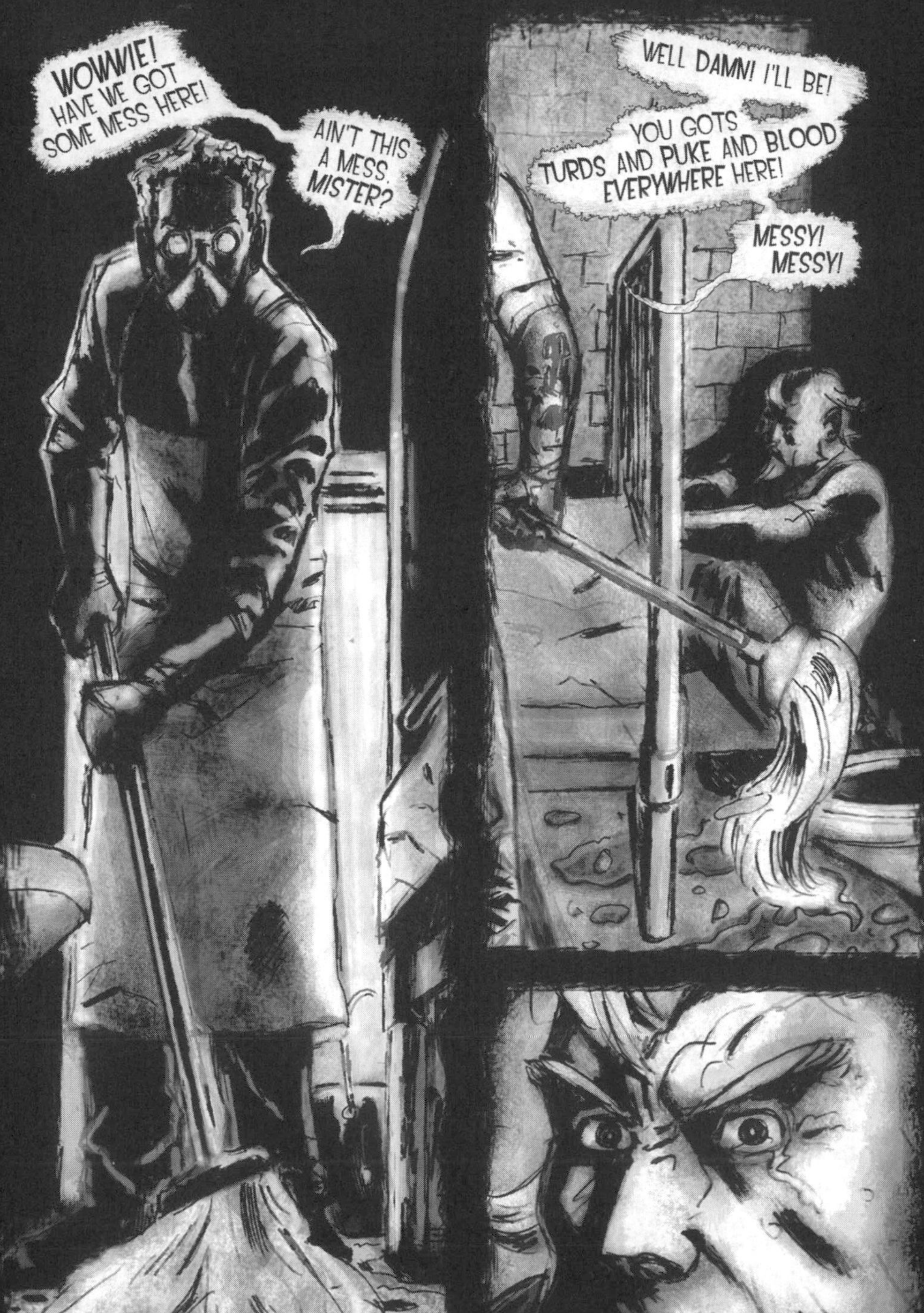
WOWWIE! HAVE WE GOT SOME MESS HERE!
AIN'T THIS A MESS, MISTER?
WELL DAMN! I'LL BE!
YOU GOTS TURDS AND PUKE AND BLOOD EVERYWHERE HERE!
MESSY! MESSY!

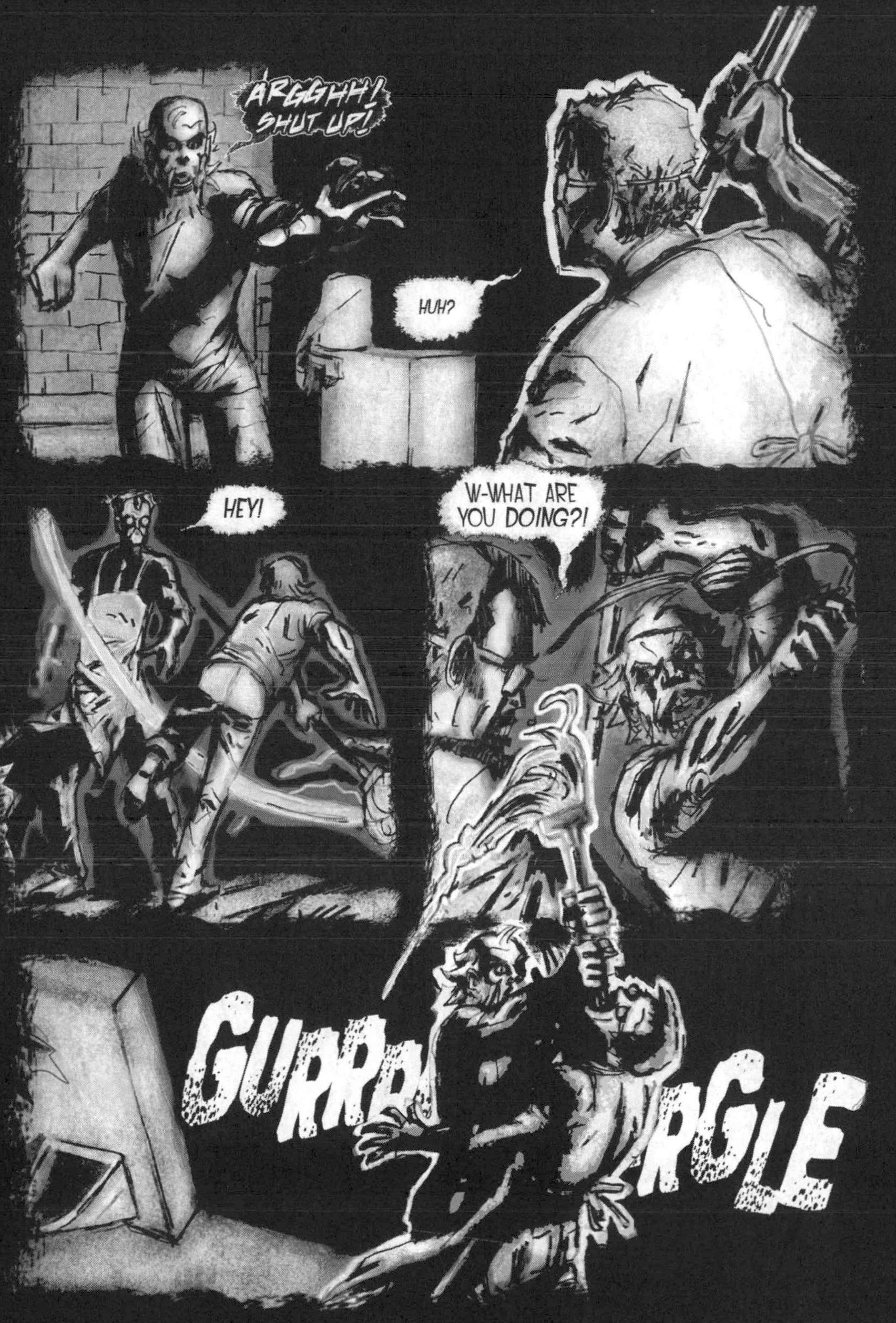
ARGGHH! SHUT UP!
HUH?
HEY!
W-WHAT ARE YOU DOING?!
GURR
RGLE

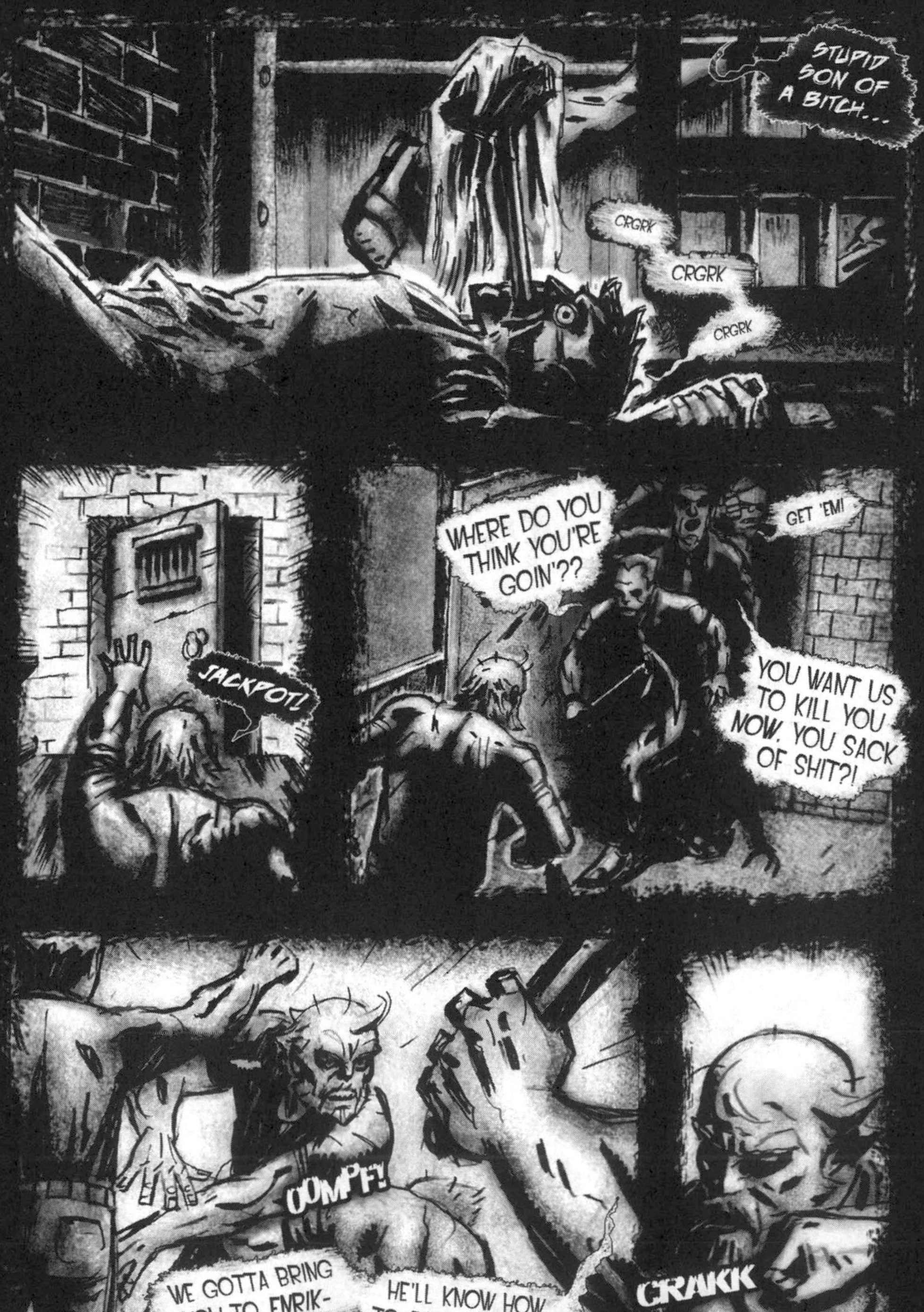
STUPID SON OF A BITCH...
CRGRK
CRGRK
CRGRK
JACKPOT!
WHERE DO YOU THINK YOU'RE GOIN'??
GET 'EM!
YOU WANT US TO KILL YOU NOW, YOU SACK OF SHIT?!
OOMPF!
WE GOTTA BRING YOU TO ENRIK-
HE'LL KNOW HOW TO FIX YOU RIGHT!
CRAKK

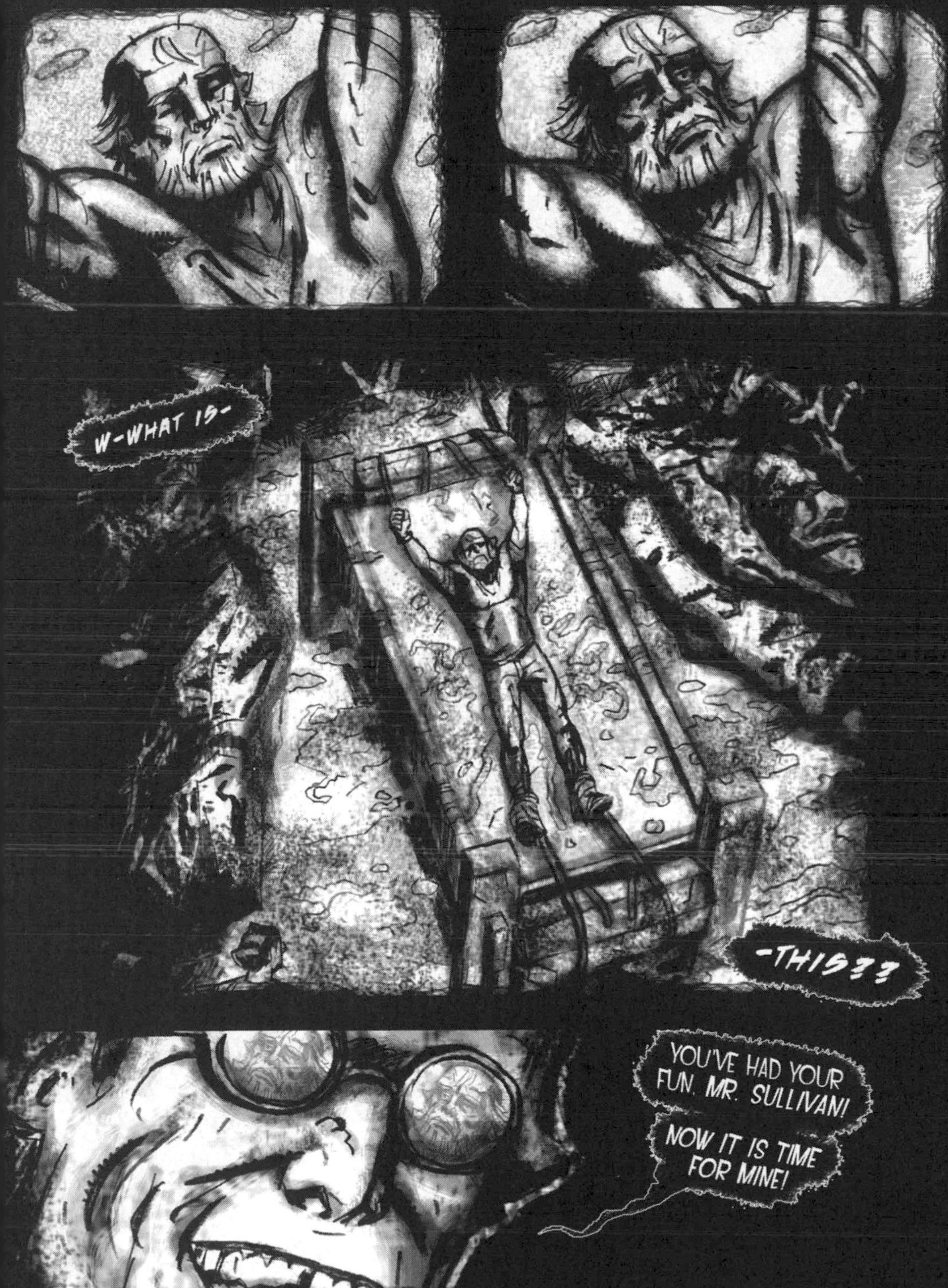
W-WHAT IS-
-THIS???
YOU'VE HAD YOUR FUN, MR. SULLIVAN!
NOW IT IS TIME FOR MINE!

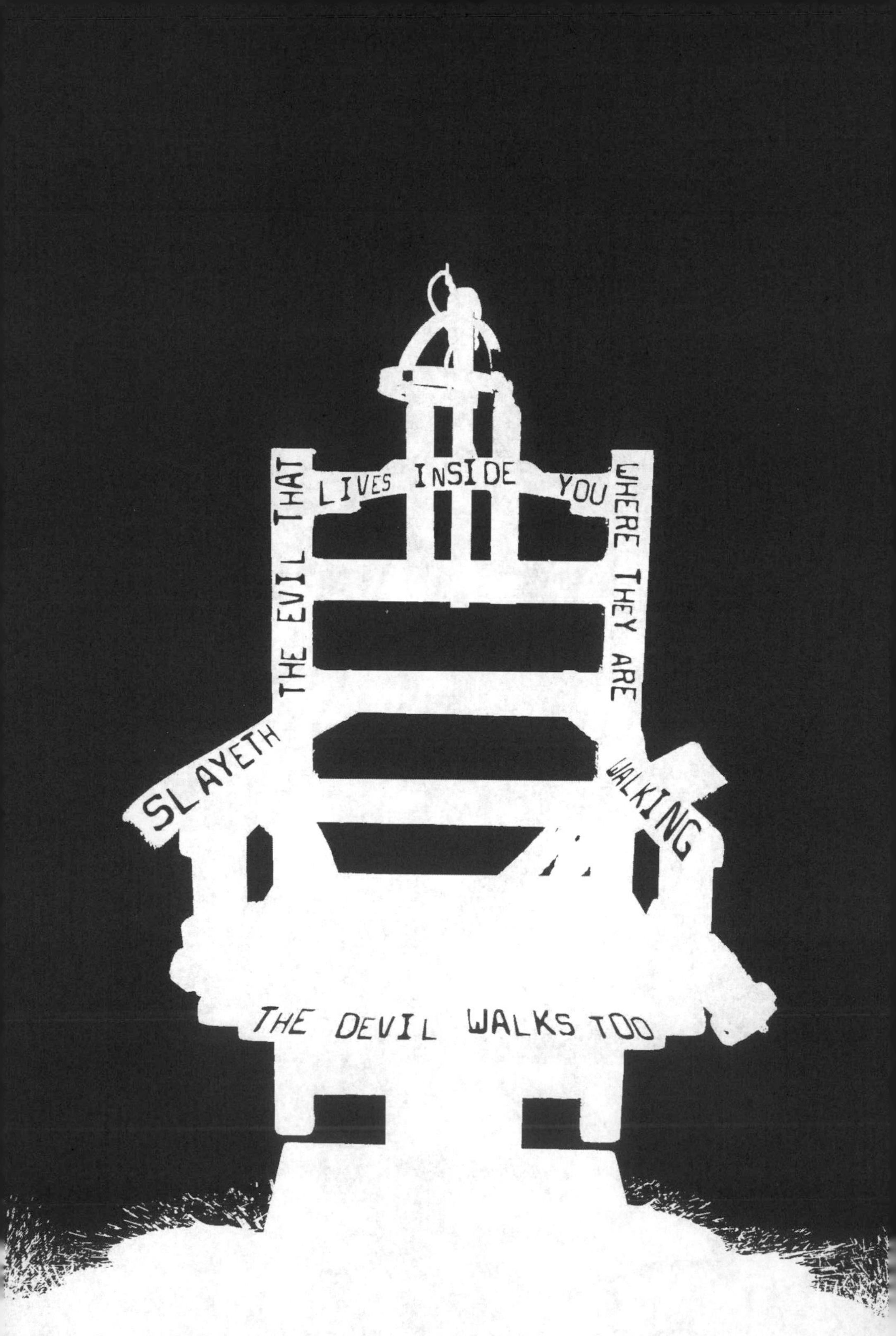
SLAYETH
THE EVIL THAT
LIVES
INSIDE
YOU
WHERE THEY ARE
WALKING
THE DEVIL WALKS TOO

ACT THREE: PEACE & QUIET

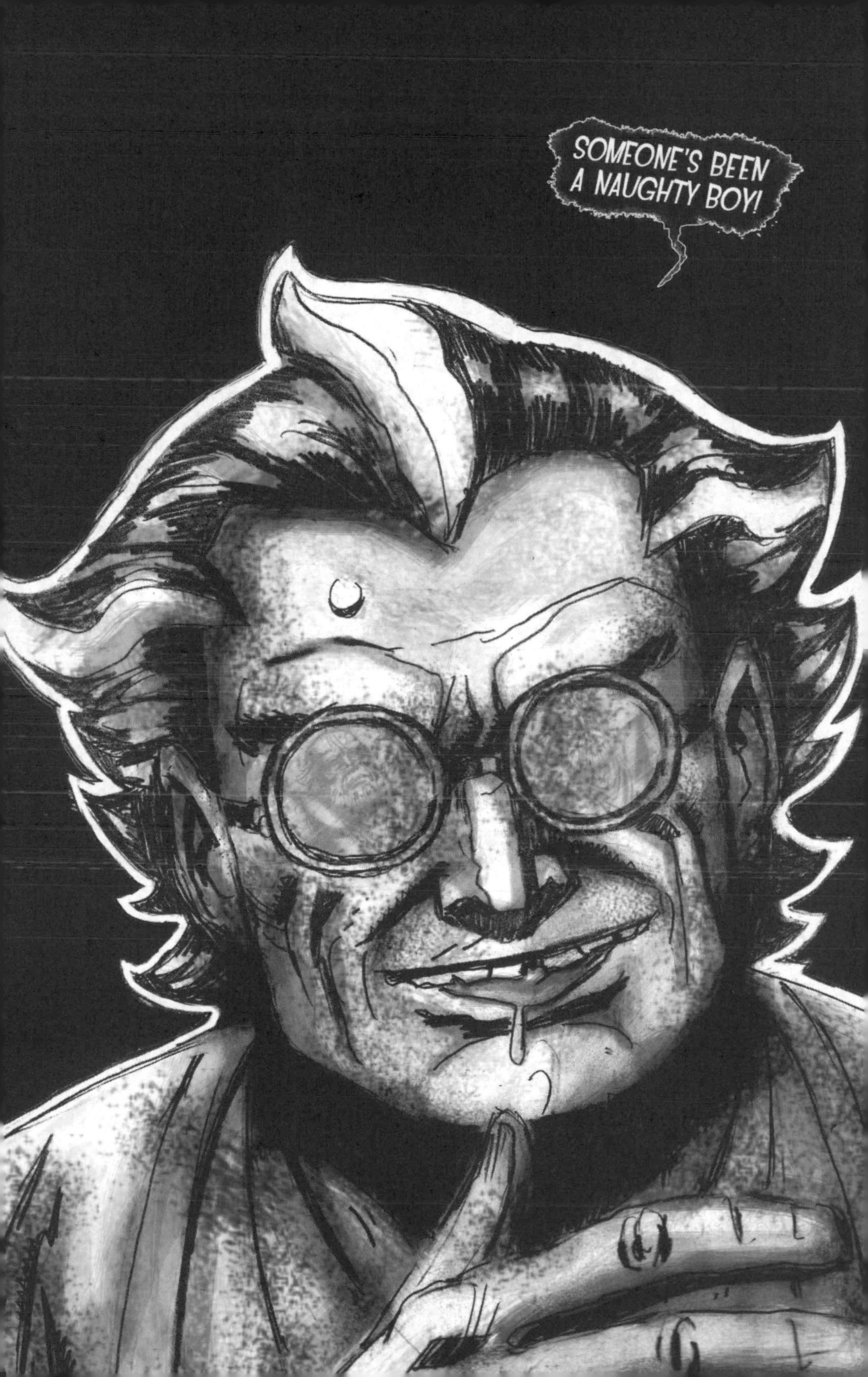
SOMEONE'S BEEN A NAUGHTY BOY!

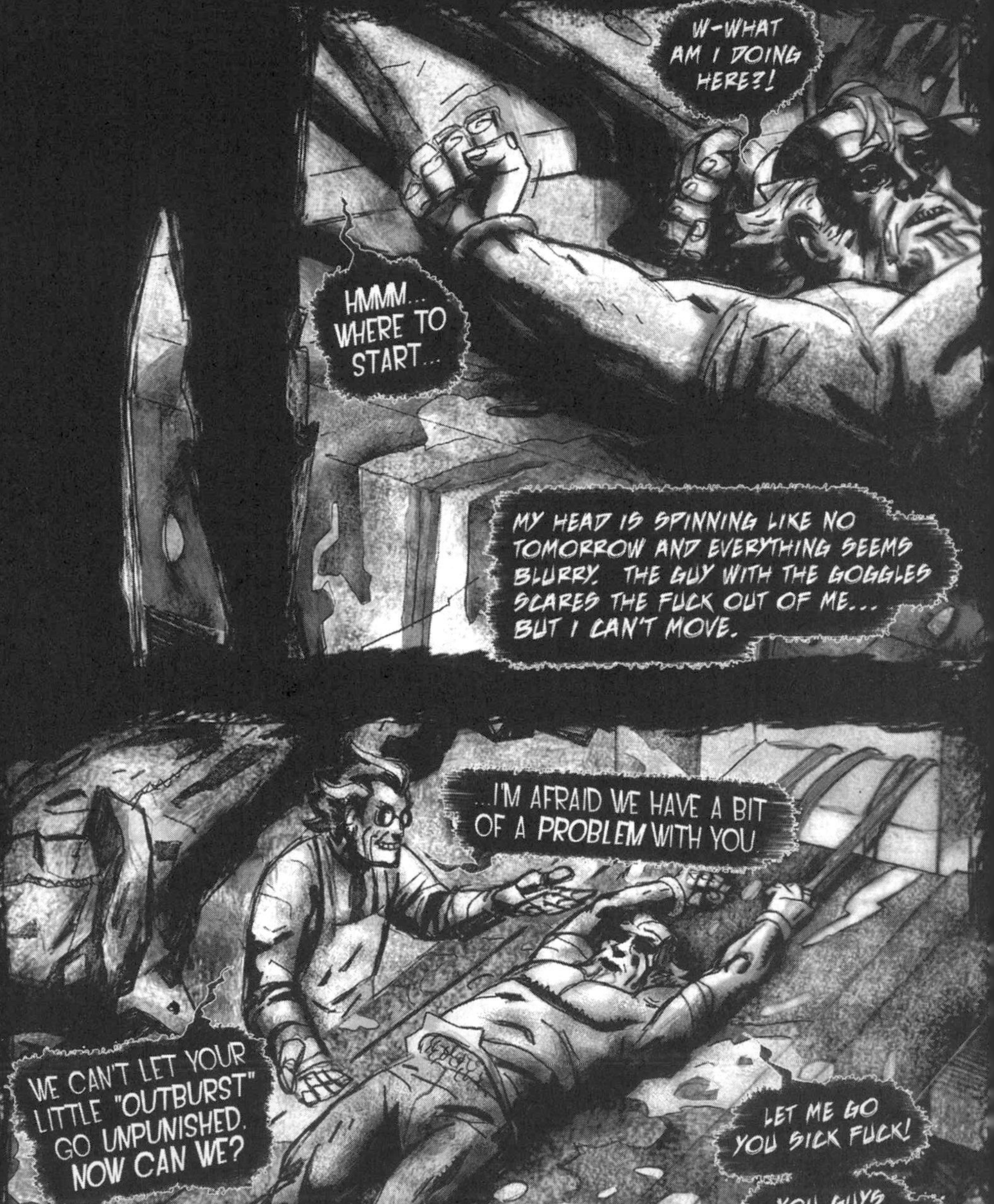
W-WHAT AM I DOING HERE?!
HMMM... WHERE TO START...
MY HEAD IS SPINNING LIKE NO TOMORROW AND EVERYTHING SEEMS BLURRY. THE GUY WITH THE GOGGLES SCARES THE FUCK OUT OF ME... BUT I CAN'T MOVE.
...I'M AFRAID WE HAVE A BIT OF A PROBLEM WITH YOU
WE CAN'T LET YOUR LITTLE "OUTBURST" GO UNPUNISHED. NOW CAN WE?
LET ME GO YOU SICK FUCK!
YOU GUYS MURDERED JIMMY!
YOU'VE BEEN MURDERING ALL THE INMATES HERE!

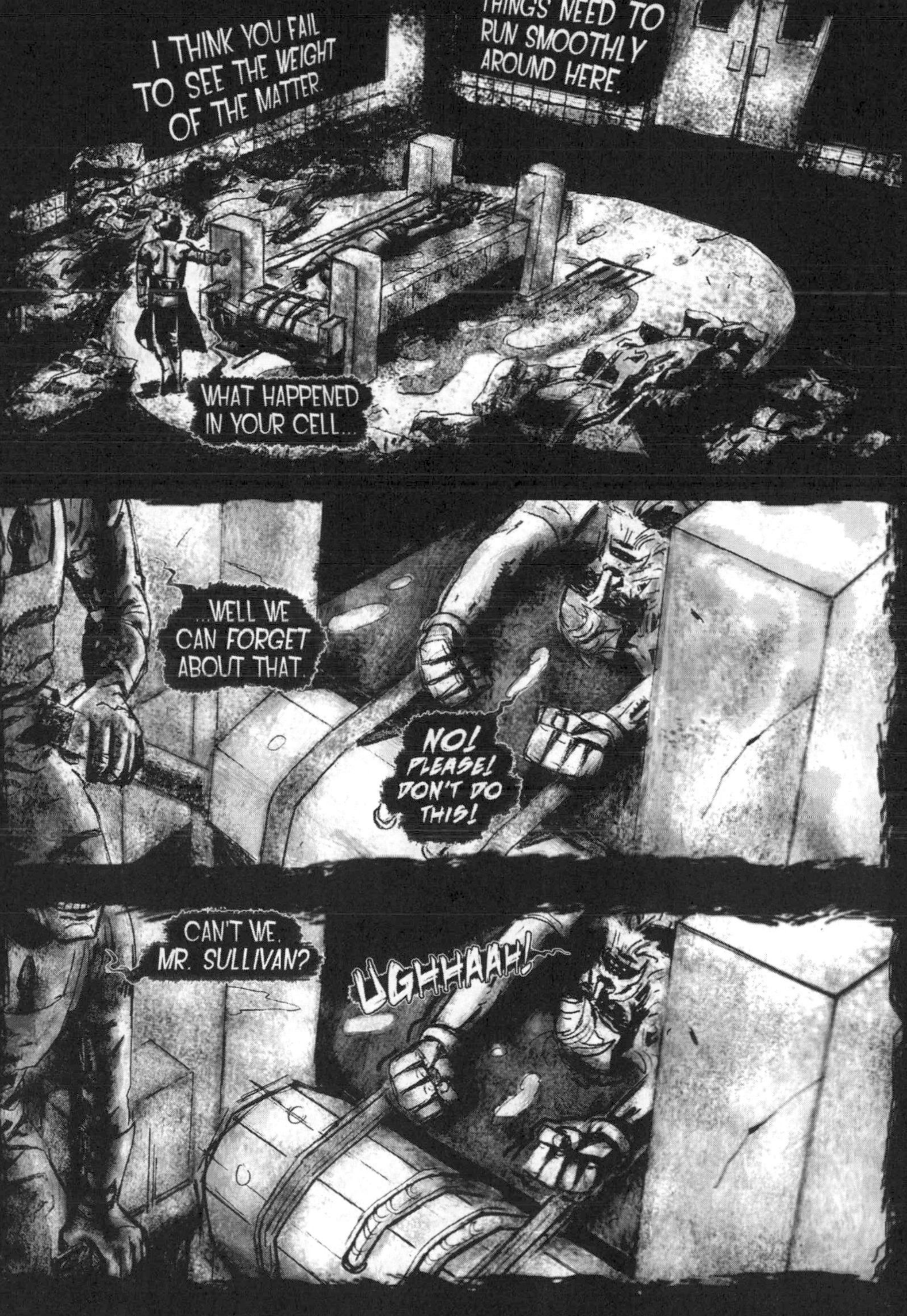
I THINK YOU FAIL TO SEE THE WEIGHT OF THE MATTER.
THINGS NEED TO RUN SMOOTHLY AROUND HERE.
WHAT HAPPENED IN YOUR CELL...
...WELL WE CAN FORGET ABOUT THAT.
NO! PLEASE! DON'T DO THIS!
CAN'T WE, MR. SULLIVAN?
UGHHAAH!

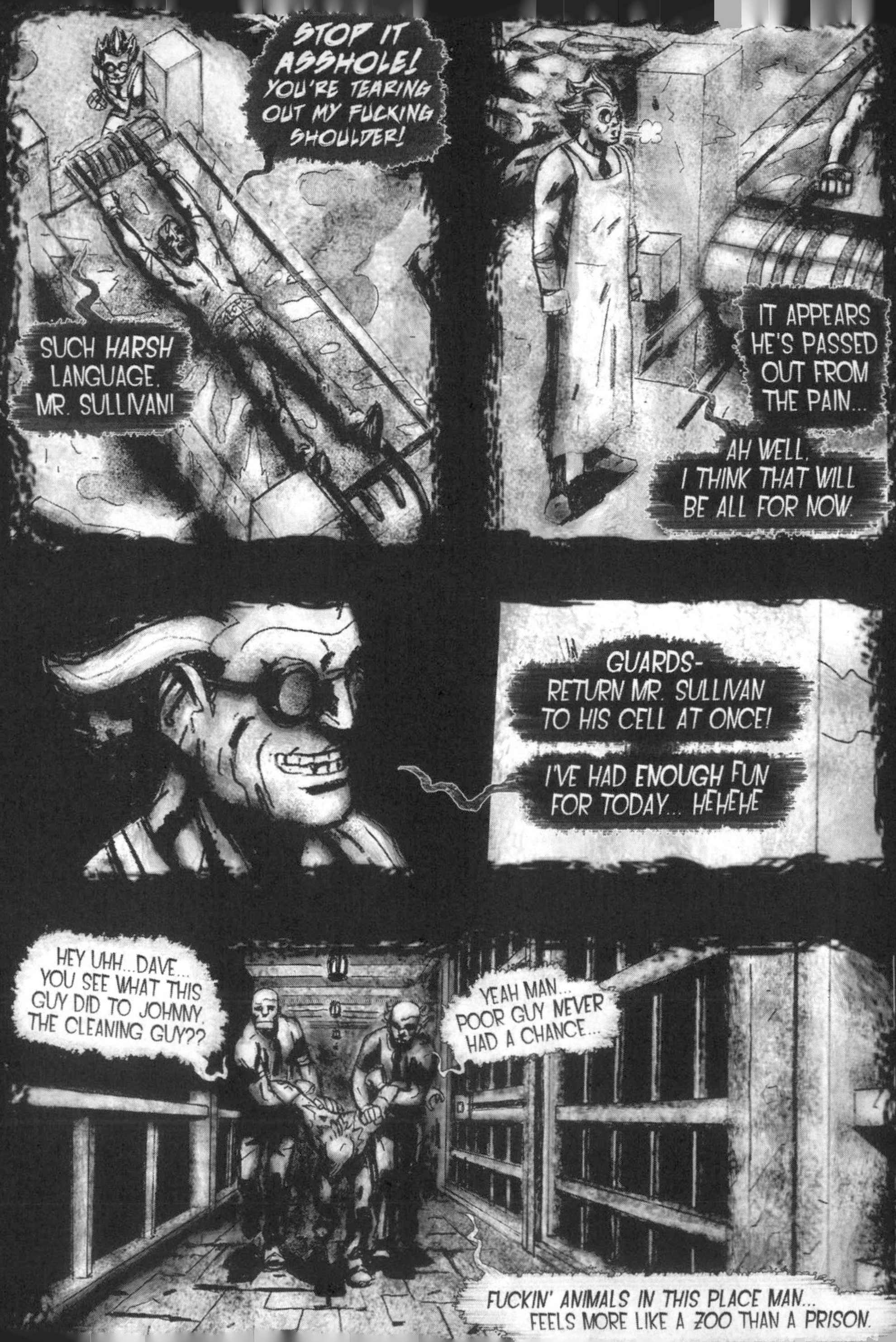
STOP IT ASSHOLE! YOU'RE TEARING OUT MY FUCKING SHOULDER!
SUCH HARSH LANGUAGE, MR. SULLIVAN!
IT APPEARS HE'S PASSED OUT FROM THE PAIN...
AH WELL, I THINK THAT WILL BE ALL FOR NOW.
GUARDS- RETURN MR. SULLIVAN TO HIS CELL AT ONCE!
I'VE HAD ENOUGH FUN FOR TODAY... HEHEHE
HEY UHH...DAVE... YOU SEE WHAT THIS GUY DID TO JOHNNY, THE CLEANING GUY??
YEAH MAN... POOR GUY NEVER HAD A CHANCE...
FUCKIN' ANIMALS IN THIS PLACE MAN... FEELS MORE LIKE A ZOO THAN A PRISON.

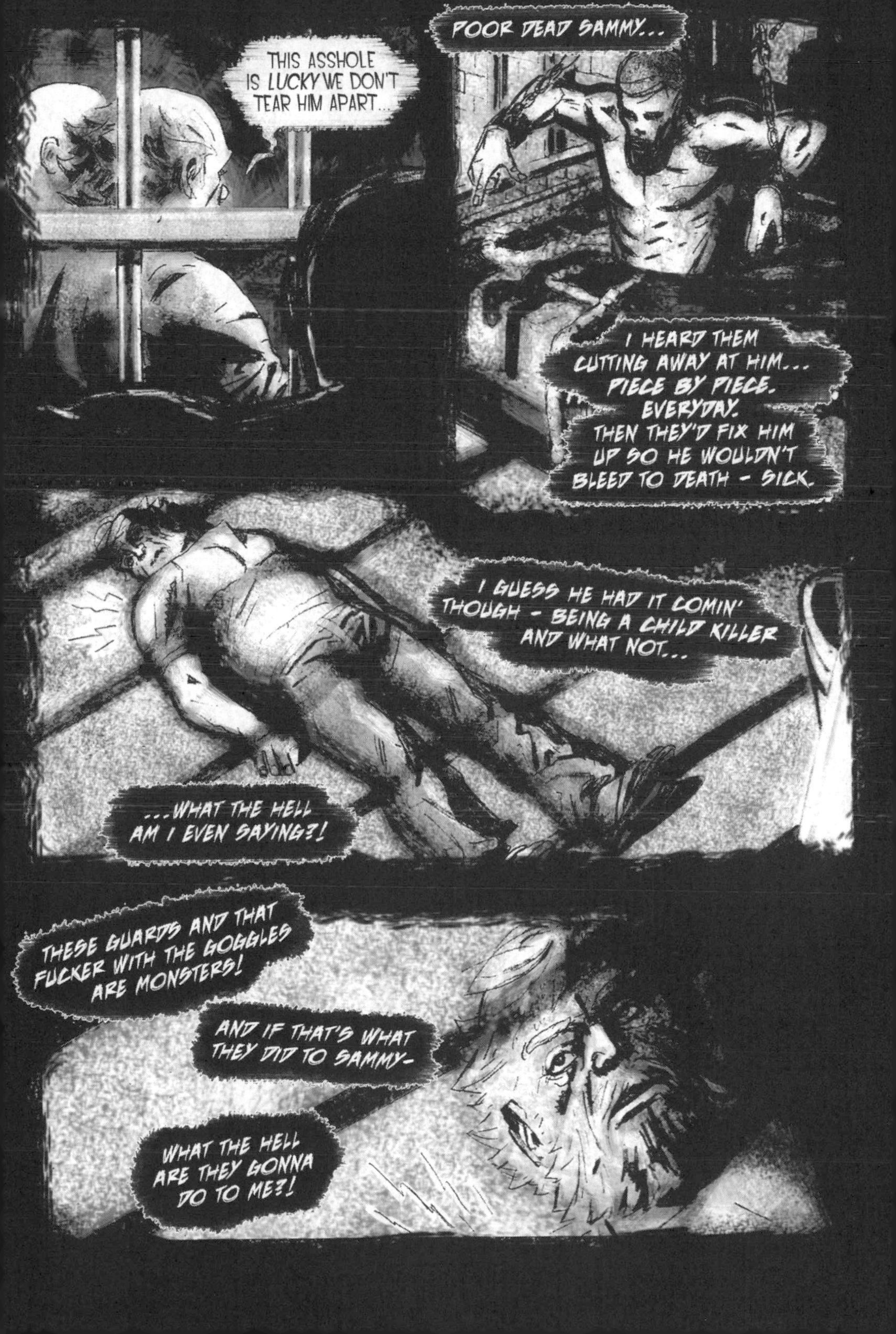
THIS ASSHOLE IS LUCKY WE DON'T TEAR HIM APART...
POOR DEAD SAMMY...
I HEARD THEM CUTTING AWAY AT HIM... PIECE BY PIECE. EVERYDAY. THEN THEY'D FIX HIM UP SO HE WOULDN'T BLEED TO DEATH - SICK.
I GUESS HE HAD IT COMIN' THOUGH - BEING A CHILD KILLER AND WHAT NOT...
...WHAT THE HELL AM I EVEN SAYING?!
THESE GUARDS AND THAT FUCKER WITH THE GOGGLES ARE MONSTERS!
AND IF THAT'S WHAT THEY DID TO SAMMY-
WHAT THE HELL ARE THEY GONNA DO TO ME?!

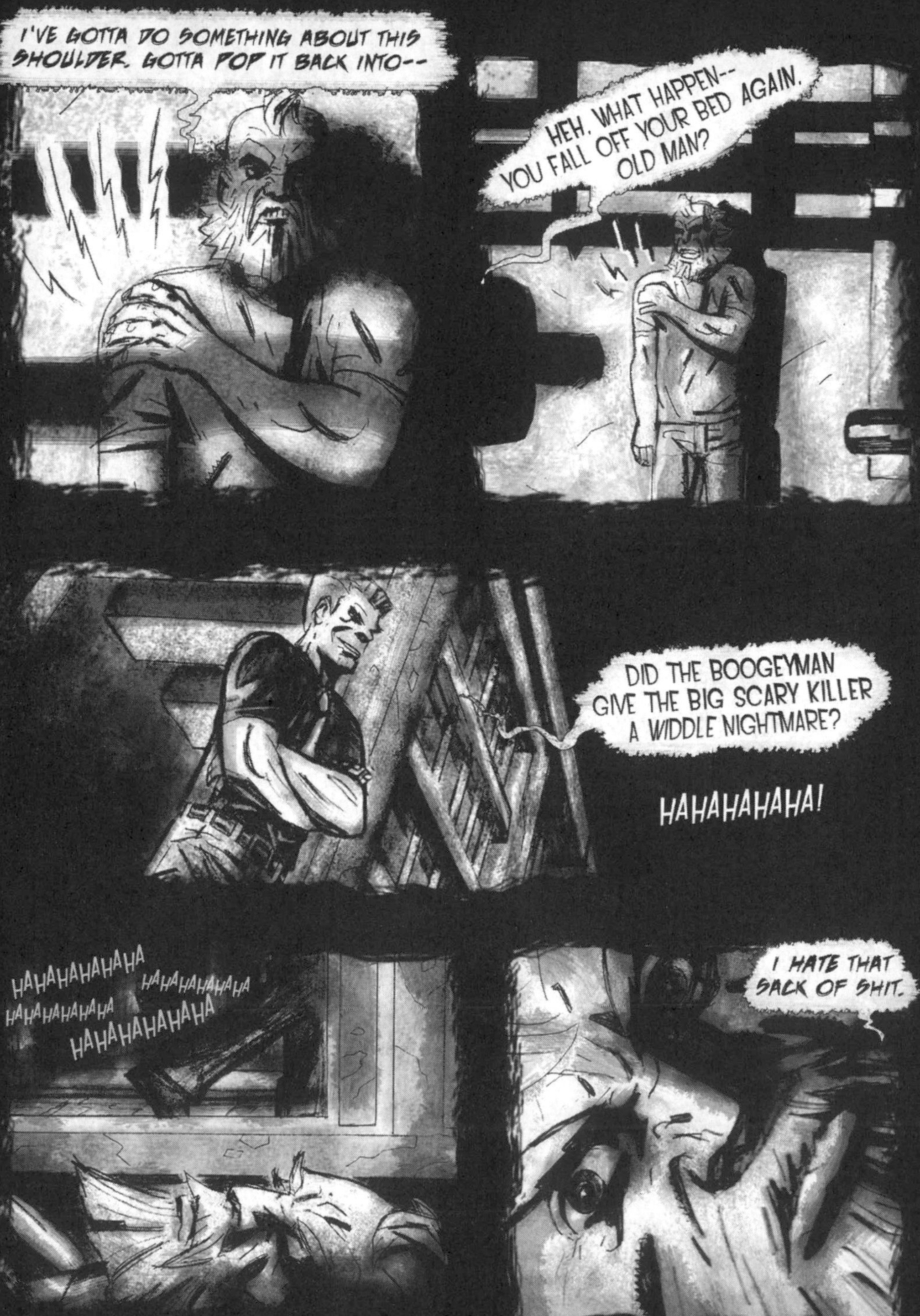
I'VE GOTTA DO SOMETHING ABOUT THIS SHOULDER. GOTTA POP IT BACK INTO--
HEH. WHAT HAPPEN-- YOU FALL OFF YOUR BED AGAIN, OLD MAN?
DID THE BOOGEYMAN GIVE THE BIG SCARY KILLER A WIDDLE NIGHTMARE?
HAHAHAHAHA!
HAHAHAHAHAHA HAHAHAHAHAHA HAHAHAHAHAHA HAHAHAHAHAHA
I HATE THAT SACK OF SHIT.

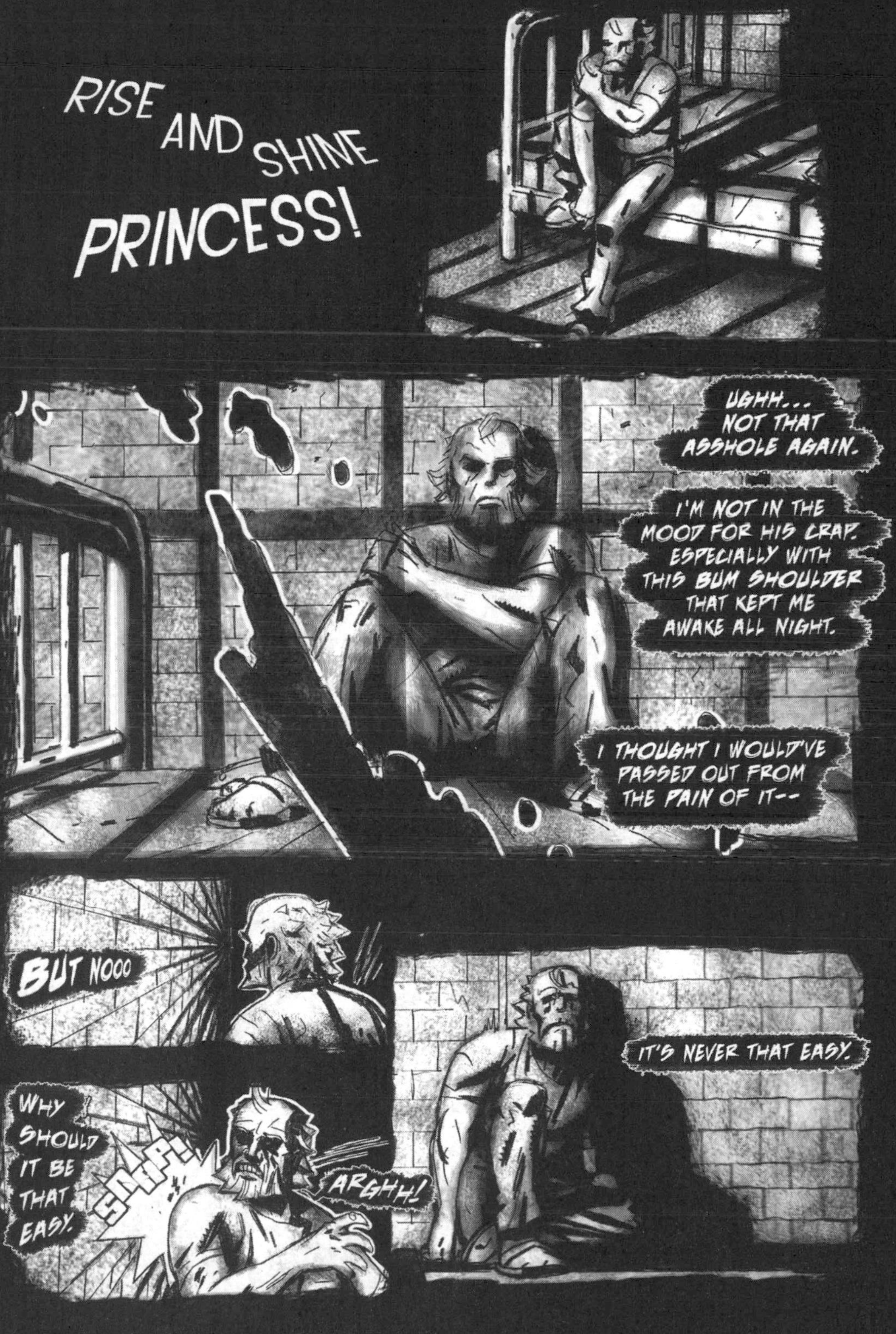
RISE AND SHINE PRINCESS!
UGHH... NOT THAT ASSHOLE AGAIN.
I'M NOT IN THE MOOD FOR HIS CRAP. ESPECIALLY WITH THIS BUM SHOULDER THAT KEPT ME AWAKE ALL NIGHT.
I THOUGHT I WOULD'VE PASSED OUT FROM THE PAIN OF IT--
BUT NOOO
IT'S NEVER THAT EASY.
WHY SHOULD IT BE THAT EASY.
ARGHH!

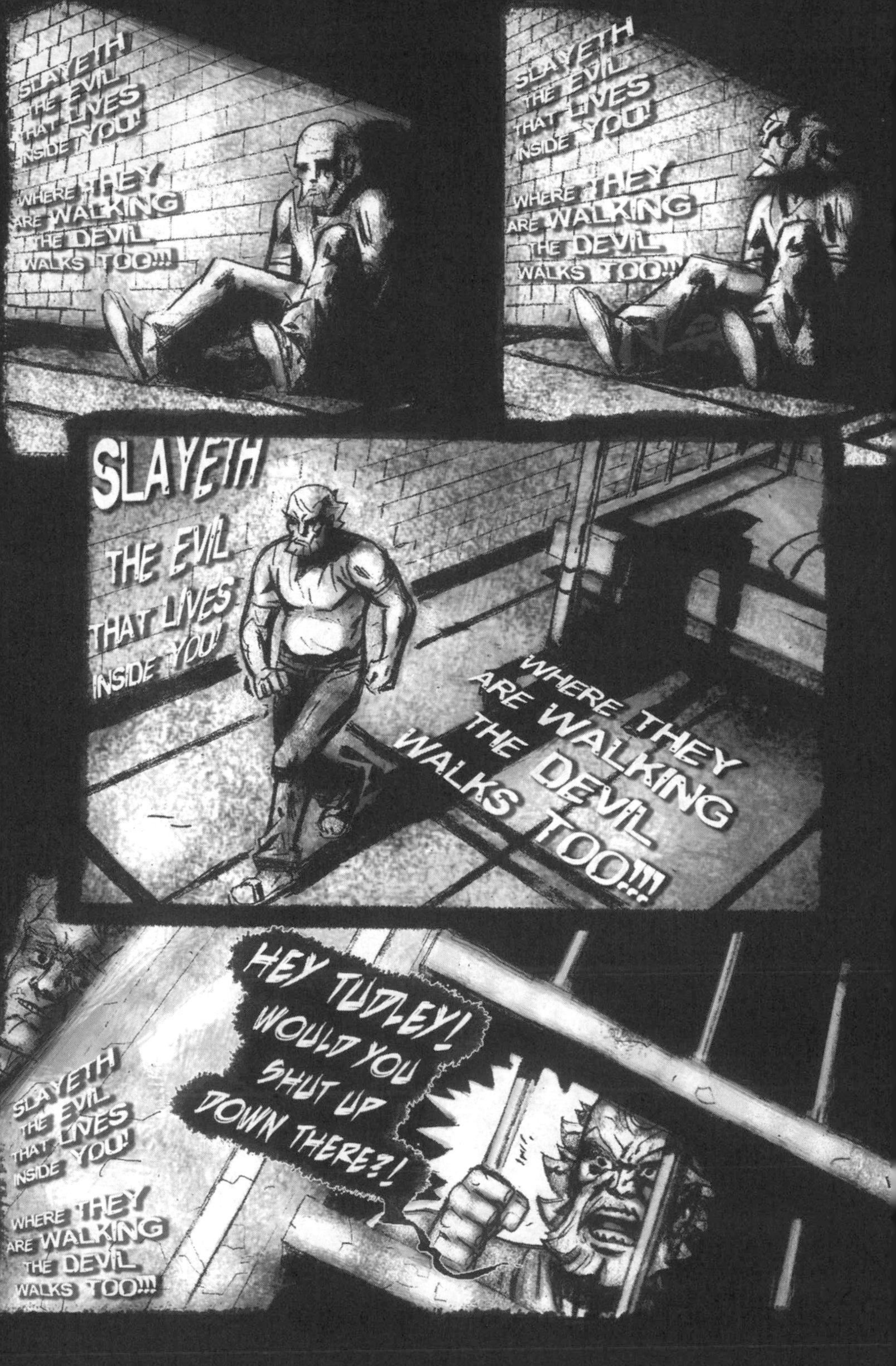
SLAYETH THE EVIL THAT LIVES INSIDE YOU!
WHERE THEY ARE WALKING THE DEVIL WALKS TOO!!!
SLAYETH THE EVIL THAT LIVES INSIDE YOU!
WHERE THEY ARE WALKING THE DEVIL WALKS TOO!!!
SLAYETH
THE EVIL THAT LIVES INSIDE YOU!
WHERE THEY ARE WALKING THE DEVIL WALKS TOO!!!
SLAYETH THE EVIL THAT LIVES INSIDE YOU!
WHERE THEY ARE WALKING THE DEVIL WALKS TOO!!!
HEY TUDLEY! WOULD YOU SHUT UP DOWN THERE?!

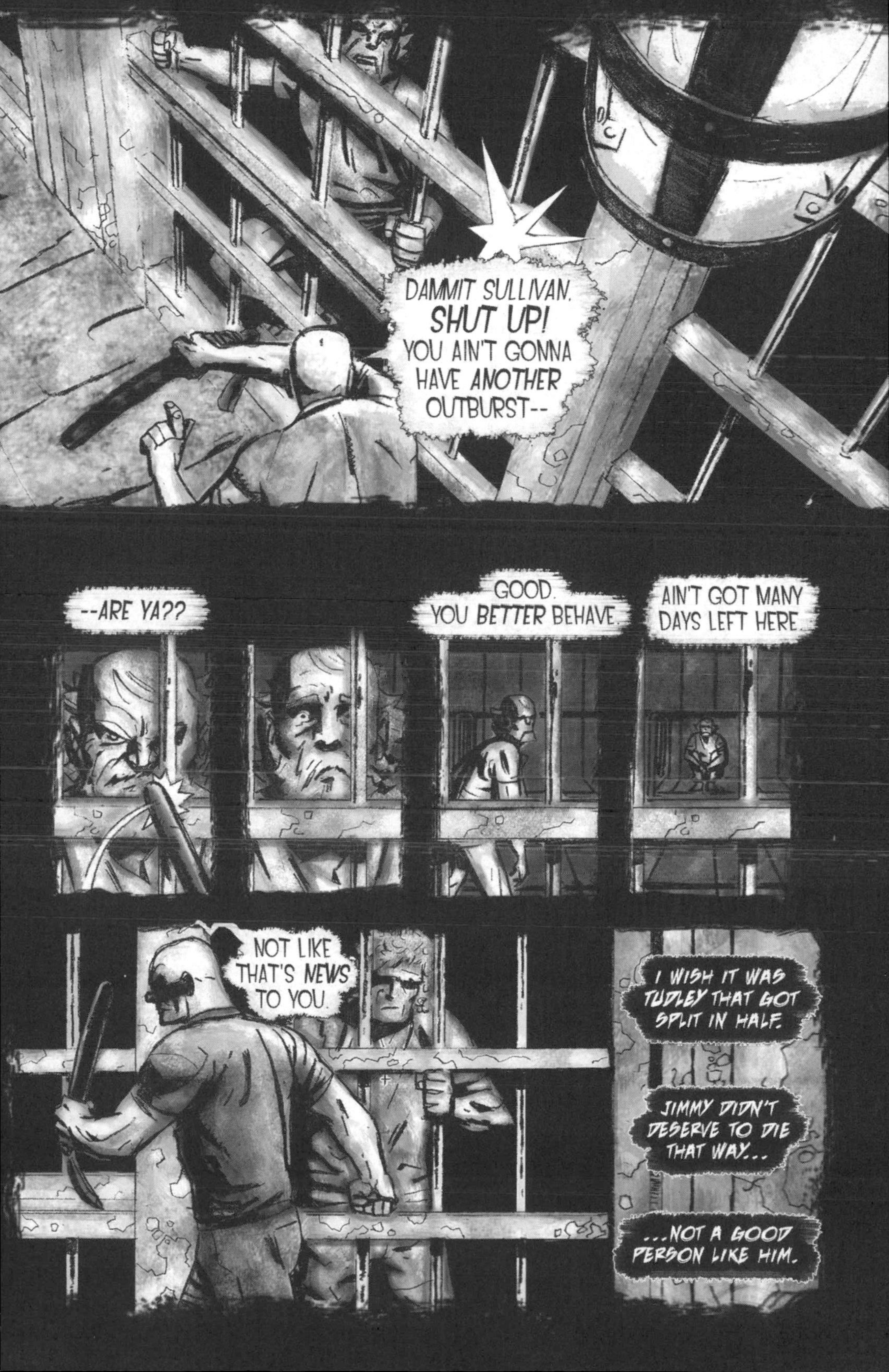
DAMMIT SULLIVAN, SHUT UP! YOU AIN'T GONNA HAVE ANOTHER OUTBURST--
--ARE YA??
GOOD. YOU BETTER BEHAVE.
AIN'T GOT MANY DAYS LEFT HERE.
NOT LIKE THAT'S NEWS TO YOU.
I WISH IT WAS TUDLEY THAT GOT SPLIT IN HALF.
JIMMY DIDN'T DESERVE TO DIE THAT WAY...
...NOT A GOOD PERSON LIKE HIM.

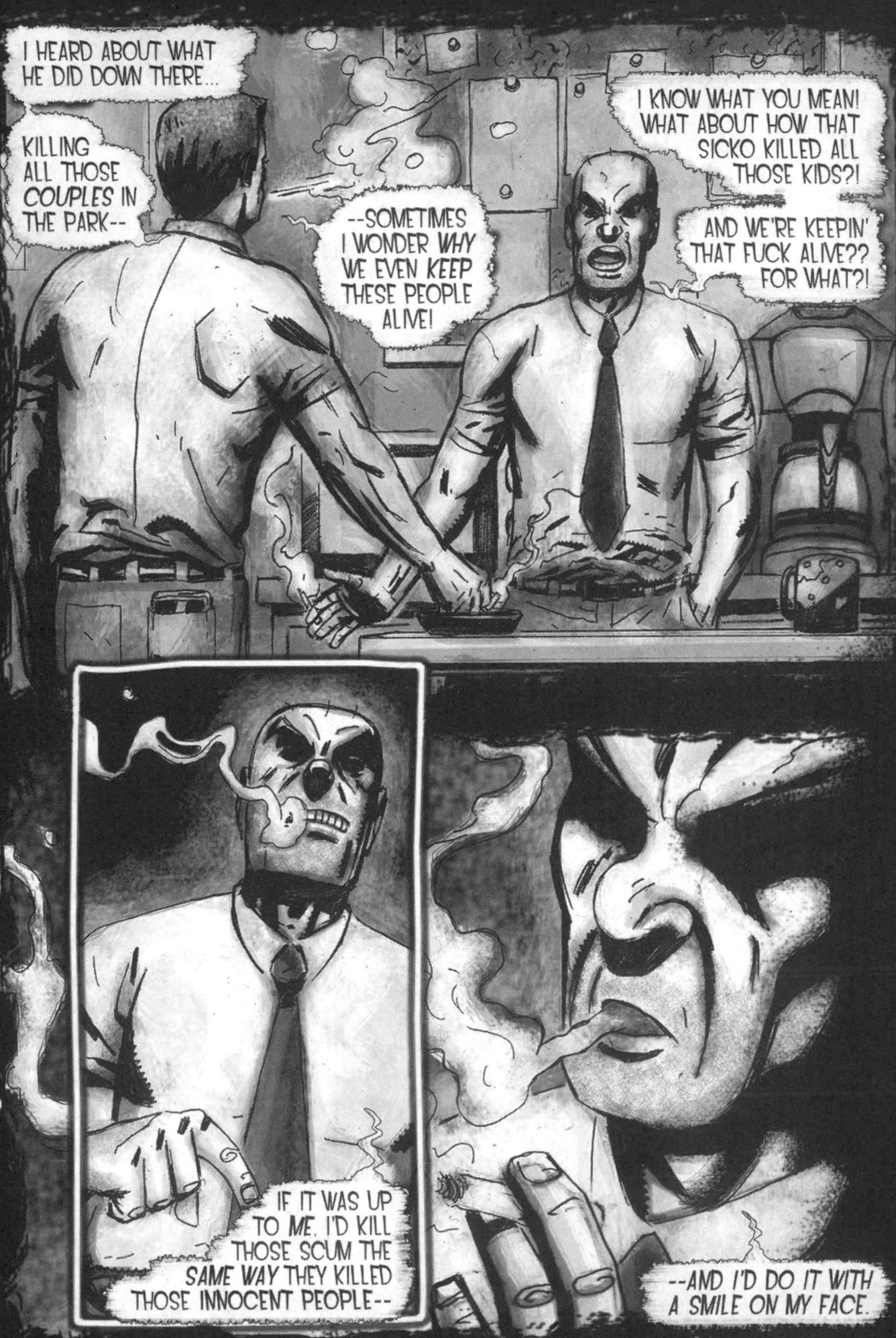
I HEARD ABOUT WHAT HE DID DOWN THERE...
KILLING ALL THOSE *COUPLES* IN THE PARK--
--SOMETIMES I WONDER *WHY* WE EVEN *KEEP* THESE PEOPLE ALIVE!
I KNOW WHAT YOU MEAN! WHAT ABOUT HOW THAT SICKO KILLED ALL THOSE KIDS?!
AND WE'RE KEEPIN' THAT FUCK ALIVE?? FOR WHAT?!
IF IT WAS UP TO *ME*, I'D KILL THOSE SCUM THE *SAME WAY* THEY KILLED THOSE INNOCENT PEOPLE--
--AND I'D DO IT WITH A SMILE ON MY FACE.

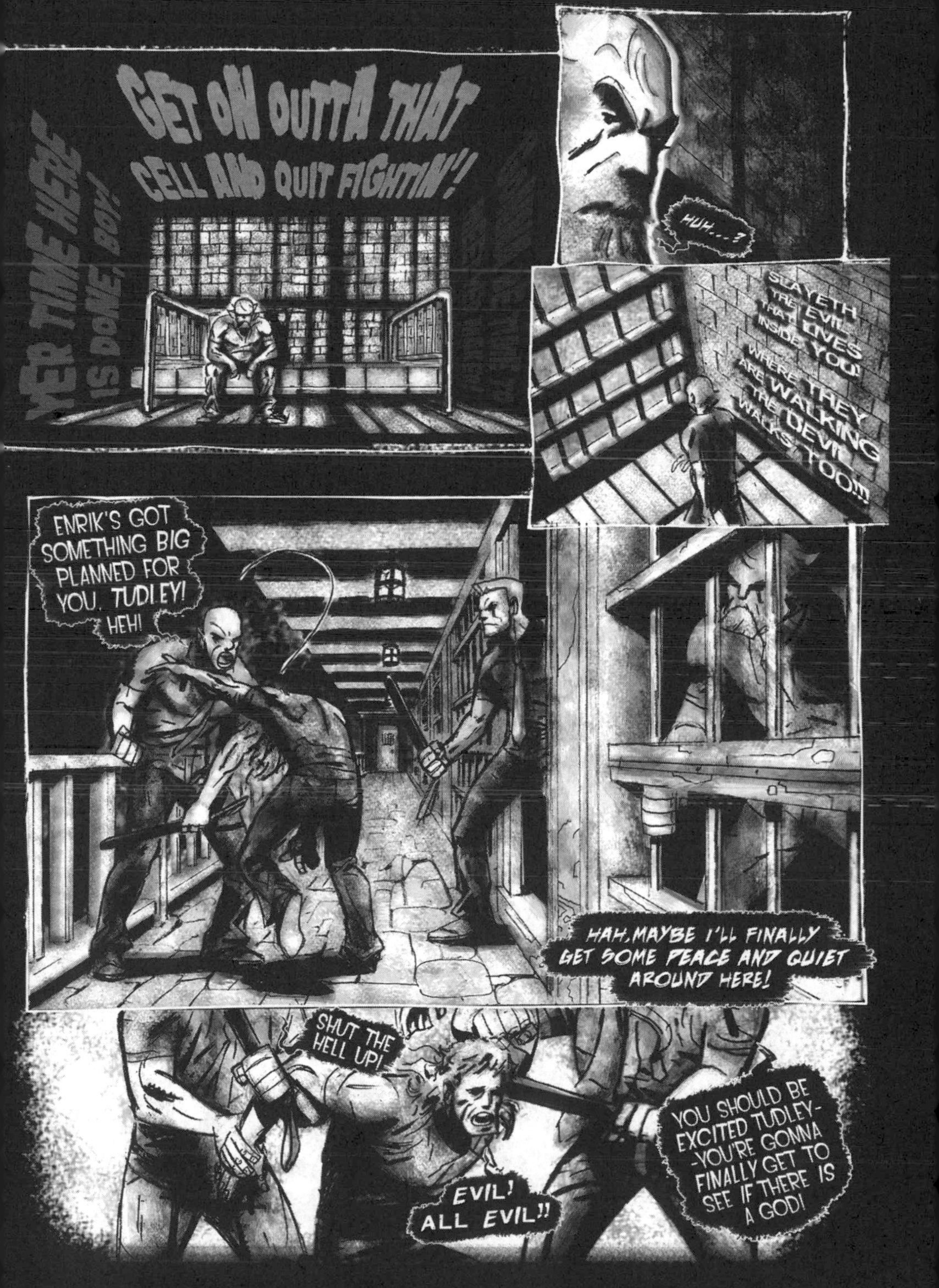

YER TIME HERE IS DONE, BOY!
GET ON OUTTA THAT CELL AND QUIT FIGHTIN'!!
HUH...?
SLAYETH THE EVIL THAT LIVES INSIDE YOU! WHERE THEY ARE WALKING THE DEVIL WALKS, TOO!!!
ENRIK'S GOT SOMETHING BIG PLANNED FOR YOU, TUDLEY! HEH!
HAH, MAYBE I'LL FINALLY GET SOME PEACE AND QUIET AROUND HERE!
SHUT THE HELL UP!
YOU SHOULD BE EXCITED TUDLEY- -YOU'RE GONNA FINALLY GET TO SEE IF THERE IS A GOD!
EVIL! ALL EVIL!!

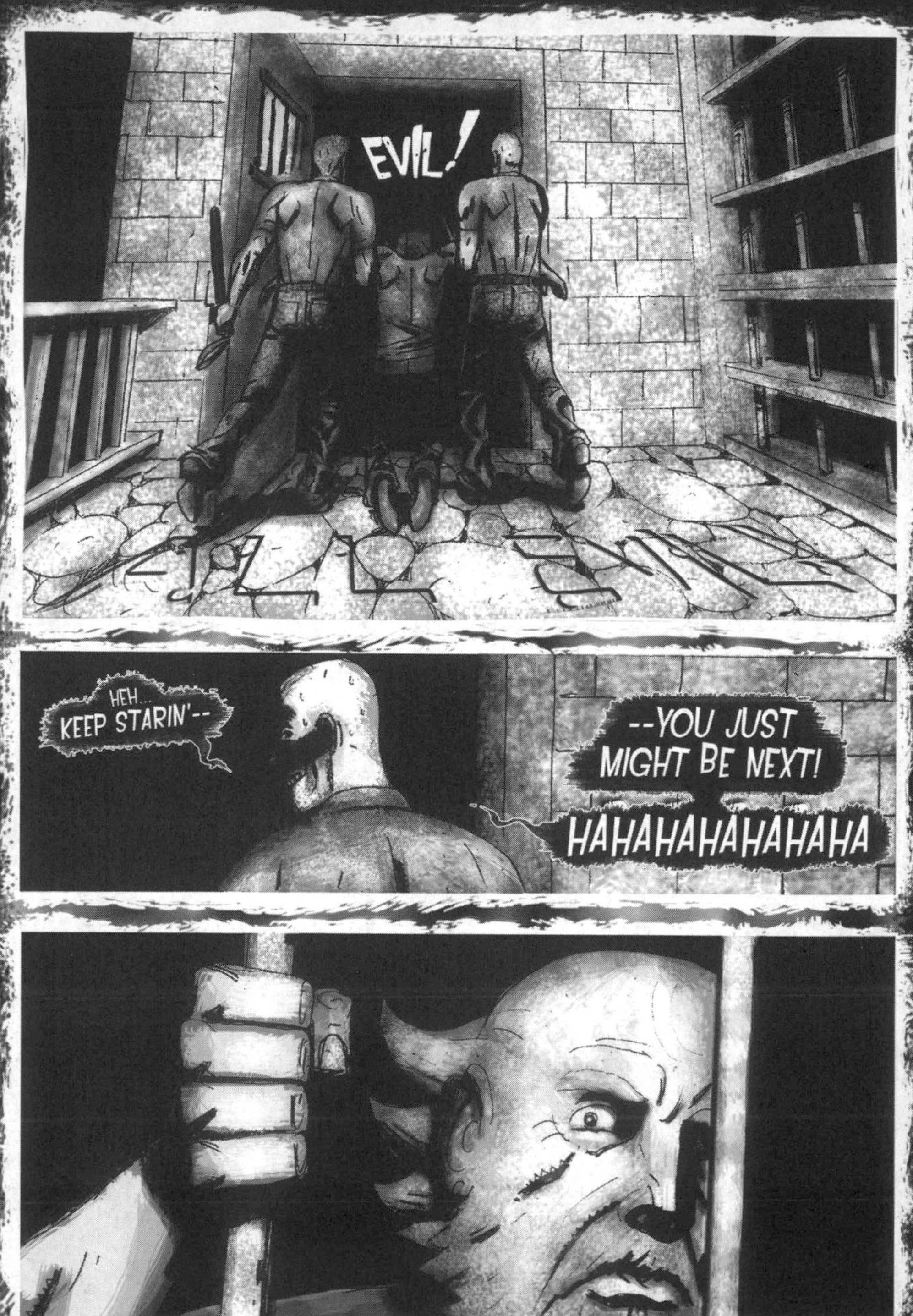
EVIL!
HEH... KEEP STARIN'--
--YOU JUST MIGHT BE NEXT!
HAHAHAHAHAHAHA

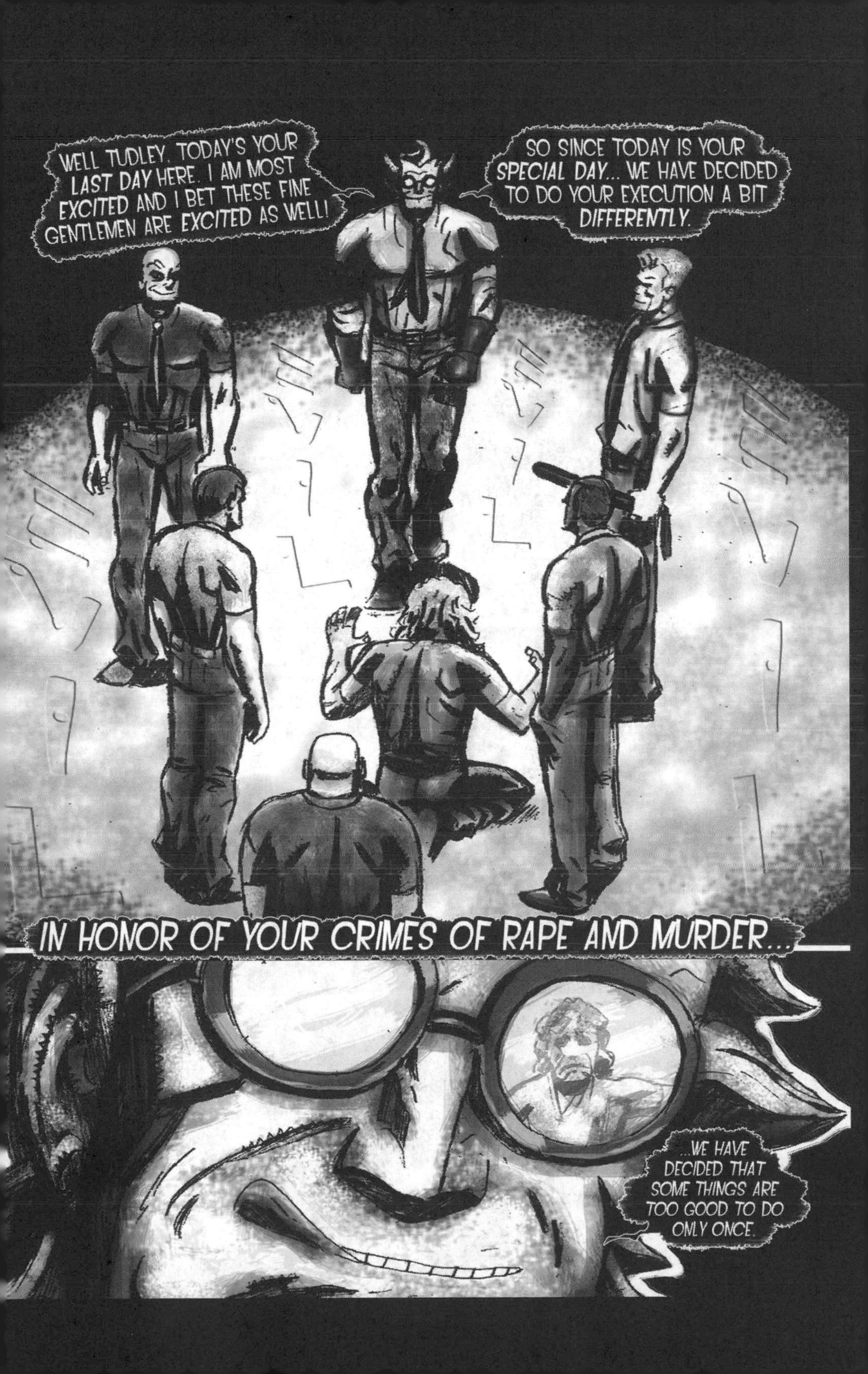
WELL TUDLEY, TODAY'S YOUR LAST DAY HERE. I AM MOST EXCITED AND I BET THESE FINE GENTLEMEN ARE EXCITED AS WELL!
SO SINCE TODAY IS YOUR SPECIAL DAY... WE HAVE DECIDED TO DO YOUR EXECUTION A BIT DIFFERENTLY.
IN HONOR OF YOUR CRIMES OF RAPE AND MURDER...
...WE HAVE DECIDED THAT SOME THINGS ARE TOO GOOD TO DO ONLY ONCE.

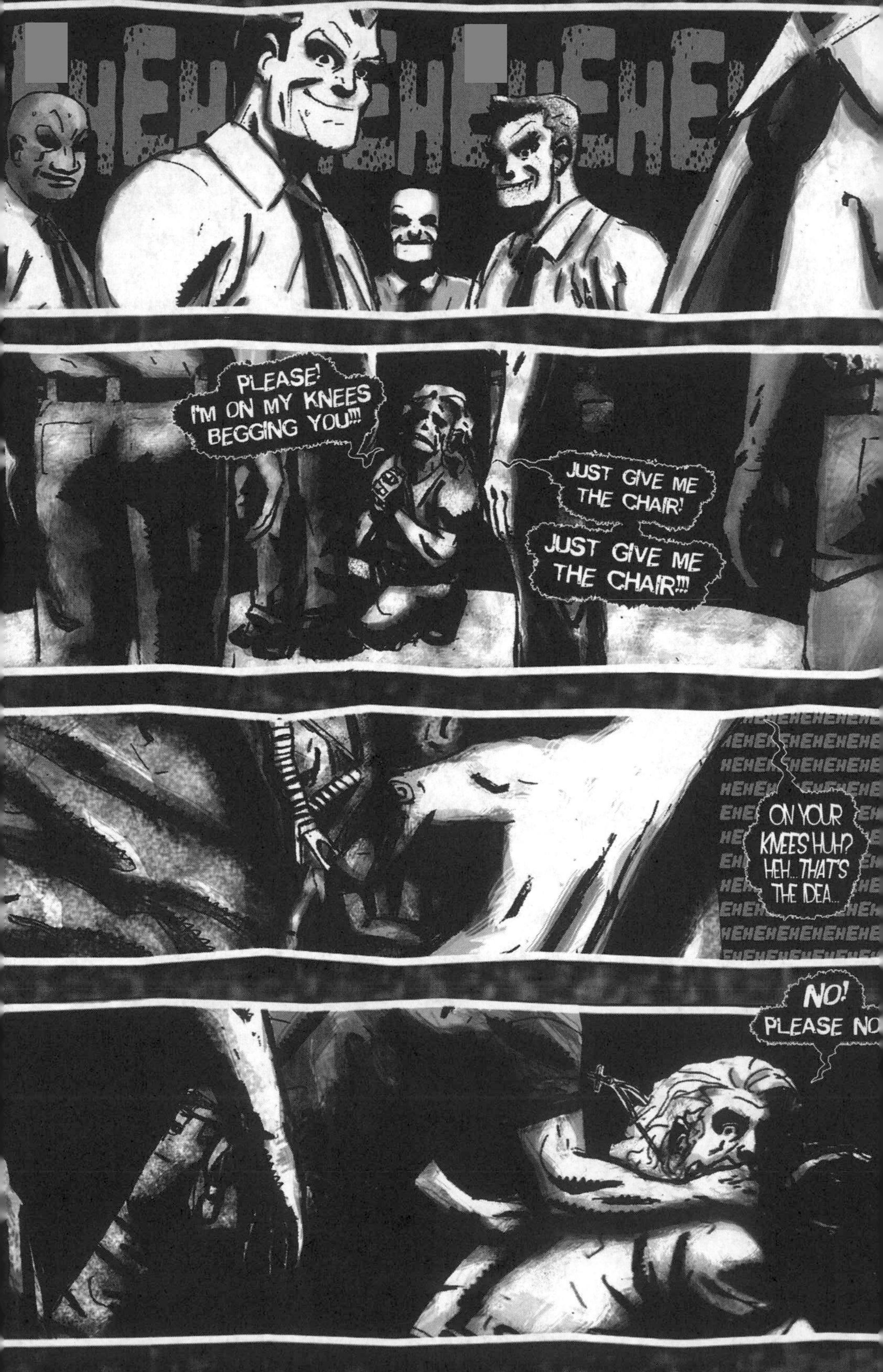
PLEASE! I'M ON MY KNEES BEGGING YOU!!!
JUST GIVE ME THE CHAIR!
JUST GIVE ME THE CHAIR!!!
ON YOUR KNEES HUH? HEH... THAT'S THE IDEA...
NO! PLEASE NO

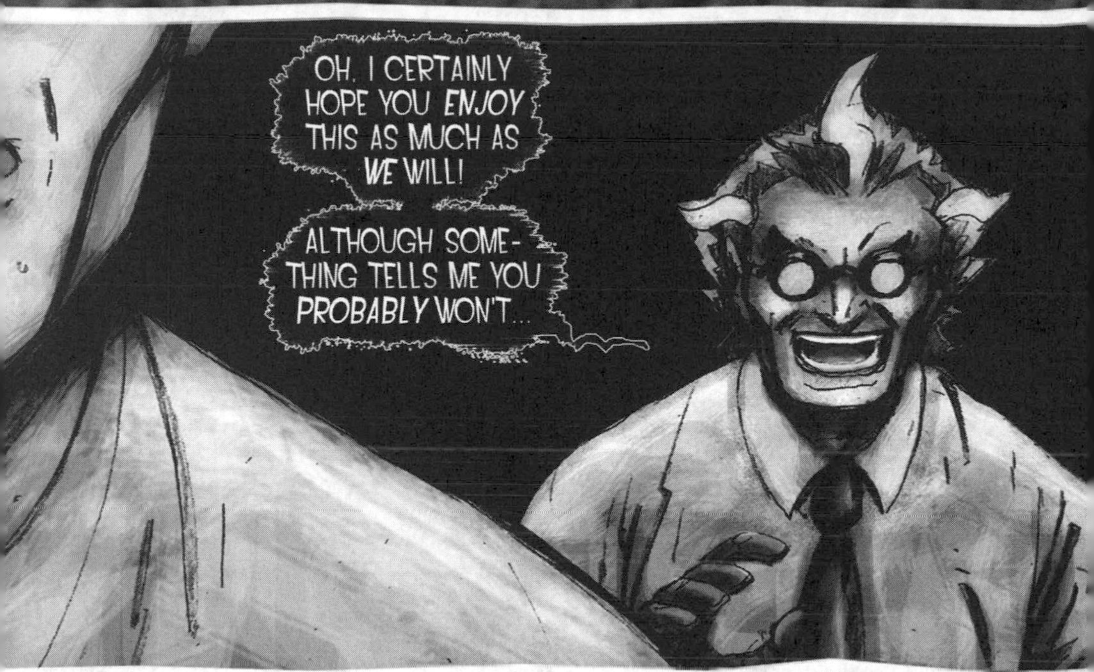

OH, I CERTAINLY HOPE YOU ENJOY THIS AS MUCH AS WE WILL!
ALTHOUGH SOMETHING TELLS ME YOU PROBABLY WON'T...

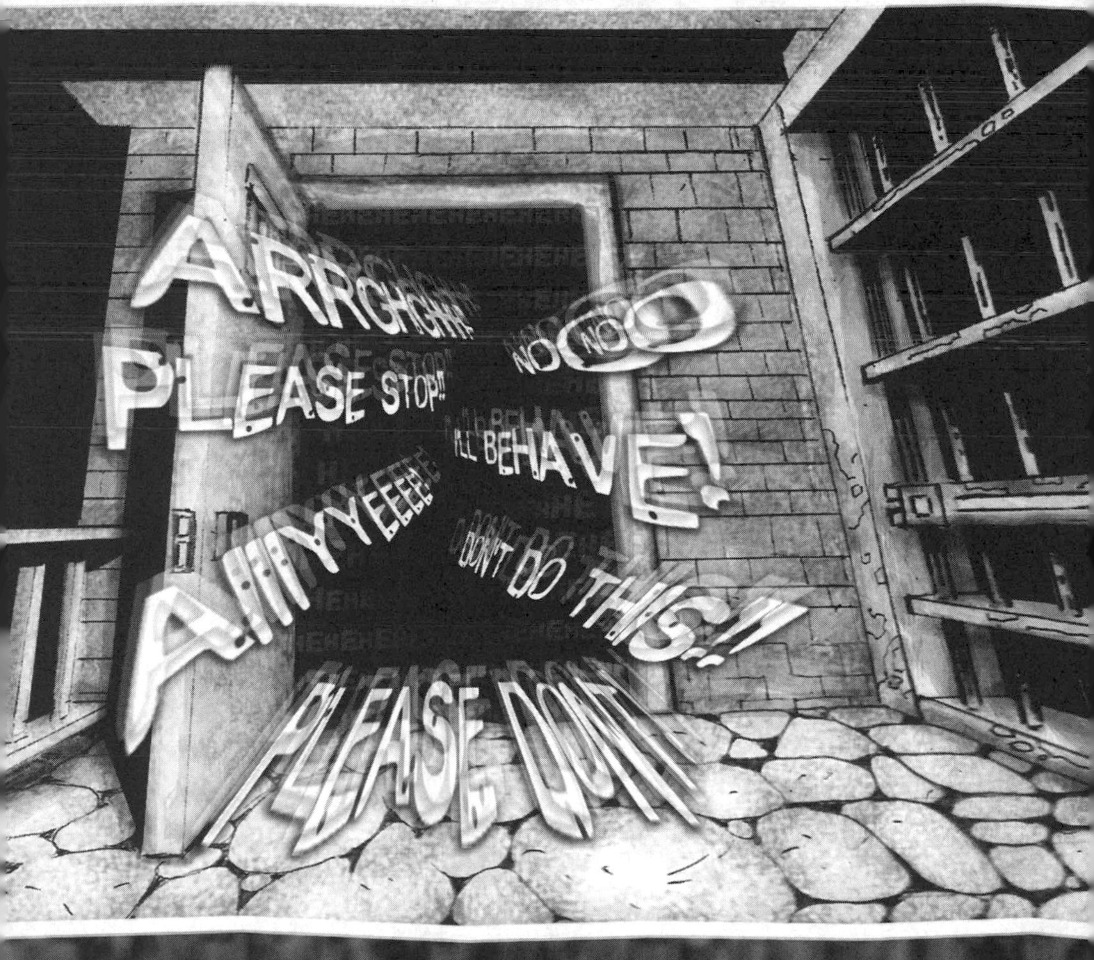

ARRGHGHH!!
PLEASE STOP!!
NO NO NOOO
I'LL BEHAVE!
AIIIYYEEEEE
DON'T DO THIS!!
PLEASE DON'T

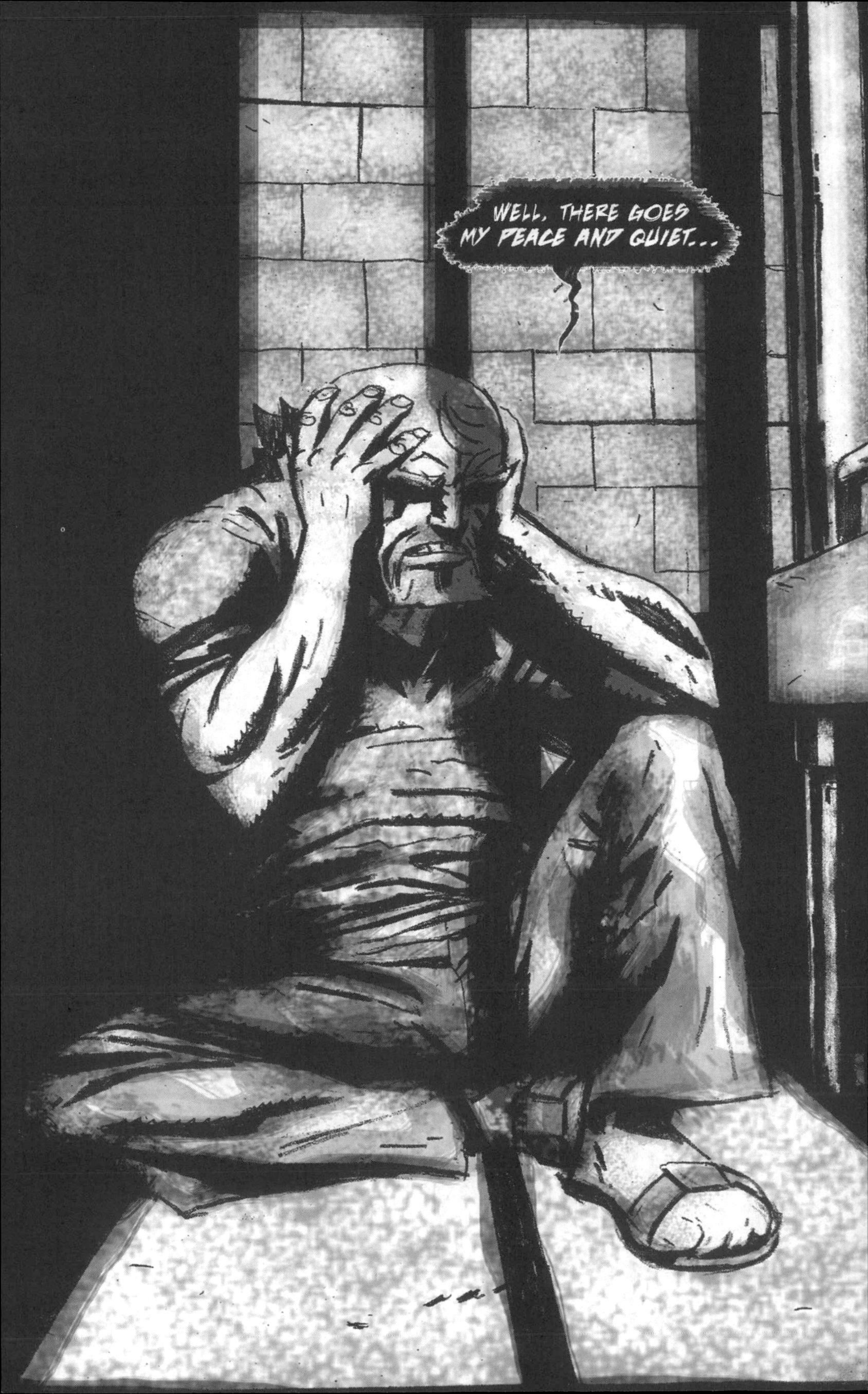
WELL, THERE GOES MY PEACE AND QUIET...

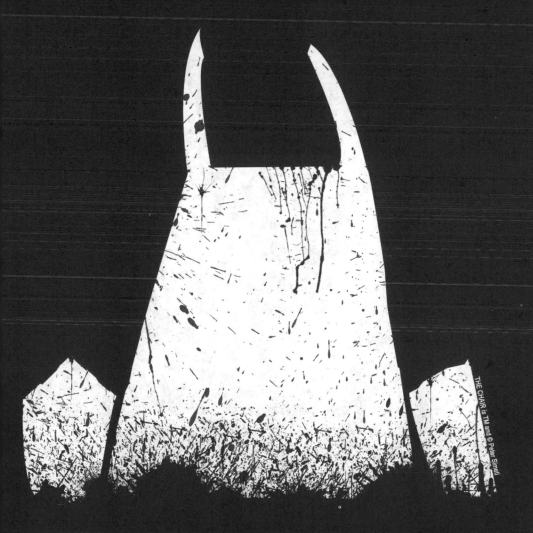

THE CHAIR is TM and © Peter Simeti

ACT FOUR: MONSTERS

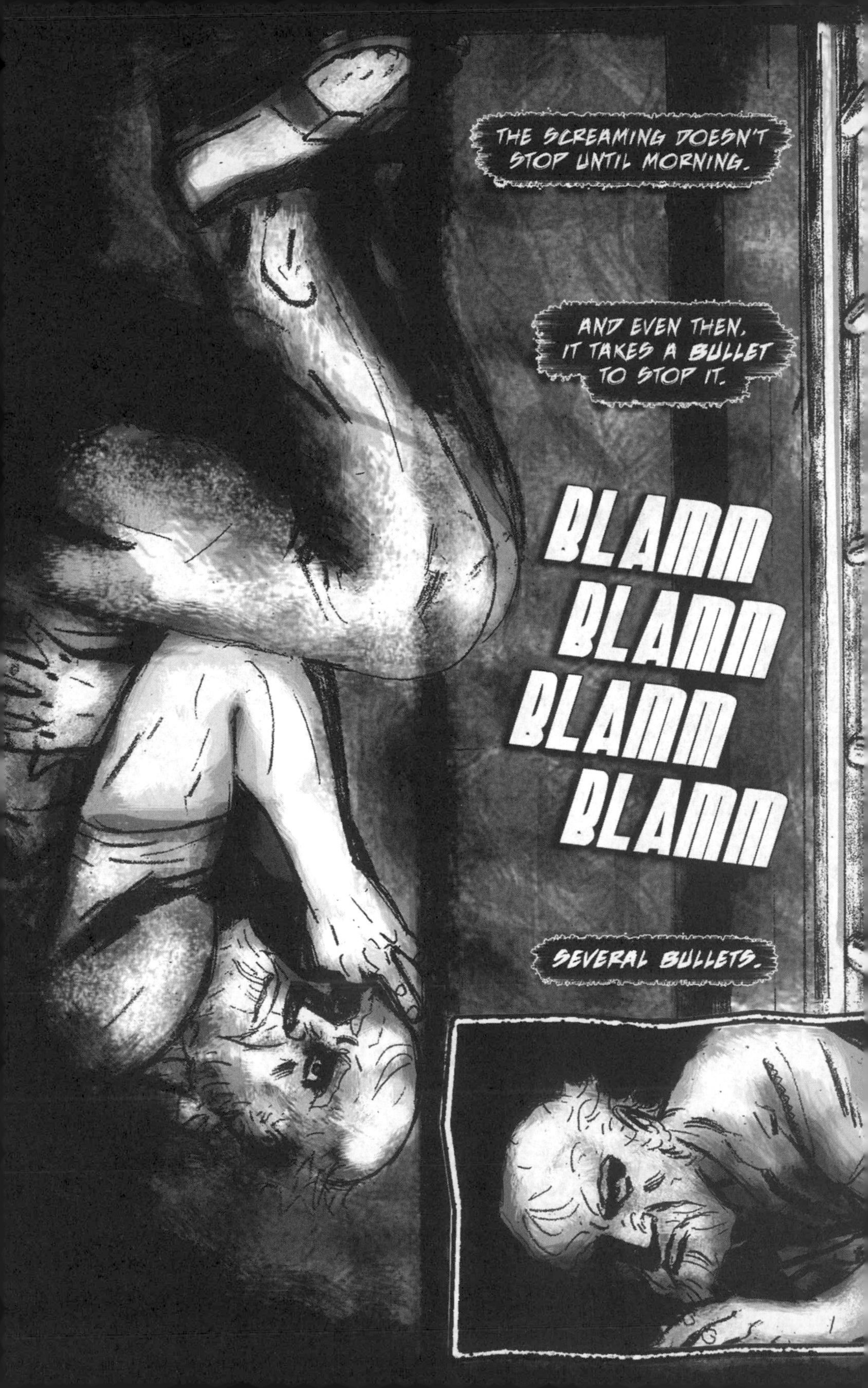
THE SCREAMING DOESN'T STOP UNTIL MORNING.
AND EVEN THEN, IT TAKES A BULLET TO STOP IT.
BLAMM BLAMM BLAMM BLAMM
SEVERAL BULLETS.

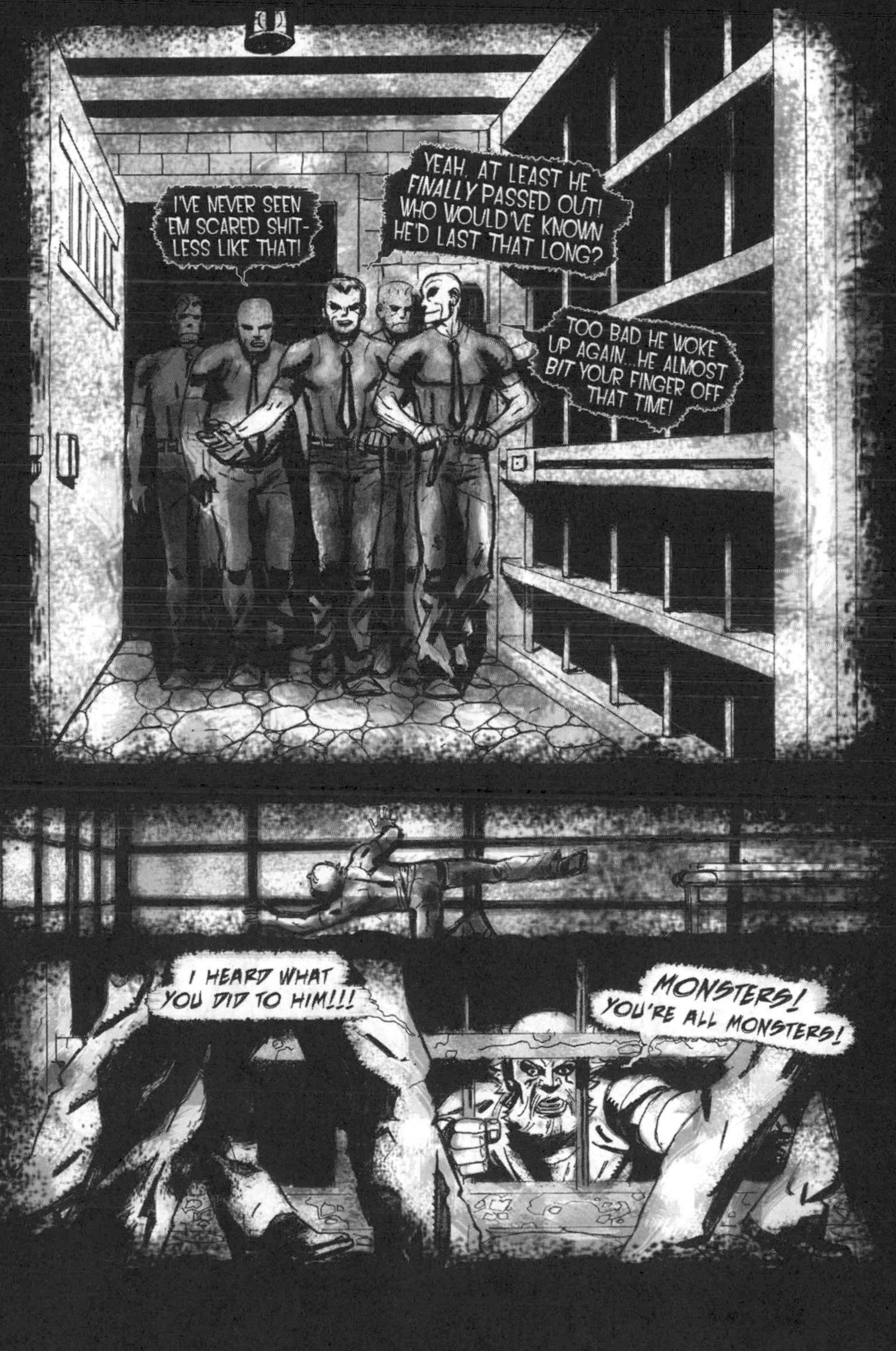
I'VE NEVER SEEN 'EM SCARED SHIT-LESS LIKE THAT!
YEAH, AT LEAST HE FINALLY PASSED OUT! WHO WOULD'VE KNOWN HE'D LAST THAT LONG?
TOO BAD HE WOKE UP AGAIN...HE ALMOST BIT YOUR FINGER OFF THAT TIME!
I HEARD WHAT YOU DID TO HIM!!!
MONSTERS! YOU'RE ALL MONSTERS!

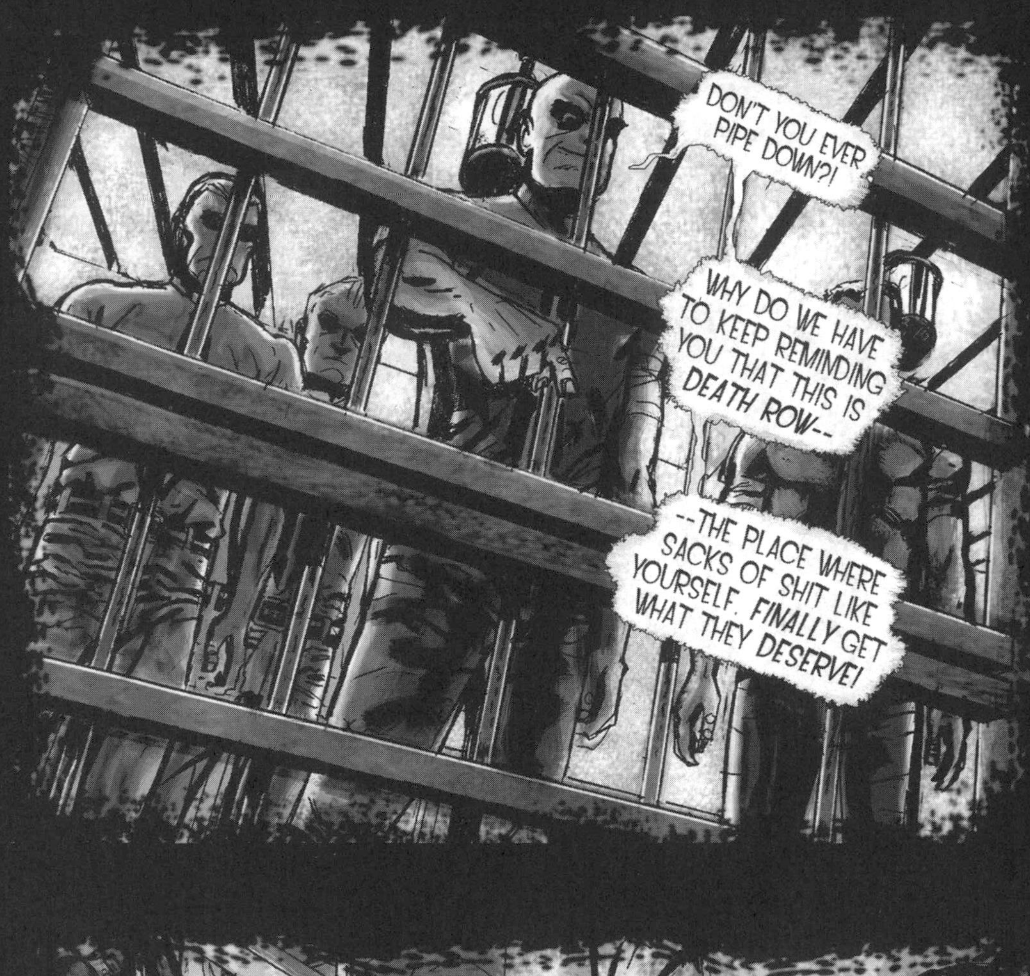
DON'T YOU EVER PIPE DOWN?!
WHY DO WE HAVE TO KEEP REMINDING YOU THAT THIS IS DEATH ROW--
--THE PLACE WHERE SACKS OF SHIT LIKE YOURSELF, FINALLY GET WHAT THEY DESERVE!
GET BACK HERE YOU ASSHOLE!
TRY SAYING THAT TO ME WHEN I'M NOT LOCKED IN HERE!
SORRY SULLIVAN. I FORGOT WE'RE NOT ALLOWED TO TEASE THE ANIMALS - HAHAHA!

"ANIMALS"...
LIKE HE'S ANY BETTER?
JUST KNOWING WHAT THEY DID TO TUDLEY REALLY TURNS MY STOMACH...
THE WAY HE SCREAMED LAST NIGHT...I DON'T EVEN THINK HIS VICTIMS SUFFERED THAT MUCH...
IT'S ALWAYS BEEN BAD HERE... BUT THINGS HAVE BEEN A LOT WORSE SINCE THEY GOT THAT NEW WARDEN.
HE'S AS MUCH A MONSTER AS SOME OF THESE INMATES.

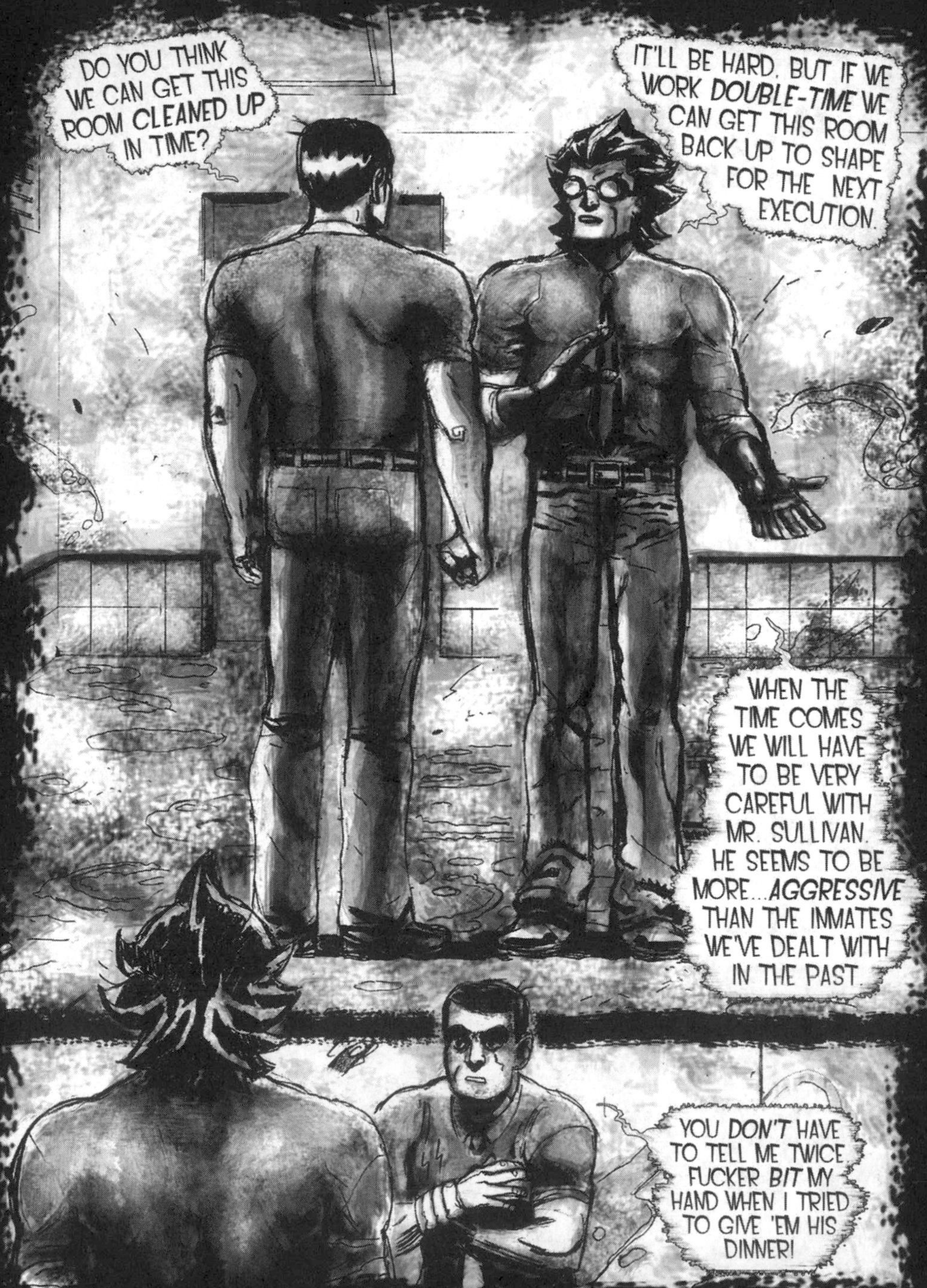
DO YOU THINK WE CAN GET THIS ROOM CLEANED UP IN TIME?
IT'LL BE HARD, BUT IF WE WORK DOUBLE-TIME WE CAN GET THIS ROOM BACK UP TO SHAPE FOR THE NEXT EXECUTION.
WHEN THE TIME COMES WE WILL HAVE TO BE VERY CAREFUL WITH MR. SULLIVAN. HE SEEMS TO BE MORE...AGGRESSIVE THAN THE IMMATES WE'VE DEALT WITH IN THE PAST.
YOU DON'T HAVE TO TELL ME TWICE. FUCKER BIT MY HAND WHEN I TRIED TO GIVE 'EM HIS DINNER!

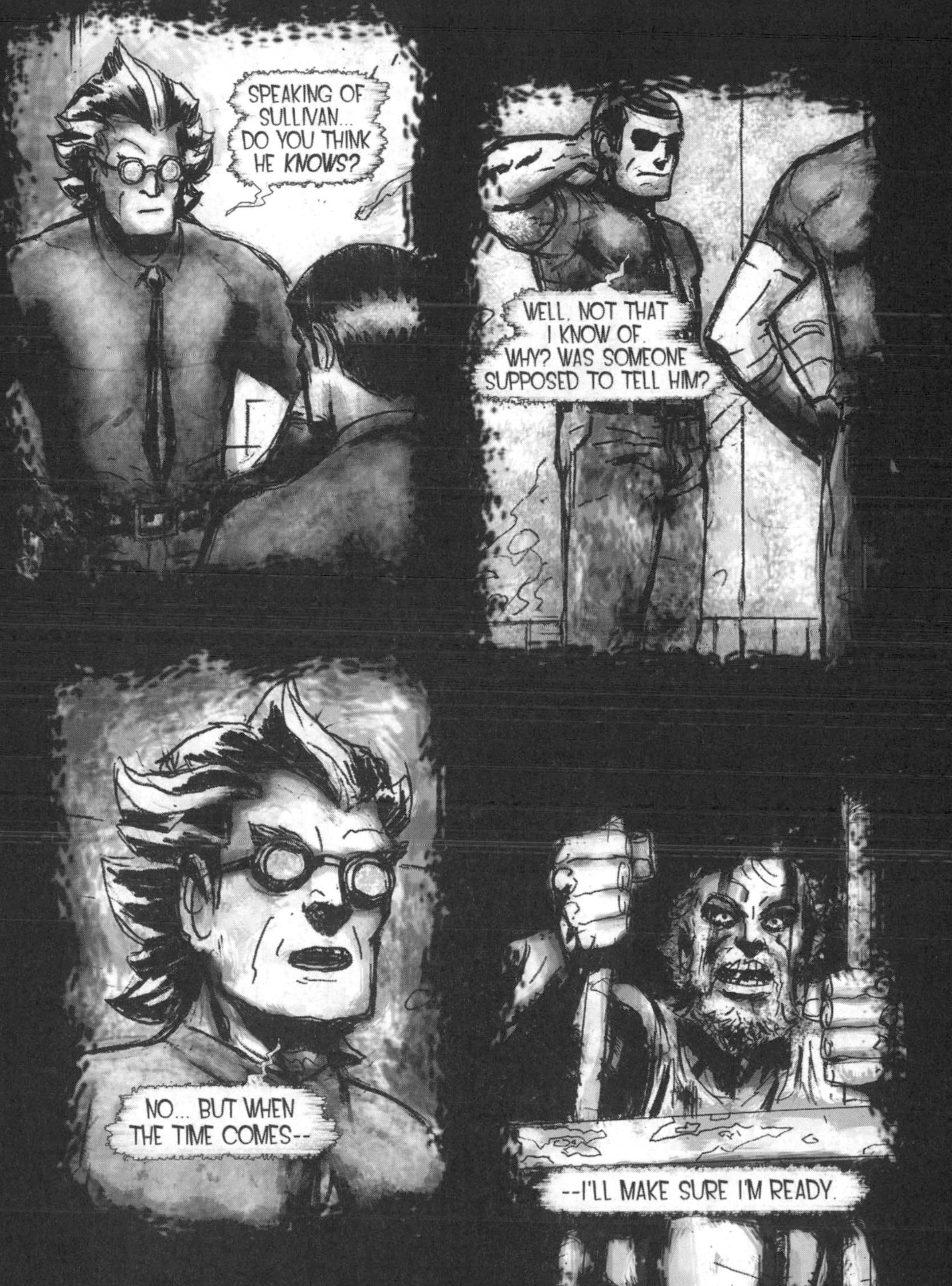
SPEAKING OF SULLIVAN... DO YOU THINK HE KNOWS?
WELL, NOT THAT I KNOW OF. WHY? WAS SOMEONE SUPPOSED TO TELL HIM?
NO... BUT WHEN THE TIME COMES--
--I'LL MAKE SURE I'M READY.

HEY WHAT THE HELL IS GOING ON DOWN THERE!?
ANYBODY HEAR ME?! I NEVER GOT MY DINNER!
NOT LIKE I WANT IT ANYWAY. I JUST HAVEN'T SEEN ANYONE SINCE THOSE GUARDS THIS MORNING... AND IN A PLACE FILLED WITH WEIRD SHIT, NOT SEEING ANY GUARDS OR IN-MATES IS EVEN WEIRDER.
IT'S GOTTA BE AT LEAST AN HOUR OR TWO SINCE I LAST TRIED CALLING OUT...
THIS WHOLE THING FEELS LIKE ONE OF THOSE DREAMS WHERE YOU'RE RUNNING YOUR HEART OUT...BUT YOU'RE JUST NOT GETTING ANYWHERE; LIKE RUNNING IN QUICKSAND.
ONLY THING IS--

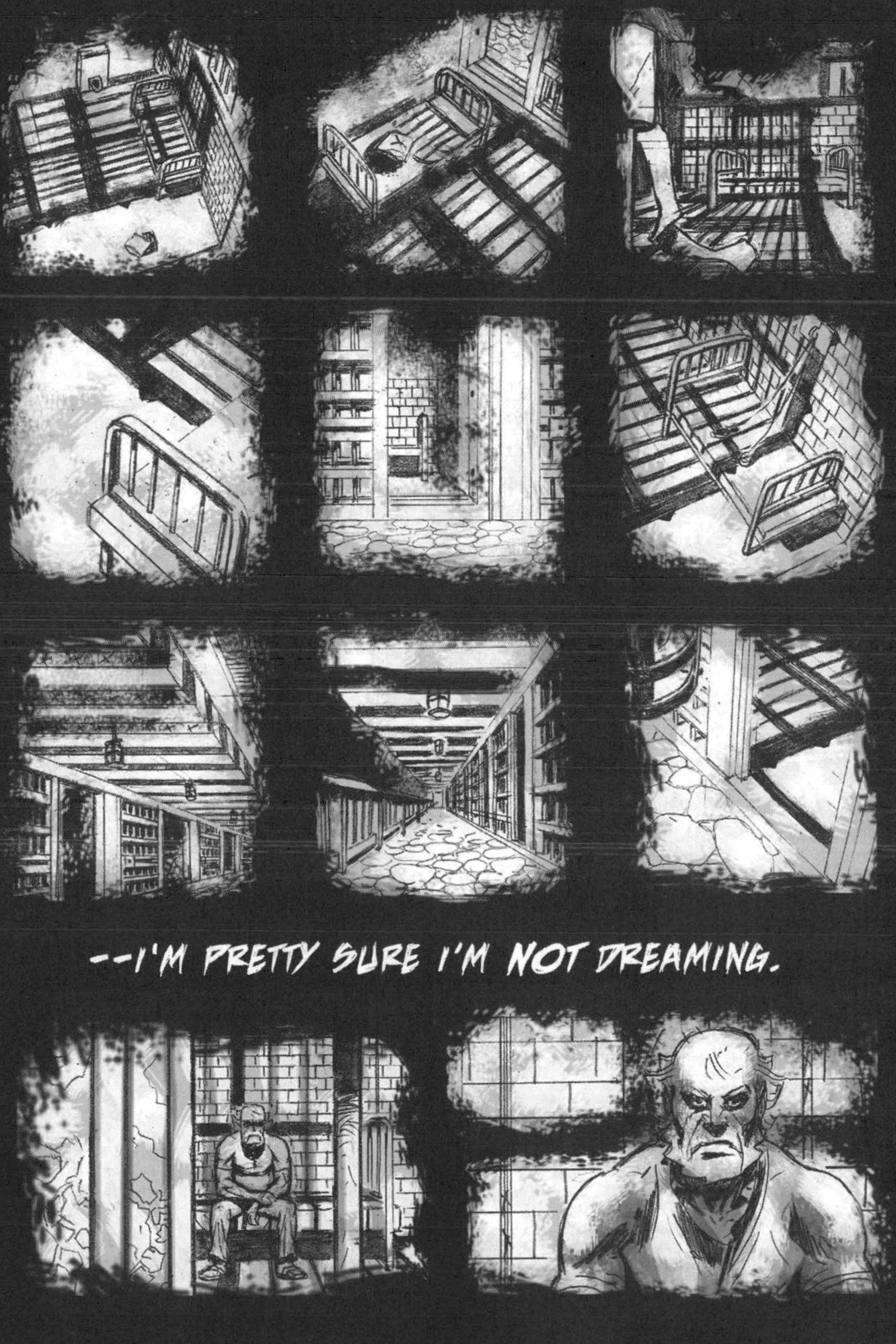
--I'M PRETTY SURE I'M NOT DREAMING.

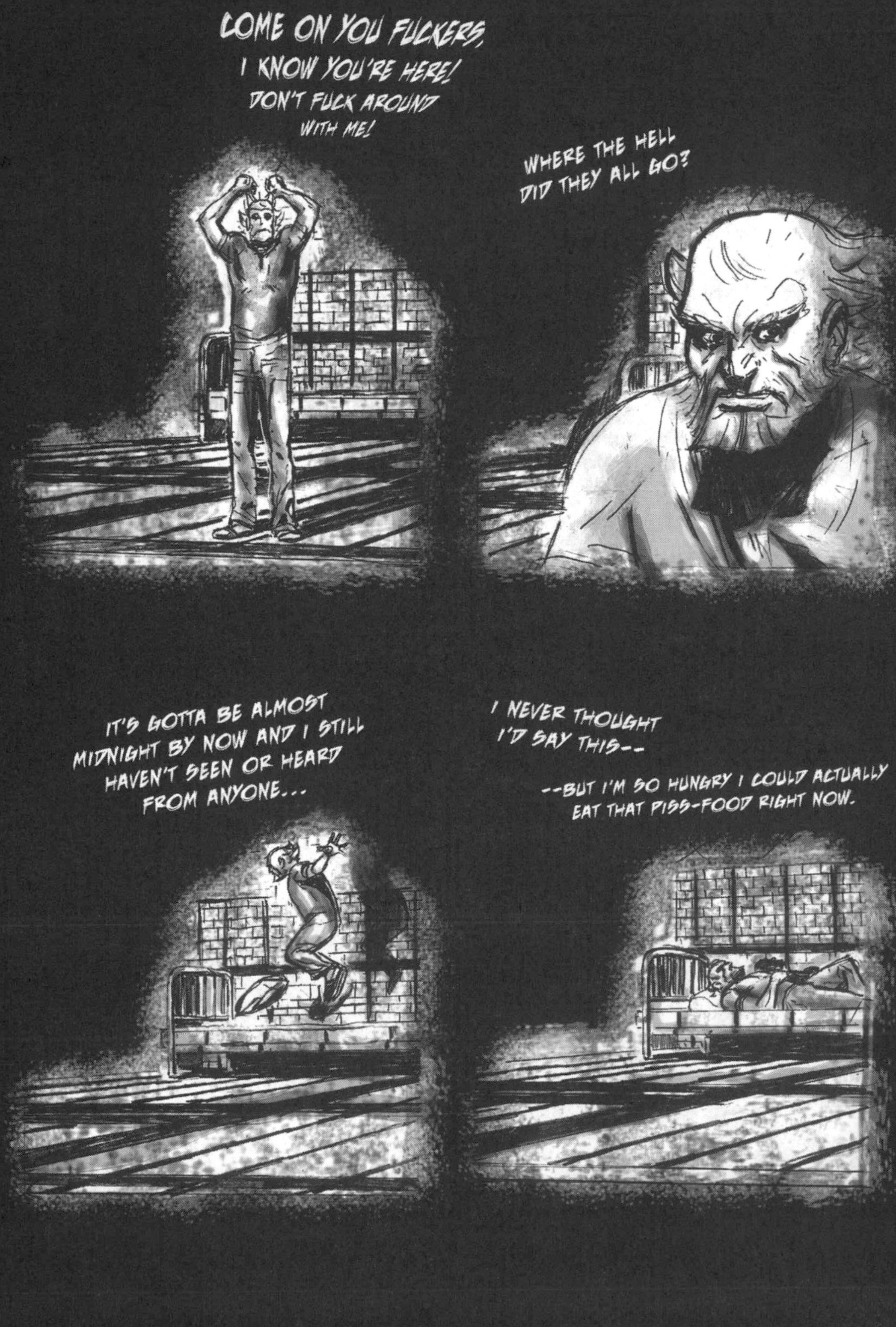
COME ON YOU FUCKERS, I KNOW YOU'RE HERE! DON'T FUCK AROUND WITH ME!
WHERE THE HELL DID THEY ALL GO?
IT'S GOTTA BE ALMOST MIDNIGHT BY NOW AND I STILL HAVEN'T SEEN OR HEARD FROM ANYONE...
I NEVER THOUGHT I'D SAY THIS--
--BUT I'M SO HUNGRY I COULD ACTUALLY EAT THAT PISS-FOOD RIGHT NOW.

EVER SINCE THAT GUARD SAID SOMETHING ABOUT MY TIME COMING UP SOON, ALL I CAN THINK ABOUT IS SEEING MY FAMILY ONE MORE TIME.
I BET MY KIDS ARE SO BIG NOW...
UGH...I HOPE THEY NEVER FIND OUT ABOUT ME BEING IN HERE.
MAYBE MY WIFE LIED TO THEM AND SAID I WENT OFF TO SOME WAR AND DIED.
ANYTHING'S BETTER THAN HAVING THEM THINK THEIR FATHER IS A CONVICTED MURDERER.

I KNOW THINGS ARE ALMOST AT AN END FOR ME...

I WISH THIS WAS LIKE ONE OF THOSE MOVIES; YOU KNOW THE KIND--

--GOVERNOR CALLS AT THE LAST SECOND...SAVES SOME INNOCENT PERSON FROM BEING EXECUTED.

BUT IF THE LAST 20 YEARS IN HERE HAVE TAUGHT ME ANYTHING... IT'S THAT EVERYTHING I USED TO KNOW WAS A LIE.

PEOPLE LIE.

YOU LIE.

EVERYONE FUCKIN' LIES.

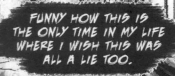

FUNNY HOW THIS IS THE ONLY TIME IN MY LIFE WHERE I WISH THIS WAS ALL A LIE TOO.

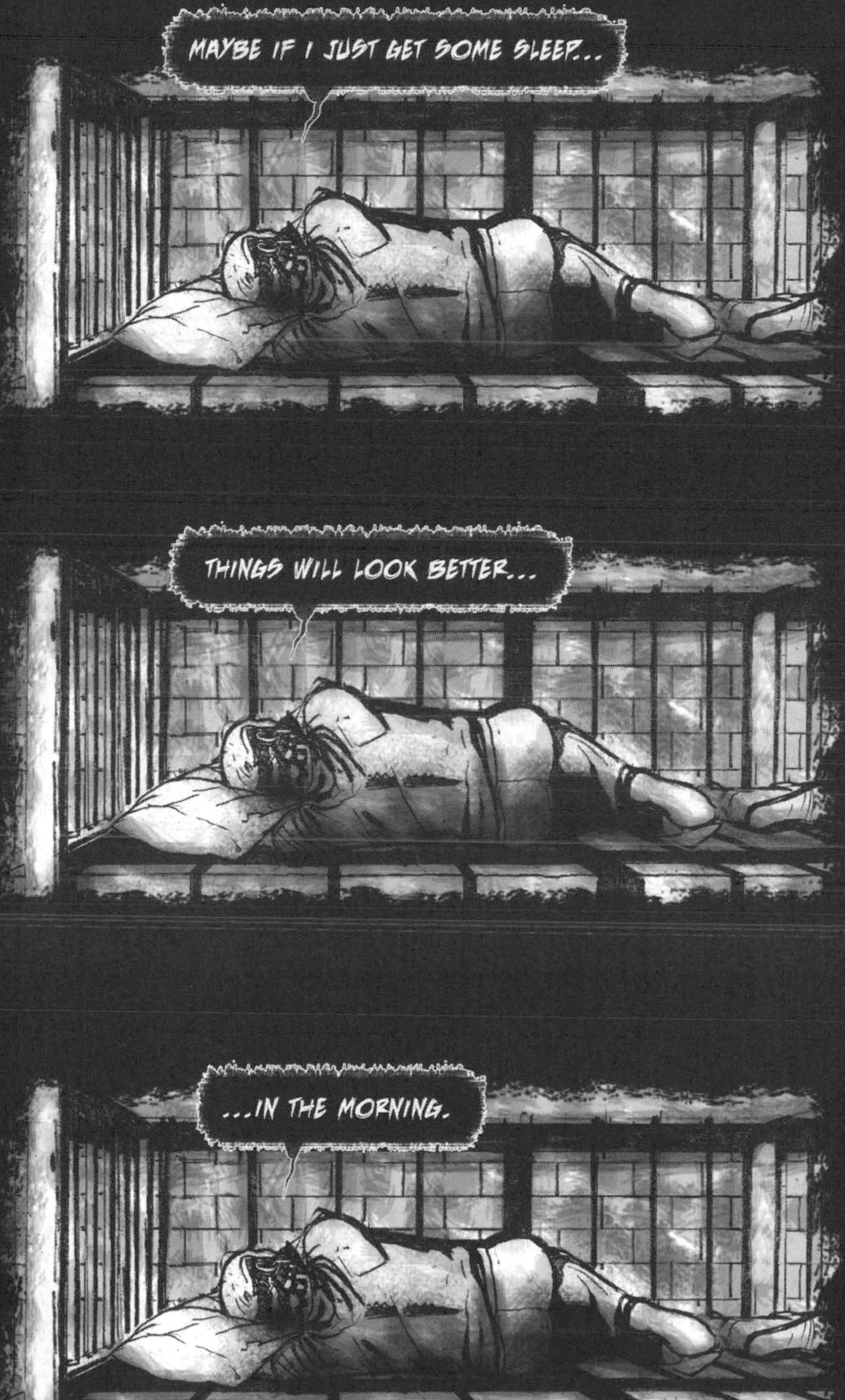
MAYBE IF I JUST GET SOME SLEEP...
THINGS WILL LOOK BETTER...
...IN THE MORNING.

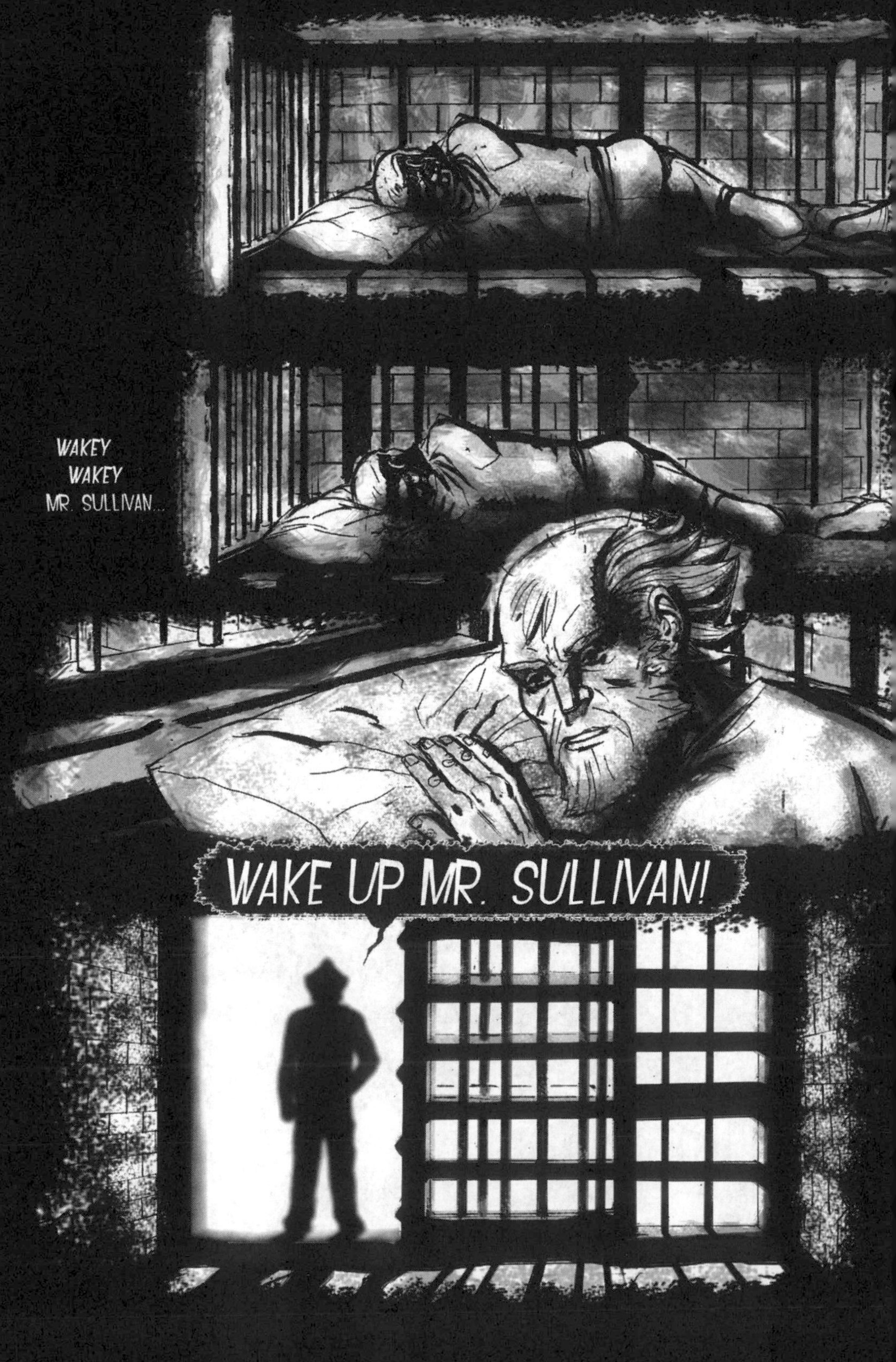
WAKEY WAKEY MR. SULLIVAN...
WAKE UP MR. SULLIVAN!

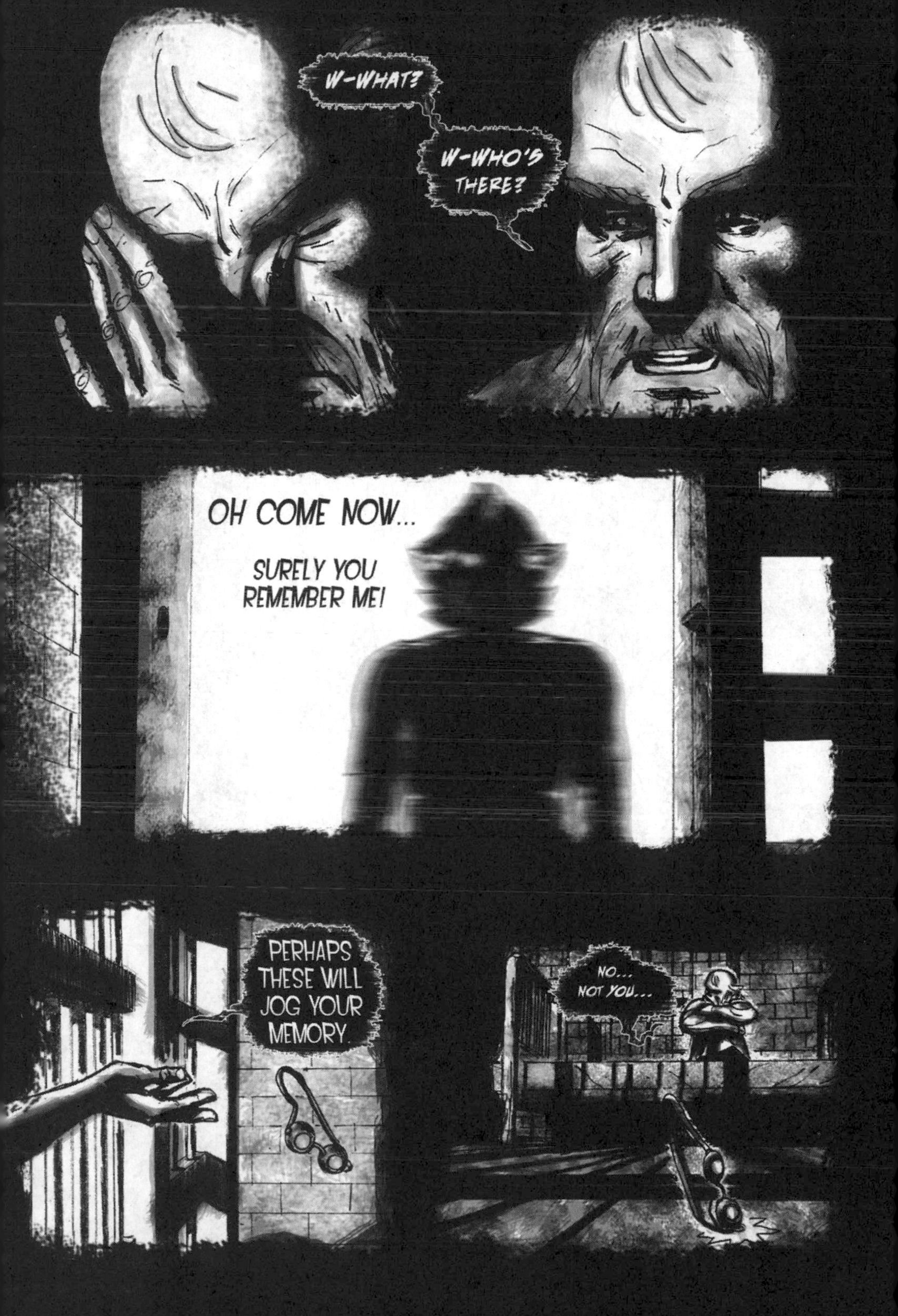
W-WHAT?
W-WHO'S THERE?
OH COME NOW...
SURELY YOU REMEMBER ME!
PERHAPS THESE WILL JOG YOUR MEMORY.
NO... NOT YOU...

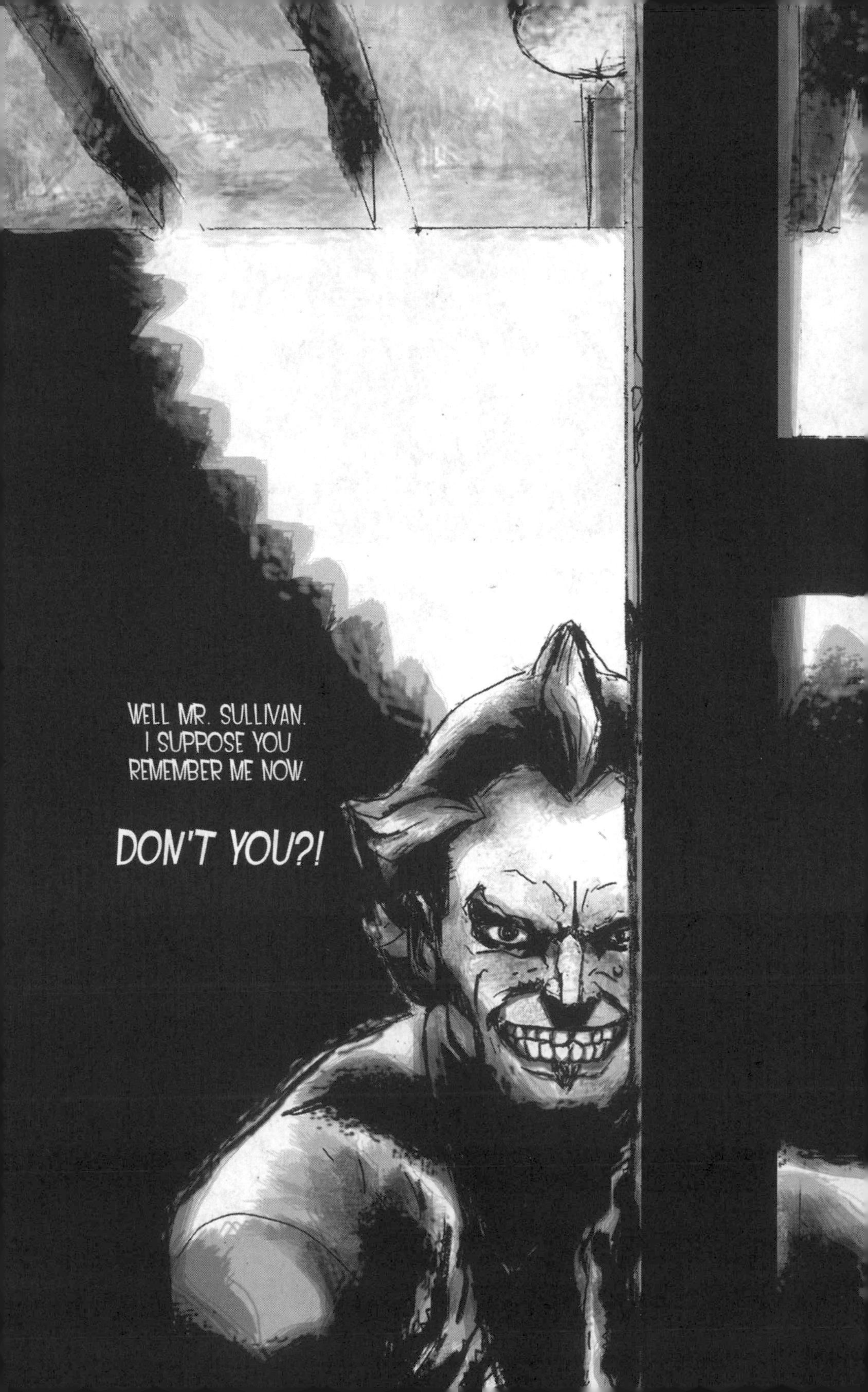
WELL MR. SULLIVAN.
I SUPPOSE YOU
REMEMBER ME NOW.
DON'T YOU?!

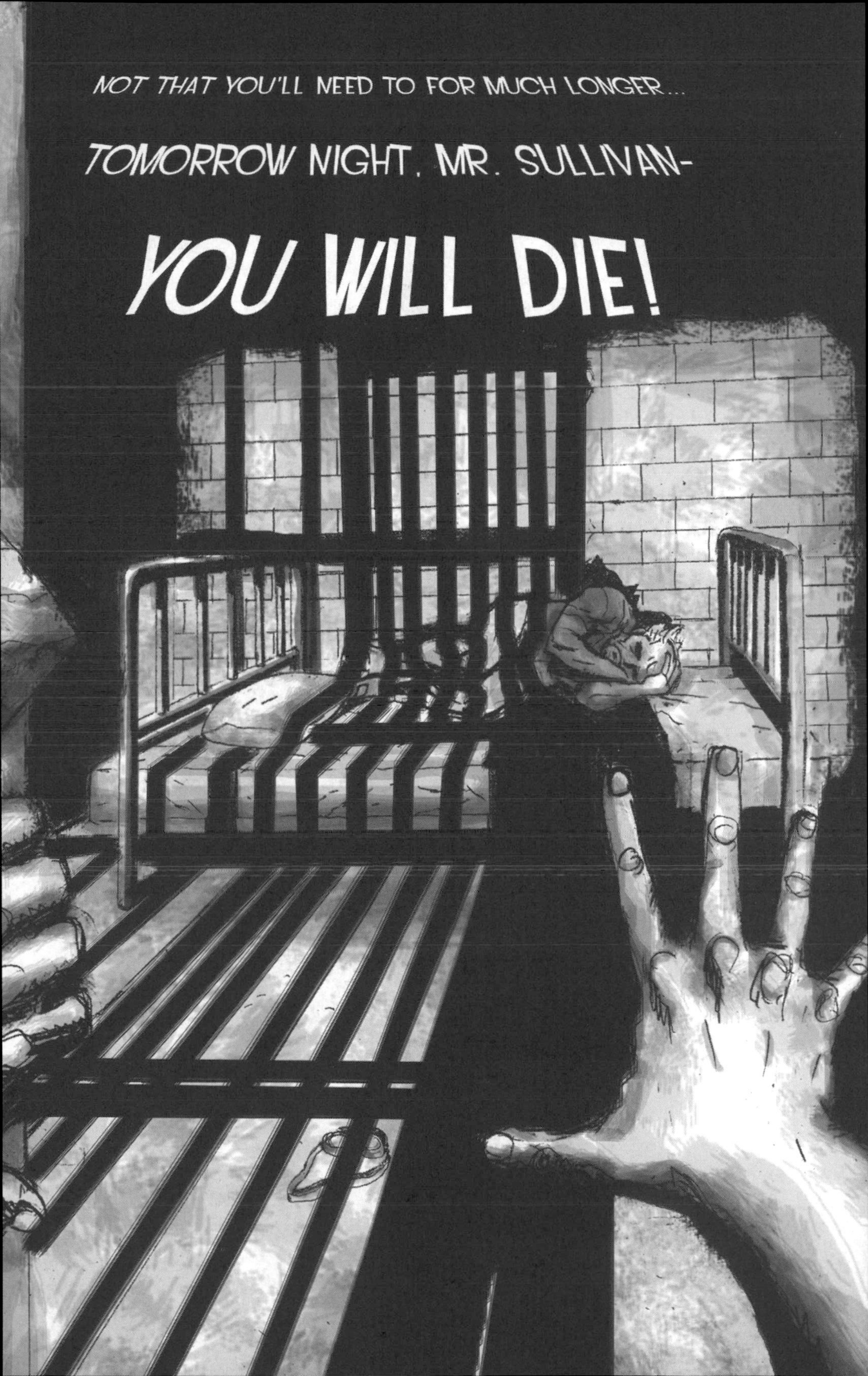
NOT THAT YOU'LL NEED TO FOR MUCH LONGER...
TOMORROW NIGHT, MR. SULLIVAN-
YOU WILL DIE!

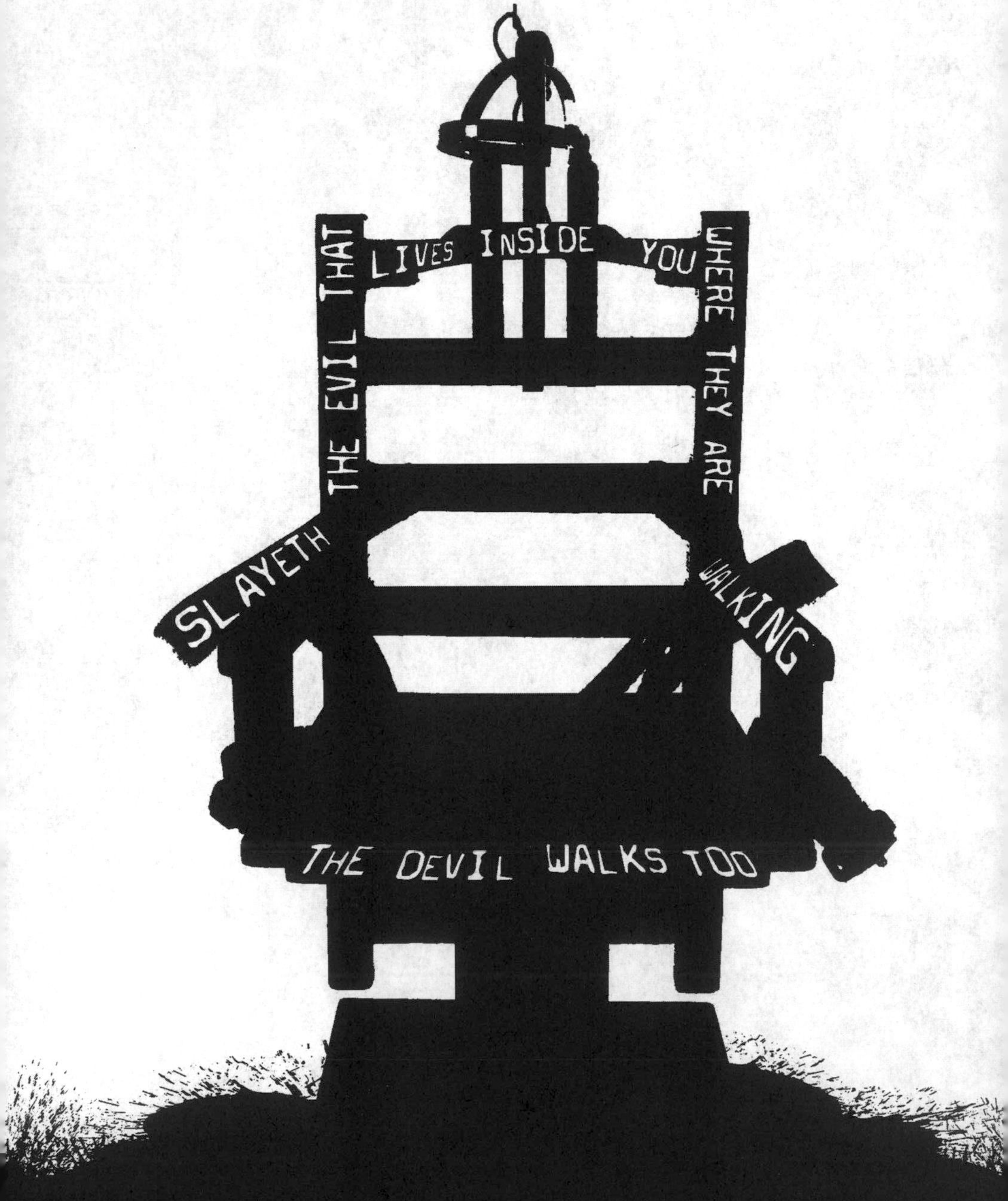
SLAYETH
THE EVIL THAT
LIVES INSIDE
YOU
WHERE THEY ARE
WALKING
THE DEVIL WALKS TOO

ACT FIVE: *ILLUSIONS*

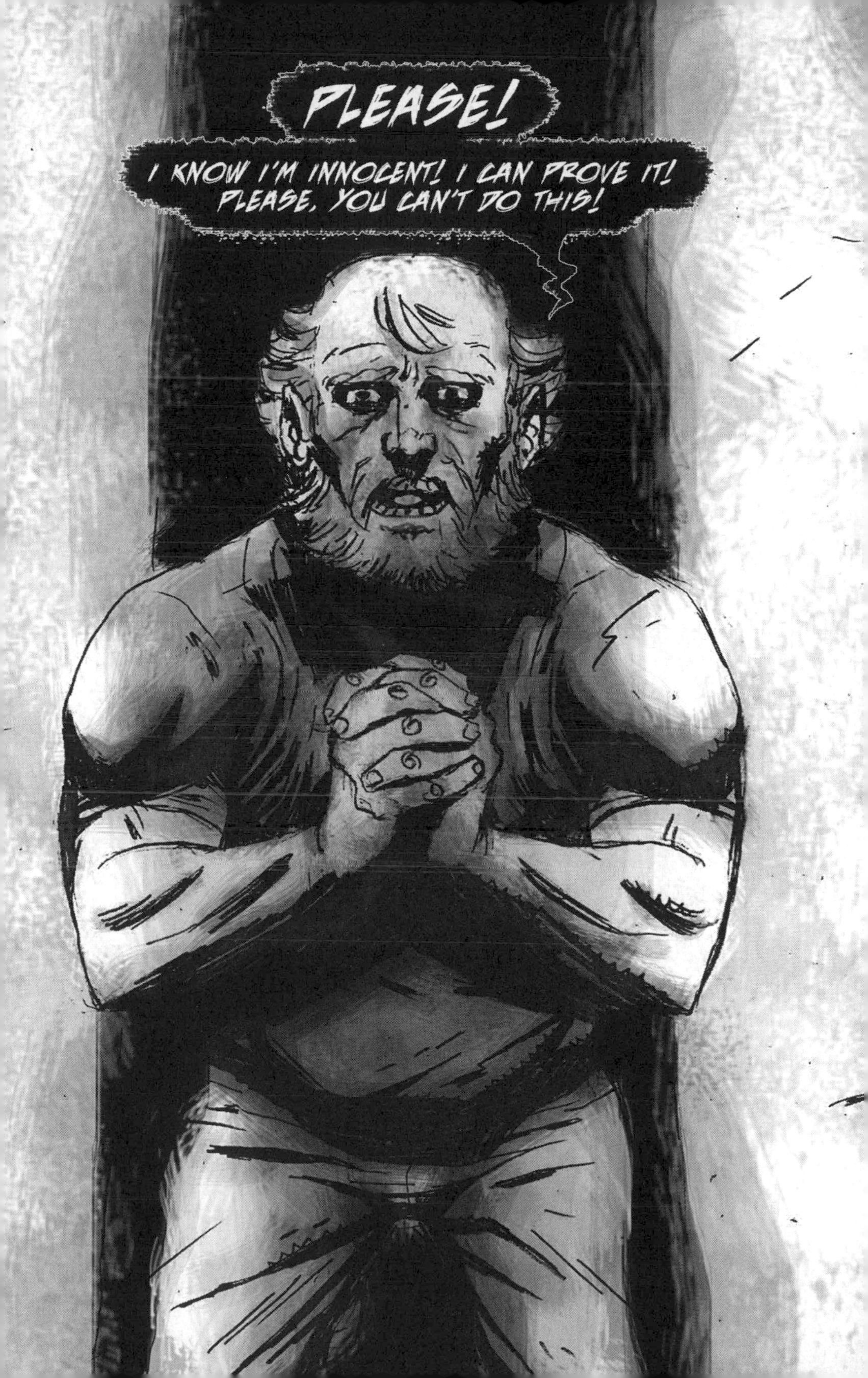
PLEASE!
I KNOW I'M INNOCENT! I CAN PROVE IT! PLEASE, YOU CAN'T DO THIS!

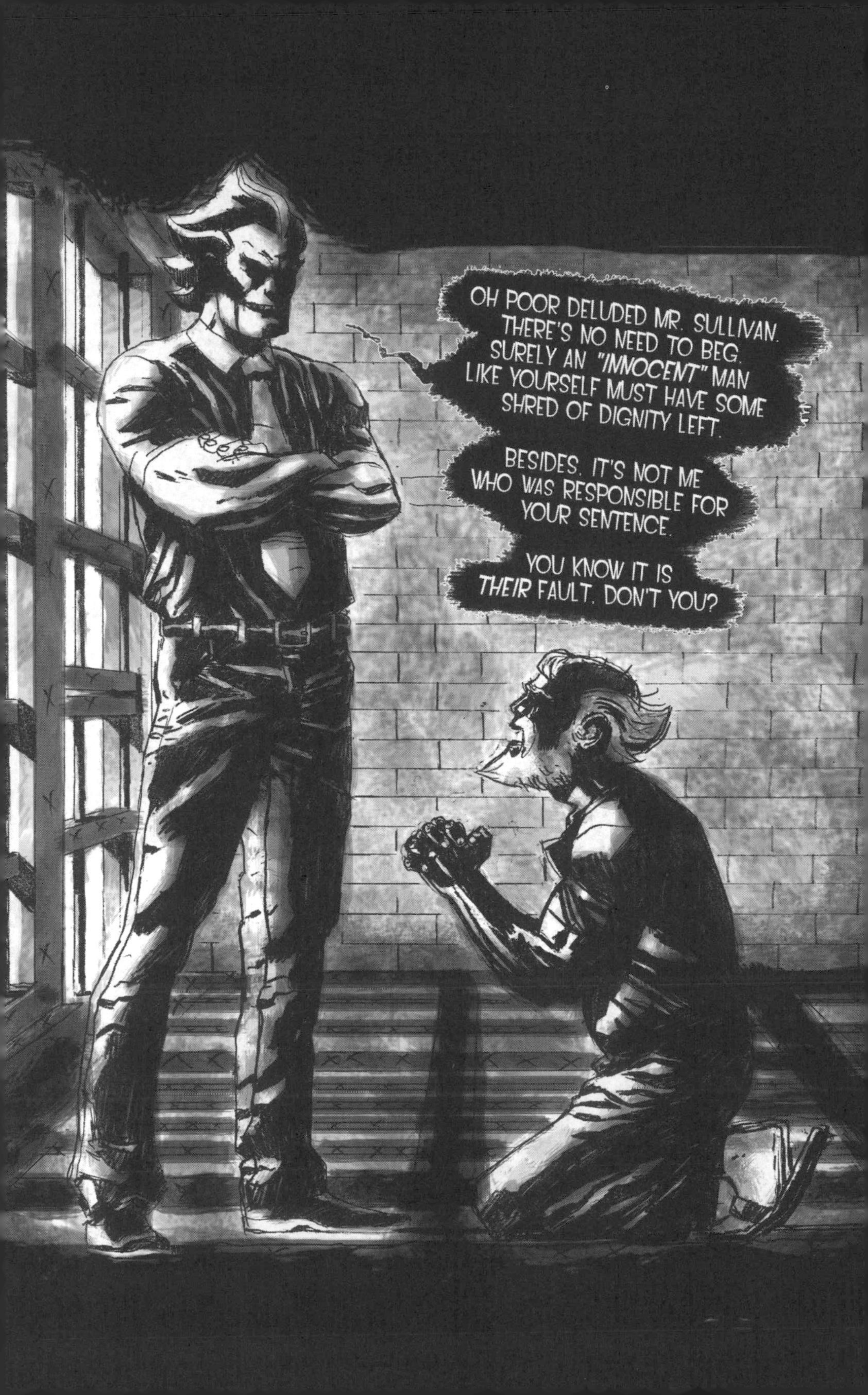
OH POOR DELUDED MR. SULLIVAN. THERE'S NO NEED TO BEG. SURELY AN "INNOCENT" MAN LIKE YOURSELF MUST HAVE SOME SHRED OF DIGNITY LEFT.
BESIDES, IT'S NOT ME WHO WAS RESPONSIBLE FOR YOUR SENTENCE.
YOU KNOW IT IS THEIR FAULT, DON'T YOU?

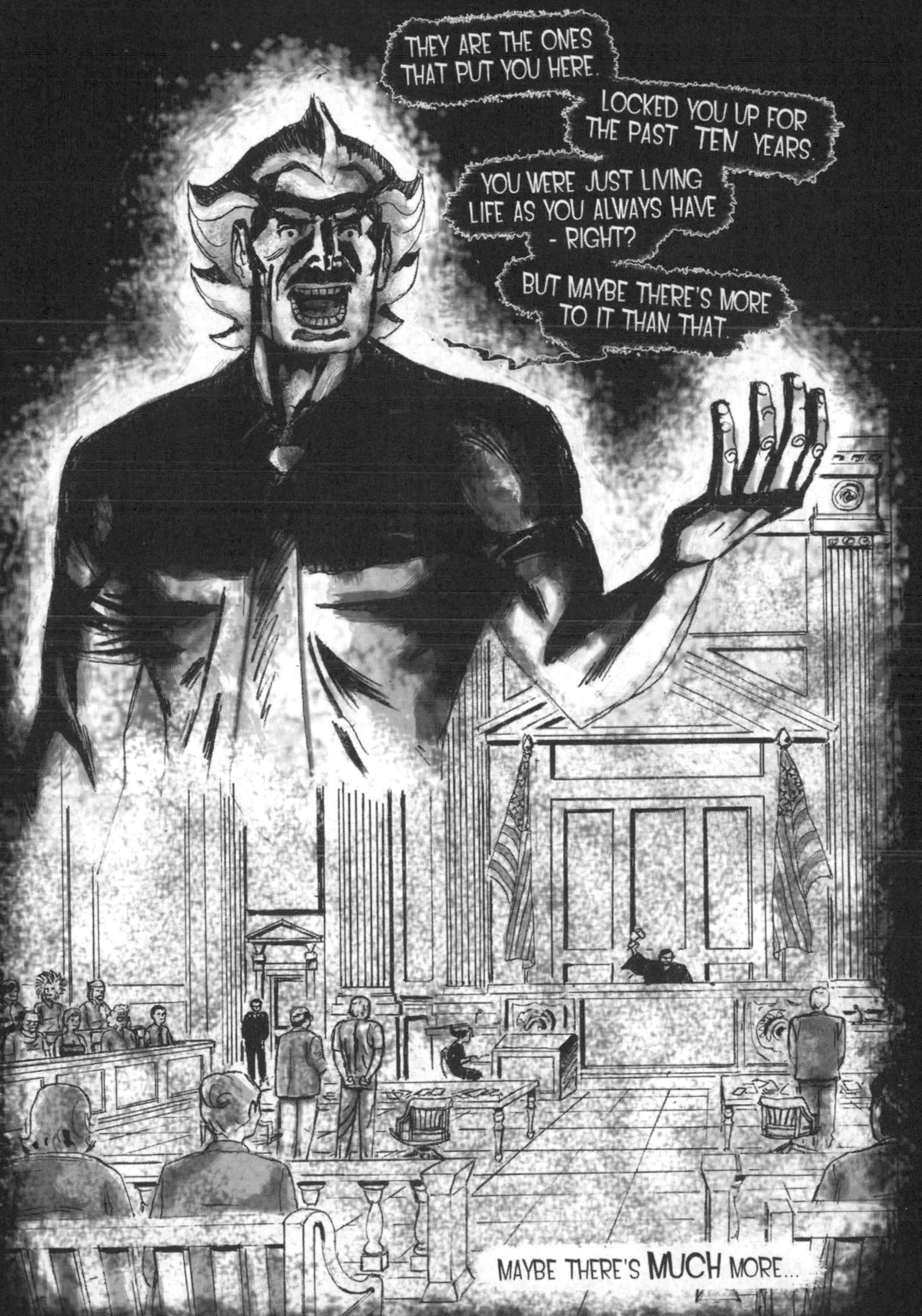
THEY ARE THE ONES THAT PUT YOU HERE.
LOCKED YOU UP FOR THE PAST TEN YEARS.
YOU WERE JUST LIVING LIFE AS YOU ALWAYS HAVE - RIGHT?
BUT MAYBE THERE'S MORE TO IT THAN THAT.
MAYBE THERE'S **MUCH** MORE...

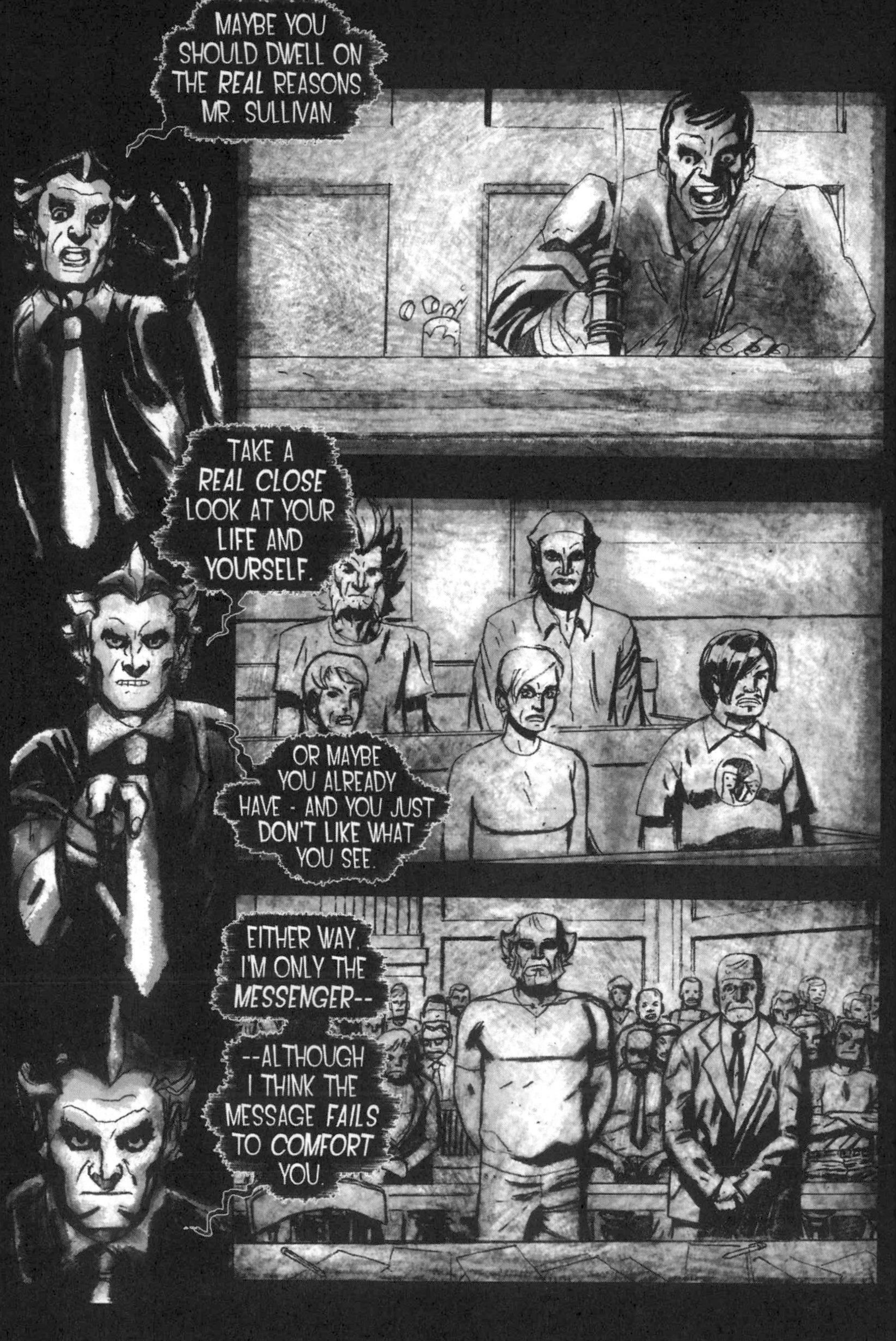
MAYBE YOU SHOULD DWELL ON THE REAL REASONS, MR. SULLIVAN.
TAKE A REAL CLOSE LOOK AT YOUR LIFE AND YOURSELF.
OR MAYBE YOU ALREADY HAVE - AND YOU JUST DON'T LIKE WHAT YOU SEE.
EITHER WAY, I'M ONLY THE MESSENGER--
--ALTHOUGH I THINK THE MESSAGE FAILS TO COMFORT YOU.

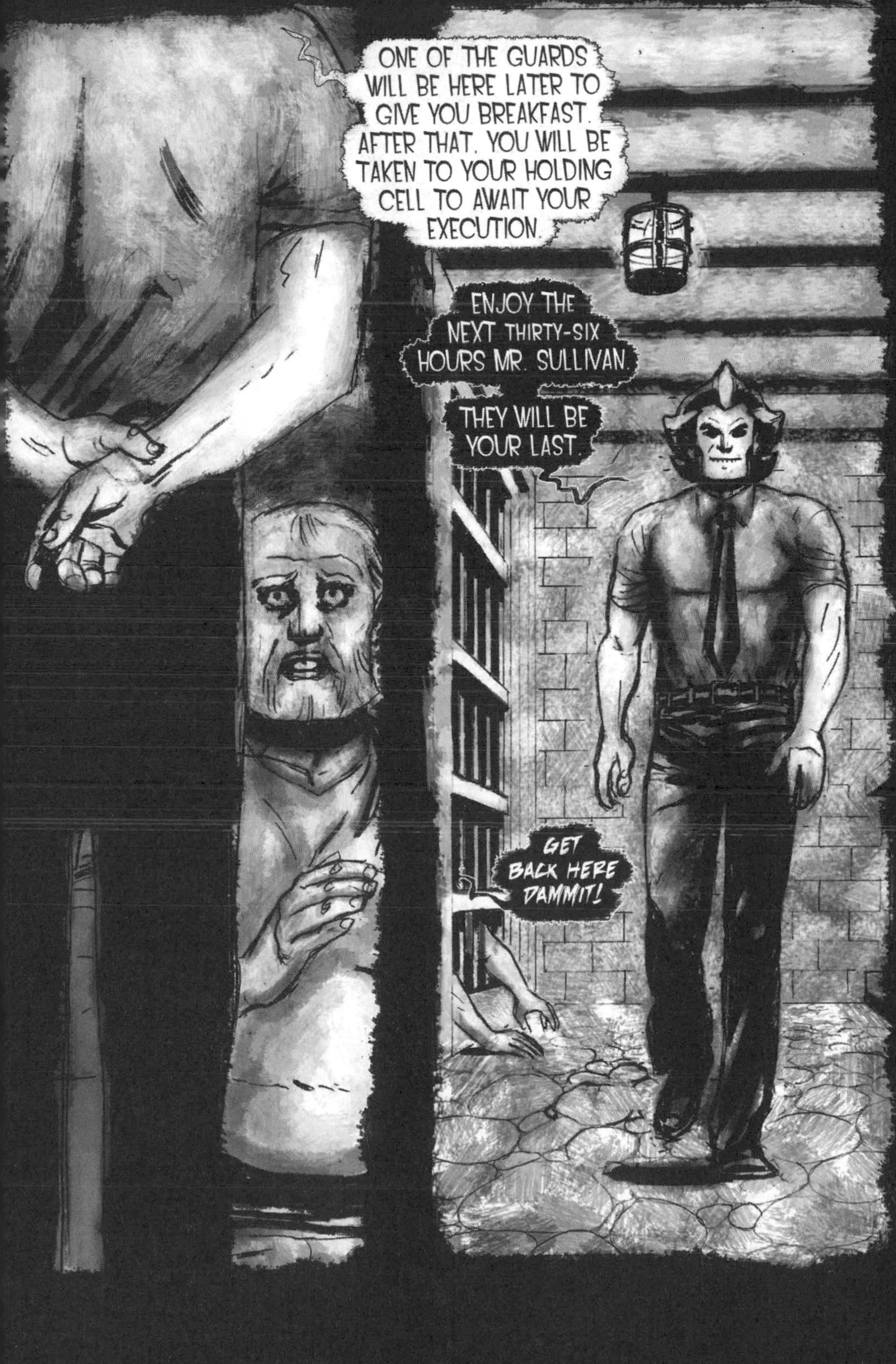
ONE OF THE GUARDS WILL BE HERE LATER TO GIVE YOU BREAKFAST. AFTER THAT, YOU WILL BE TAKEN TO YOUR HOLDING CELL TO AWAIT YOUR EXECUTION.
ENJOY THE NEXT THIRTY-SIX HOURS MR. SULLIVAN.
THEY WILL BE YOUR LAST.
GET BACK HERE DAMMIT!

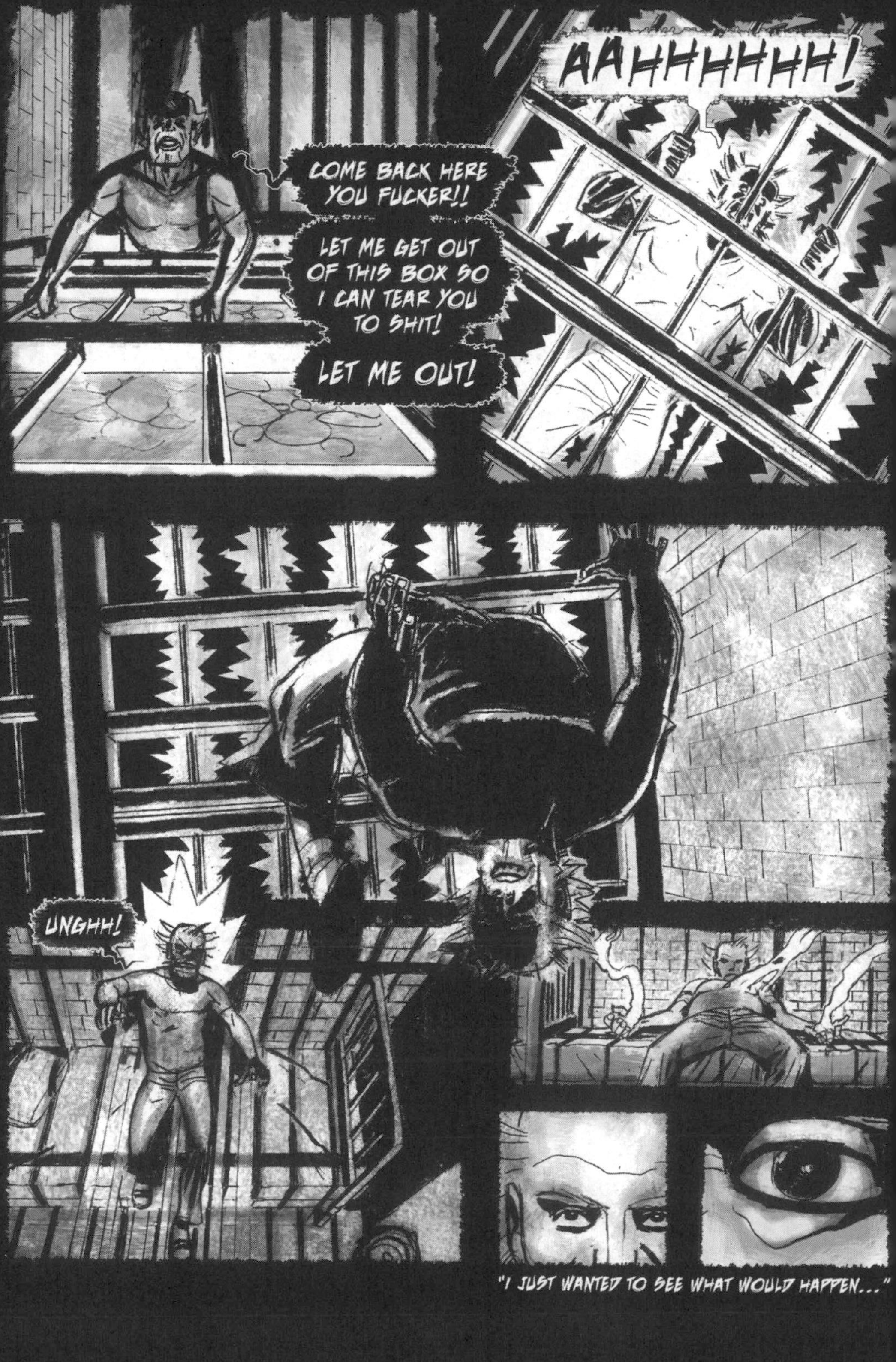
COME BACK HERE YOU FUCKER!!
LET ME GET OUT OF THIS BOX SO I CAN TEAR YOU TO SHIT!
LET ME OUT!
AAHHHHHH!
UNGHH!
"I JUST WANTED TO SEE WHAT WOULD HAPPEN..."

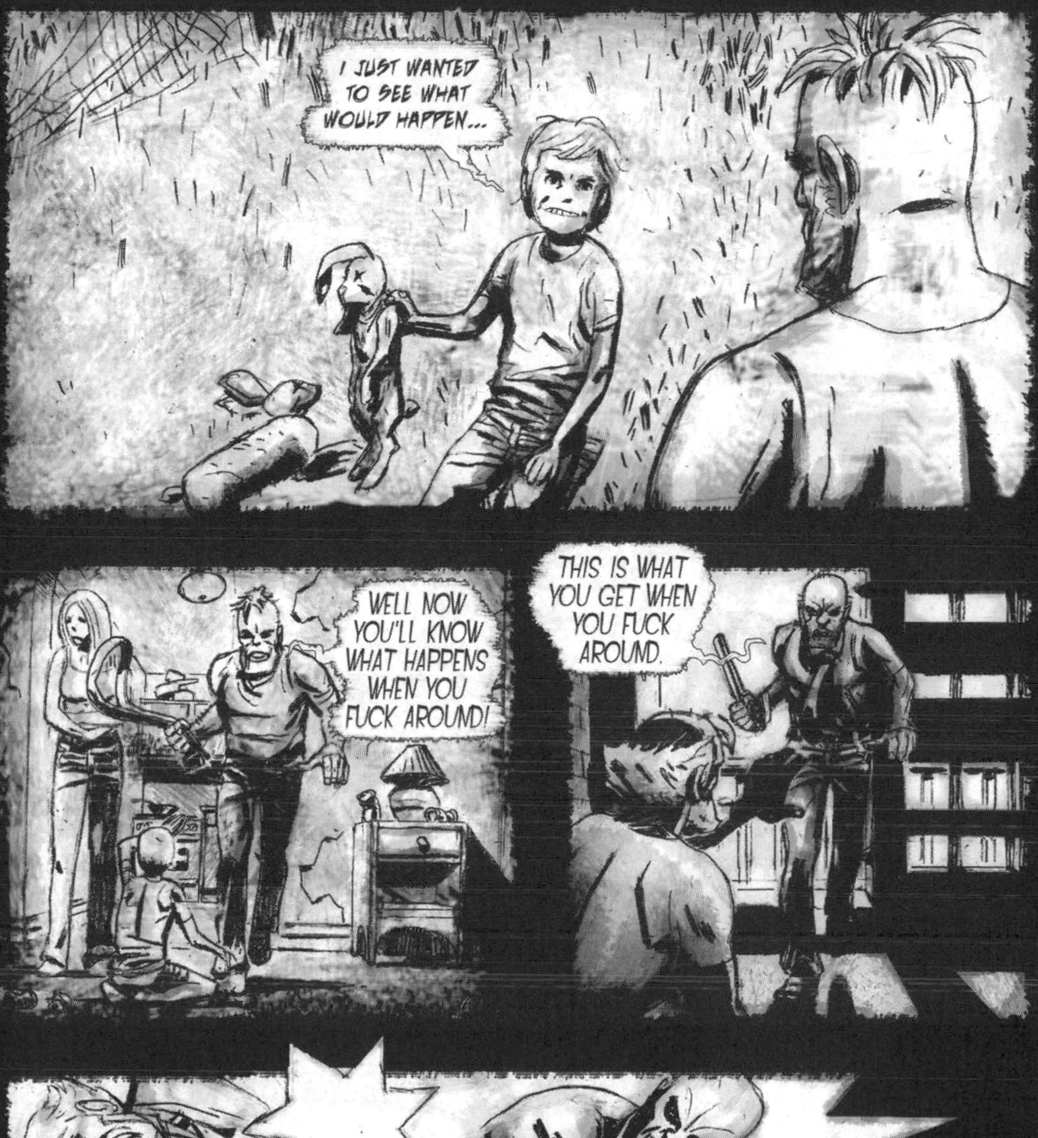
I JUST WANTED TO SEE WHAT WOULD HAPPEN...
WELL NOW YOU'LL KNOW WHAT HAPPENS WHEN YOU FUCK AROUND!
THIS IS WHAT YOU GET WHEN YOU FUCK AROUND.
AND THAT'S FOR BITING MY HAND YOU PSYCHO!

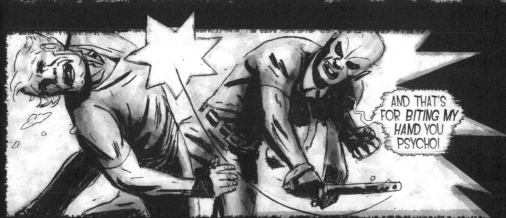

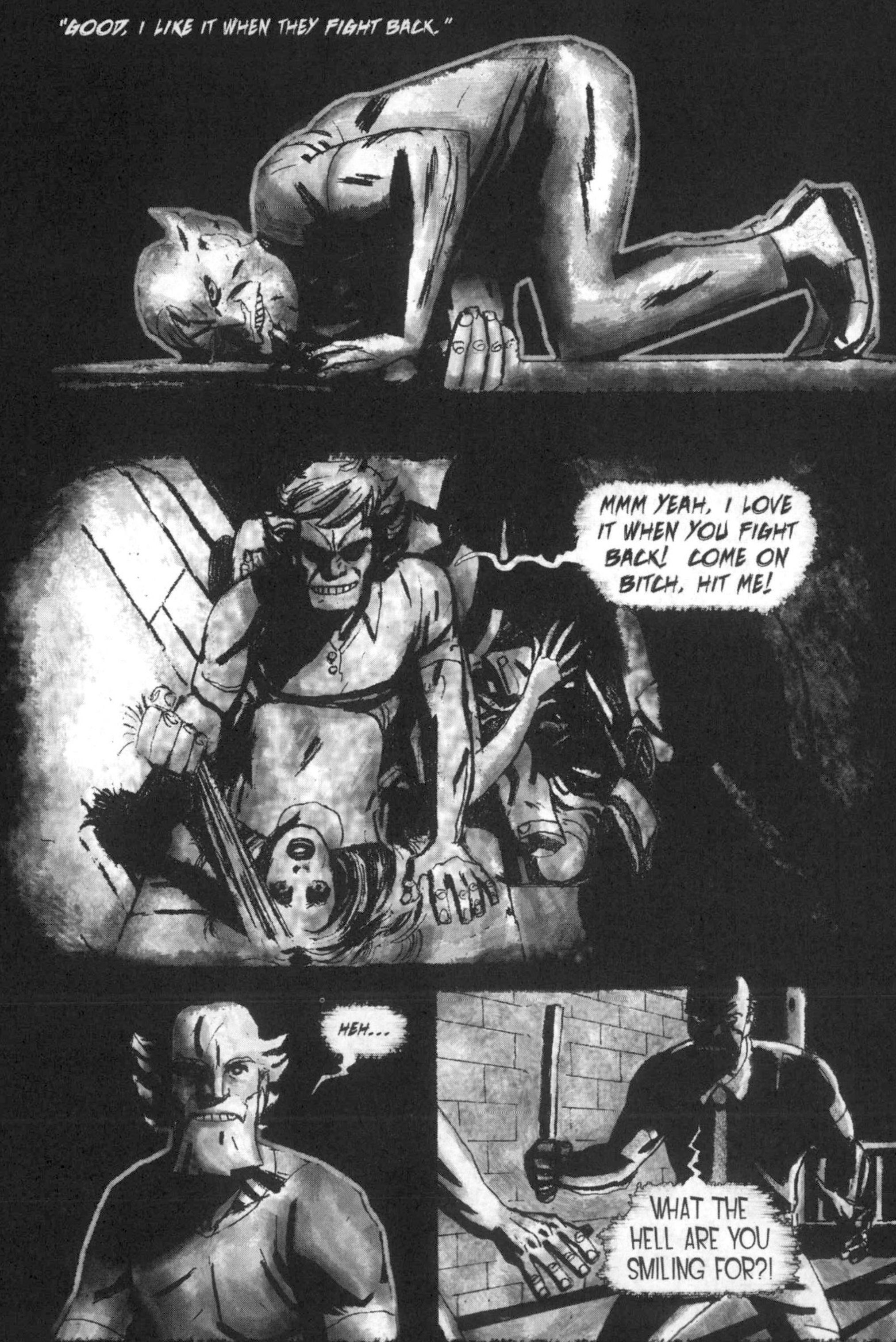
"GOOD. I LIKE IT WHEN THEY FIGHT BACK."
MMM YEAH, I LOVE IT WHEN YOU FIGHT BACK! COME ON BITCH, HIT ME!
HEH...
WHAT THE HELL ARE YOU SMILING FOR?!

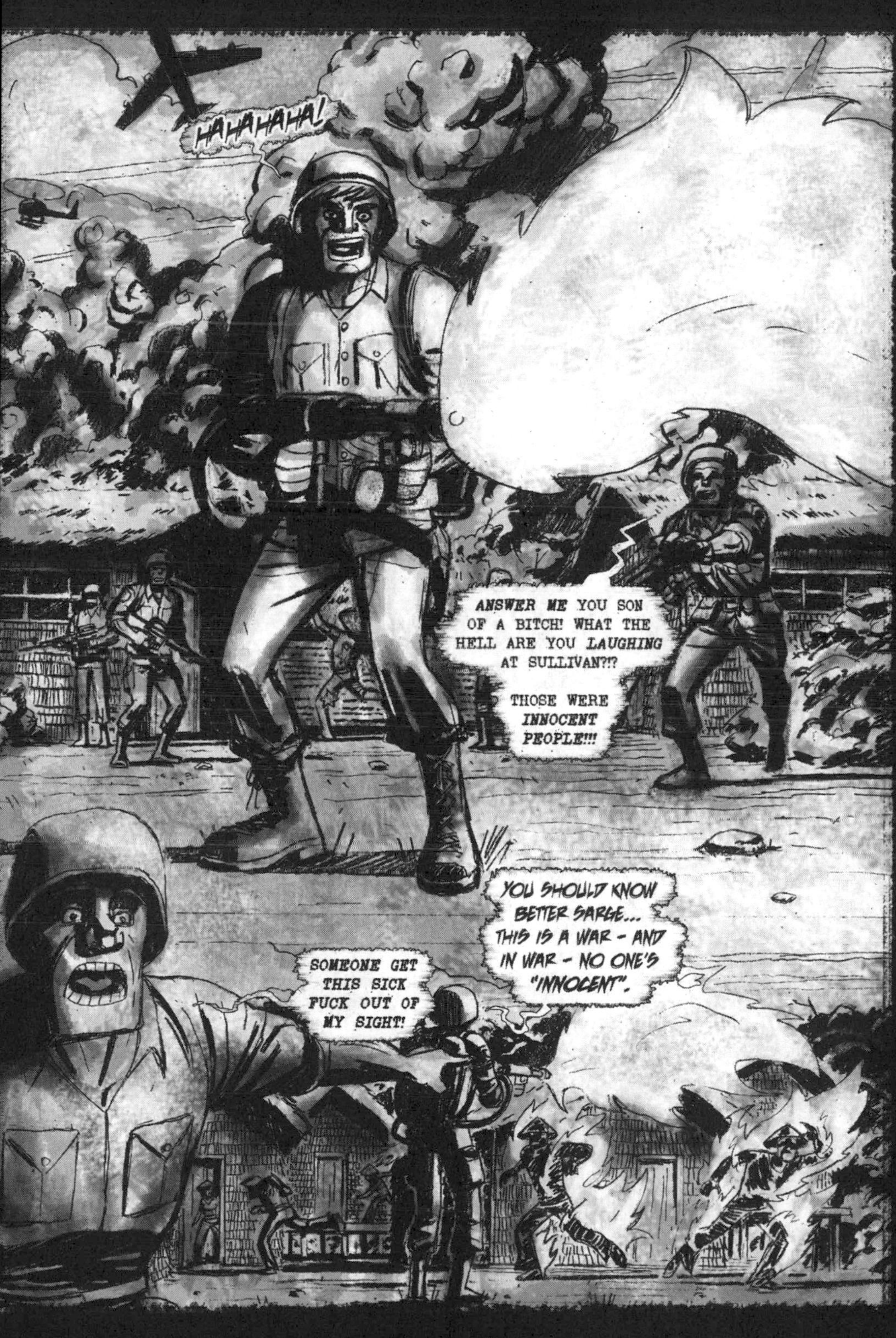
HAHAHAHA!
ANSWER ME YOU SON OF A BITCH! WHAT THE HELL ARE YOU LAUGHING AT SULLIVAN?!?
THOSE WERE INNOCENT PEOPLE!!!
YOU SHOULD KNOW BETTER SARGE... THIS IS A WAR - AND IN WAR - NO ONE'S "INNOCENT".
SOMEONE GET THIS SICK FUCK OUT OF MY SIGHT!

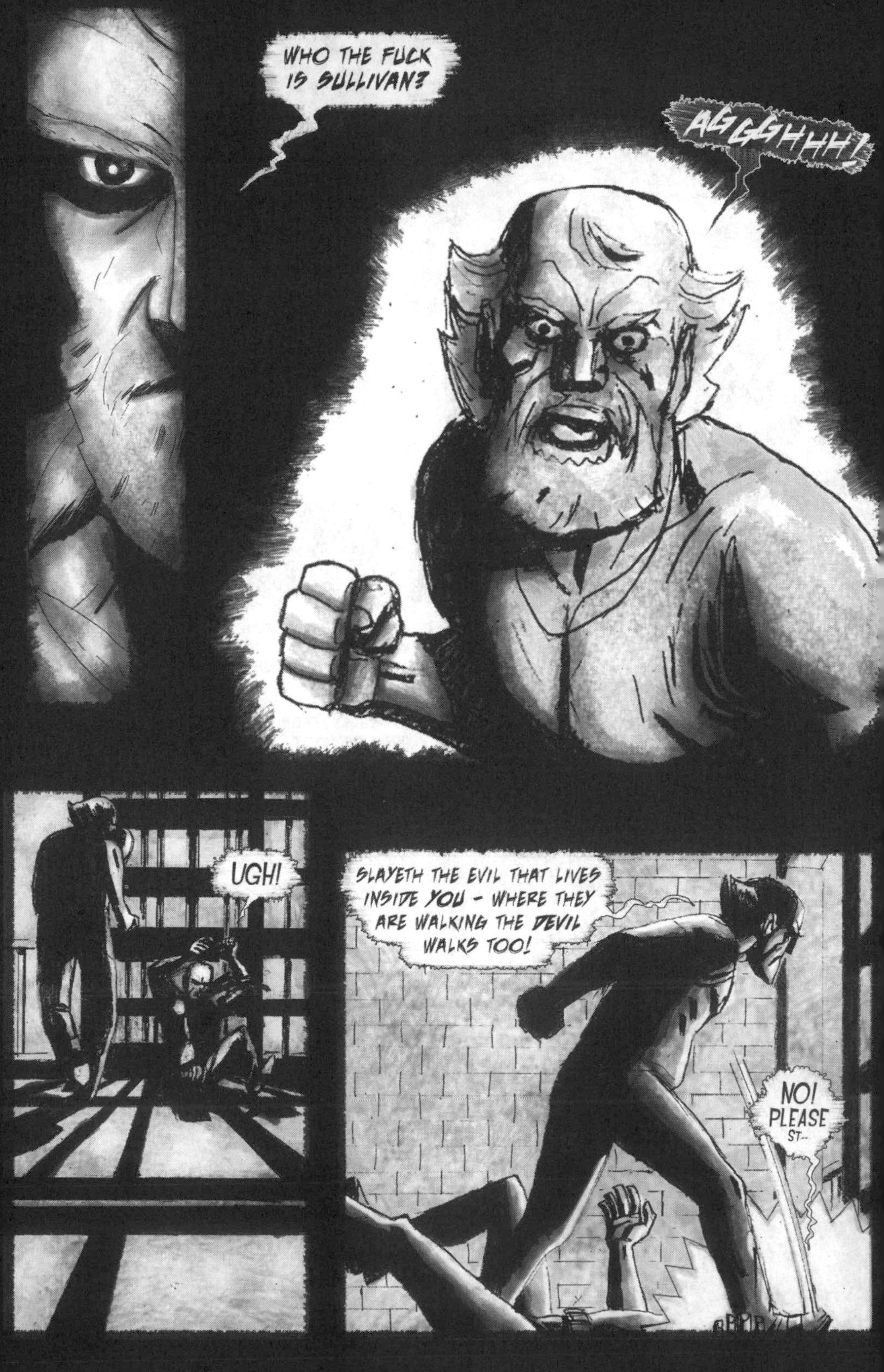
WHO THE FUCK IS SULLIVAN?
AGGGHHH!
UGH!
SLAYETH THE EVIL THAT LIVES INSIDE YOU - WHERE THEY ARE WALKING THE DEVIL WALKS TOO!
NO! PLEASE ST--

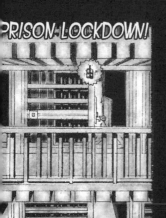

PRISON LOCKDOWN!

PRISON LOCKDOWN!

PRISON LOCKDOWN!

WE HAVE A PRISONER TRYING TO ESCAPE CELL 8--

COMMENCING PRISON LOCKDOWN!

SLAMM

SLAMM

SLAMM

AHH SHIT...

"YOU KNOW, I HAVE PLENTY MORE INSIDE."

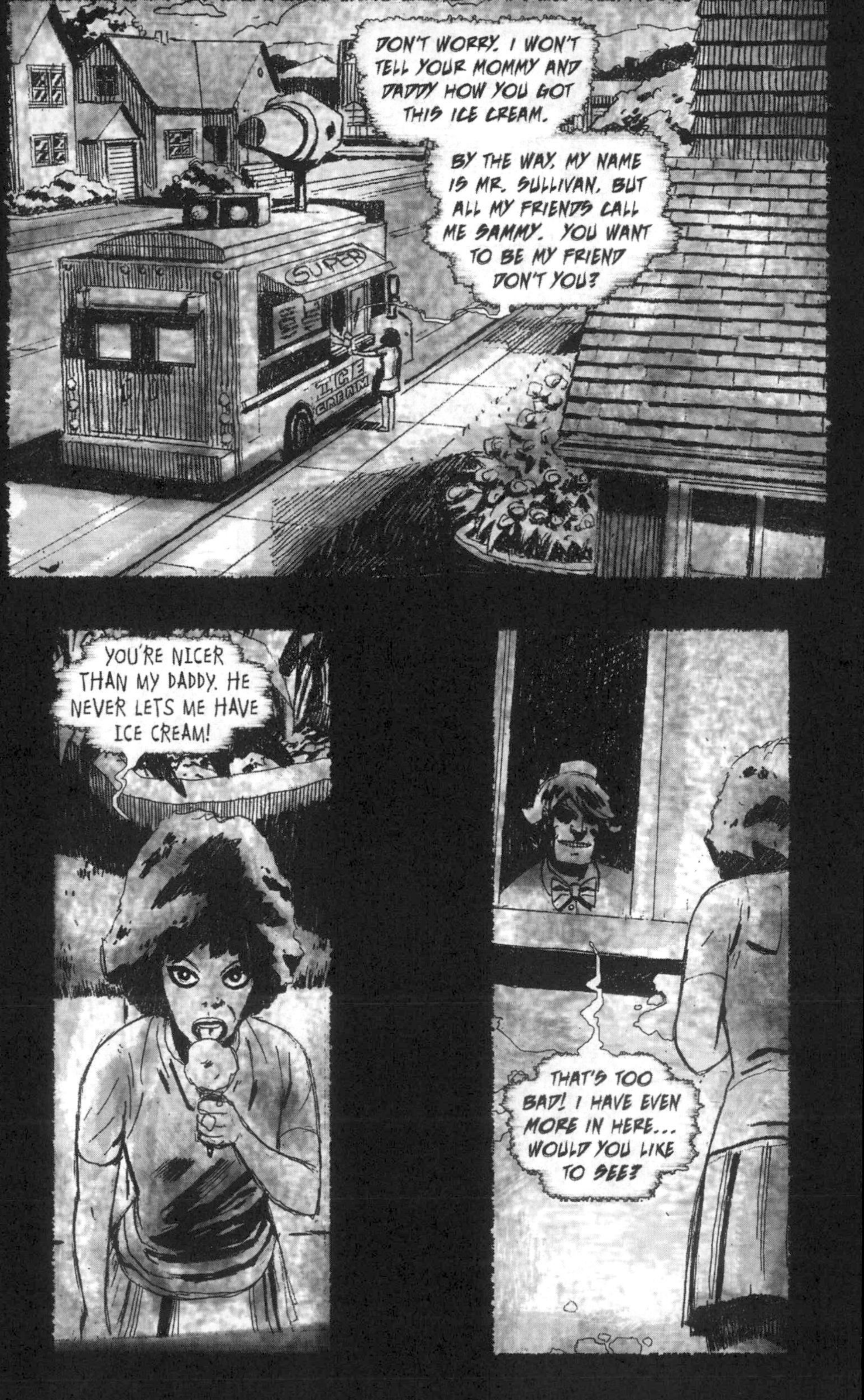
DON'T WORRY. I WON'T TELL YOUR MOMMY AND DADDY HOW YOU GOT THIS ICE CREAM.
BY THE WAY, MY NAME IS MR. SULLIVAN, BUT ALL MY FRIENDS CALL ME SAMMY. YOU WANT TO BE MY FRIEND DON'T YOU?
SUPER
ICE CREAM
YOU'RE NICER THAN MY DADDY. HE NEVER LETS ME HAVE ICE CREAM!
THAT'S TOO BAD! I HAVE EVEN MORE IN HERE... WOULD YOU LIKE TO SEE?

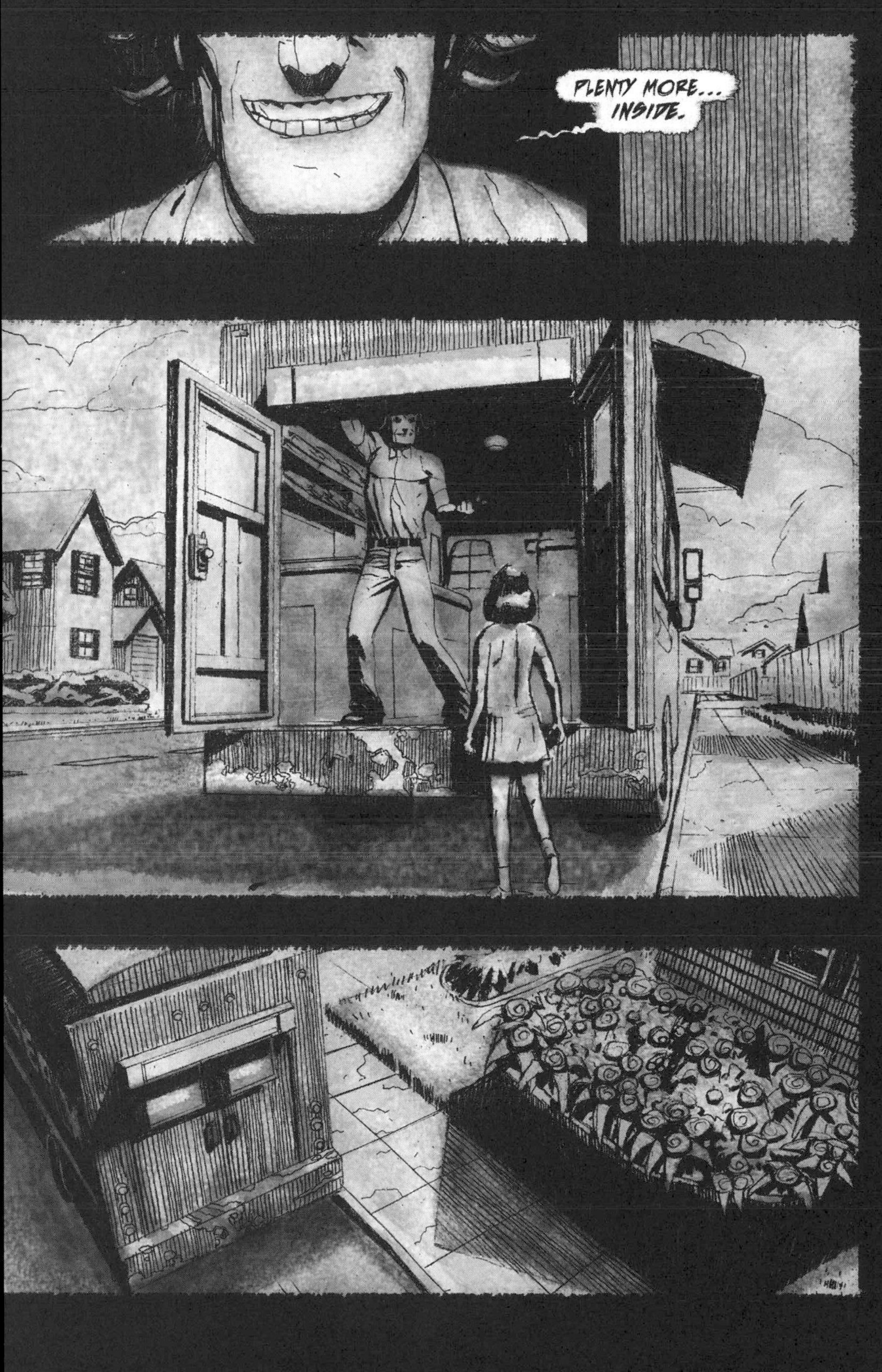
PLENTY MORE... INSIDE.

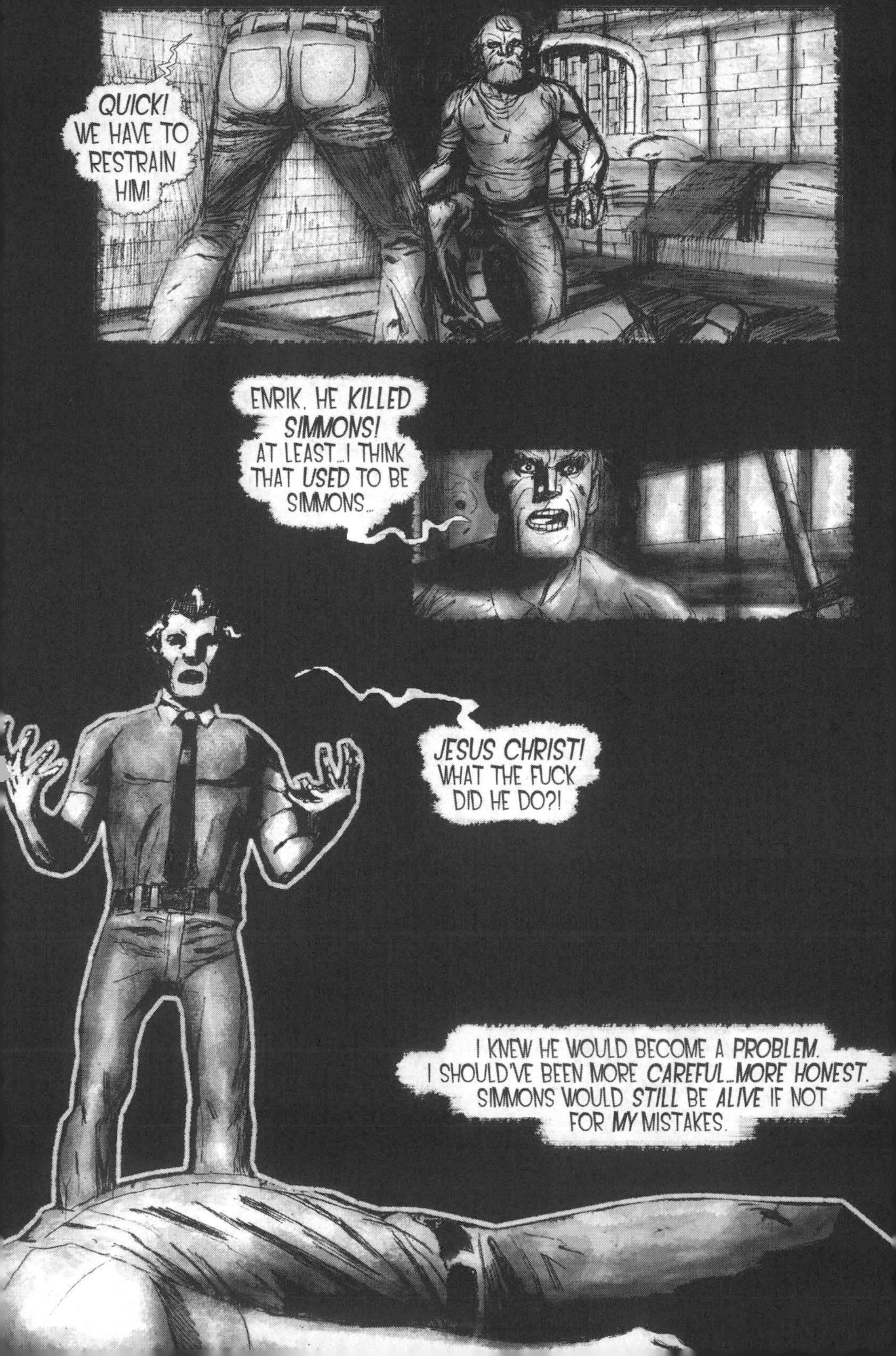
QUICK! WE HAVE TO RESTRAIN HIM!
ENRIK, HE KILLED SIMMONS! AT LEAST...I THINK THAT USED TO BE SIMMONS...
JESUS CHRIST! WHAT THE FUCK DID HE DO?!
I KNEW HE WOULD BECOME A PROBLEM. I SHOULD'VE BEEN MORE CAREFUL...MORE HONEST. SIMMONS WOULD STILL BE ALIVE IF NOT FOR MY MISTAKES.

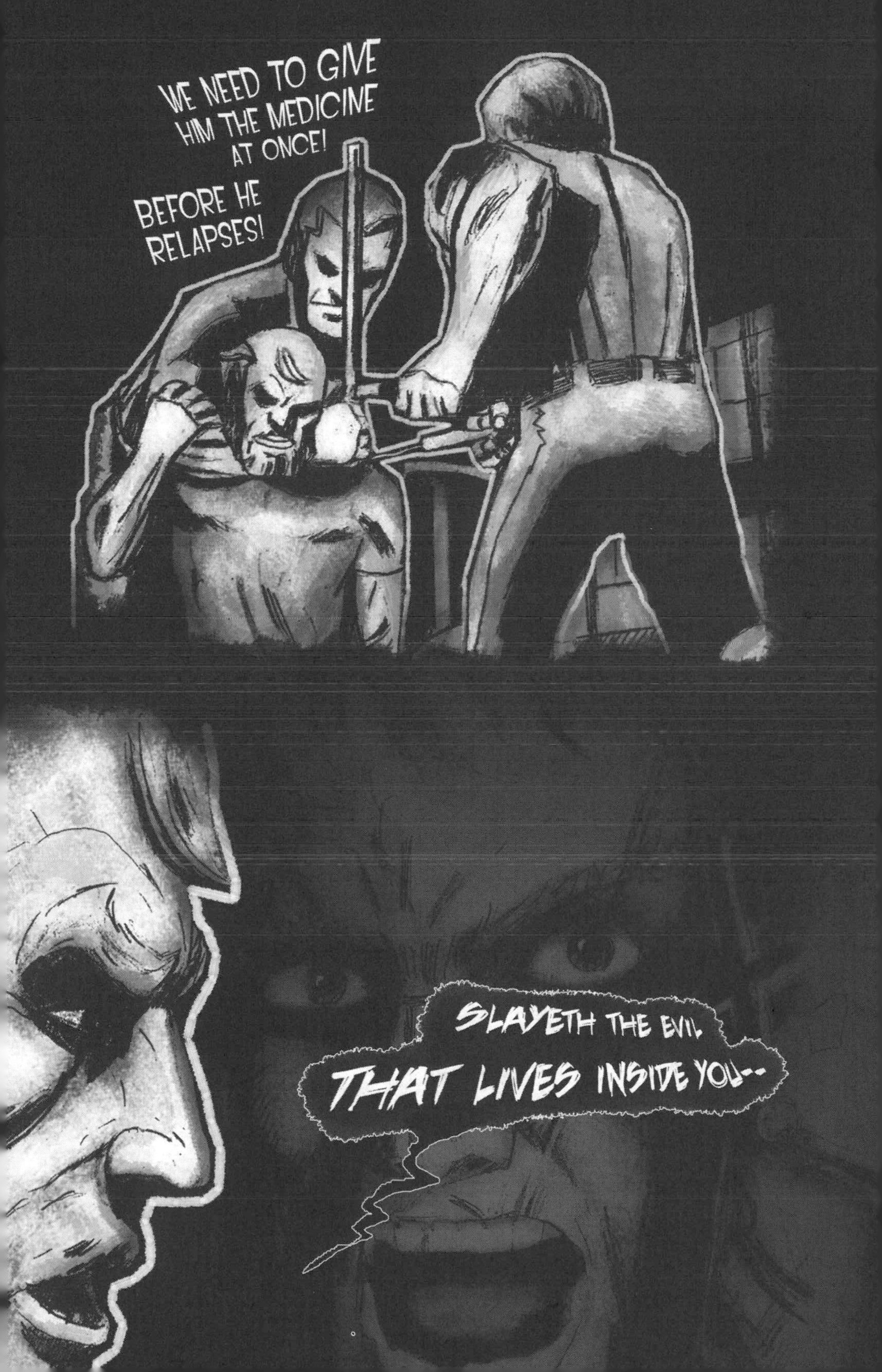
WE NEED TO GIVE HIM THE MEDICINE AT ONCE!
BEFORE HE RELAPSES!
SLAYETH THE EVIL THAT LIVES INSIDE YOU--

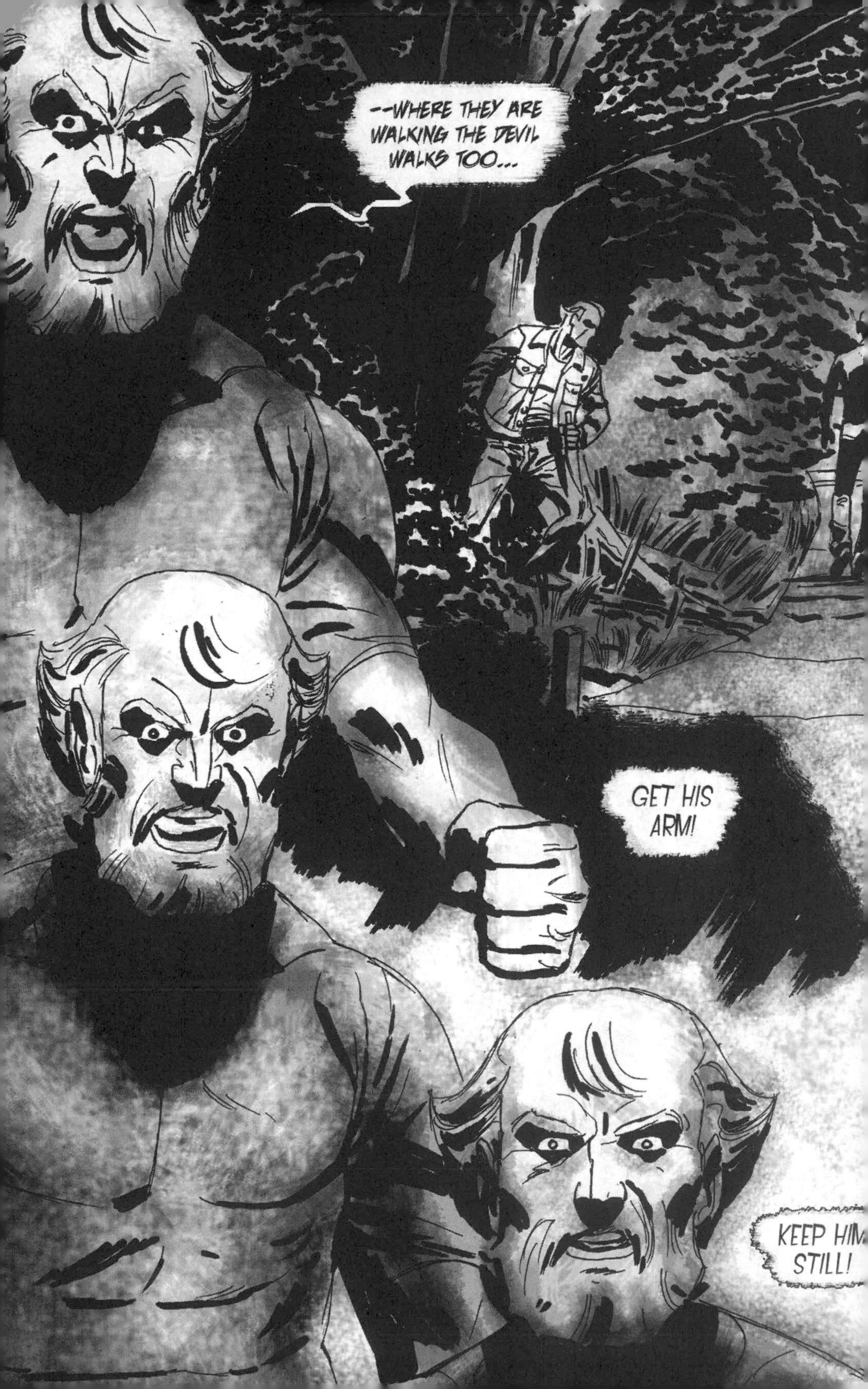
--WHERE THEY ARE WALKING THE DEVIL WALKS TOO...
GET HIS ARM!
KEEP HIM STILL!

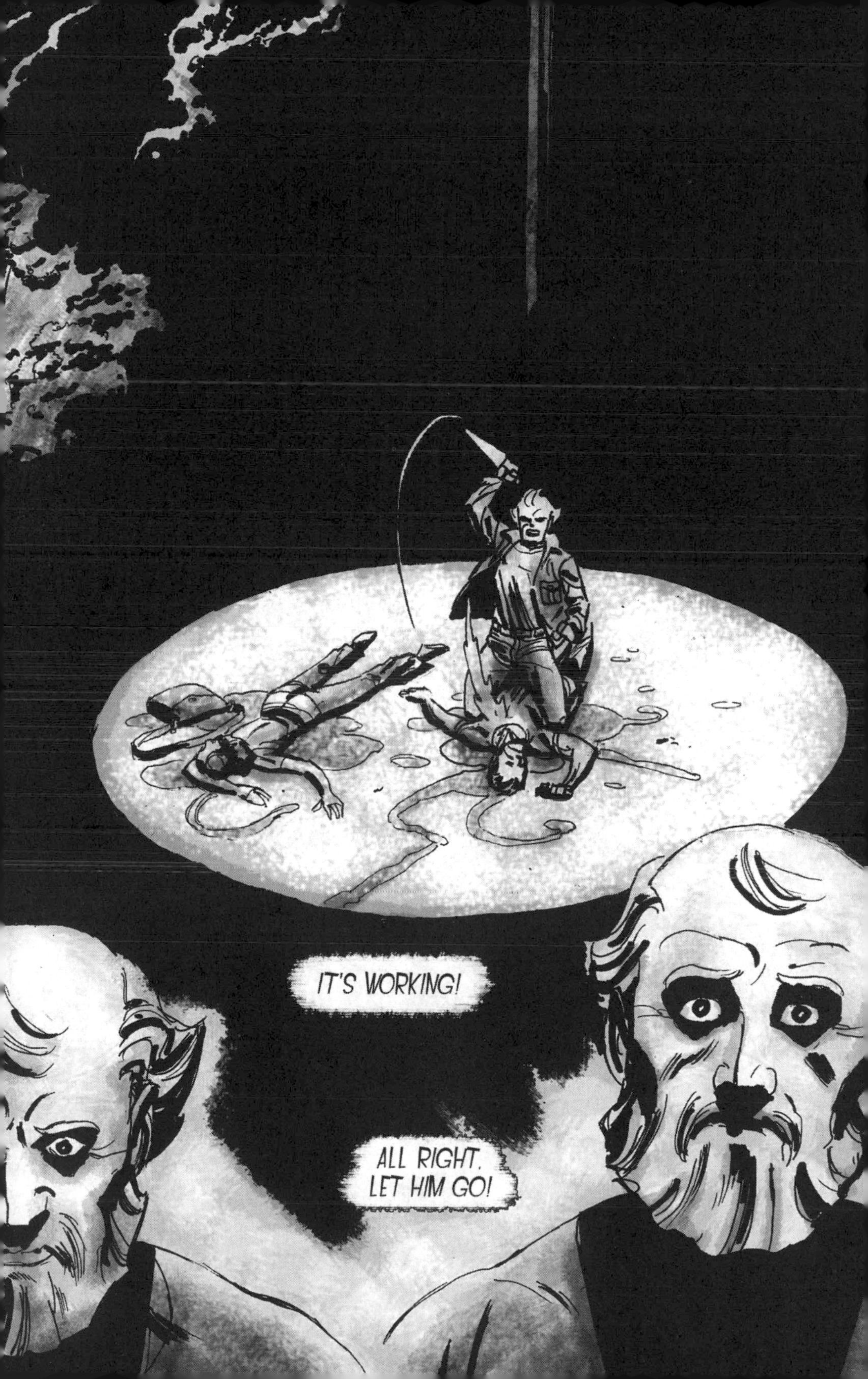
IT'S WORKING!
ALL RIGHT. LET HIM GO!

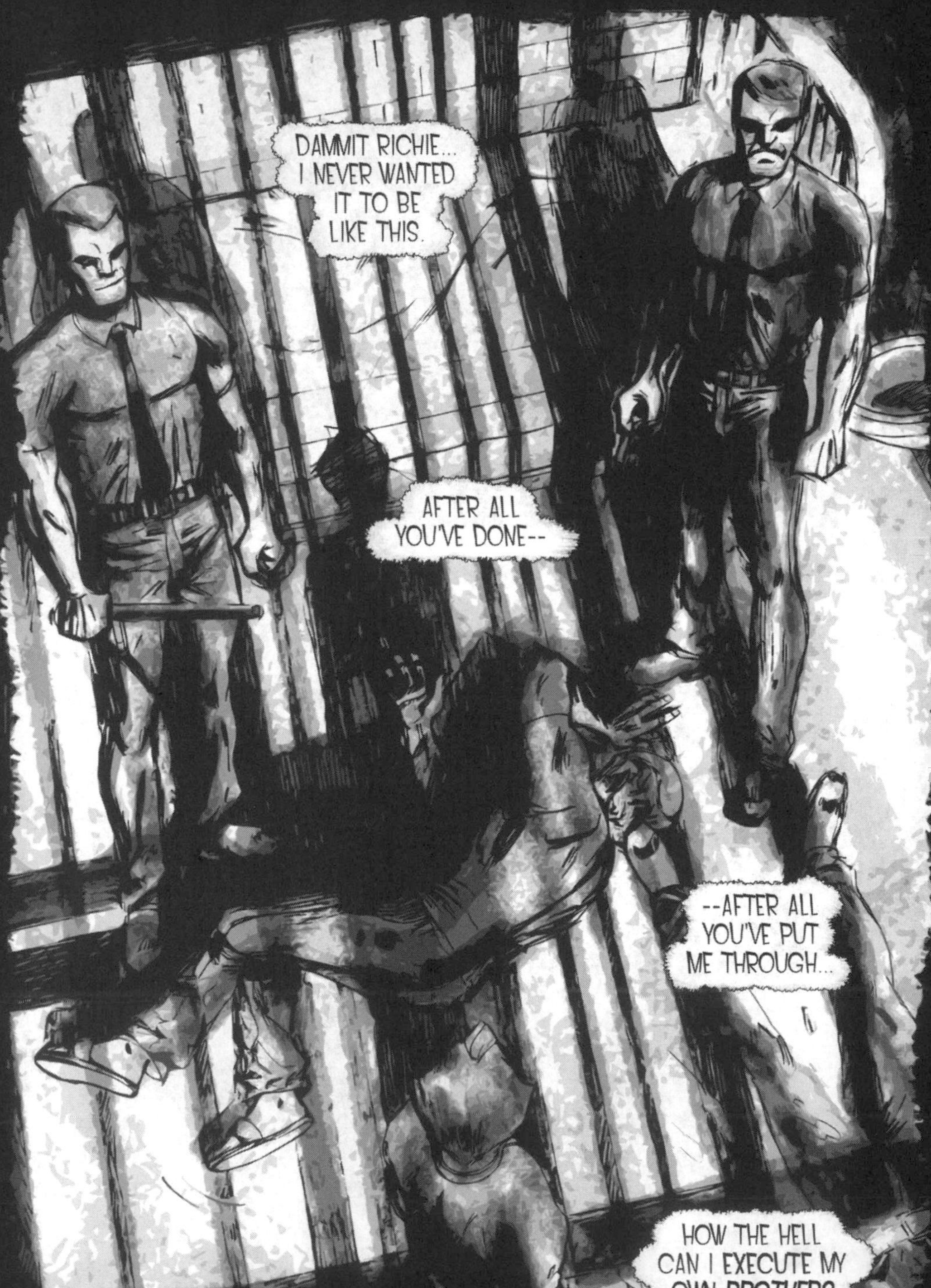
DAMMIT RICHIE... I NEVER WANTED IT TO BE LIKE THIS.
AFTER ALL YOU'VE DONE--
--AFTER ALL YOU'VE PUT ME THROUGH...
HOW THE HELL CAN I EXECUTE MY OWN BROTHER?

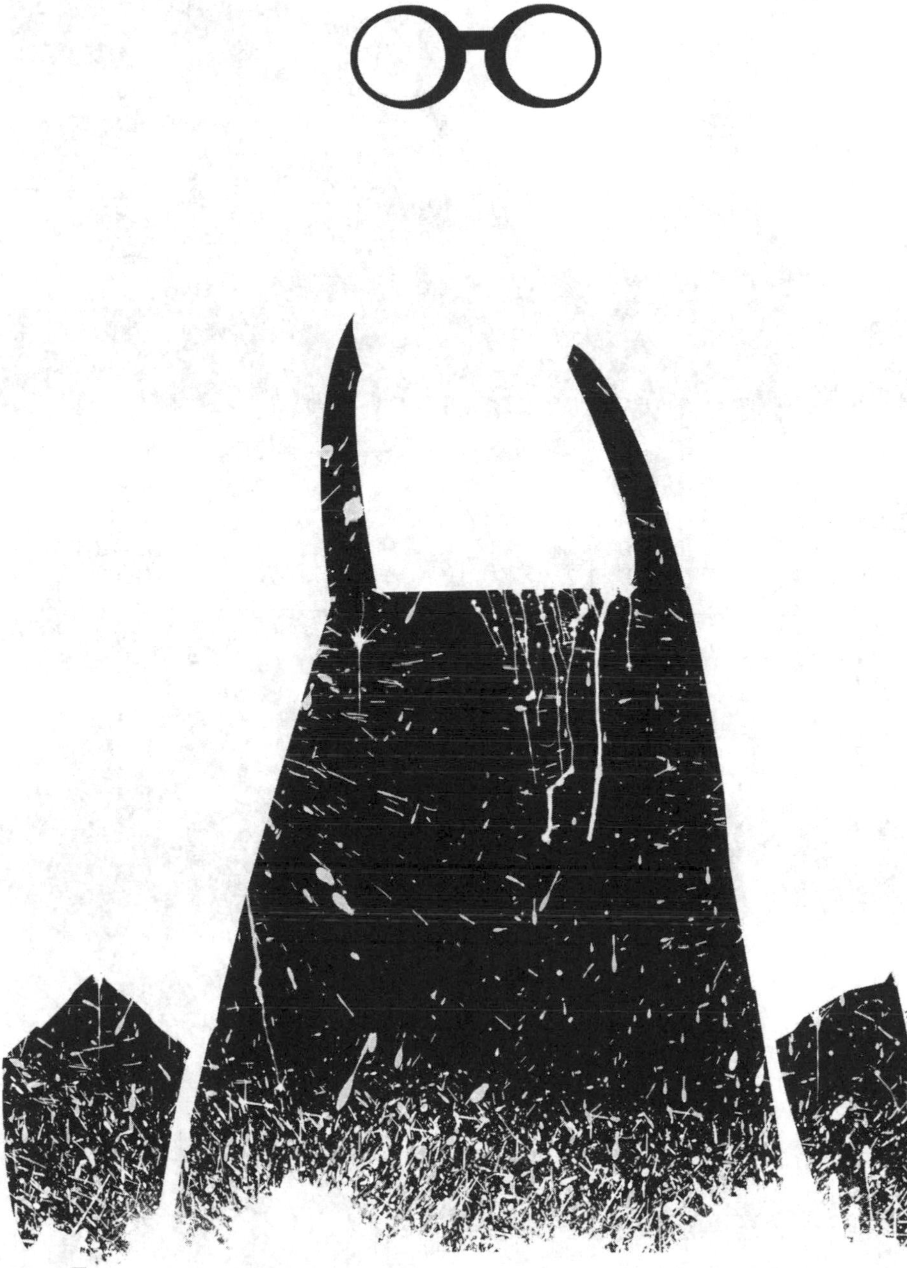

ACT SIX: TRUTH & CONSEQUENCE

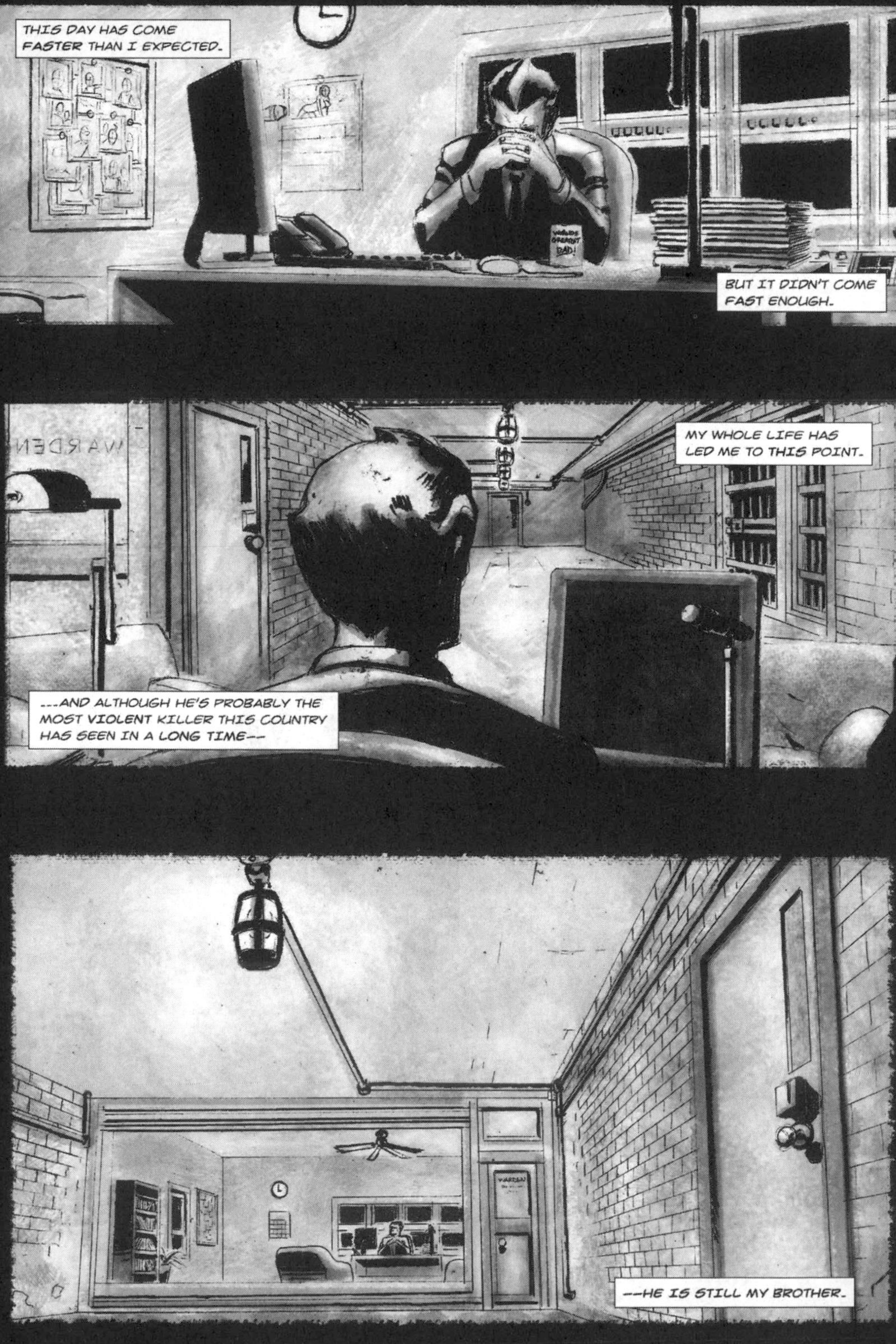
THIS DAY HAS COME FASTER THAN I EXPECTED.
BUT IT DIDN'T COME FAST ENOUGH.
MY WHOLE LIFE HAS LED ME TO THIS POINT.
---AND ALTHOUGH HE'S PROBABLY THE MOST VIOLENT KILLER THIS COUNTRY HAS SEEN IN A LONG TIME--
--HE IS STILL MY BROTHER.

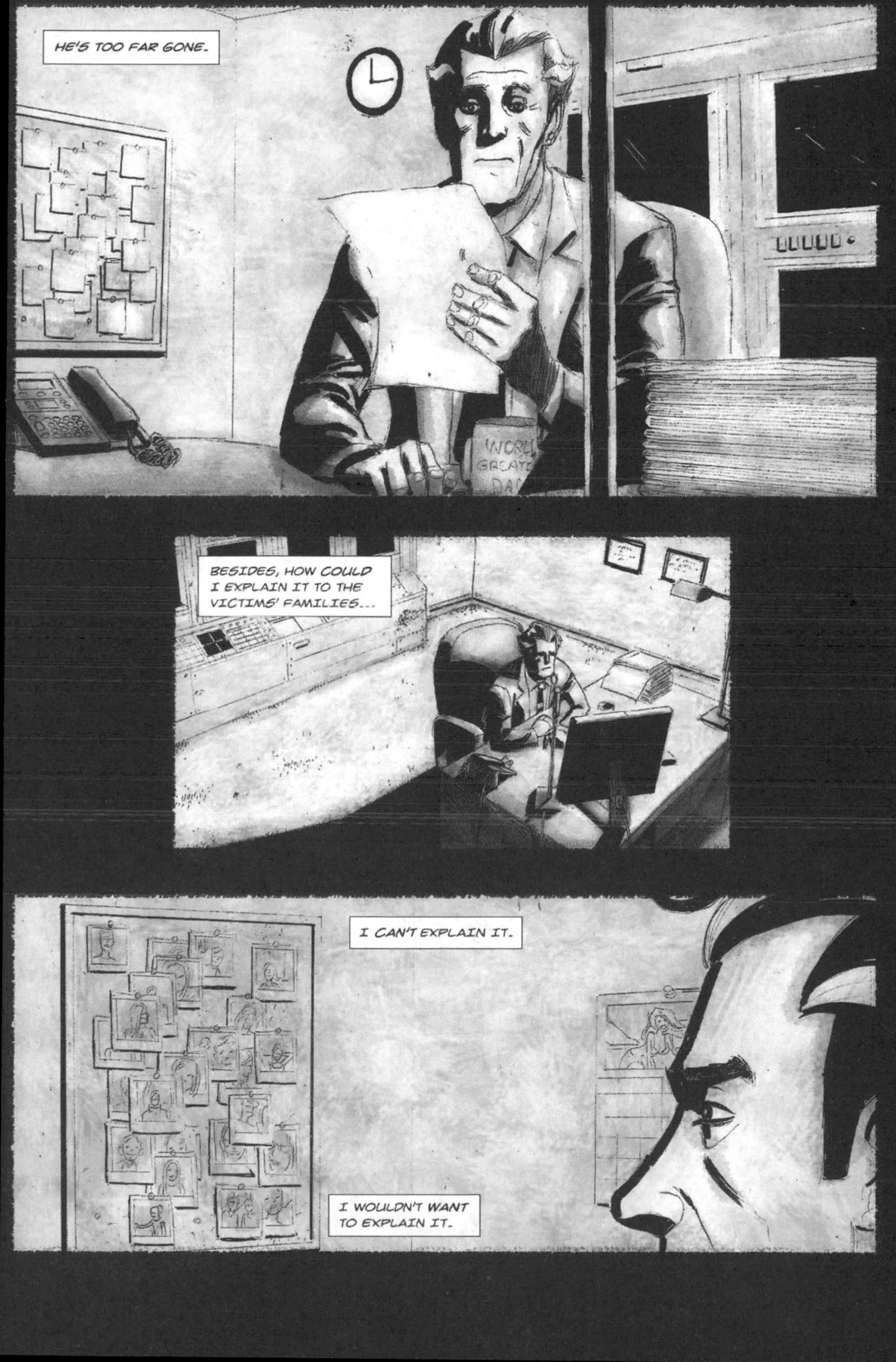
HE'S TOO FAR GONE.
BESIDES, HOW COULD I EXPLAIN IT TO THE VICTIMS' FAMILIES...
I CAN'T EXPLAIN IT.
I WOULDN'T WANT TO EXPLAIN IT.

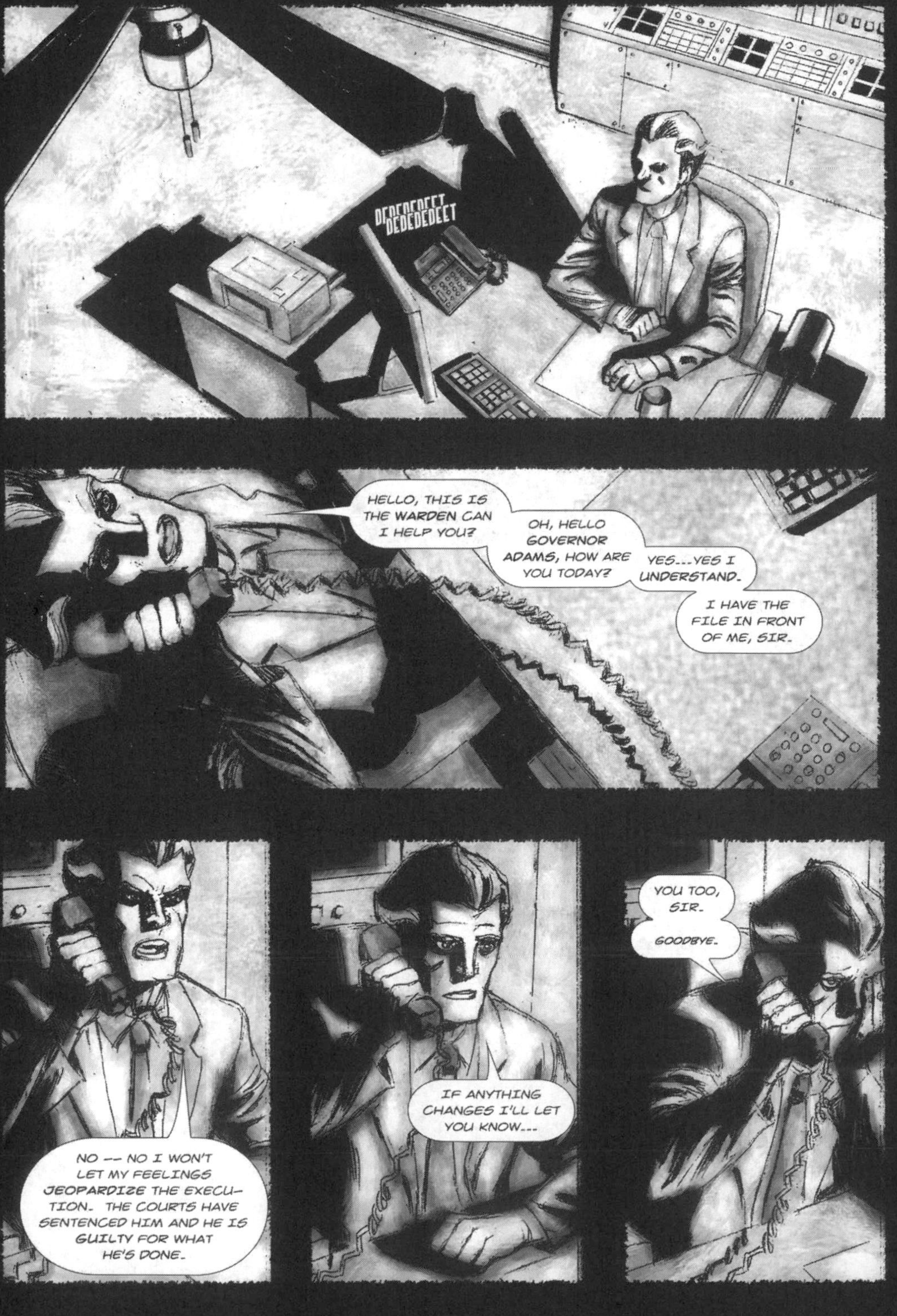
DEDEDEDEET DEDEDEDEET
HELLO, THIS IS THE WARDEN CAN I HELP YOU?
OH, HELLO GOVERNOR ADAMS, HOW ARE YOU TODAY?
YES...YES I UNDERSTAND.
I HAVE THE FILE IN FRONT OF ME, SIR.
NO -- NO I WON'T LET MY FEELINGS JEOPARDIZE THE EXECUTION. THE COURTS HAVE SENTENCED HIM AND HE IS GUILTY FOR WHAT HE'S DONE.
IF ANYTHING CHANGES I'LL LET YOU KNOW...
YOU TOO, SIR.
GOODBYE.

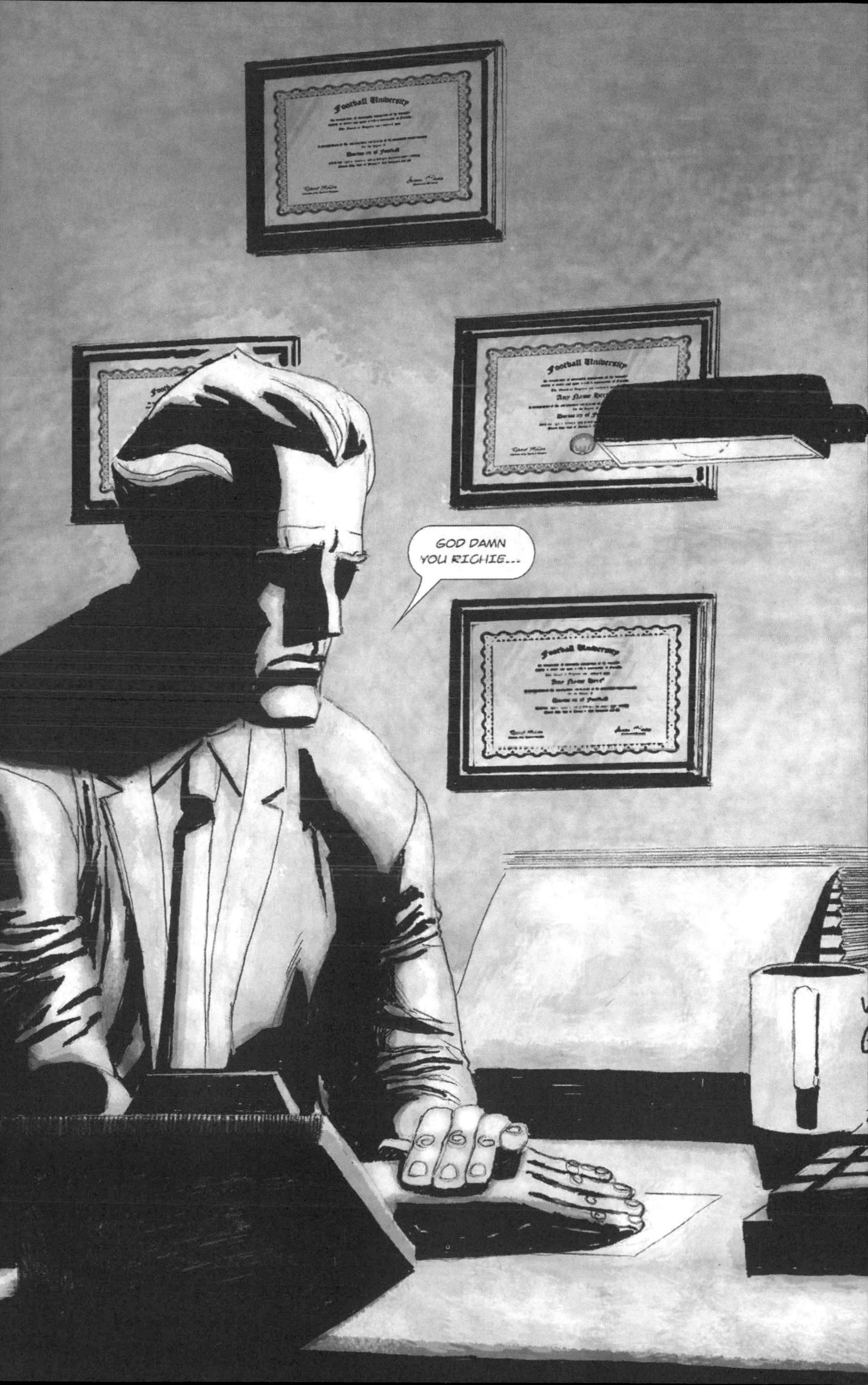
GOD DAMN YOU RICHIE...

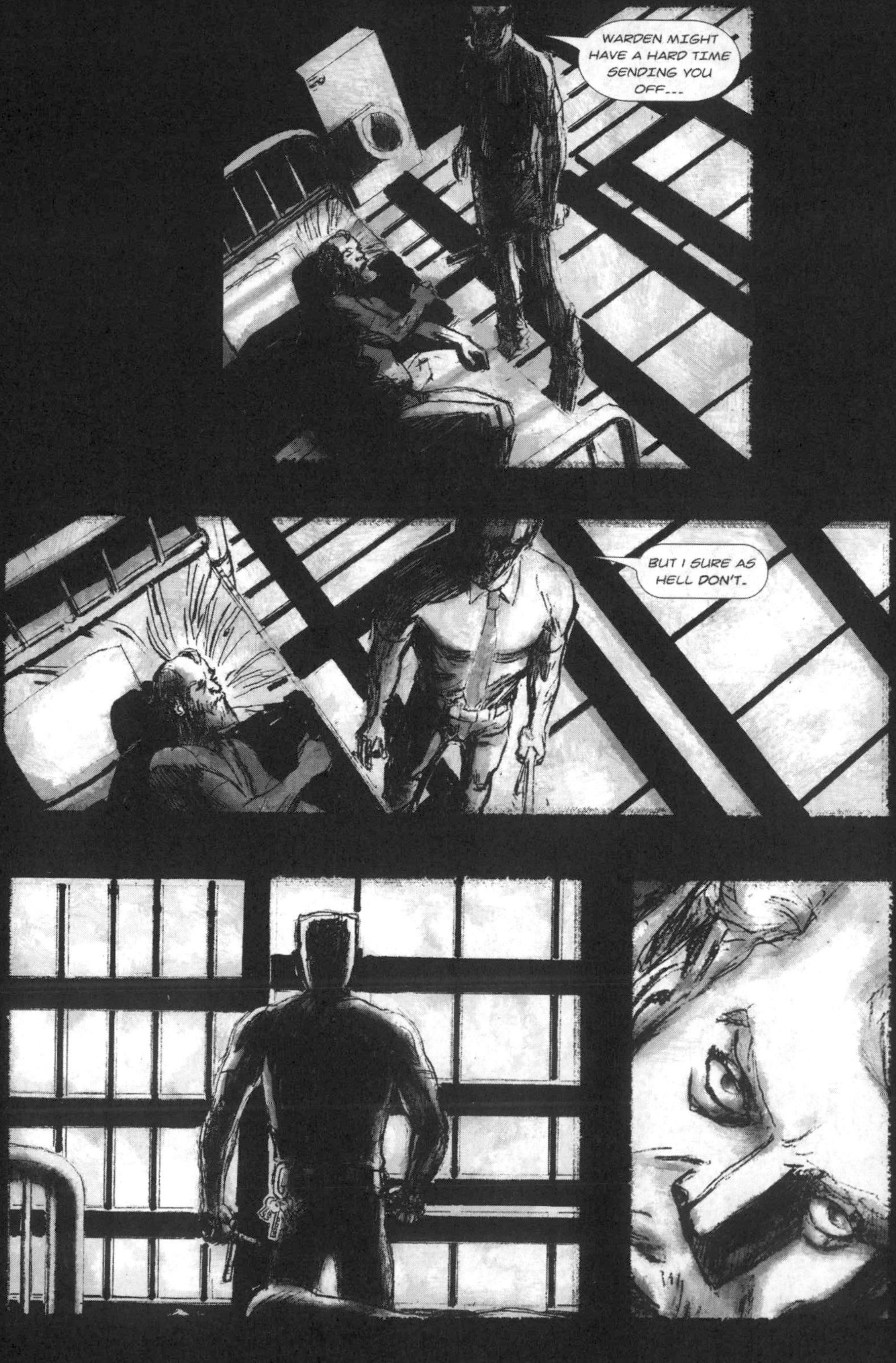
WARDEN MIGHT HAVE A HARD TIME SENDING YOU OFF...
BUT I SURE AS HELL DON'T.

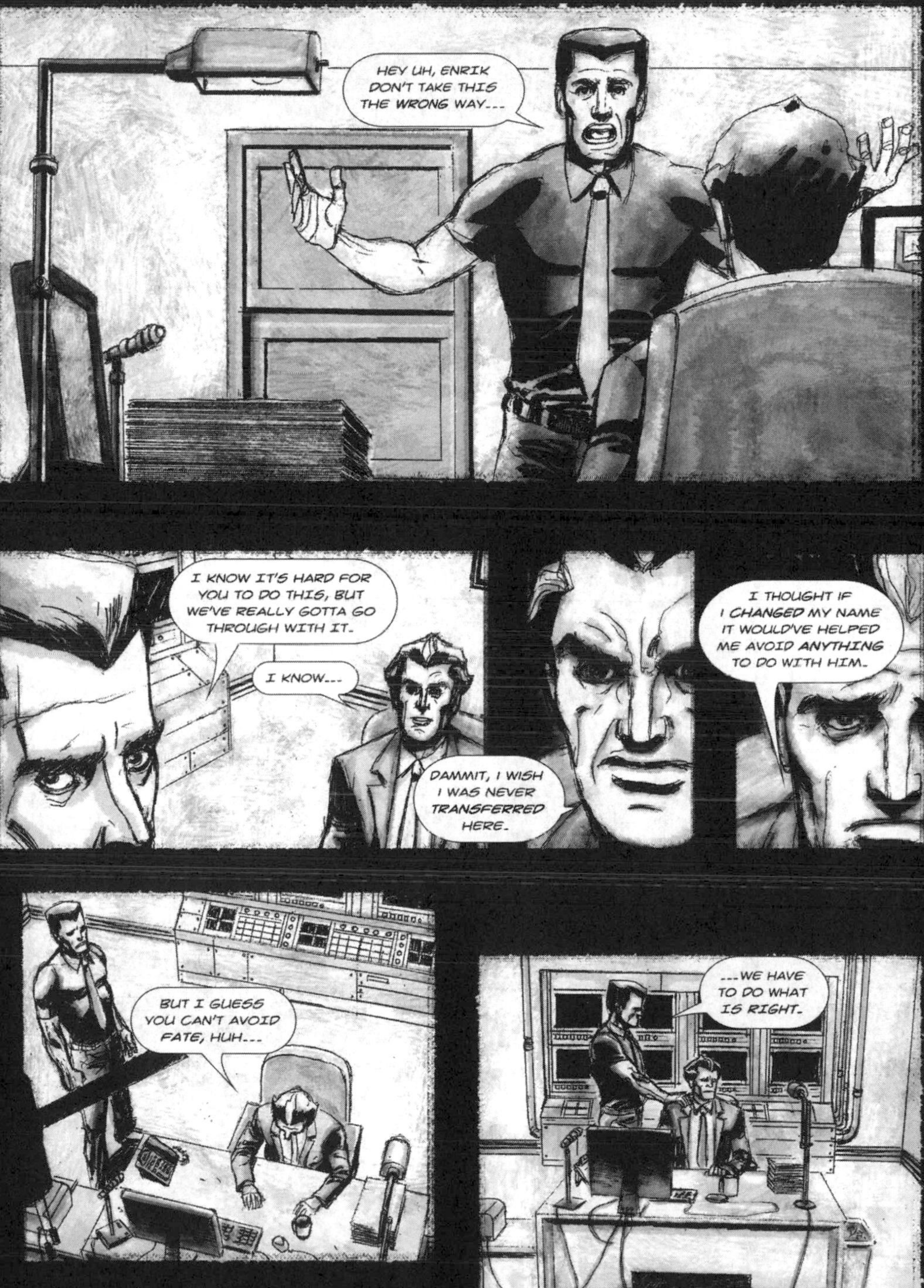
HEY UH, ENRIK DON'T TAKE THIS THE WRONG WAY...
I KNOW IT'S HARD FOR YOU TO DO THIS, BUT WE'VE REALLY GOTTA GO THROUGH WITH IT.
I KNOW...
DAMMIT, I WISH I WAS NEVER TRANSFERRED HERE.
I THOUGHT IF I CHANGED MY NAME IT WOULD'VE HELPED ME AVOID ANYTHING TO DO WITH HIM.
BUT I GUESS YOU CAN'T AVOID FATE, HUH...
...WE HAVE TO DO WHAT IS RIGHT.

I'LL SEE YOU LATER, ENRIK. JUST THINK ABOUT WHAT I SAID.

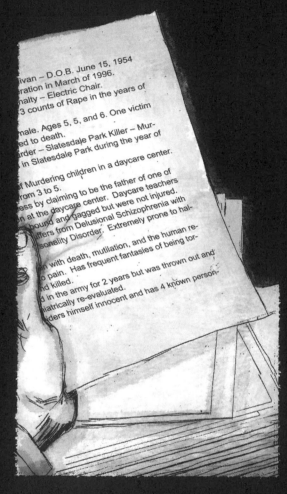

...ivan – D.O.B. June 15, 1954
...eration in March of 1996.
...nalty – Electric Chair.
...3 counts of Rape in the years of

...male. Ages 5, 5, and 6. One victim
...ed to death.
...rder – Slatesdale Park Killer – Mur-
...urder – Slatesdale Park during the year of
...t in Slatesdale Park during the year of

...f Murdering children in a daycare center.
...rom 3 to 5.
...ess by claiming to be the father of one of
...n at the daycare center. Daycare teachers
...bound and gagged but were not injured.
...ffers from Delusional Schizophrenia with
...sonality Disorder. Extremely prone to hal-

...n with death, mutilation, and the human re-
...o pain. Has frequent fantasies of being tor-
...d killed.
...d in the army for 2 years but was thrown out and
...iatrically re-evaluated.
...ders himself innocent and has 4 known person-

I GUESS WE CAN ADD ANOTHER COUNT OF MURDER...

DAMMIT SIMMONS!

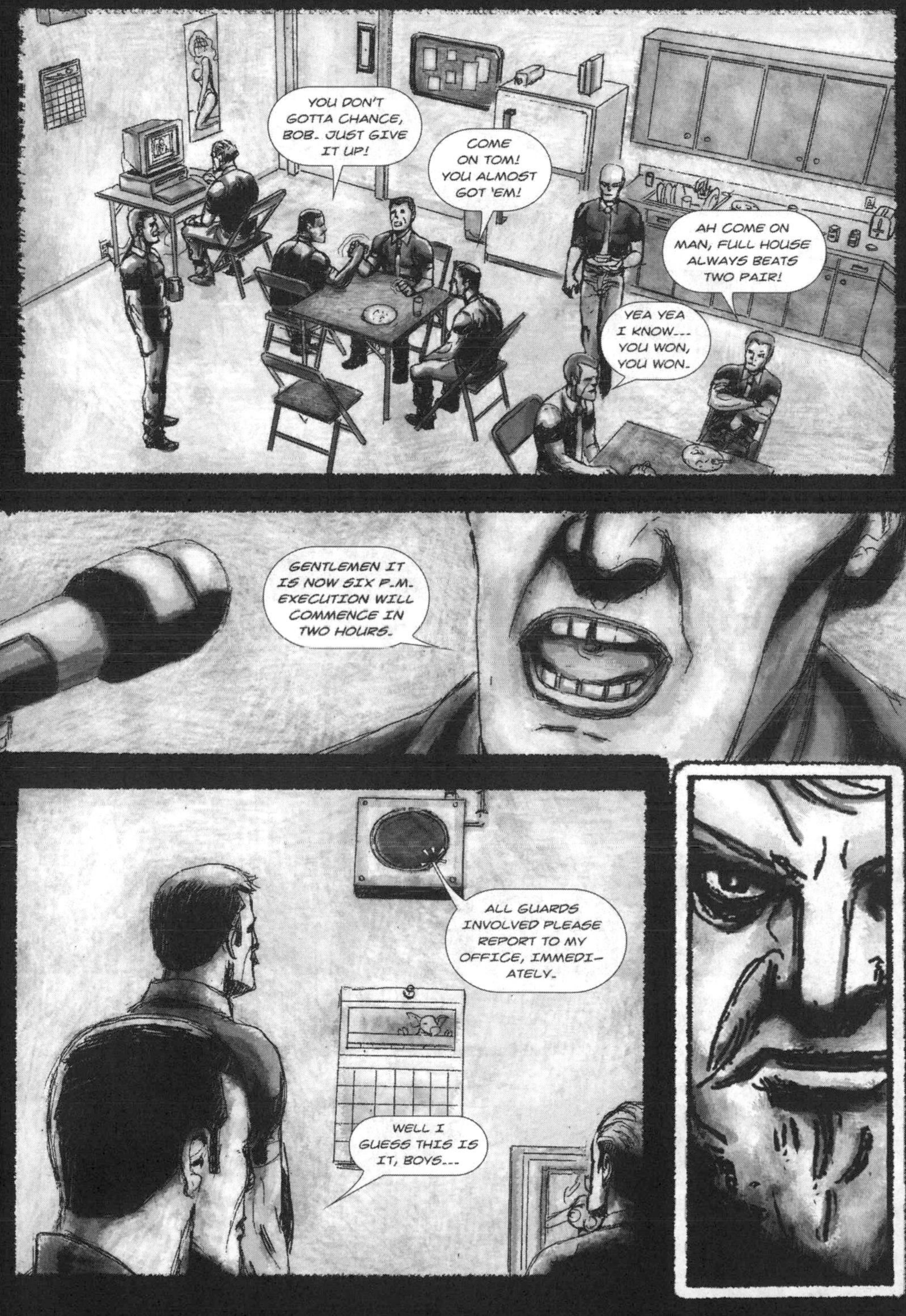
YOU DON'T GOTTA CHANCE, BOB. JUST GIVE IT UP!
COME ON TOM! YOU ALMOST GOT 'EM!
AH COME ON MAN, FULL HOUSE ALWAYS BEATS TWO PAIR!
YEA YEA I KNOW... YOU WON, YOU WON.
GENTLEMEN IT IS NOW SIX P.M. EXECUTION WILL COMMENCE IN TWO HOURS.
ALL GUARDS INVOLVED PLEASE REPORT TO MY OFFICE, IMMEDI-ATELY.
WELL I GUESS THIS IS IT, BOYS...

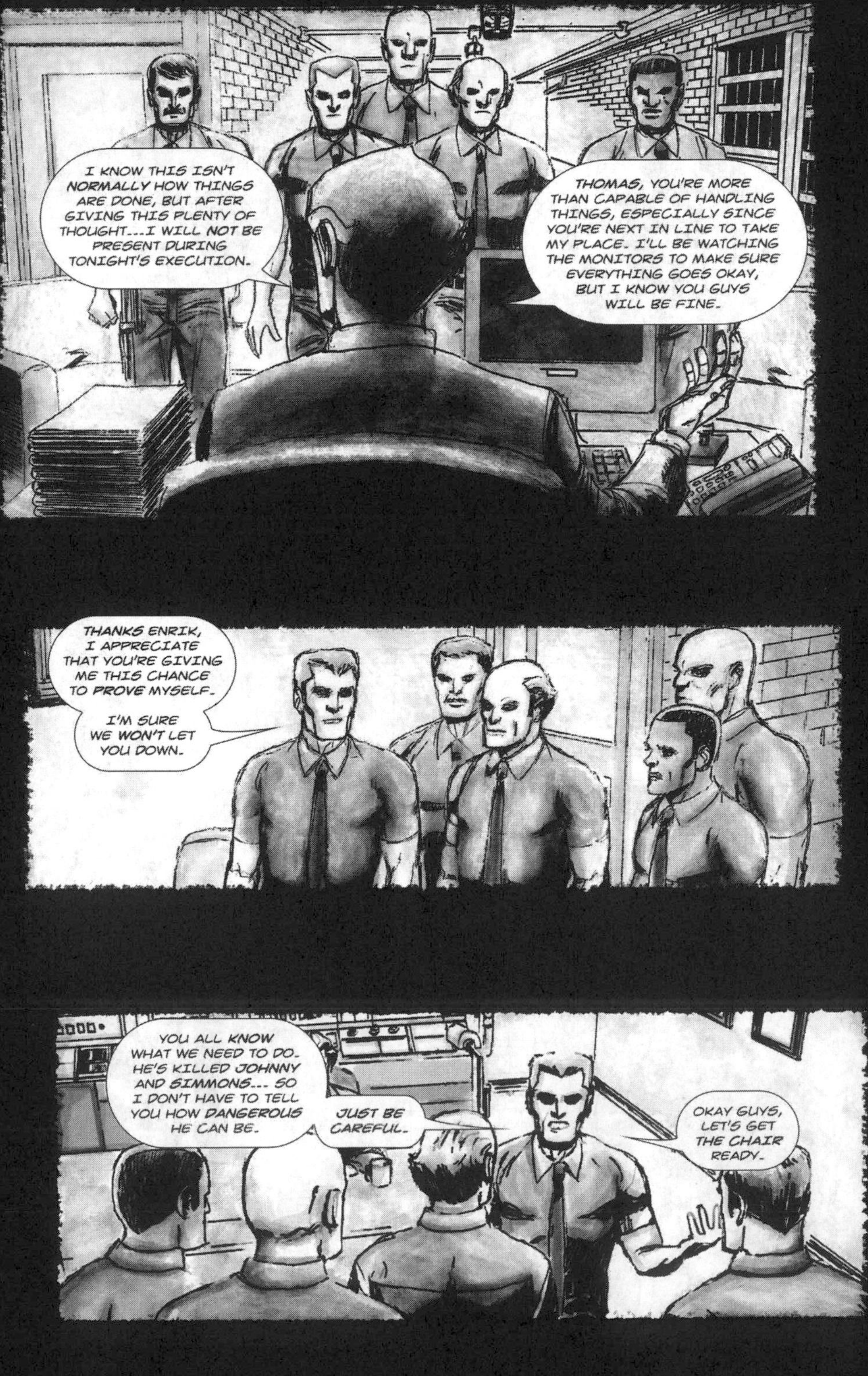
I KNOW THIS ISN'T NORMALLY HOW THINGS ARE DONE, BUT AFTER GIVING THIS PLENTY OF THOUGHT...I WILL NOT BE PRESENT DURING TONIGHT'S EXECUTION.
THOMAS, YOU'RE MORE THAN CAPABLE OF HANDLING THINGS, ESPECIALLY SINCE YOU'RE NEXT IN LINE TO TAKE MY PLACE. I'LL BE WATCHING THE MONITORS TO MAKE SURE EVERYTHING GOES OKAY, BUT I KNOW YOU GUYS WILL BE FINE.
THANKS ENRIK, I APPRECIATE THAT YOU'RE GIVING ME THIS CHANCE TO PROVE MYSELF.
I'M SURE WE WON'T LET YOU DOWN.
YOU ALL KNOW WHAT WE NEED TO DO. HE'S KILLED JOHNNY AND SIMMONS... SO I DON'T HAVE TO TELL YOU HOW DANGEROUS HE CAN BE.
JUST BE CAREFUL.
OKAY GUYS, LET'S GET THE CHAIR READY.

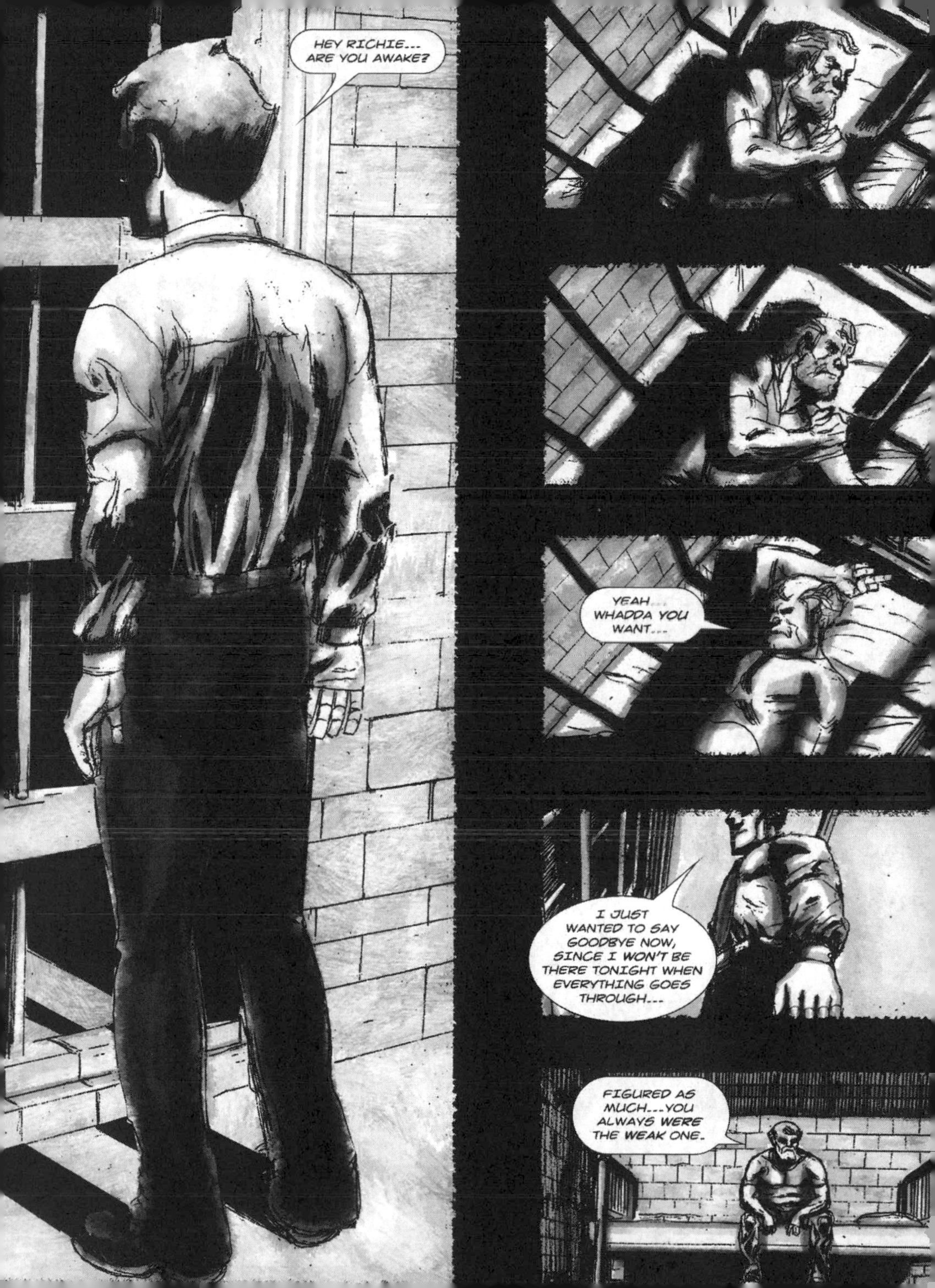
HEY RICHIE... ARE YOU AWAKE?
YEAH... WHADDA YOU WANT...
I JUST WANTED TO SAY GOODBYE NOW, SINCE I WON'T BE THERE TONIGHT WHEN EVERYTHING GOES THROUGH...
FIGURED AS MUCH...YOU ALWAYS WERE THE WEAK ONE.

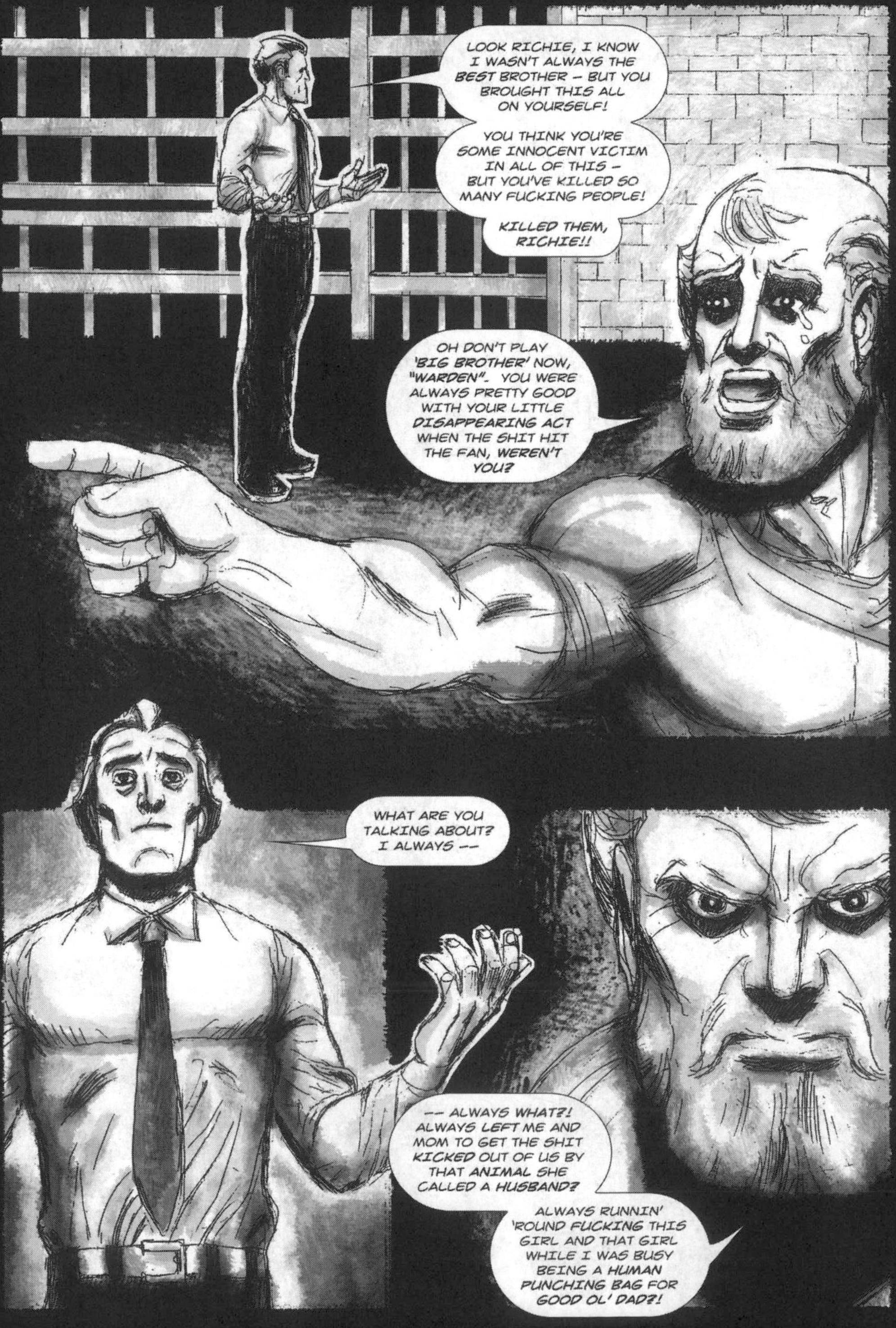
LOOK RICHIE, I KNOW I WASN'T ALWAYS THE BEST BROTHER -- BUT YOU BROUGHT THIS ALL ON YOURSELF!
YOU THINK YOU'RE SOME INNOCENT VICTIM IN ALL OF THIS -- BUT YOU'VE KILLED SO MANY FUCKING PEOPLE!
KILLED THEM, RICHIE!!
OH DON'T PLAY 'BIG BROTHER' NOW, "WARDEN". YOU WERE ALWAYS PRETTY GOOD WITH YOUR LITTLE DISAPPEARING ACT WHEN THE SHIT HIT THE FAN, WEREN'T YOU?
WHAT ARE YOU TALKING ABOUT? I ALWAYS --
-- ALWAYS WHAT?! ALWAYS LEFT ME AND MOM TO GET THE SHIT KICKED OUT OF US BY THAT ANIMAL SHE CALLED A HUSBAND?
ALWAYS RUNNIN' 'ROUND FUCKING THIS GIRL AND THAT GIRL WHILE I WAS BUSY BEING A HUMAN PUNCHING BAG FOR GOOD OL' DAD?!

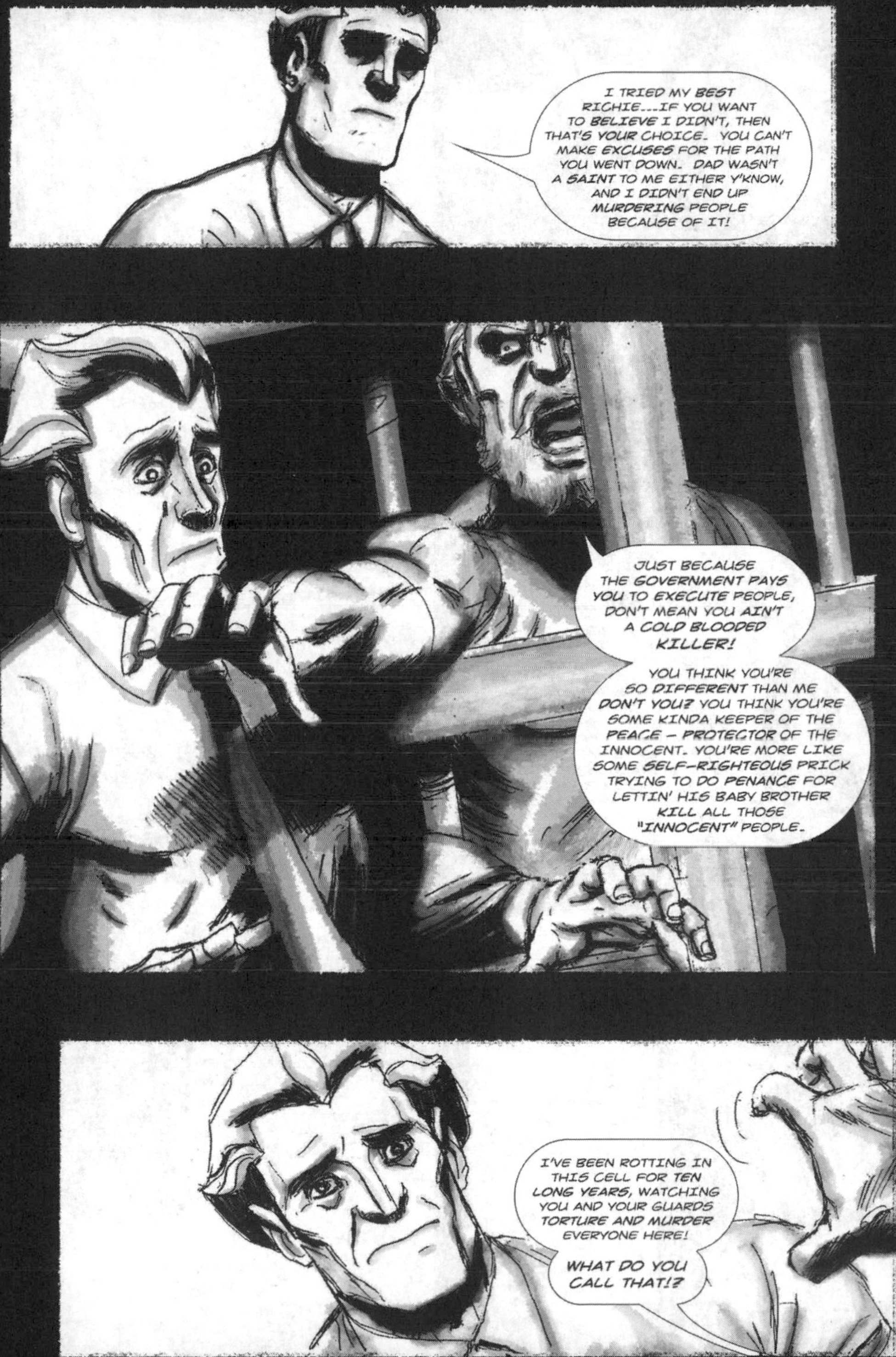
I TRIED MY BEST RICHIE...IF YOU WANT TO BELIEVE I DIDN'T, THEN THAT'S YOUR CHOICE. YOU CAN'T MAKE EXCUSES FOR THE PATH YOU WENT DOWN. DAD WASN'T A SAINT TO ME EITHER Y'KNOW, AND I DIDN'T END UP MURDERING PEOPLE BECAUSE OF IT!
JUST BECAUSE THE GOVERNMENT PAYS YOU TO EXECUTE PEOPLE, DON'T MEAN YOU AIN'T A COLD BLOODED KILLER!
YOU THINK YOU'RE SO DIFFERENT THAN ME DON'T YOU? YOU THINK YOU'RE SOME KINDA KEEPER OF THE PEACE – PROTECTOR OF THE INNOCENT. YOU'RE MORE LIKE SOME SELF-RIGHTEOUS PRICK TRYING TO DO PENANCE FOR LETTIN' HIS BABY BROTHER KILL ALL THOSE "INNOCENT" PEOPLE.
I'VE BEEN ROTTING IN THIS CELL FOR TEN LONG YEARS, WATCHING YOU AND YOUR GUARDS TORTURE AND MURDER EVERYONE HERE!
WHAT DO YOU CALL THAT!?

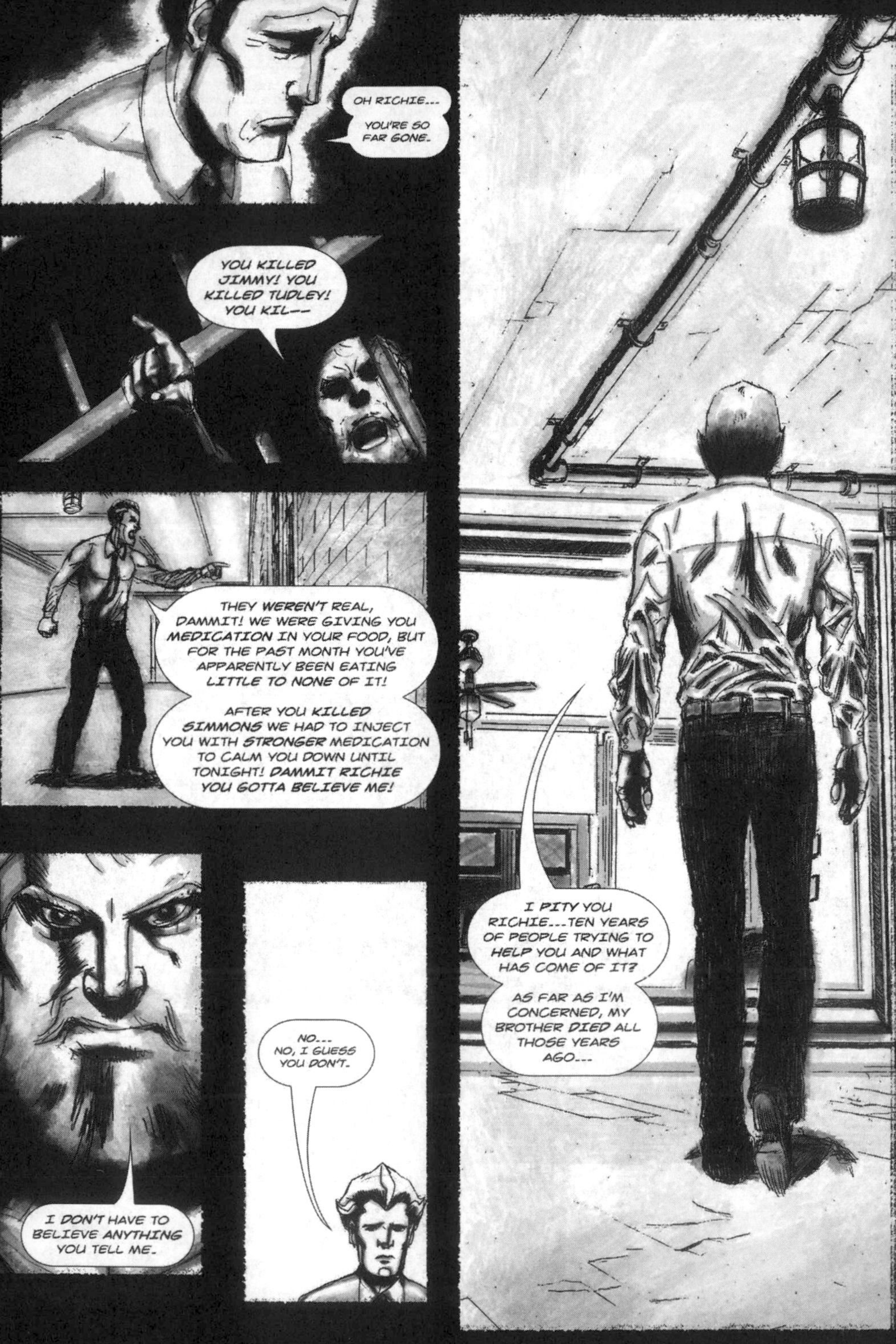
OH RICHIE...
YOU'RE SO FAR GONE.
YOU KILLED JIMMY! YOU KILLED TUDLEY! YOU KIL--
THEY WEREN'T REAL, DAMMIT! WE WERE GIVING YOU MEDICATION IN YOUR FOOD, BUT FOR THE PAST MONTH YOU'VE APPARENTLY BEEN EATING LITTLE TO NONE OF IT!
AFTER YOU KILLED SIMMONS WE HAD TO INJECT YOU WITH STRONGER MEDICATION TO CALM YOU DOWN UNTIL TONIGHT! DAMMIT RICHIE YOU GOTTA BELIEVE ME!
I DON'T HAVE TO BELIEVE ANYTHING YOU TELL ME.
NO... NO, I GUESS YOU DON'T.
I PITY YOU RICHIE...TEN YEARS OF PEOPLE TRYING TO HELP YOU AND WHAT HAS COME OF IT?
AS FAR AS I'M CONCERNED, MY BROTHER DIED ALL THOSE YEARS AGO...

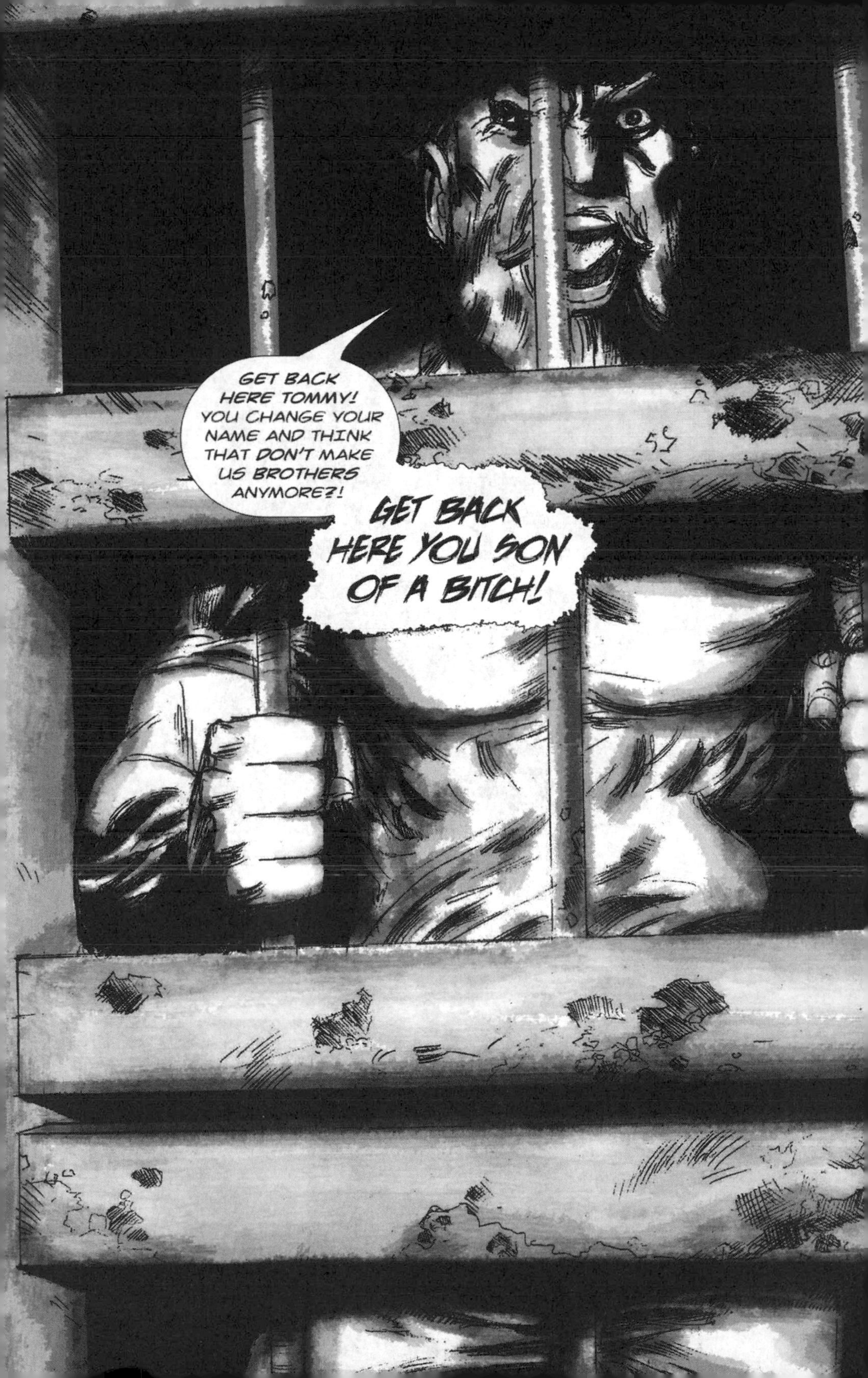
GET BACK HERE TOMMY! YOU CHANGE YOUR NAME AND THINK THAT DON'T MAKE US BROTHERS ANYMORE?!
GET BACK HERE YOU SON OF A BITCH!

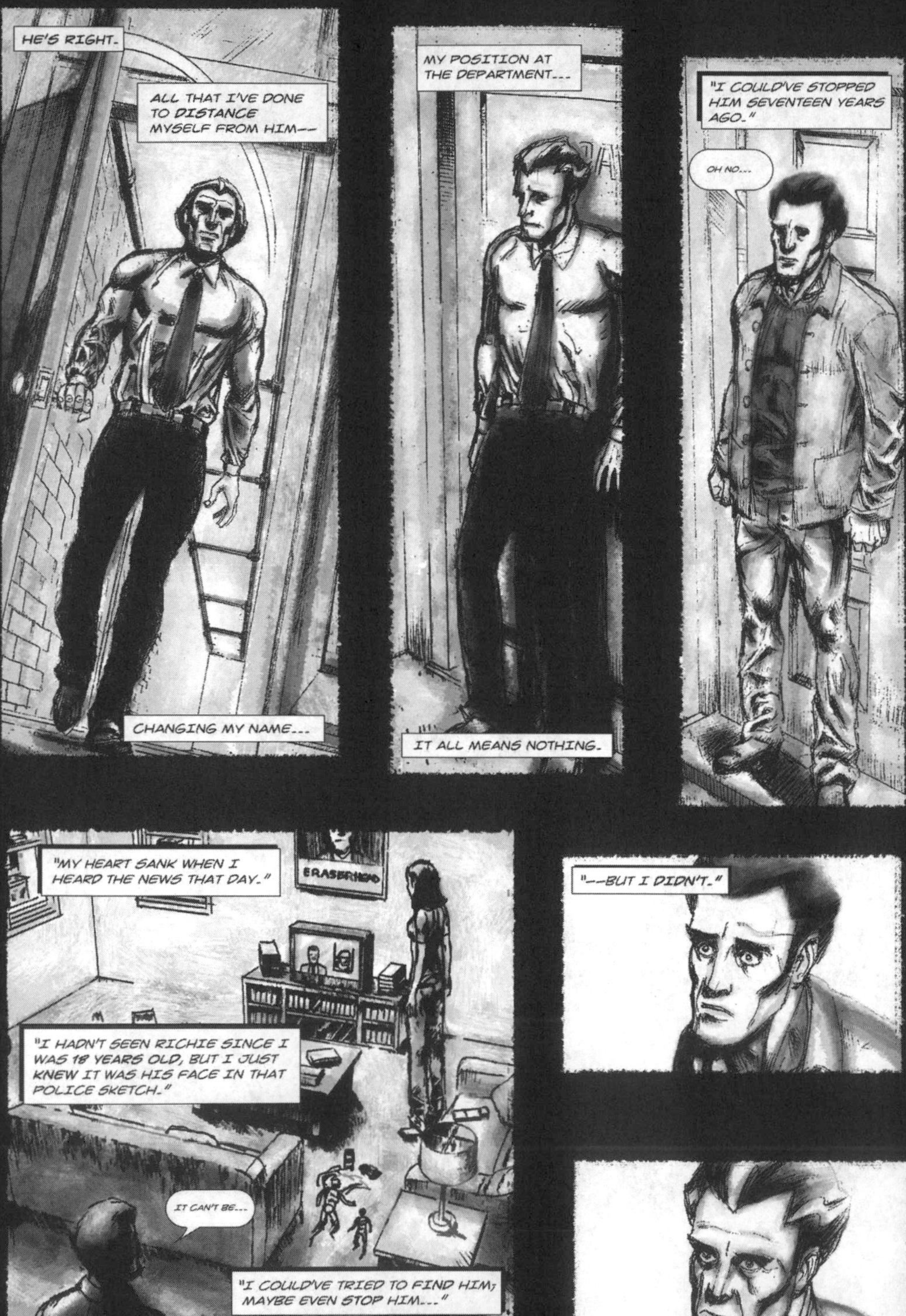

HE'S RIGHT.
ALL THAT I'VE DONE TO DISTANCE MYSELF FROM HIM--
CHANGING MY NAME...
MY POSITION AT THE DEPARTMENT...
IT ALL MEANS NOTHING.
"I COULD'VE STOPPED HIM SEVENTEEN YEARS AGO."
OH NO...
"MY HEART SANK WHEN I HEARD THE NEWS THAT DAY."
ERASERHEAD
"I HADN'T SEEN RICHIE SINCE I WAS 18 YEARS OLD, BUT I JUST KNEW IT WAS HIS FACE IN THAT POLICE SKETCH."
IT CAN'T BE...
"I COULD'VE TRIED TO FIND HIM; MAYBE EVEN STOP HIM..."
"--BUT I DIDN'T."
I COULDN'T.

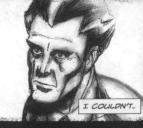

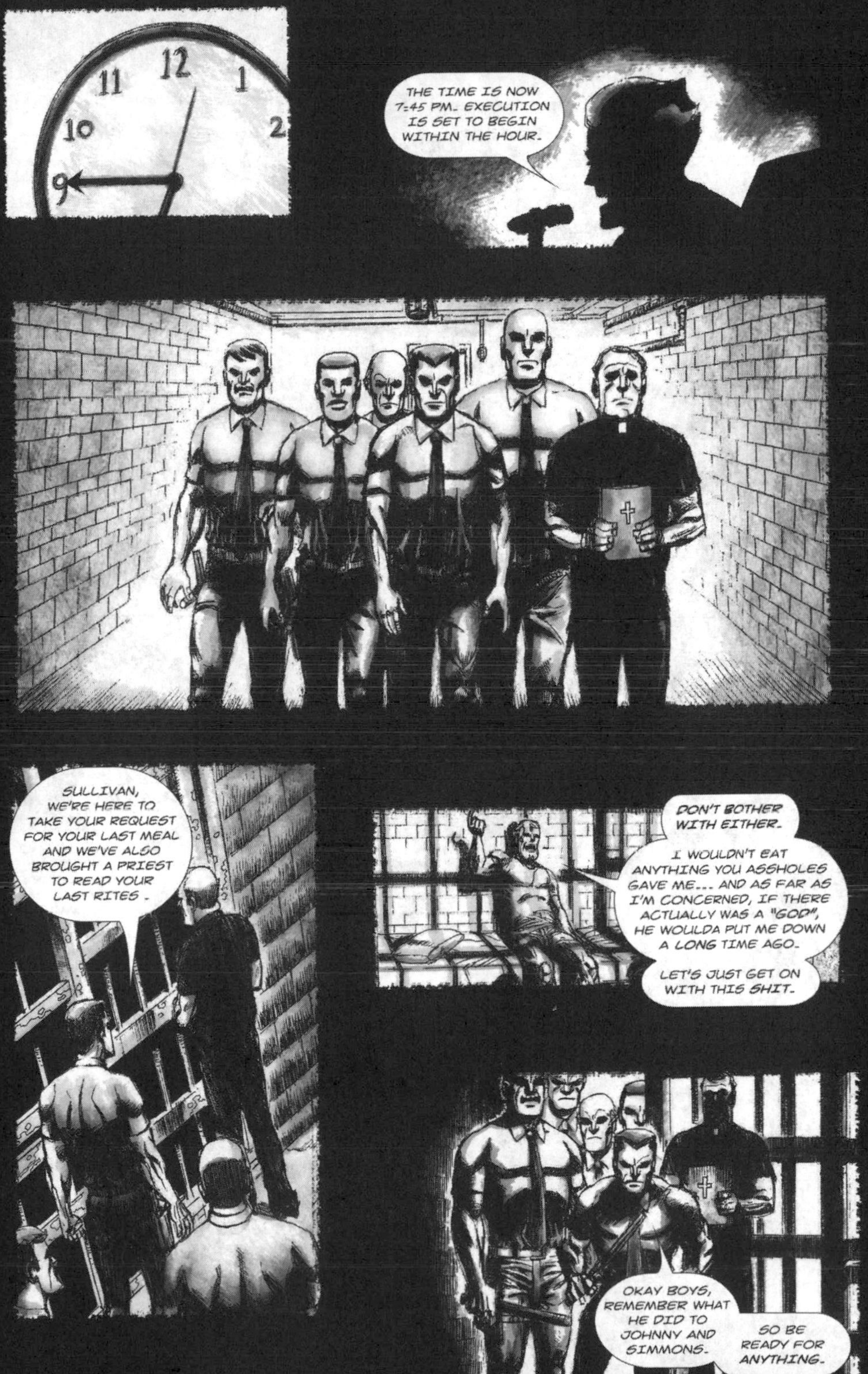
THE TIME IS NOW 7:45 PM. EXECUTION IS SET TO BEGIN WITHIN THE HOUR.
SULLIVAN, WE'RE HERE TO TAKE YOUR REQUEST FOR YOUR LAST MEAL AND WE'VE ALSO BROUGHT A PRIEST TO READ YOUR LAST RITES.
DON'T BOTHER WITH EITHER.
I WOULDN'T EAT ANYTHING YOU ASSHOLES GAVE ME... AND AS FAR AS I'M CONCERNED, IF THERE ACTUALLY WAS A "GOD", HE WOULDA PUT ME DOWN A LONG TIME AGO.
LET'S JUST GET ON WITH THIS SHIT.
OKAY BOYS, REMEMBER WHAT HE DID TO JOHNNY AND SIMMONS.
SO BE READY FOR ANYTHING.

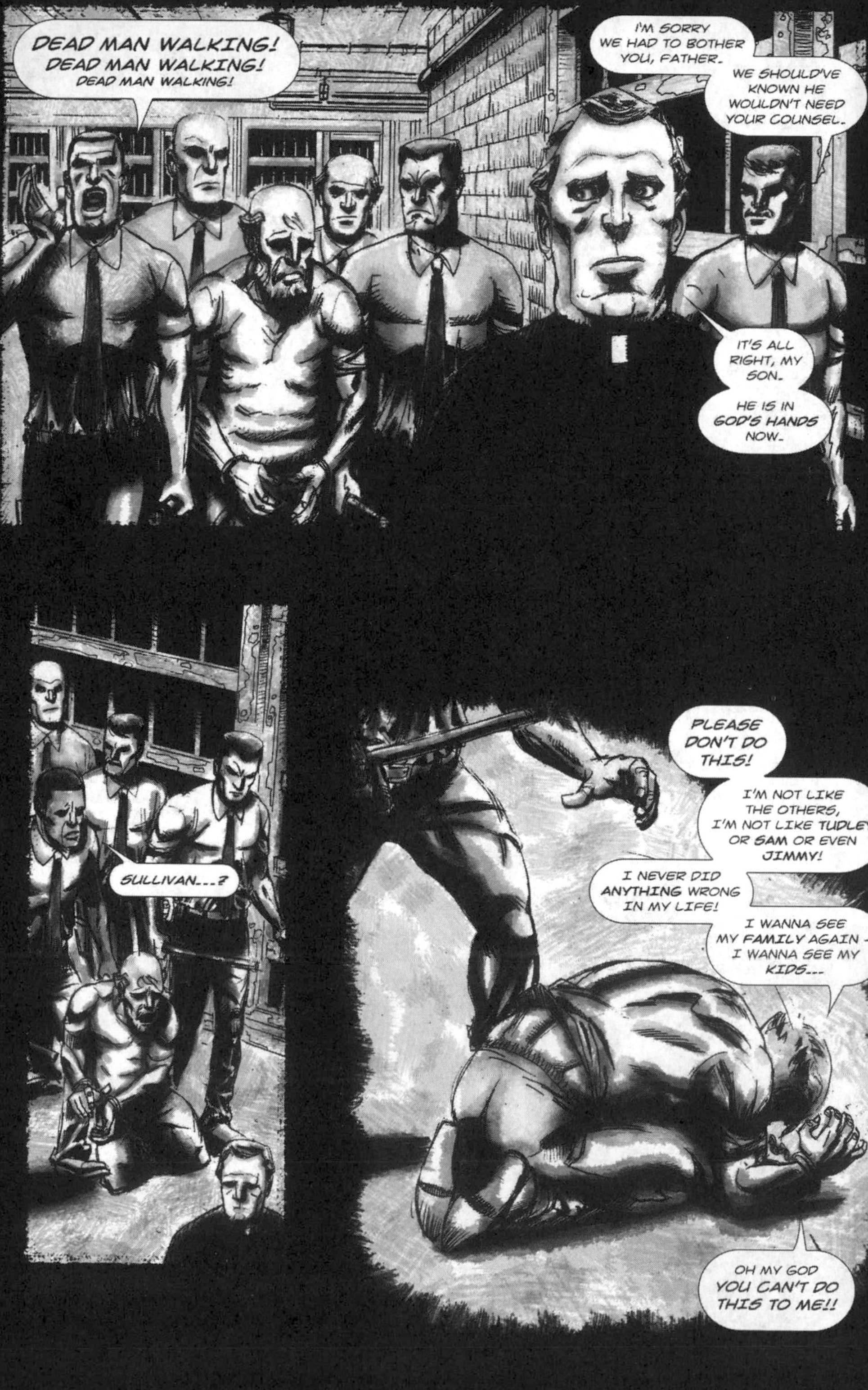
DEAD MAN WALKING! DEAD MAN WALKING! DEAD MAN WALKING!
I'M SORRY WE HAD TO BOTHER YOU, FATHER.
WE SHOULD'VE KNOWN HE WOULDN'T NEED YOUR COUNSEL.
IT'S ALL RIGHT, MY SON.
HE IS IN GOD'S HANDS NOW.
SULLIVAN...?
PLEASE DON'T DO THIS!
I'M NOT LIKE THE OTHERS, I'M NOT LIKE TUDLEY OR SAM OR EVEN JIMMY!
I NEVER DID ANYTHING WRONG IN MY LIFE!
I WANNA SEE MY FAMILY AGAIN – I WANNA SEE MY KIDS...
OH MY GOD YOU CAN'T DO THIS TO ME!!

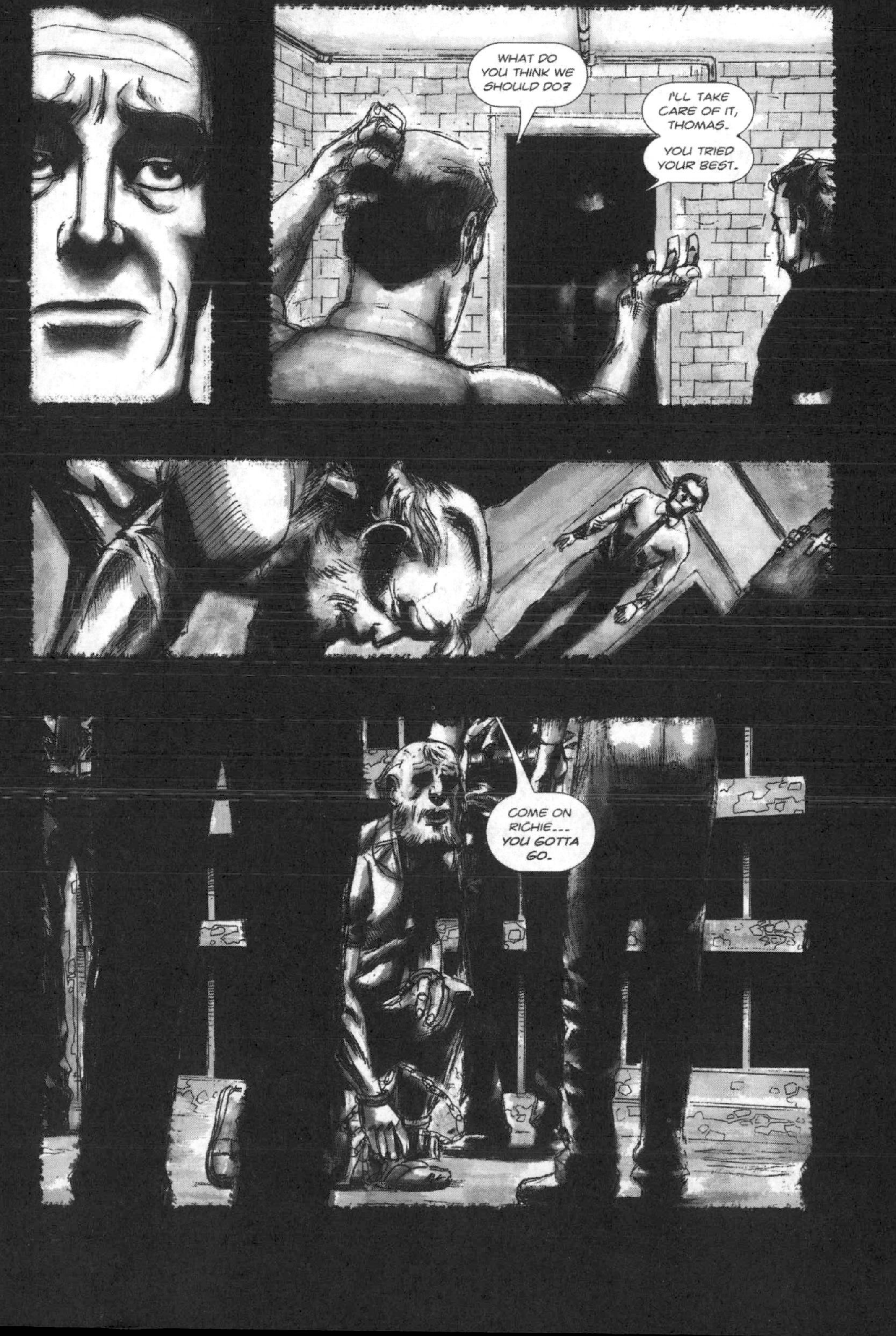
WHAT DO YOU THINK WE SHOULD DO?
I'LL TAKE CARE OF IT, THOMAS.
YOU TRIED YOUR BEST.
COME ON RICHIE... YOU GOTTA GO.

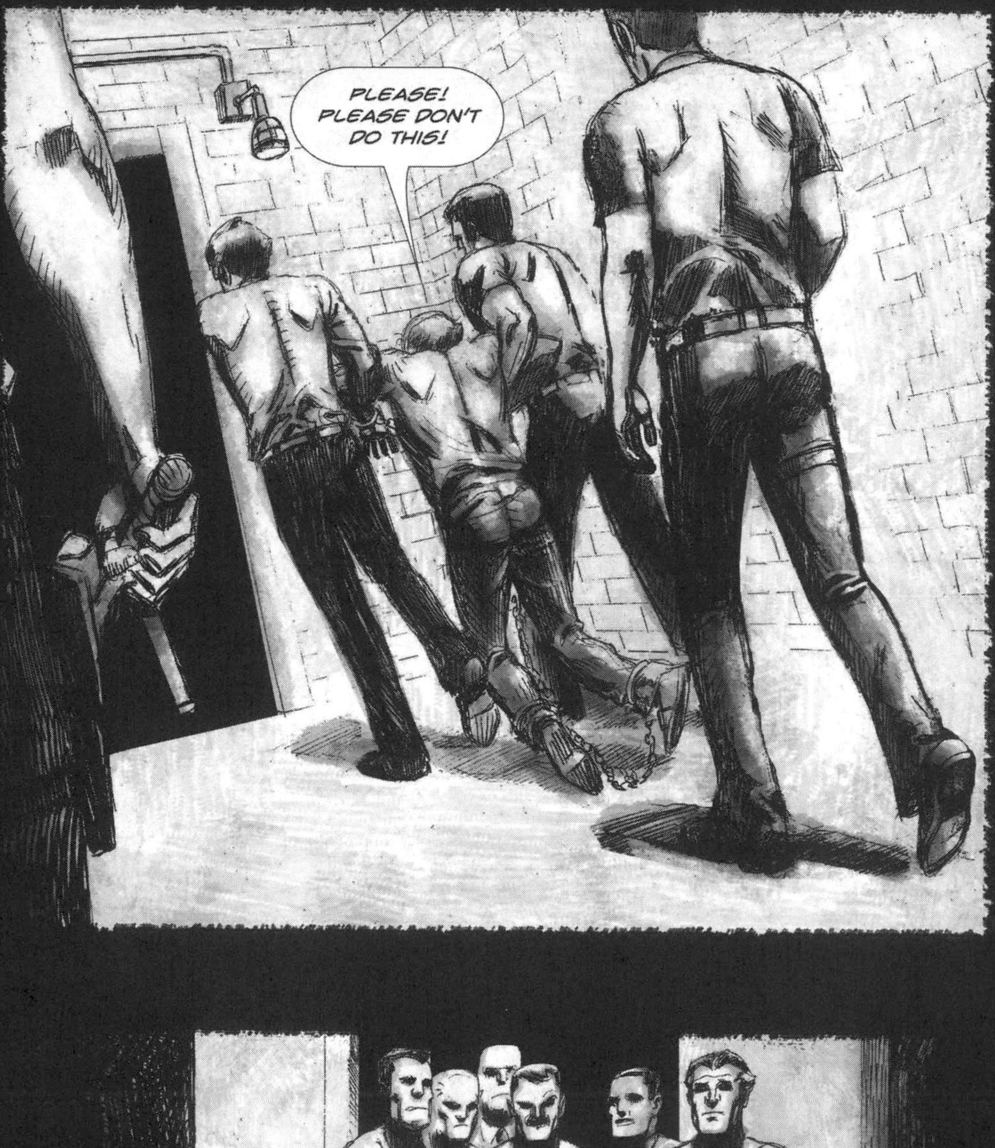
PLEASE! PLEASE DON'T DO THIS!
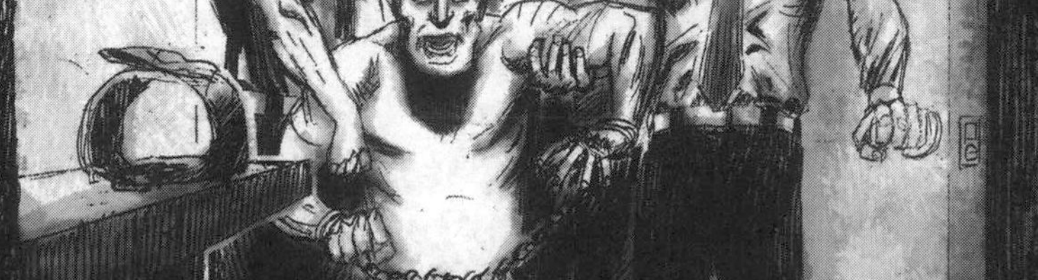
OH GOD...

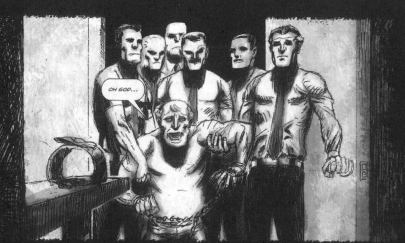

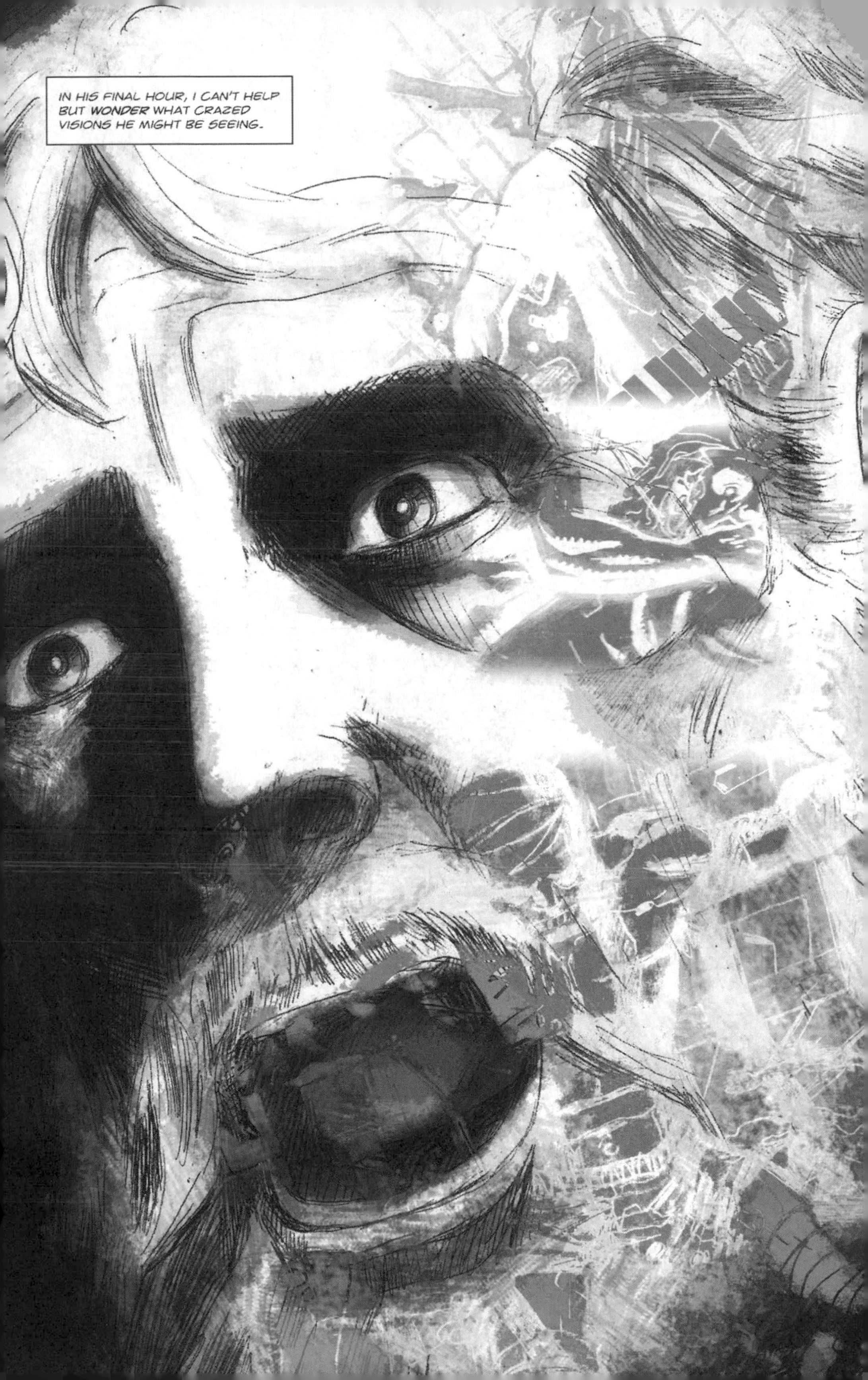
IN HIS FINAL HOUR, I CAN'T HELP BUT WONDER WHAT CRAZED VISIONS HE MIGHT BE SEEING.

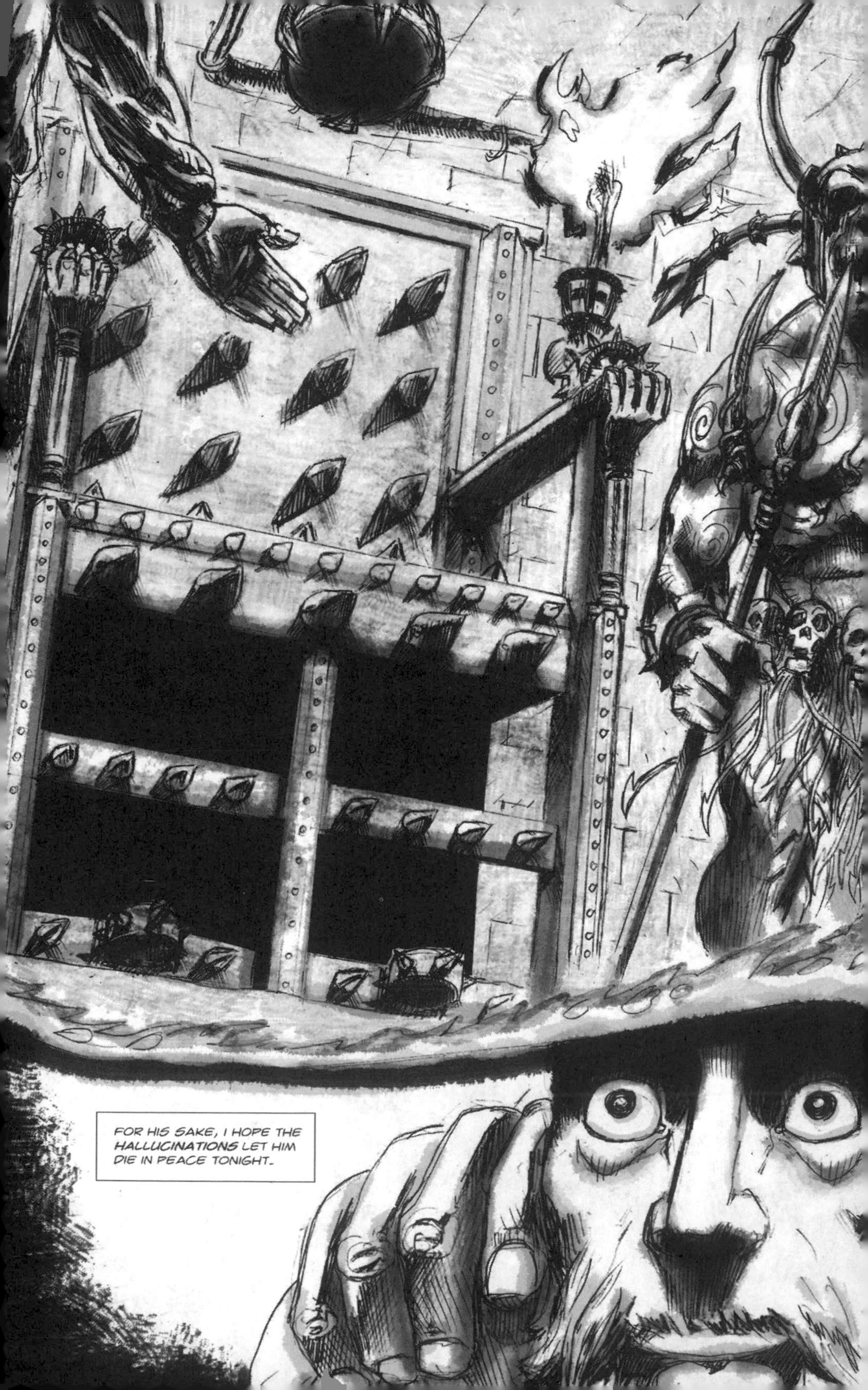
FOR HIS SAKE, I HOPE THE HALLUCINATIONS LET HIM DIE IN PEACE TONIGHT.

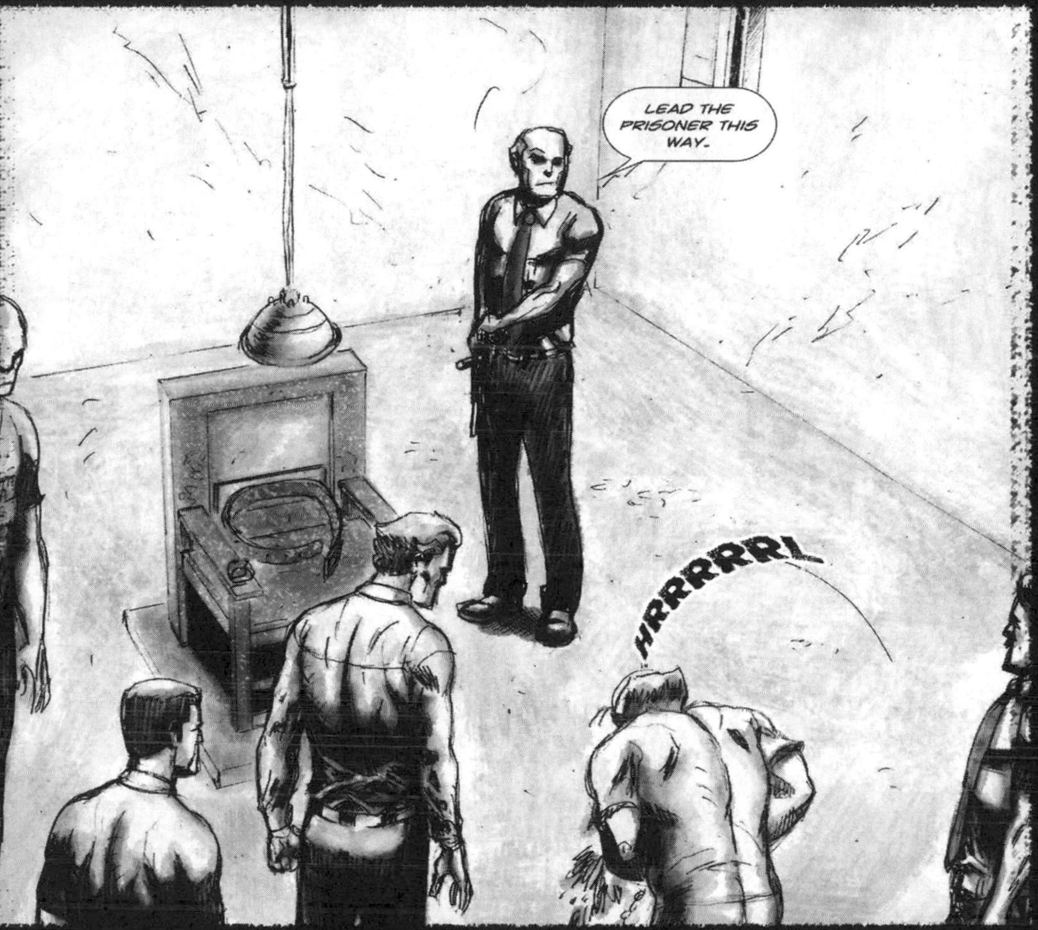
LEAD THE PRISONER THIS WAY.
HRRRRRL

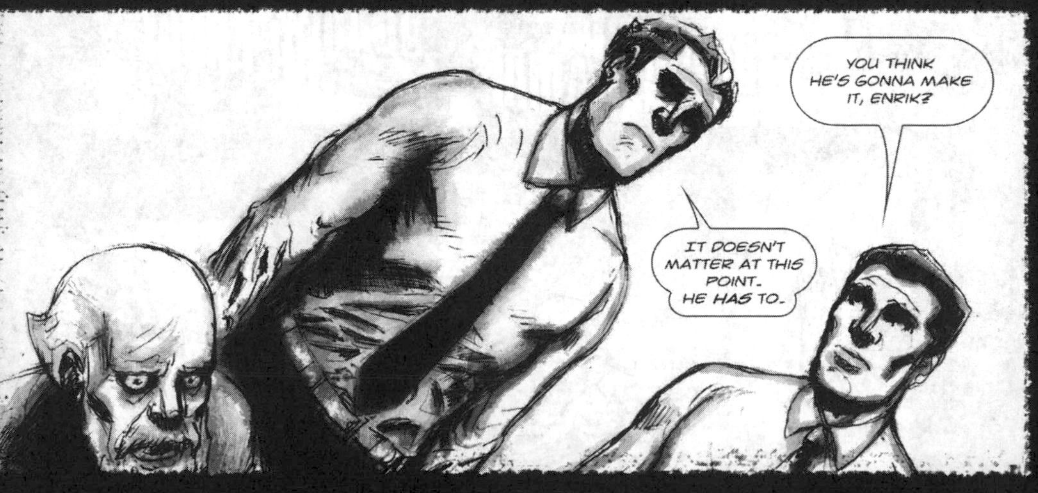
YOU THINK HE'S GONNA MAKE IT, ENRIK?
IT DOESN'T MATTER AT THIS POINT. HE HAS TO.

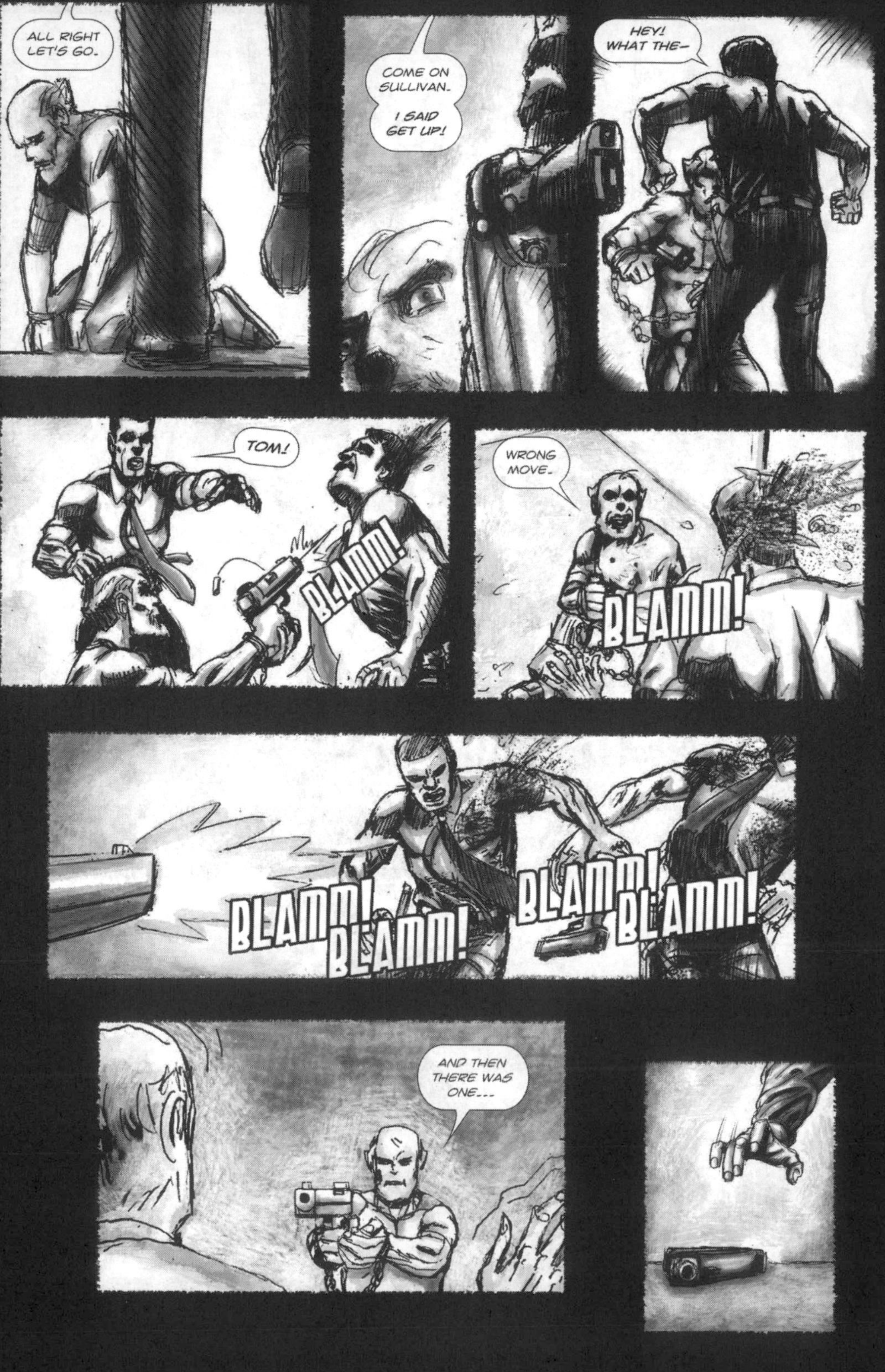
ALL RIGHT LET'S GO.
COME ON SULLIVAN.
I SAID GET UP!
HEY! WHAT THE–
TOM!
BLAMM!
WRONG MOVE.
BLAMM!
BLAMM!
BLAMM!
BLAMM!
BLAMM!
AND THEN THERE WAS ONE...

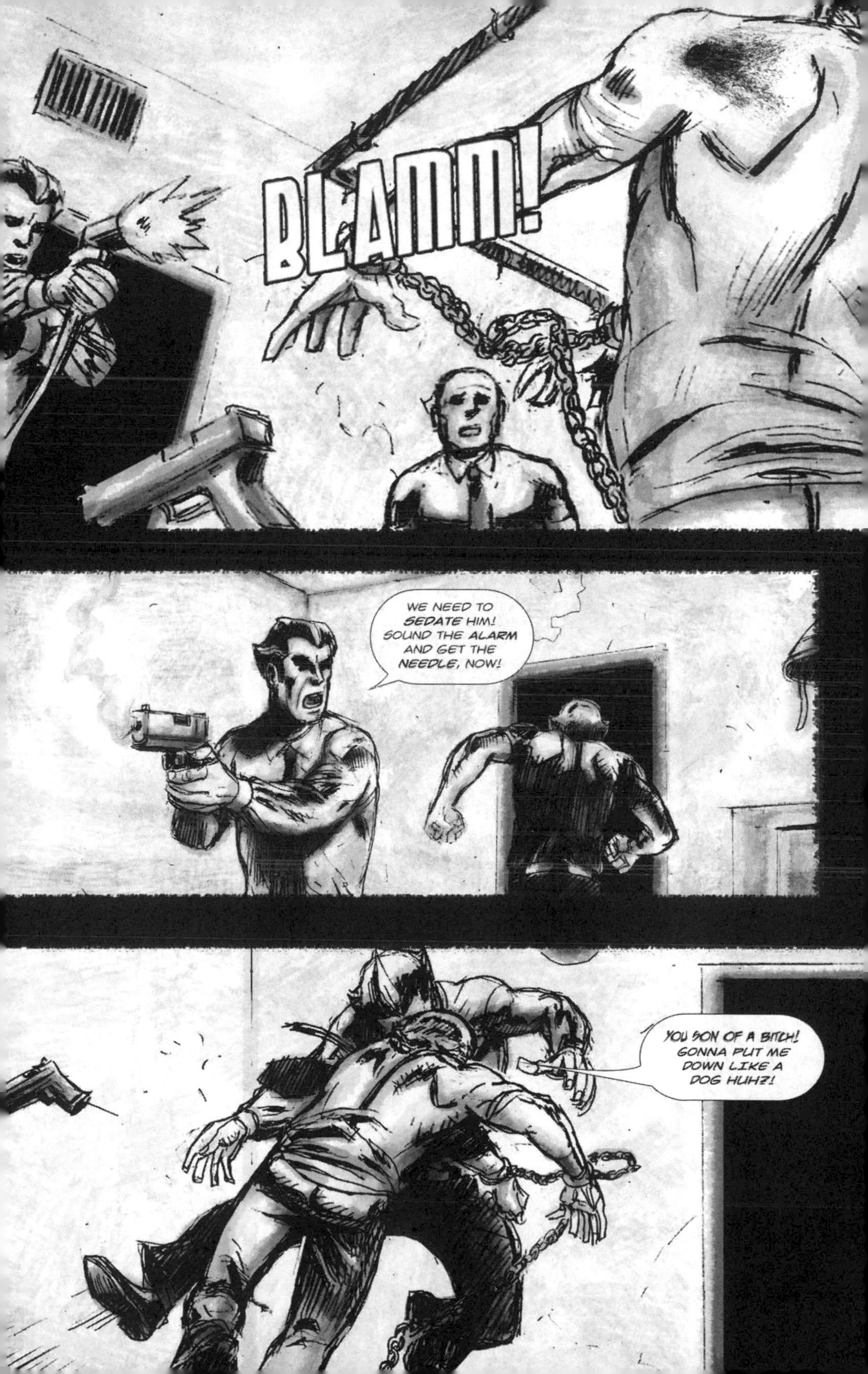
BLAMM!
WE NEED TO SEDATE HIM! SOUND THE ALARM AND GET THE NEEDLE, NOW!
YOU SON OF A BITCH! GONNA PUT ME DOWN LIKE A DOG HUH?!

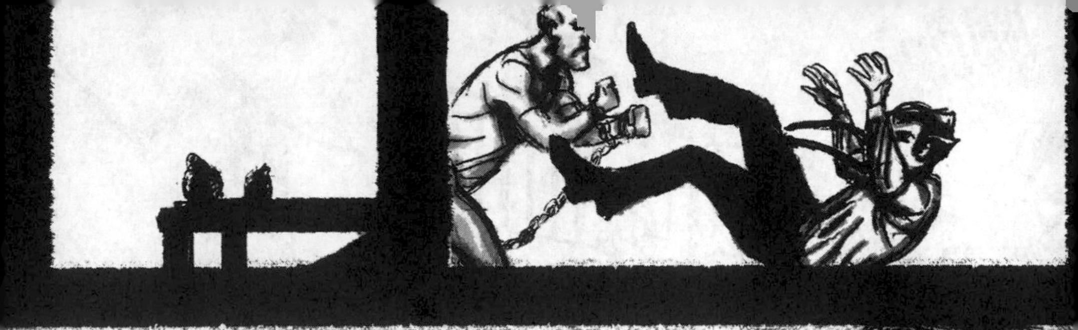

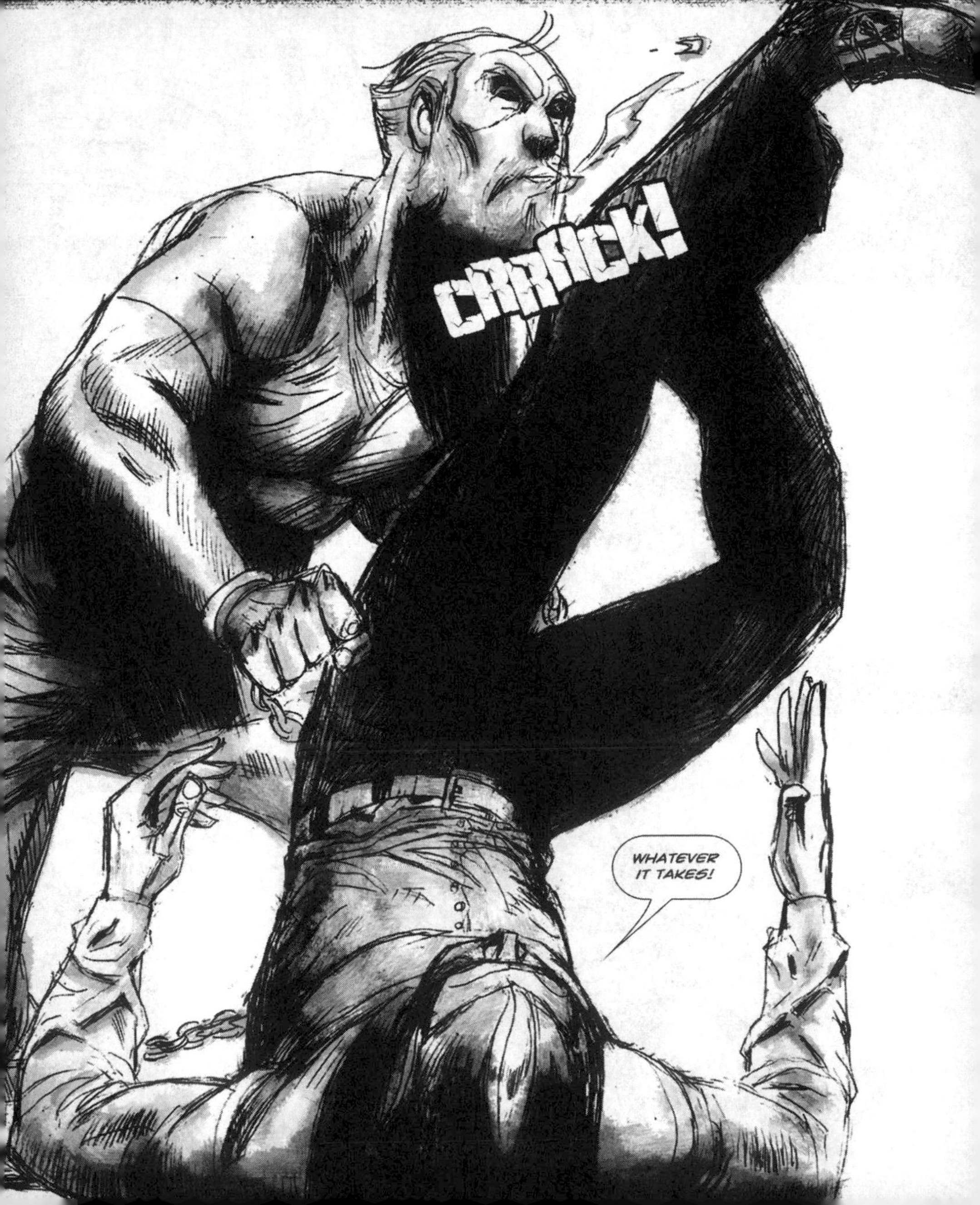
CRRACK!
WHATEVER IT TAKES!

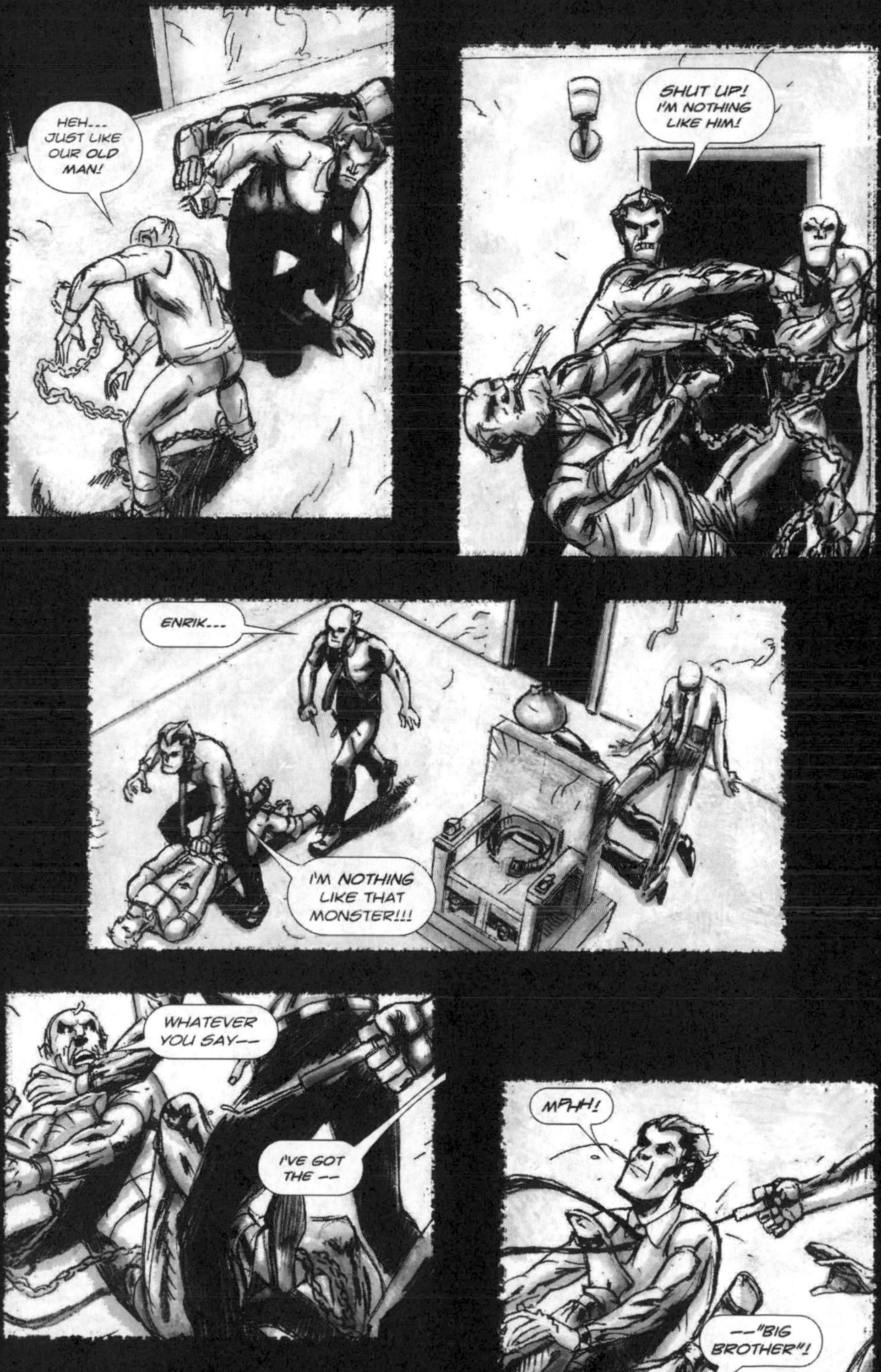
HEH--- JUST LIKE OUR OLD MAN!
SHUT UP! I'M NOTHING LIKE HIM!
ENRIK---
I'M NOTHING LIKE THAT MONSTER!!!
WHATEVER YOU SAY--
I'VE GOT THE --
MPHH!
--"BIG BROTHER"!

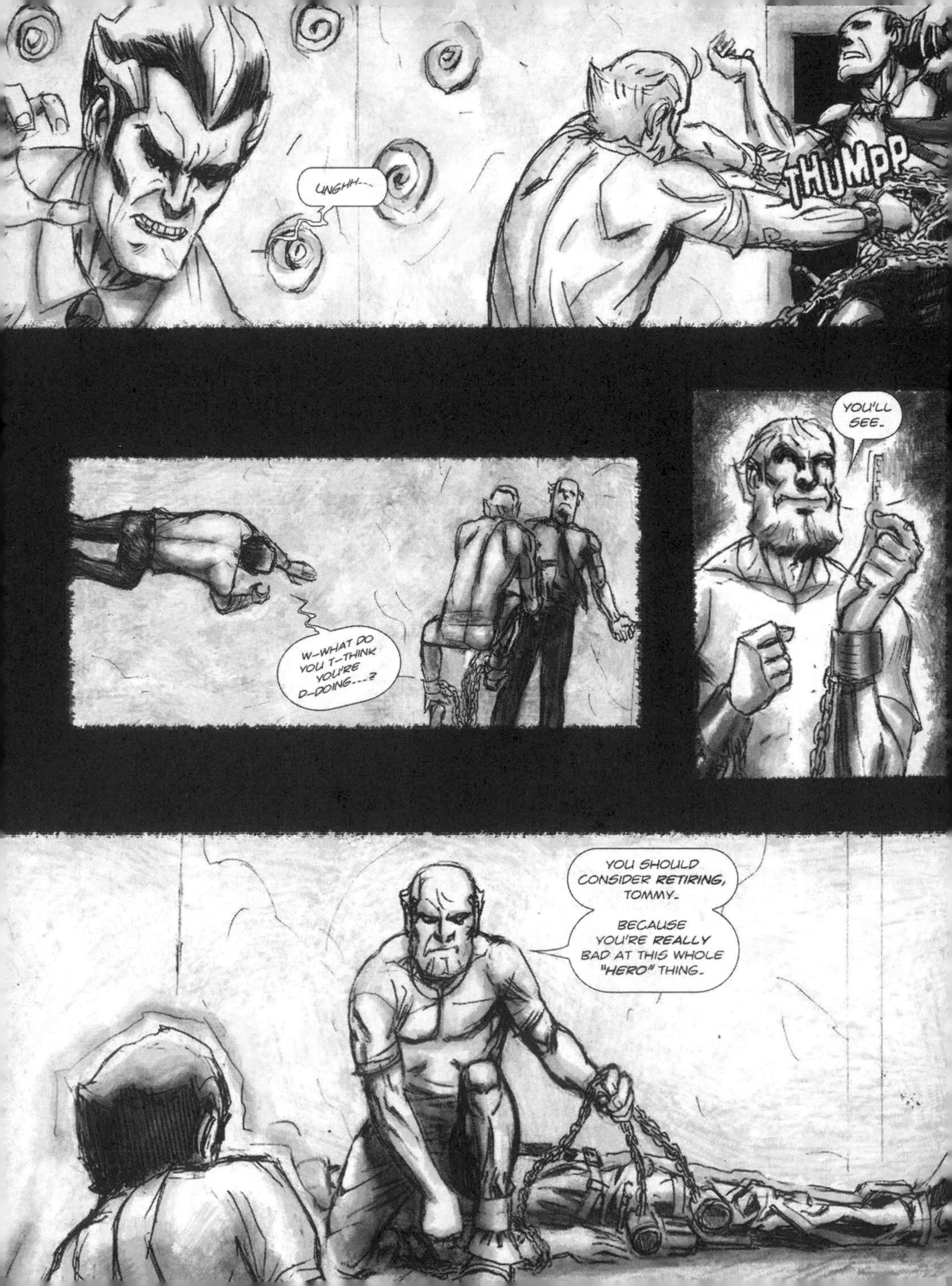
UNGHH...
THUMPP
W--WHAT DO YOU T--THINK YOU'RE D--DOING...?
YOU'LL SEE.
YOU SHOULD CONSIDER RETIRING, TOMMY.
BECAUSE YOU'RE REALLY BAD AT THIS WHOLE "HERO" THING.

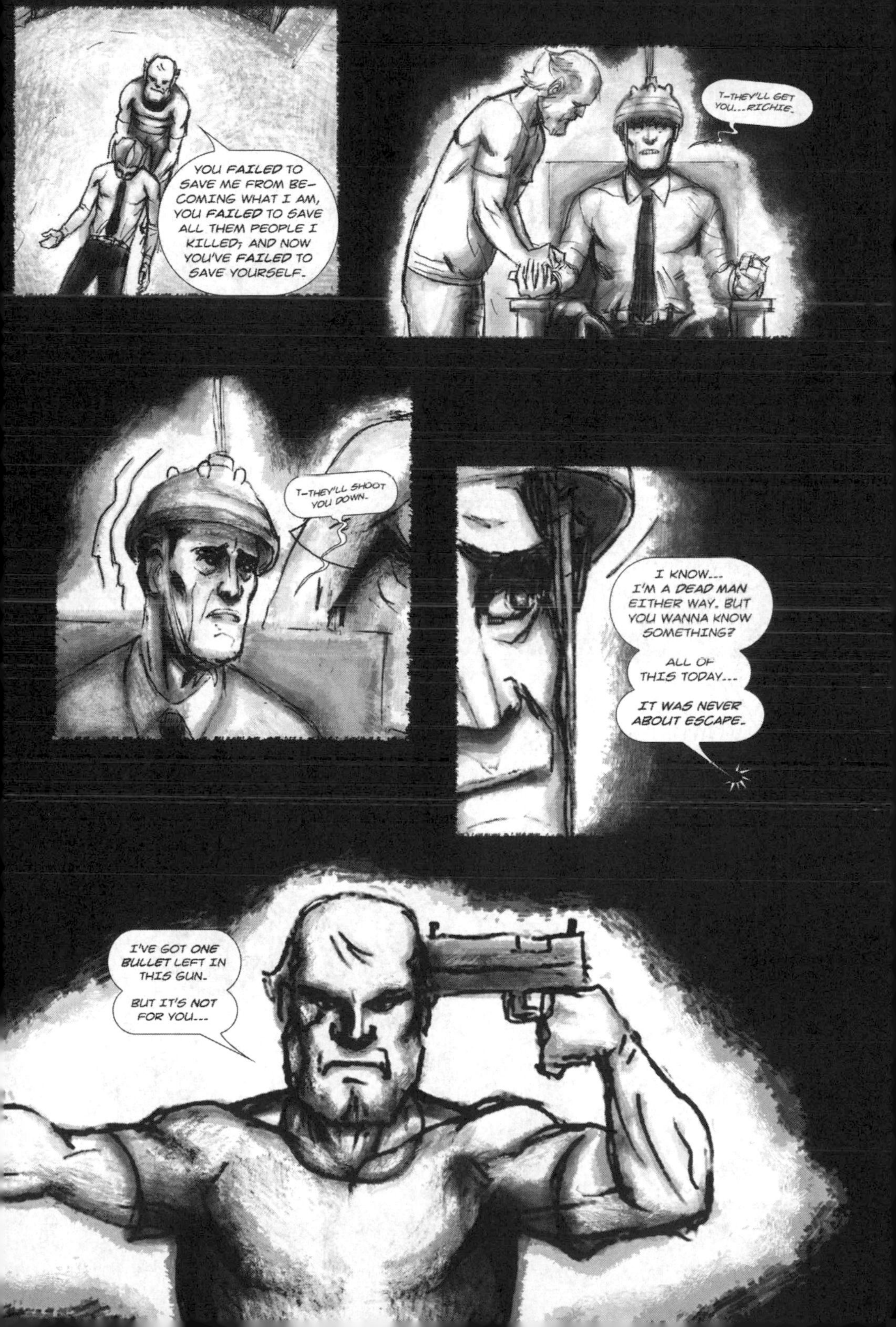
YOU FAILED TO SAVE ME FROM BE- COMING WHAT I AM, YOU FAILED TO SAVE ALL THEM PEOPLE I KILLED; AND NOW YOU'VE FAILED TO SAVE YOURSELF.
T-THEY'LL GET YOU...RICHIE.
T-THEY'LL SHOOT YOU DOWN.
I KNOW... I'M A DEAD MAN EITHER WAY. BUT YOU WANNA KNOW SOMETHING?
ALL OF THIS TODAY...
IT WAS NEVER ABOUT ESCAPE.
I'VE GOT ONE BULLET LEFT IN THIS GUN.
BUT IT'S NOT FOR YOU...

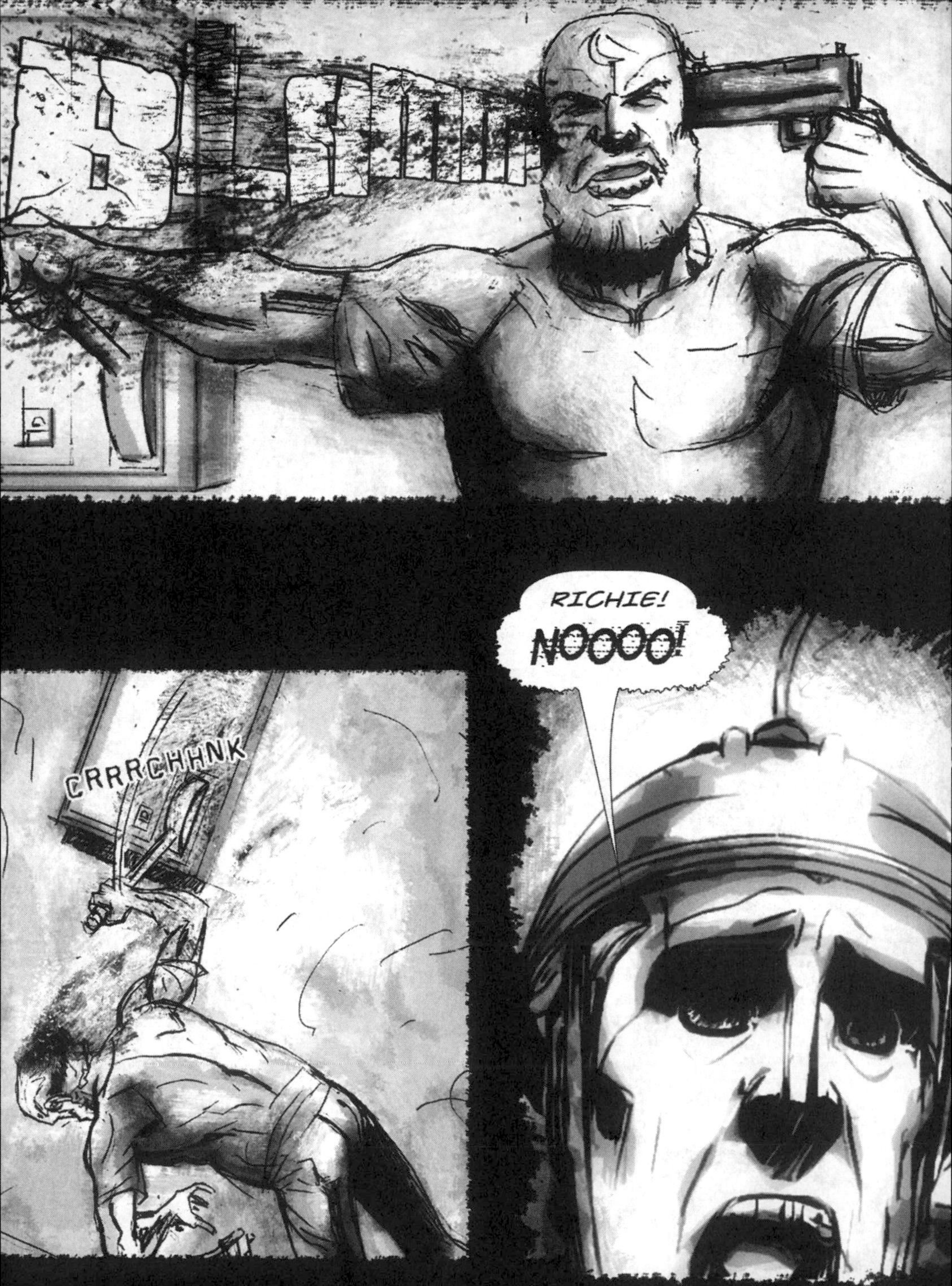
CRRRCHHNK
RICHIE!
NOOOO!

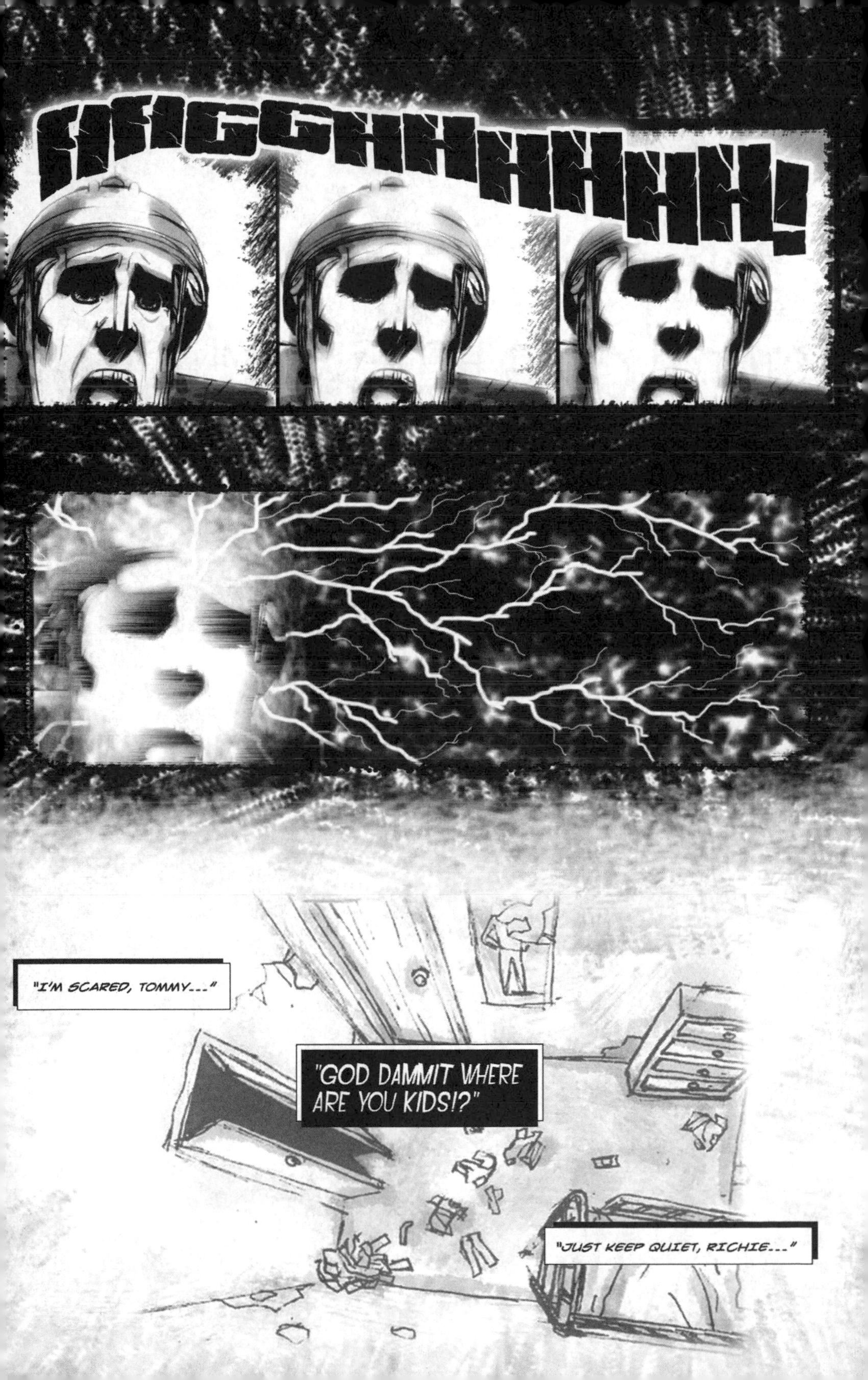
"I'M SCARED, TOMMY..."
"GOD DAMMIT WHERE ARE YOU KIDS!?"
"JUST KEEP QUIET, RICHIE..."

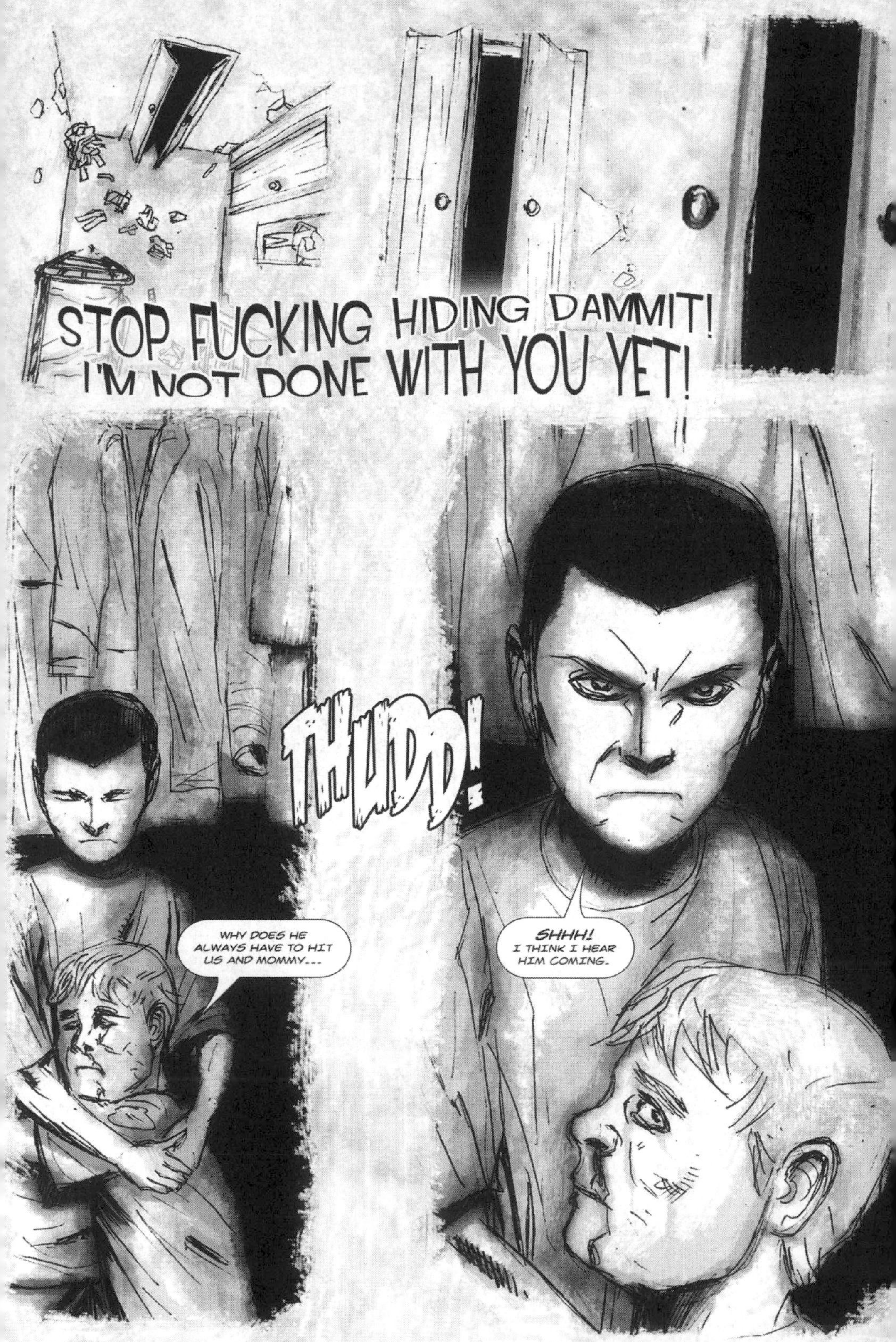
STOP FUCKING HIDING DAMMIT!
I'M NOT DONE WITH YOU YET!
THUDD!
WHY DOES HE ALWAYS HAVE TO HIT US AND MOMMY...
SHHH! I THINK I HEAR HIM COMING.

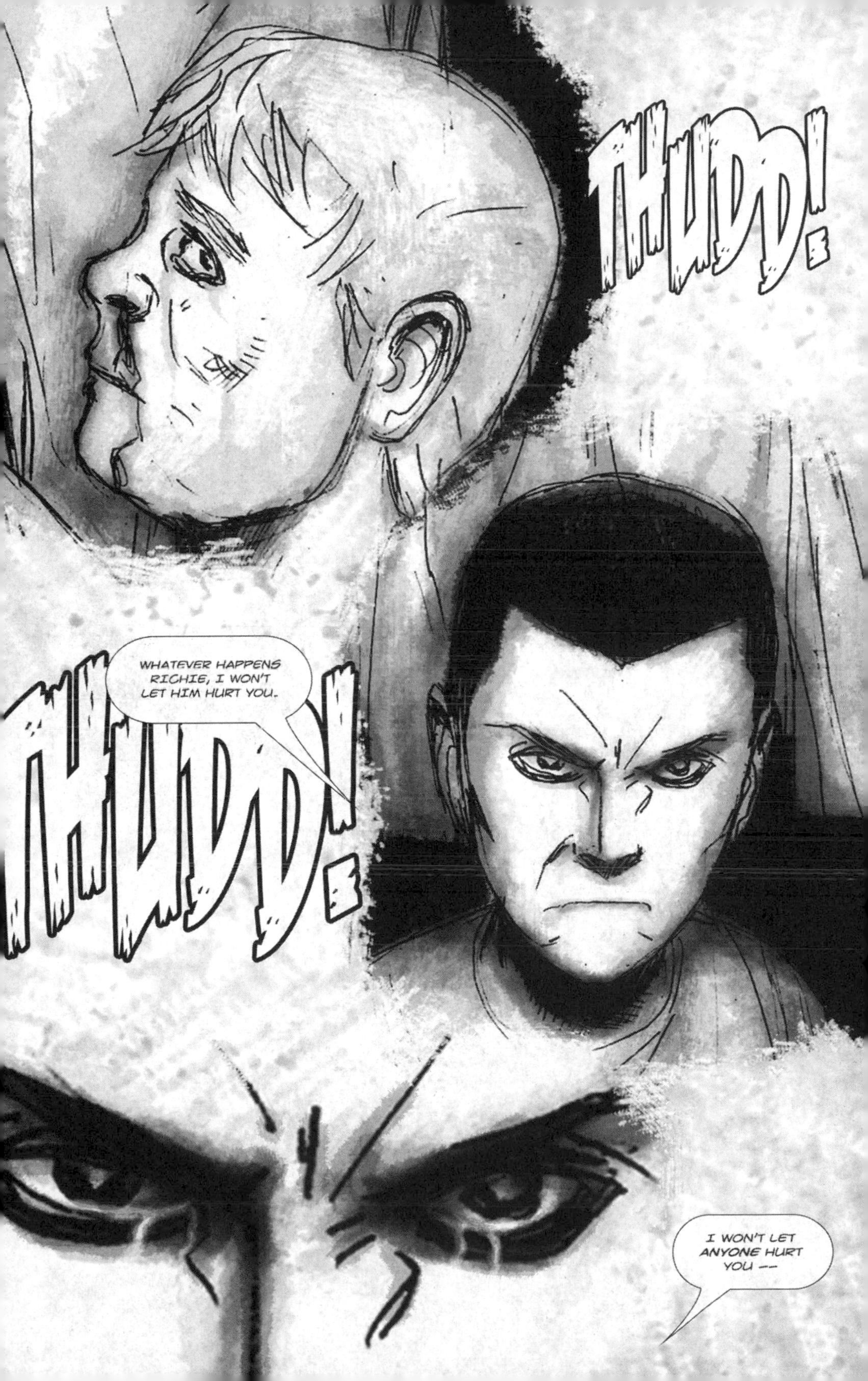
THUDD!
WHATEVER HAPPENS RICHIE, I WON'T LET HIM HURT YOU.
THUDD!
I WON'T LET ANYONE HURT YOU --

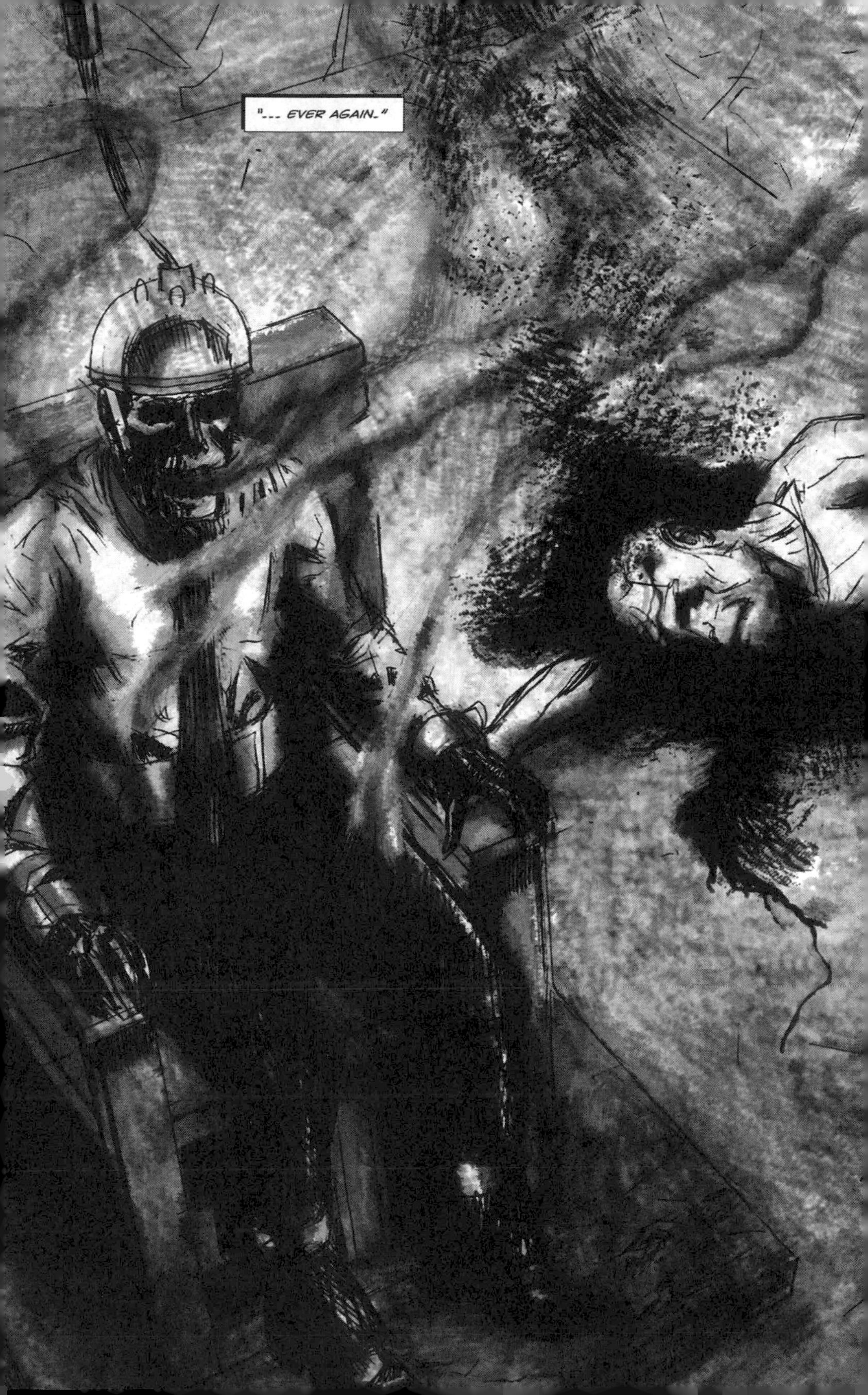
"... EVER AGAIN."

THE END.

"THE CHAIR"
SCREENPLAY
WRITTEN BY
ERIN KOHUT
AND
PETER SIMETI

BASED ON THE
GRAPHIC NOVEL
THE CHAIR
WRITTEN BY
PETER SIMETI

1 INT. A SOLID BLACK SCREEN

A barrage of sound fills the blackness - Alarm bell RINGING. Numerous FOOTSTEPS
running down hall. Frantic fists POUNDING on steel door. BANG! a gunshot goes
off, and within the same second we hear the HUM of something electric warming
up.

> MALE VOICE
> *(off screen - screaming)*
> No!

ELECTRIC BUZZ of the electric chair cancels out all other sounds.

SILENCE

CREDIT SEQUENCE: over montage of prison images. TITLE CARD

> THE CHAIR

FADE TO BLACK:

> SULLIVAN(V.O.)
> I didn't do it.
> *(pause)*
> I know what you're thinking, that's what they all
>
> say, only thing is, I'm telling the truth.

FADE IN:

2 INT. PRISON - SULLIVAN'S CELL - TIME OF DAY CANNOT BE DETERMINED

Everything is gloomy and grey.

RICHARD SULLIVAN, a rough-looking 50 year old death row inmate is sitting on the
edge of his bed. He is somewhat out of shape, balding with longer hair around
the edges of his head, and a shaggy medium sized beard upon his weathered face.

We can partially see down the angled walkway outside of his cell. OUT OF FOCUS -
image of guard pushing cart cell to cell down walkway. SOUND OF SQUEAKING WHEEL
echos in the SILENCE.

2A INT. PRISON - WALKWAY - SAME

CLOSE ON wheel of food cart rolling. Stops. A food tray overflowing with rancid
mush clatters to floor of cell in BACK GROUND. CAMERA RISES from wheel/floor
level to CLOSE ON - MURPHY, 50 year old prison guard that has been walking this
floor a very long time and has seen it all and does not hide his contempt for
the inmates. Tooth pick dangling from his lip, he mumbles as he turns from the
cell, looking ahead his profile fills the FRAME. Slowly, he begins pushing the
food cart CARMERA FOLLOWS to next cell.

ABOVE ANGLE as metal ladle dips into the large metal pot atop the cart and draws
out a heaping helping of mush, sloppily plopping it onto a dinged up metal tray.

2B INT. PRISON - SULLIVAN CELL - SAME

ANGLE ON hand mirror through bars - reflection of Murphy dropping food tray into
another cell down walkway. Slowly, Sullivan draws the mirror back into his cell.

> SULLIVAN(V.O)
> When I think of how I got here, four years of trials,

two appeals, it's kind of ridiculous.
                    (pause)
    I guess that's where all my tax dollars went.

The reflection in the mirror/camera slowly pans around the tiny cell to CLOSE ON Sullivan's PAINED FACE. He gives a snort at his reflection. CAMERA DOLLY to head on Sullivan - as he lowers the mirror. He stares straight ahead.

                    SULLIVAN(V.O.)
    Been here so long, I can barely remember
    a time before it, a time when I had a life.
    Had a good job, a loving wife, great family.
    Yeah... the whole thing.

CUT TO:

3 INT. OFFICE BUILDING - MR.BATES OFFICE - MORNING

CLOSE ON - Sullivan, in his 40s, dressed in a business suit, SLIGHT PAN THEN DOLLY BACK TO TWO SHOT to reveal him sitting in a chair across from his Boss, MR. BATES, a well dressed business man sitting behind a large desk.

The two men arguing about something, but we can only hear Sullivan's narration.

CLOSE ON Bates - his gaping mouth spitting out unheard words, clenching teeth. Sweat running down forehead.

CLOSE ON Sullivan - eyes bulging with rage.

                    SULLIVAN(V.O.)
    Seems like one minute I was talking to my boss...

Sullivan remains seated, but keeps slapping his hands on the arms of his chair out of anger.

CLOSE ON Sullivan's hands - grip chair hard. SLAP.

                    SULLIVAN(V.O.)
    I wanted to take an early retirement,
    he disagreed. . .

OVER SHOULDER Sullivan - as he leans forward, slaps his palms on the front of Mr. Bates' desk. Terrified, Bates leans back in chair.

                    SULLIVAN(V.O.)
    . . .and the next minute the police were taking
    me out of the fucking building.

Sullivan turns head toward door, his profile fills the FRAME from same OVER SHOULDER ANGLE.

V.O. Narration ends and we can now hear the dialog of the current scene.

WIDE REVERSE - OFFICER CHRIS BELL, OFFICER #2 and SECURITY GUARD enter the office. Security Guard motions towards Richard Sullivan.

                    SECURITY GUARD
    That's him.

OFFICER CHRIS BELL
    Richard Sullivan?

OVER SHOULDER Bates on Sullivan - as he looks at the cop then back to his boss confused because he believes that they are there because of the argument.

SULLIVAN
(to boss)
    What the hell is this?

ZOOM IN DOLLY BACK ON Bates - he rolls in his chair as far back as possible, as he nods, 'yes', this is Richard Sullivan.

OFFICER CHRIS BELL
    Sir, please place your hands flat out on the desk   and do NOT
make a move!

OVER SHOULDER Bates on Sullivan - as he straightens up, glaring with a perplexed look through Bates. Takes a deep breath.

WIDE OVERHEAD SHOT - as Officer #2 pats Sullivan down, Officer Chris Bell reads him his rights.

OFFICER CHRIS BELL
    You have the right to remain silent, any-

SULLIVAN
(angry)
    Are you fucking kidding me?
    Since when can't a man argue with his God-damn-boss?

INSERTS - Cuffs LOCKING, ECU Badge, gun, baton, name tag.

The police officers escort a cuffed Sullivan from the office. Security guard stands with Bates next to the desk.

3A INT. OFFICE BUILDING - OUTER HALL - CONTINUEOUS

MED ON Sullivan fidgeting, slightly kicks the open door as he passes by it. SLO-MO DOLLY BACK as they walk toward CAMERA down the long hallway.

Sound in the scene fades out as Sullivan's V.O. narration continues over remainder of the scene.

SULLIVAN(V.O.)
    Turned out some psycho killed twelve kids in the
    building's daycare center, and since my boss' kid
    was one of them, I became the prime suspect.

CUT TO:

4 INT. DAYCARE CENTER - MORNING

CAMERA ON DOLLY ALONG WITH MAN - SLIGHT HIGH ANGLE with back of man to CAMERA, his face unseen. He walks through the daycare center swinging a blood covered knife in his right hand, as he passes numerous dead children strewn across the floor. The sound of loud to fading HEART BEAT is heard. The further in he goes the room's shadows begin to cross causing the space to become darker, darker...until complete blackness.

FADE IN:

5 INT. PRISON - SULLIVAN'S CELL - TIME OF DAY UNDETERMINED

MED LOW ANGLE Sullivan - sitting on the bed in his cell as his V.O. continues.

> SULLIVAN(V.O.)
> Heh...almost fifteen years have passed since that
> day.
> > *(pause)*
> It's amazing what that time can do to a man waiting
> on death row.

CLANK! Murphy purposely pushes the food too quickly through the slot and it
falls onto the ground, splattering everywhere. WHIP PAN from Sullivan to food on
floor. SLOW PAN UP to Murphy.

> MURPHY
> Hey Sullivan! Rise and shine bitch! It's meal time!

Looking to mess on floor, flipping tooth pick in mouth.

> MURPHY
> Oops!! Clumsy me!!
> > *(softer to himself)*
> heh, fucker...

EXITS FRAME. CAMERA PANS BACK TO Sullivan. SLOW PUSH TO CU.

FLASH INSERT - urine spraying on food/tray.

> SULLIVAN(V.O.)
> Wasn't planning on eatin' anyway, that asshole
> pisses in the food.
> The night guard only spits in it.

FLASH INSERT - spit splattering on food/tray.

> SULLIVAN(V.O.)
> Once you get used to it, it's not too bad.

Sullivan's hand mirror peeks through bars. In reflection:
The end of the death row walkway, a large ominous metal door SLAMS open.

Standing, Sullivan presses up against the bars of his cell, looks down towards
door, but barely reacts as he has been here for so long that nothing surprises
him anymore.

5A INT. PRISON - WALKWAY - SAME

DOLLY - RILEY AND BOWEN, two prison guards, emerge wheeling an old gurney down
the walkway.

ABOVE ANGLE - someone is laying on their back covered mostly by a dirty white
sheet.

The wheels SQUEAK and cause it to not roll smoothly.

WIDE ANGLE - Riley and Bowen are being so haphazard with it that it keeps
KNOCKING into passing cells.
It SMASHES right into Sullivan's cell, but he barely flinches.

The gurney takes a sharp turn and is wheeled into the empty cell directly across from Sullivan's.

5B INT.PRISON - SULLIVAN'S CELL - SAME

OVER SHOULDER Sullivan - watching Riley and Bowen.

> SULLIVAN(V.O.)
> I know they treat us like shit because they
> think we're all monsters,
> and for the most part they're right. . .
>> (pause)
> . . .but it goes beyond that.

During Sullivan's V.O., we see the guards removing a prison inmate from the gurney and placing him in dungeon-like shackles on the wall. Riley and Bowen are being rougher than they need to.

We see glimpses of blood stains and the inmate is wincing in pain, but doesn't have much fight left in him.

> SULLIVAN(V.O.)
> It's like the world forgot about us.
> No letters from family.
> No bullshit interviews and book deals.
> Just a bunch of sadistic
> bastards who call themselves prison guards.

INSERT: SLOW ZOOM INTO THE METAL DOOR.

> SULLIVAN(V.O.)
> And the screams that come from behind that door...
> It's like nothing I've ever heard.

LOW ANGLE - Riley and Bowen exit the cell pulling along the empty gurney. CELL DOOR CLOSES with a CLANK. Trough the bars, on the floor of cell, shadowed in darkness against the wall is a man, his hands held above his head in iron shackles.

INCHING CLOSER AND CLOSER TO CAMERA is a growing pool of blood on the floor as it gets closer CAMERA BEGINS PUSH IN/ SLOW ZOOM TO CU ON this prisoner, SAMMY. He is missing one leg from his knee down, and the remaining stump has been bandaged sloppily.

Sullivan's V.O. continues over this image as follows.

> SULLIVAN(V.O.)
> Just take a look at Sammy over there...
>> (pause)
> he's torn to pieces over the subject.

FADE OUT:

FADE IN:

6 INT. PRISON - SULLIVAN'S CELL - DAY

C.U. of a tray of uneaten food on a small table. It looks like it has been
sitting there a while. The gravy on the mystery-meatloaf has a coagulated film.

PAN FROM FOOD TO MED ON Sullivan - sitting on his bunk again staring across at
Sammy, who is unconscious but not dead.

                              WARDEN
                    (off screen over intercom)
                    (an evil menacing voice)
          Do you know what time it is gentlemen?
          Well of course you don't,
          I had all the clocks removed!

INSERT: Speaker hung from above metal door at end of walkway.
                              WARDEN(O.S.)
                    (laughs and then collects himself)
          It's time again to stretch those legs
          and get to know each other
          just a little bit better.
                              (laughs)

6A INT. PRISON - WALKWAY - SAME

PULL BACK FROM SPEAKER TO WIDE ANGLE - as the cell door locks CLICK
automatically. Slowly, the inmates open their doors and step into the doorways
all except for Sammy.

HAND HELD CAMERA ON Sullivan, next to him is BONES, a skinny weak looking man,
and TUDLEY who is also on the thin side, has hair and a beard in the style of
Jesus Christ and wears a wooden rosary around his neck.

INSERT ON - Tudley's rosary.

Tudley and Bones appear more nervous than a typical death row prisoner would be,
as if they are afraid of something other than the fact that they will all be
eventually electrocuted.

LONG SHOT - Murphy, along with ALVAREZ, a younger male guard who is new to the
prison, are standing by at the end of the walkway.

TWO SHOT ON Murphy and Alvarez.

                              MURPHY
                    (banging his club on the cell bars)
          Come on, everyone out, you heard the Warden!

CLOSE ON Alvarez - feeling unsure of what to do, he just stands there, letting
Murphy handle it.

MED ANGLE ON Sullivan - he steps out of his cell and just stands there.

SLIGHT PAN TO TWO SHOT as Bones creeps cautiously out of his and heads toward
Sullivan.

IN BACKGROUND OF SHOT Tudley leaves his cell and goes in the opposite direction
to stand in a corner by the outer bars of the cell and the small space of
concrete wall by the metal door.

ANGLE ON Tudley - he grips his rosaries mouthing prayers to himself.

LOW ANGLE TWO SHOT Alvarez and Murphy.

                              ALVAREZ
                        (softly to Murphy)
         Hey... is it really a good idea letting these
         maniacs out together?

                              MURPHY
                   (Flips tooth pick around in mouth)
         The Warden is what you'd call... an eccentric genius.

                              ALVAREZ
                           (confused)
          Huh?

                              MURPHY
                   (smugly taps his club on the bars)
         It's all electrified. The bars, the floors, the
         toilets-

                              ALVAREZ
                           (puzzled)
          -the fucking toilets?

                              MURPHY
                           (laughing)
          Gotcha!

Alvarez laughs nervously and looks around to make sure the inmates are all
behaving.

                              MURPHY
                           (serious)
         Nah, but seriously, just one flip of a switch,
         and the whole place becomes
         one giant electric chair. . .

OVER SHOULDER Murphy - his view of inmates PUSH IN ON BARE FEET walking along
walkway.

                              MURPHY
                            (pause)
         Why do you think they're all barefoot...
                        (gestures to inmates)
          ...budget cuts?

CLOSE ON Alvarez - laughing nervously, still unsure of what to make of this
prison and Murphy.

The intercom clicks on again with a BUZZ. LOW ANGLE ON Murphy and Alvarez - they
look up toward speaker, their faces suddenly turn serious.

                              WARDEN
                     (off screen over intercom)
         Oh, by the way, Sammy, since you can't run around
         and play with everyone else, you and I are going
         to spend some quality time!
                        (laughs menacingly)

Intercom CLICKS off, abruptly cutting off laughter.

ANGLE ON Metal door end of walkway, it SLAMS open, startling every inmate.

PUSH IN CLOSE ON Tudley - his face pressed into the corner, he begins uttering indecipherable prayers. His lips flutter against the concrete wall as if at any moment the hand of the good LORD will pull him through to freedom.

PUSH IN CLOSE ON Bones, terrified, backs against the outside of the cell he is in front of as tightly as he can.

PUSH IN CLOSE ON Sullivan holds his ground, unfazed.

PUSH IN CLOSE ON Sammy still passed out in cell. He did not hear the announcement.

WIDE/LONG SHOT Riley and Bowen emerge through metal door pushing the gurney toward Sammy's cell.

6B INT. PRISON - SAMMY'S CELL - SAME

LOW ANGLE ON Sammy - Bowen and Riley look down at the mass of human wreckage with just a slight glint of pity in their eyes.

> BOWEN
> (gesturing to a sleeping Sammy)
> Wonder why he'd want this guy again so soon?

> RILEY
> (dryly)
> I gave up trying to figure out how that one thinks a long time ago...

Riley begins to unshackle his arms.

OVER SHOULDER Riley - Sammy as he wakes up, instantly realizing what is going on, he starts SCREAMING, begins a to struggle.

7 INT. PRISION - WALKWAY - SAME

ABOVE SHOT ON the three men.

> RILEY
> (annoyed/dryly)
> Yeah yeah yeah. . .you don't want to go, no big surprise there.

> BOWEN
> Can't say I blame him...
> (laughs)

PULL BACK HIGHER ON SAME ANGLE as Riley and Bowen roughly throw him onto the gurney. As his door cell SLAMS shut CAMERA PANS WITH MOTION to screaming Sammy being wheeled toward metal door at end of walkway, CONTINUE PAN TO WIDE of other inmates as Sammy's SCREAMS ECHO. Tudley - remains muttering in his corner.

Bones creeps back out into the walkway, sees Sullivan, and heads towards him.

Sullivan looks towards Bones, who is still shaking as he approaches, a look of pity etched across his face.

Unfazed by the incident, Sullivan gives a slight smile to to Bones.

OVER SHOULDER Bones - on Sullivan.

                              SULLIVAN
          Hey Bones, how you holdin' up?

OVER SHOULDER Sullivan - on Bones.

                              BONES
                        (shaky and weak)
          Not so good Sully, I haven't eaten in four days...
          I've survived worse though... I'll get through this.

TWO SHOT.

                              SULLIVAN
          What the hell is worse than this?

                              BONES
                (shaky and distant, lost in thought)
          War.
                              (pause)
          Anyway, you know that guard, right?

                              SULLIVAN
          The one that pees in the food?

                              BONES
          Yeah, well, lately that's not all I'm
          getting in mine. . .

FLASH INSERT: Guard squatting over food tray.

CLOSE ON Sullivan.

                              SULLIVAN
          Ugh, fucking disgusting.
                              (motions to cell)
          I got food in my cell from last night,
          it's cold, but take it if you want.
          Looks like you could use it more than me.

CLOSE ON Bones.

                              BONES
          Thanks man, I really appreciate it.

TWO SHOT.

                              SULLIVAN
          Don't worry about it.

SLIGHT PAN FOLLOWS Bones as he turns and enters Sullivan's cell. Begins to pick
at the tray of food. Sullivan in edge of FRAME. SOUNDS OF Bones' eating with
gusto FADES OUT.

PUSH CLOSE ON Sullivan - he remains in place watching Bones eat.

                              SULLIVAN(V.O.)
          Bones was a private in the army but had a breakdown

and went AWOL. When they found him, they charged him
with desertion and sentenced him to death.

SOUNDS OF COMBAT - EXPLOSIONS/GUN FIRE BLEND INTO JUDGE'S GAVEL HITTING HARD.
Sullivan closes his eyes tight.

Opening his eyes, with a slight shake off of Bones' situation, Sullivan looks
over toward the far end of the walkway. CAMERA PANS WITH his head catching sight
of Tudley slowly coming toward him, sticking close to the cells as some form of
false security. RACK FOCUS TO BACKGROUND - Alvarez and Murphy are discussing
sports and not paying attention to the inmates.

RACK FOCUS BACK as Tudley reaches Sullivan, creeping too close for comfort.

>   TUDLEY
>   (whispering)
>   Slayeth the Evil that lives inside you-

PAN TO TWO SHOT.

>   SULLIVAN
>   (annoyed)
>   - ahh, fuck off Tudley... -

>   TUDLEY
>   -where they are walking the Devil walks too-

>   SULLIVAN
>   (louder)
>   - Leave me alone you freak!

ANGLE ON Alvarez and Murphy - stopping their conversation when they hear
Sullivan raising his voice.

>   MURPHY
>   (yelling)
>   Hey you assholes! Keep it down over there!

CLOSE ON Tudley - he stays glued to Sullivan's side, puts up a finger to his
lips in a "shhh" motion.

>   TUDLEY
>   (whispering)
>   We know what you did-

TWO SHOT.

>   SULLIVAN
>   (furious)
>   - I said get the hell away from me!
>   (shoves Tudley)

LOW ANGLE ON Tudley - falls to the floor and starts screaming in "pain", having
a tantrum. SAME LOW ANGLE RACK FOCUS as Murphy and Alvarez pull out their clubs
and walk towards Sullivan and Tudley.

CLOSE ON Sullivan looks from Tudley to Murphy and Alvarez walking toward them.

MED DOLLY WITH Murphy and Alvarez as they march fourth. When they stop CAMERA
PANS BETWEEN THEM ONTO Sullivan and Tudley.

>   MURPHY
>   (angry)
>   Are you guys deaf?! I said break it up!

DIRTY OVER SHOULDER Murphy - he motions like he's going to hit Tudley with his club. Tudley straightens up off the floor but is still clutching his rosary and is now laughing uncontrollably.

> MURPHY
> *(gesturing with his club)*
> All right Tudley, back in your cell.

LOW ANGLE SKATEBOARD DOLLY ON Tudley - as he starts crawling towards his cell like an animal. Murphy behind/over him following.

> MURPHY
> Stand the fuck up, you can at least *walk* like a
> normal person.

OVER SHOULDER Murphy - before reaching his cell Tudley rolls onto his back like a dog with his legs in the air, LAUGHING insanely. Murphy reaches down and grabs Tudley hard by the arm. Looks over his shoulder his profile into FRAME.

> MURPHY
> *(frustrated)*
> Jesus Christ
> *(to Alvarez)*
> Grab his other arm.

LOW ANGLE WIDE - Stepping over, Alvarez grabs Tudley's other arm.

CAMERA ON Tudley's body like a human dolly as they drag him toward his cell.

MED ON Sullivan's cell as Bones steps out of the shadows halfway into the walkway to see what is going on. He leans his back against the cell opening, continues eating, looks over to Sullivan.

SLIGHT PAN PUSH CLOSE ON Sullivan - he blankly watches Murphy and Alvarez drag Tudley, kicking and wriggling, to into his cell.

Murphy and Alvarez step out of Tudley's cell and stand before it.

CLOSE ON Murphy.

> MURPHY
> *(looks up)*
> Close number two.

TWO SHOT BETWEEN Murphy and Alvarez - on Tudley cell.
Just as the door starts to remotely slide shut, Tudley GROWLS and lunges at the cell door, which locks shut just in time as his face SLAMS into the bars.

7A INT. PRISON - TUDLEY CELL - CONTINUEOUS

Startled, Alvarez and Murphy leap back from Tudley's reaching arms.

Tudley starts hanging on the cell bars, shaking back and forth and YELLING.

> ALVAREZ
> *(to Murphy)*
> *(softly)*
> What do we do now?

                                    MURPHY
                                   (smiles)
        Just wait and watch. . .

INSERT C.U. of a hand in a black vinyl glove turning an antique looking dial
until it clicks. SOUND of an electric HUM slowly builds up.

FROM BETWEEN Murphy and Alvarez CAMERA PUSHES CLOSE ON Tudley - as his body
seizes and clenches against the bars.

7B INT. PRISON - SULLIVAN'S CELL - MOMENTS LATER

HANDHELD ANGLE ON Sullivan - he recognizes the SOUND instantly, and yells out to
Bones, leaning against the cell door, which has now become electrified.

                                   SULLIVAN
                                  (yelling)
        Bones, MOVE!

WHIP PAN FROM Sullivan to Bones as, an electric charge runs through all the cell
bars ZAPPING Bones in place.

SOUND OF ELECTRICITY SWITCHING OFF.

Bones falls to the ground convulsing. From the waist down he is inside the cell,
and from the waist up he is in the walkway.

LOW ANGLE ON Bones with Sullivan in background. SLOW MOTION Sullivan begins to
rush toward the cell to see if Bones is okay.

ECU ANGLE ON Murphy - LAUGHING.

ECU ANGLE ON Alvarez - looks shaken up, nervous.

INSERT C.U. gloved hand pulling down an antique metal lever.

A brief CREAKING METAL SOUND can be heard before every cell door slams shut with
a loud CLANG.

OVER SHOULDER Sullivan as he dives forward, reaching to Bones, grabbing his hand
just as the door closes cutting him in half at the waist. In an instant,
Sullivan YANKS BACK with all of his might to save him, but it's too late as the
severed torso of Bones falls back with Sullivan into the walkway.

OVERHEAD ON carnage - Sullivan with Bones on top of him, convulsing but not yet
dead. Blood pooling all around.

LOW ANGLE TWO SHOT ON Sullivan on his back and Bones atop - they're face to
face.

                                    BONES
        Can't feel my legs.

CLOSE ON Sullivan - looks just past Bones' face.

Sullivan's POV - Bones' entrails connected to his severed legs inside the cell.

CLOSE ON Sullivan - swallows hard. Tries to hide the site of horror from his
eyes as looks into Bones' eyes.

OVERHEAD ANGLE - dying, Bones begins to convulse as his blood pumps out.
Sullivan becomes hysterical, crying and screaming.

                        SULLIVAN
   Oh my God! BONES!
   You fucking MONSTERS, help him!!

Murphy and Alvarez step into FRAME - standing above Bones and Sullivan. Raising
his club, Murphy knocks Sullivan across the head.

                        MURPHY
                     (angrily)
      That's enough out of you!

PUSH IN CLOSE ON Sullivan - he loses consciousness as the screen fades to black.

FADE IN:

8 INT. PRISON - SULLIVAN'S CELL - LATER

The screen is still black as the intercom CLICKS back on. OVER HEAD SLOW FOCUS
IN on Sullivan as Warden's speech begins.

                        WARDEN
                 (off screen over intercom)
                   (dark and angry)
      It seems there's been an "accident", Mr. Sullivan.
      Someone will be there soon to
      clean that crap out of your cell...

DUTCH LOW ANGLE ON Sullivan - he wakes from his fog, tries to collect himself.
Rolling to his side in bed, he rubs his face and feels something wet/sticky.

Sullivan POV - his hands covered in blood. RACK FOCUS through his spread fingers
to Bones' severed legs on the floor of his cell. The horror floods back.

DUTCH LOW ANGLE ON Sullivan - completely overwhelmed, he vomits and cowers into
the corner of his bunk.

SOUND OF the metal door down the walkway SLAMS open.

8A INT. PRISON - WALKWAY - SAME

WIDE ANGLE ON Doorway - the ominous silhouette of JOHNNY THE JANITOR stands in
the doorway, he emerges into the walkway. The door SLAMS loudly behind him.

Johnny is tall, thin and wearing a black butcher's apron, protective goggles,
and black gloves up to the elbow. He begins to whistle as he wheels along a mop
resting inside a rusty old bucket.

CLOSE ON Johnny - sees the blood and guts. Stops whistling.

                        JOHNNY
                  (ominously playful)
      Wowwie! Have we got some mess here!
      Ain't this a mess, mister?!

OVER SHOULDER ON Johnny rolls the bucket into the blood, dips the mop, and slops it to the floor. Sullivan doesn't say a word, remains huddled in his bunk.

> JOHNNY
> Hmmm... quiet type huh? Well, damn, I'll be!
> You gots turds and blood and puke everywhere in here.
> Wild party last night, huh? HAH!

8B INT. PRISON - SULLIVAN'S CELL - SAME

WIDE TWO SHOT ON Johnny and Sullivan - he waves a finger back and forth at Sullivan, to say, 'No, no'.

> JOHNNY
> Messy, messy!

Sullivan can't take anymore, loses all control and lunges at Johnny.

> SULLIVAN
> SHUT UP!

> JOHNNY
> (looks up confused)
> Wuh?

OVER SHOULDER Sullivan - he grabs the mop through the bars with both hands.

> JOHNNY
> Hey! That's MY mop! GUARDS!

In a flash, Sullivan JABS the tip of the mop handle through Johnny's teeth and into the roof of Johnny's mouth pushing his head back, lifting him up off his feet.

CLOSE ON Johnny - broken teeth and blood running down the sides of his mouth, he struggles to pull free. His choking and gurgling noises fill the cell block.

CLOSE ON Sullivan - teeth clenched, struggling with all his might.

INSERT: Tudley - cheering to the sounds of murder.

WIDE ANGLE - Johnny is lifted higher off the ground.

LOW ANGLE ON mop - with the leverage of the vertical bars of the cell, Sullivan puts his knee on the end of the mop.

ABOVE ANGLE BEHIND Johnny - Sullivan reaches both hands through the bars, grabbing the sides of Johnny's head. And with all his might, he pulls forward. SPLAT! The tip of the mop handle pops down Johnny's throat, bulging at the back of his neck.

OVER SHOULDER Sullivan - Johnny's front teeth drag along the handle...closer...closer until his face SLAMS into the bars, cracking his skull with the force, near pulling the top of his head into the cell.

Exhausted, Sullivan drops to his knees. Looks up to what he's wrought.

8C INT. PRISON - WALKWAY - MOMENTS LATER

Murphy and Alvarez run into the cell and freeze for a second at the grisly sight of it all, not knowing how to handle this.

> ALVAREZ
> *(completely shocked at what he's seeing)*

What the fuck...

POV Murphy - Sullivan looks up and makes eye contact with Murphy. PAN FROM Sullivan up Johnny's dangling legs to his crumpled head lodge between the top bars of the cell. Dead.

WHIP PAN DOWN TO Sullivan.

> SULLIVAN
> (growls)

You mother-fuckers...

There is a wildness in Sullivan's eyes, as he lunges through the bars at Murphy and Alvarez.

ANGLE ON Murphy and Alvarez as they quickly step back. RACK FOCUS as the door at the end of the walkway bursts open.

HANDHELD ON SIMMONS, RILEY, and BOWEN, running down the walkway armed with billy-clubs. Simmons gets in front of everyone. CLOSE ON each guard as they ready for combat.

Fearless, Murphy spits out toothpick. Gives a WIDE smile.

Nervous, Alvarez wipes sweat from brow with sleeve.

Crazed excitement, Bowen tilts his head back and fourth cracking his neck.

Riley begins to breath fast and slow like a prize fighter trying to focus before a title bout.

Calmly, through grit teeth, Simmons peers through the bars at Sullivan.

> SIMMONS
> *(fearless)*

What the hell is going on here!?
You want us to kill you NOW you sack of shit!?
> (looks up. Yells)

OPEN IT!

Murphy turns the key in the cell door lock. Pulls it open.

> SIMMONS
> *(to the other guards)*

Quick! Pin him down!

LOW ANGLE OVER SHOULDER Sullivan as all the guards dog pile him.

ABOVE ANGLE on fight - as clubs fly, Sullivan tries to but stand but slips on blood and vomit. Finally, they pin him down.

CLOSE ON Simmons as he sticks him with a syringe.

INSERT: syringe with yellowish liquid injected into Sullivan's neck.

ECU Sullivan's eyes roll back.

CLOSE ON Sullivan - his struggle fades. Motionless, his eyes flutter.

Sullivan's POV - guards looming above him.

                        SIMMONS
        We gotta bring you to Enrik, he'll know how
        to fix you up.

                        BOWEN
                     (snickering)
            Yeah...the Warden will make you allll better.

SOUND and image distort/blur as Sullivan goes unconscious.

FADE TO BLACK

FADE IN

9 INT. PRISON - WARDEN'S OPERATING ROOM/TORTURE CHAMBER - UNABLE TO DISCERN TIME
OF DAY

Sullivan POV starts to wake up, his vision is slightly blurred going in and out
of FOCUS. An antique operating room light above his head. He looks down to his
barefoot.

ECU Sullivan's eyes - he quickly realizes where he must be and his eyes snap
open all the way. Tries to pull his arms, legs free. No luck.

WIDE OVER HEAD ON Sullivan - he's strapped to a metal gurney in the center of
Warden's operating room/torture chamber. He starts to wriggle his entire body,
trying to get free of the restraints.

CLOSE ON Sullivan - scanning the room.

Sullivan POV - there are two ways in and out of this room, one door, guarded by
Bowen leads back to death row and the other door guarded by Riley leads to the
other blocks of the prison.

CLOSE ON Sullivan - leaning his head back as far as possible into the gurney.

Sullivan POV image upside down - his back to Sullivan, working at a table is
ENRIK THE WARDEN the man behind the voice heard over the intercom previously.

He is around 50 years old, tall and thin, wearing black pants, black shoes, a
white dress shirt, a black vinyl apron, black vinyl gloves and steampunk welder
goggles.

WIDE ABOVE ANGLE ON Sullivan.

                        SULLIVAN
                     (scared)
            W-what *is* this?

Warden turns, looming over Sullivan.

LONG SHOT CAMERA ON gurney at Sullivan's feet slight DUTCH as Enrik leans over.

                     ENRIK THE WARDEN
        You've had your fun Mr. Sullivan,
        now it's time for mine.
        The guards have informed me that someone has
        been a *very* naughty boy.

                              SULLIVAN
     W-what am I doing here?

                              ENRIK
          Hmm, where to start? I'm afraid we have a
          bit of a problem with you.
          We can't let your little... outburst... go
          unpunished, now can we?

A MOANING sound erupts from the other side of the room.

CLOSE ON Sullivan - he strains to look, tilting his chin into his neck.

OVER SHOULDER Sullivan - PUSH CLOSE TO Sammy atop a gurney in the far corner.
He's been completely severed in half and is bleeding profusely from Enrik's
surgical experiments.

MED ON Enrik.

                              ENRIK
                           (politely)
          Forgive me for the *mess*.
          I usually clean up before company arrives,
          but your visit was a bit unexpected.
                       (yelling to a guard off-screen)
          Get him out of here!
                              (calmly to himself)
          I can't even hear myself think...

Sullivan POV - Bowen and Riley push the gurney with Sammy atop out of the room.

OVER HEAD CLOSE ON Sullivan.

                              SULLIVAN
                           (terrified)
          Let me go you sick fuck!

HAND HELD OVER SHOULDER ON Enrik as he pulls a metal table with a tray of
surgical tools on it over to Sullivan's bedside. The tools are rusty and old,
with fresh and dried blood on them and on the tray itself.

LOW ANGLE FROM TRAY UP ON Enrik - looking them over carefully, caressing them
longingly with his right hand, he decides on a scalpel and picks it up. CAMERA
RISES WITH MOVEMENT PANS WITH Enrik as he walks next to Sullivan's legs.

                              ENRIK
          Now where were we... ah yes...
          I think you fail to see the weight of the matter,
          things need to run smoothly around here-

OVER SHOULDER ON Enrik - as he lightly glides the scalpel along Sullivan's pant
leg, towards his feet. Once his pant leg ends, the scalpel blade runs along the
skin of his ankle, making a very light cut and drawing blood.

                              ENRIK
          -what happened to Bones, well, we can forget
          about that, right Mr. Sullivan?

LOW ANGLE FROM HIS FEET ON Sullivan - he assumes that what happened to Sammy is
now going to happen to him.

                              SULLIVAN

                              (terrified)
          No! Please don't do this!

INSERT: ON BLADE as it pushes harder into ankle.

DIRTY OVER SHOULDER Sullivan on Enrik.

                              ENRIK
          Do what, exactly, Mr. Sullivan?

Enrik grins coldly as Sullivan becomes more terrified.

Enrik pulls the blade away, LAUGHS SOFTLY to himself, steps to the end of the
gurney, stares down at Sullivan's feet.

                              ENRIK
                             (calmly)
          Have you ever heard the story of Achilles?

                              SULLIVAN
          What?! Are you fucking kidding me??

                              ENRIK
                             (calmly)
          Well, Mr. Sullivan, when Achilles was just a baby,
          it was foretold that he would die young, so in
          order to prevent this, his
                             (sarcastic)
          ever-so-loving-mother
                             (calmly)
          dipped him into the River Styx.

WIDE OVERHEAD - as Enrik talks he begins walking in a circle around Sullivan.

                              ENRIK
                (growing more agitated as the story continues)
          Well, wouldn't you just know that the
          STUPID BITCH dipped his entire body into the water...

LOW ANGLE TWO SHOT.

                              ENRIK
          (leans over, smiles wide, and yells into Sullivan's face)
             except... his heel!

Sullivan WINCES from the yell.

DOGGIECAM/CAMERA ATTACHED TO Enrik as he continues walking around the gurney.

                              ENRIK
                (calmer at first, then more agitated)
          Shh, I know what you're thinking, well, she
          had to hold onto him somehow, right?
          Well, of course, Mr. Sullivan, but did it
          ever occur to you that she could have dipped him in
          twice?

> *(softly laughs to himself)*
> I mean, why not?
> *(shaking with anger)*
> It seems pretty fucking obvious to me!

Enrik covers his face with his hands, shaking in anger, then suddenly pulls them away, with an eerie calm expression once again.

Sullivan too scared to speak, just listens silently.

                    ENRIK
                (calmly)
> But, as we all know, that's not how the story goes
> and because of her stupidity...

                (agitated)
> his enemies were able to kill him

                    (amused)
> by shooting a poisonous arrow into his heel.
> Now, I bet you are wondering what any of
> this has to do with you-

Enrik completes walking in a circle and now is back by Sullivan's feet.

DIRTY OVER SHOULDER Sullivan - on Enrik with the scalpel in hand he very lightly traces along Sullivan's Achilles tendon.

                    ENRIK
        -do you know what this is Mr. Sullivan?

Terrified that Enrik intends to sever his Achilles tendon, he manages to answer him, hoping it might slow him down.

                    SULLIVAN
> My Achilles tendon...

WIDE OVERHEAD.

                    ENRIK
                (happily surprised)
> Very good! I'm impressed! And, do you know
> what would happen if I were to. . .
>   *(short pause)*
> . . .slice. . .
>   *(short pause)*
> . . .it. . .
>   *(short pause)*
> . . .off?

Sullivan doesn't reply, looks away.

                    ENRIK
                (impatient)
> Well?

                    SULLIVAN

(softly)
I wouldn't be able to walk.

                    ENRIK
              (sarcastically)
Wow! Give this man a prize! Were you a doctor
before joining us here?

Enrik picks up a clipboard and starts excitedly flipping through the pages,
looking for this information, then he throws the clipboard across the room.

It slams against the floor, pages go everywhere.

                    ENRIK
                (yelling)
    No, no, that's right!
    You weren't a Doctor!
    You were a child killer!

In one quick motion Enrik picks up the metal tray, surgical tools scatter onto
the floor, and he whacks Sullivan right in the forehead/top of the head with it.

LOW ANGLE ON Sullivan blacks out, head tilts into CAMERA. Blood running down
his face. IN BACKGROUND - Enrik paces around a bit, collecting himself until he
is calm again.

Bowen and Riley push the empty gurney trough the door.

                    ENRIK
              (to both guards)
    Guards, return Mr. Sullivan to his cell,
    I've had enough *fun* for today.

CUT TO:

10 INT. PRISON - WALKWAY - LATER

CAMERA ON gurney - Bowen and Riley are wheeling Sullivan down walkway.

                    BOWEN
    Still can't believe what this monster did
    to the janitor...

                    RILEY
    Yeah, thank God Simmons stuck him in time,
    or else we might all be like Johnny. . .dead.

                    BOWEN
    Fucking animals in this place, feels
    more like a zoo than a prison.

                    RILEY
    Are you kidding me? I ain't never seen an
    animal torture another animal just for kicks.

Bowen shrugs.

10A INT. PRISON - SULLIVAN'S CELL - CONTINUEOUS

HIGH WIDE ANGLE - rolling gurney in, they struggle to toss Sullivan onto his
bunk. THUD! Unconscious, Sullivan plops onto the hard mattress.

> RILEY
> If it were up to me this fucker right here would
> be dead today. Just one bullet, bam, right in the
> head.

They chuckle in agreement as they wheel the gurney out. Cell door closes.

FADE OUT:

FADE IN:

11 INT. PRISON - SULLIVAN'S CELL - LATER

OVERHEAD ANGLE ON Sullivan - lying in bed. His eyelids flutter a few times but
he doesn't wake up.

CLOSE ON Murphy - watching Sullivan sleep. He flips the toothpick in his mouth
with his tongue.

> MURPHY
> Rise and Shine princess! Dinner time!

OVER SHOULDER Murphy - on Sullivan stirring in his bed.

> MURPHY
> I said rise and shine!

Sullivan is startled awake and starts wriggling as if still strapped to Enrik's
gurney.

He rolls right off the edge of his bed and onto the floor, landing hard on his
shoulder.

> MURPHY
> You fall outta bed again old man!?
> (babytalk)
> Did the boogeyman give the big scary killer
> a widdle nightmare?
> (laughs)
> Dinner time, bitch!

WIDE LOW ANGLE - Murphy shoves the food tray intentionally too hard and it falls
to the floor.

Laughing to himself, Murphy walks away down the walkway.

Sullivan just glares forward too weak to do anything else.
Feeling hungry after everything that's happened, he crawls over to the food.

OVER SHOULDER Sullivan on floor as he grabs the spoon and starts scooping some
cleaner parts back onto the tray.

A very slow moving red trickle of blood enters FRAME on the floor.

CLOSE ON Sullivan - looks up to see where it is coming from.

Sullivan POV - Sammy across the walkway in his own cell. He is gone from the waist down and there is blood coating the floor. He is obviously dead.

PAN FROM SAMMY DOWN TO FLOOR - blood actually touches some of the food.

CLOSE ON Sullivan - looking down at it all, disgusted, he throws the spoon and tray into the corner of the room.

Exhausted, Sullivan leans back into the wall of his cell, staring at Sammy.

CUT TO:

12 INT. PRISON - SULLIVAN'S CELL - LATER

HIGH ANGLE Sullivan - pacing around his cell like a caged animal, agitated that he can't sleep.

OFF SCREEN Tudley - starts mumbling something from his cell. It starts off softly and builds in volume.

CLOSE ON Sullivan - he tries to listen, pressing closer to the bars.

> TUDLEY
> *(a whisper off screen)*
> Slayeth the evil that lives inside you,
> where they are walking the Devil walks too.
> *(just a hush)*
> Slayeth the evil that lives inside you,
> where they are walking the Devil walks too.
> *(a normal volume)*
> Slayeth the evil that lives inside you,
> where they are walking the Devil walks too.

12A INT. PRISON - WALKWAY - TUDLEY CELL - CONTINUEOUS

CAMERA DOLLIES TO Tudley's cell. He is clinging to the bars, practically trying to push himself through.

> TUDLEY
> *(louder)*
> Slayeth the evil that lives inside
> where they are walking the Devil walks too!
> *(yelling)*
> Slayeth the evil that lives inside you,
> where they are walking the Devil walks too!!

Sullivan is annoyed at this point and shouts from his end.

> SULLIVAN
> *(off screen)*
> Hey Tudley, would you shut the fuck up down there!!?

Simmons is patrolling the walkway. He whacks the bars of Sullivan's cell with his club.

TWO SHOT ON Simmons and Sullivan.

> SIMMONS

Dammit Sullivan, shut up!
You're not gonna have another out-burst
> *(pause)*

now are you?

Timidly, Sullivan steps backward to the wall of his cell.

CLOSE ON Simmons - leans close to bars of Sullivan's cell.

> SIMMONS

Good. You better behave, not many days
left here anyway, not like that's news to you...

> TUDLEY
> *(off screen screaming)*

Slayeth the evil that lives inside you,
where they are walking the Devil walks too.

> SIMMONS
> *(yelling at Tudley)*

Shut up!!!

PULL BACK WIDE as Simmons starts to walk away from Sullivan's cell. EDGE OF
FRAME - Sullivan starts yelling too. He lunges forward GRABBING the bars of his
cell.

> SULLIVAN
> *(yelling at Tudley)*

Should've been you Tudley! Bones was a good person!
It should've been you!

Prison intercom CLICKS on.

> ENRIK
> *(off screen over intercom)*

Oooh! What a splendid idea Mr. Sullivan,
Mr. Tudley *has* begun to wear out his welcome...
but electrocution? Cutting? Chopping?
> *(pause)*

I think we can be more creative than thaaaat.

Looking up toward the sound, a look of terror etches across Sullivan's face as
he hears the warden's voice. Slowly, he backs toward the shadows of his cell, as
far from the bars and guards as possible.

> ENRIK
> *(off screen over intercom)*

You know what to do boys. Bring him in...

Intercom CLICKS off.

The door at the end of the walkway SLAMS open and Alvarez and Murphy come out to
help Simmons. DOLLY BACK as they all walk toward Tudley's cell. PAN TO cell as
door slides open and Alvarez and Murphy enter. Simmons watches from the walkway.

Cowering in the corner of his bed, as tight as he can be with his legs drawn up
in front of him, Tudley lets out a guttural yell.

> TUDLEY

(yelling)
Slayeth the evil that lives inside you!
Where they are walking the devil walks too!

12B INT.PRISON - TUDLEY CELL - SAME

LOW ANGLE DIRTY OVER SHOULDER Tudley - as the guards get closer to him he
becomes louder and more agitated.

                    ALVAREZ
     Let's go Tudley...
     It's time.

                    MURPHY
                 (to Alvarez)
     Make sure you got a good hold on 'em.
     This fucker's a live one!!
                 (laughs)

Alvarez and Murphy each grab one of Tudley's shoulders/upper arms and try to
stand him up off of the bed, but he resists.

12C INT. PRISON - WALKWAY - SAME

OVER SHOULDER Simmons - as he watches the scene play out.

                    MURPHY
                 (to Tudley)
     God, don't you ever shut the fuck up!?

                    TUDLEY
                 (louder)
     Slayeth the evil that lives inside you!
     Where they are walking the devil walks too!

                    SIMMONS
            (to Alvarez and Murphy)
     Get him up already! Enrik won't fucking
     mind if you bruise him a bit for Christ's sake.

Alvarez and Murphy drag a kicking and screaming Tudley out into the walkway.

INSERT: LOW ANGLE PUSH IN ON Sullivan - trembling against the wall of his cell.

CAMERA ON Tudley's chest(human dolly) ANGLED ON his face with Alvarez to LEFT
and Murphy to RIGHT of FRAME pulling him down walkway.

                    TUDLEY
            (yelling and crying)
     Slayeth the evil that lives inside you!
     Where they are walking the devil walks too!

SPLIT DIAPTER CLOSE ON Simmons face in FRAME as is Tudley's futile struggle down
the entire length of the walkway.

                    SIMMONS
                 (to Tudley)
     Look on the bright side Tudley, you're gonna
     finally get to see if there really *is* a God!

Alvarez and Murphy reach the metal door and drag him through. It SLAMS shut.
Simmons looks toward Sullivan, gestures towards the door with his club.

> SIMMONS
> One more word outta you --
> and I'll drag you in there myself.

Simmons walks to the metal door. Opens. SLAMS shut.

12D INT.PRISON - SULLIVAN'S CELL - MOMENTS LATER

CLOSE ON Sullivan - shaking as he leans his head back against the wall. He
closes his eyes as he tries to drown out Tudley's screams.

CUT TO:

13 INT. PRISON - OPERATING ROOM/TORTURE CHAMBER - LATER

HIGH WIDE ANGLE - the gurneys and operating equipment has been pushed up against
the walls, to make as much free space in the center of the room as possible.

Riley, and Bowen are standing in the center of the room as Alvarez and Murphy
enter dragging Tudley behind them.
Alvarez looks weary and nervous. Murphy looks thrilled.

Simmons enters right after they do and closes the door.

Alvarez and Murphy throw Tudley HARD to the center of the room.

LOW ANGLE on Tudley as he hits the floor. Terrified, he keeps his head down, not
wanting to know what is about to happen.

HIGH WIDE ANGLE - the guards circle around him. Enrik enters from the opposite
door wearing black dress pants, a white shirt, and a black tie. He looks sharp.
He walks into the circle of guards and right up to Tudley, cowering on the
floor.

LOW ANGLE DIRTY OVER SHOULDER Tudley - on Enrik looming over.

> ENRIK
> Well Tudley, I am very excited to announce that
> today will be your last day here.
> *(to guards)*
> Boys, I think this deserves a round of applause...

OVER SHOULDER Enrik PAN - to all the guards as they begin clapping. They are
clearly very into what is going on, and smile and elbow each other knowingly,
while Alvarez seems a bit apprehensive.

FINISH PAN ON Enrik looks down TO POV ON Tudley - as he rocks back and forth,
mumbling.

> ENRIK
> So, since today is your *special* day, we
> have decided to do your execution a bit...
> *(ominously)*
> ...differently.

ECU Tudley - sweat beading on his brow.

> TUDLEY
> *(whispering to himself)*
> Slayeth the evil that lives inside you...

OVER SHOULDER Tudley - on Enrik.

> ENRIK
>
> What's this now?

Enrik bends down in a mocking way, putting a hand to his ear in an exaggerated effort to hear Tudley clearer.

> TUDLEY
> *(continues whispering)*
> where they are walking the Devil walks too.

> ENRIK
>
> Oh! The Devil you say!
> *(to guards)*
> Spoooooky, right boys?
>
> *(laughs)*

WIDE ANGLE - Enrik stands back up as the guards laugh along with him. Alvarez nervously laughs.

LOW ANGLE TWO SHOT - feigning seriousness, Enrik crouches back down and puts a hand on Tudley's upper back. Tudley cringes at his touch.

> ENRIK
> *(mocking whisper)*
> Hey, Tudley, can I ask you something?

Tudley doesn't move or respond.

> ENRIK
> *(normal speaking tone)*
> I said, can I ask you a question?

Tudley doesn't move or respond. Enrik stands up throwing his arms out.

> ENRIK
> *(yelling)*
> Well now you're just being fucking rude.
> *(louder)*
> Hello Tudley! Is anybody home!?

Enrik crouches back down and puts his hand back on Tudley's back.

> ENRIK
> *(continues in a mocking whisper)*
> . . .we want you to come out and play.

Gestures to guards.
> *(yelling)*
> Or perhaps we'll just kick in your fucking skull
> *(louder)*
> until your fucking brains
> *(louder)*
> are all over the floor!

CLOSE ON Enrik - stands back up and tries to control his breathing in an attempt to calm down.

DIRTY OVER SHOULDER Tudley - on the guards stare Tudley down angrily.

CLOSE ON Alvarez - still seems uneasy, as he looks back and forth from Tudley to Enrik to his fellow guards, then to the floor as sweat from his brow splashes down. Wipes brow with sleeve.

Alvarez POV - PAN from Tudley, Enrik, guards, floor. INSERT: drop of swear splash to floor.

ECU Tudley - he continues to whisper his chant.

CLOSE ON Enrik PULL BACK as he exhales a deep breath, then a disturbing grin creeps across his face. CAMERA LOWERS TO TWO SHOT - as he bends down putting his ear closer to Tudley to exaggerate trying to hear him better.

> ENRIK
>
> What was that Tudley? I can't quite make out
> what your answer was...

> TUDLEY
> (normal tone)
>
> Slayeth the evil that lives inside you,
> where they are walking the Devil walks too.

> ENRIK
>
> Well fuck me... we have a broken record here, boys.
> Let me adjust the needle!

Standing, Enrik kicks Tudley over onto his side. He continues chanting.

> TUDLEY
> (normal tone)
>
> Slayeth the evil that lives inside you,
> where they are walking the Devil walks too.

DIRTY OVER SHOULDER Alvarez - on Enrik as he kicks Tudley HARD in the stomach. Alvarez lowers his head in disgust.

CLOSE ON Enrik.

> ENRIK
> (yelling)
>
> Did you say that to all your victims?
> Did you, you piece of shit!

LOW ANGLE CLOSE ON Tudley - as Enrik's boot SMASHES into his nose. LOUD CRUNCH SOUND - EXPLOSION of blood. Tears run down his cheeks mixing with blood, as he begins to gag.

> ENRIK
> (continued)
>
> Did you say that to the fifteen women you
> (louder)
> raped and murdered?

HIGH ANGLE ON Enrik - he kicks Tudley on the back, then as he pulls his leg back, wipes the blood from his shoe onto Tudley's back as he lays quivering in a ball on the floor.

> ENRIK
> (continued)
>
> Was that load of bullshit
> (louder)
> the last words they ever heard!?

Enrik makes the motion that he is going to stomp Tudley's head in with his boot, but stops just before he does, and walks away, collecting himself.

CLOSE ON Enrik.

> ENRIK
> *(calmly)*
> No, no, no...that would be too easy.
> You deserve much, much worse for the crimes you have
> committed, for the PAIN and SUFFERING you have
> caused.

PUSH CLOSER - as he pauses for a moment, then smiles. He nods to the guards.

OVER HEAD WIDE ANGLE ON guards - they start making a tighter circle around Tudley, laying on the floor.

CLOSE ON Tudley - as he peeks through his blood stained fingers.

LOW ANGLE Tudley POV - the guards start unzipping their flies.

CLOSE ON Tudley - he realizes what is about to happen, and tries to stand, too weak, he drops to his knees.

> TUDLEY
> *(pleading)*
> Please, no...please!
> Just give me the chair!
> Just give me the chair!!
>
> *(louder)*
> Please! I'm begging you...!
> I'm on my knees!

LOW ANGLE OVER SHOULDER Tudley - on Simmons.

> SIMMONS
> *(laughing)*
> On your knees, huh? Well, that *is* the idea...

OVER HEAD WIDE ANGLE - the guards are moving closer with their unzipped pants. Enrik steps outside the circle as the guards close in. Tudley disappearing beneath them.

> TUDLEY
> Get away from me! Stop! No!!

CLOSE ON Enrik - as he walks toward the door.

> ENRIK
> I hope you enjoy this as much as they will. . .
> *(pause)*
> . . .although something tells me you *probably* won't.

Enrik EXITS room.

HAND HELD CAMERA on Tudley - as the guards pull him to his feet, bend him over the gurney. He is screaming hysterically.

LOW ANGLE floor - Tudley's pants drop below his knees.

ECU INSERT: Guards sweaty faces, mouths, eyes, hands groping Tudley's dirty flesh. Blood spattering on thighs.

CAMERA ON gurney CLOSE ON Tudley with the guards behind him OUT OF FOCUS. The guards are all laughing and cheering as they RAPE Tudley.

SPLIT DIAPTER - ClOSE ON Alvarez - standing near the door with his head turned away from the rape in revile. As the guards take horrific pleasure in the background.

RILEY

Alvarez, come get some a this!

BOWEN

Yeah, bitch!

Alvarez clenches his eyes closed. Tears roll down his cheeks.

CUT TO:

14 INT. PRISON - SULLIVAN'S CELL - MOMENTS LATER

LOW ANGLE ON Sullivan - slumped on the floor with his hands pressed hard over his ears, rolling his head back and forth. The SOUND of Tudley's SCREAMS echo down the walkway.

SULLIVAN

No, no, no...no one deserves this...

Sullivan suddenly opens his eyes wide and takes his hands off of his ears.

SULLIVAN
(angry and gruff)

Yes, yes he does. He's a fucking rapist and a killer!
What the hell am I saying??

SOUND OF Tudley's SCREAMS begin to weaken.

CAMERA BEGINS TO SHAKE WITH Sullivan as his head rocks back and forth in an attempt to block out the mental battle going on inside his head.

He clamps his hands back over his ears and closes his eyes tightly again. CAMERA GOES STILL.

SULLIVAN
(nervously)

No, no, no...

SOUND OF Tudley's screams end abruptly and the prison is eerily quiet for a few seconds. SOUND OF DOOR OPENING.

14A INT.PRISON - WALKWAY - MOMENTS LATER

WIDE ANGLE as the guards come strolling out of the metal door and down past Sullivan's cell.

Lagging behind, Alvarez in shock at what he's witnessed.

HAND HELD OVER SHOULDER Alvarez - as he watches the others boast.

SIMMONS
(laughing)

I've never seen him scared shitless like that.

                              RILEY
          Yeah, at least he finally passed out.
          Who would have thought he'd last that long?

                             MURPHY
          Baby Jesus, I almost shit myself when he woke up
          again, the fucker damn near bit my finger off!

                            SIMMONS
                          (laughing)
          Better your finger than your dick...

                            ALVAREZ
                       (quietly to Bowen)
          This kinda stuff happens all the time around here?

                             BOWEN
          An eye for an eye, man. An eye for an eye.

Bowen leaps back as Sullivan rushes to the front of his cell, his fists CLAMP
tightly around the bars.

                            SULLIVAN
          I heard what you did!
          You're all monsters!

14B INT. PRISON - SULLIVAN'S CELL - SAME

OVER SHOULDER Sullivan - on guards.

                             RILEY
          Says the child-killer...

                            SIMMONS
          Jesus Christ, don't you ever pipe down?
          Why do we keep having to remind you that
          this is Death Row,
          you know, the place where pieces of shit like
          yourself finally get what they deserve.

The guards start to walkaway.

Sullivan loses control and sticks his right arm out of the cell as far as it
will go.

                            SULLIVAN
          Get back here you asshole!
          Try saying that to me when I'm not locked in here!

14C INT. PRISON - WALKWAY - SAME

WIDE ANGLE ON Simmons - as he turns to Sullivan and begins to walk backward
following the others.

                            SIMMONS
          Sorry Sullivan, I forgot that we're

not supposed to tease the animals.
>(laughs)
>(to Murphy)

Get this bastard his dinner before he gnaws
right through those bars.

The Guards leave the walkway.

14D INT. PRISON - SULLIVAN'S CELL - SAME

DOGGIE CAM ON Sullivan walks to the brick wall of his cell and gives it a hard
push with both hands before he turns around, putting his back against it, and
slumps down to the floor with a WINCE.

The last inmate on Death Row, Sullivan begins talking out loud just to break the
defining silence.

>SULLIVAN
>(muttering to himself)

Animals...like they're any better.
>(shakes head)

The way Tudley screamed...
>(shudders)

CUT TO:

15 INT. PRISON - THE WARDEN'S OFFICE - LATER

HIGH ANGLE ON Enrik sitting behind a desk going through paperwork when Simmons
enter.

>SIMMONS

Tudley will no longer be bothering you, Warden.

>ENRIK
>(shuffles papers)

Great, great job, and the room is being cleaned?

OVER SHOULDER Enrik on Simmons.

>SIMMONS
>(laughs)

I stuck the new guys on it, got to break them
in eventually.

>ENRIK

I heard you exchanging words with Sullivan a
moment ago?

>SIMMONS

Yeah he just can't seem to keep his damn mouth shut.

Murphy enters and stands behind the other guards. He doesn't say anything but
he is holding a bandage around his left hand.

CLOSE ON Enrik.

>ENRIK

When the time comes we will have to be very
careful with Mr. Sullivan. He seems to be more...
>(pauses)
. . .aggressive than the inmates we've dealt
with in the past.

CLOSE ON Murphy.

                               MURPHY
    You don't have to tell me twice, the fucker
    bit my hand when I insisted he eat his dinner.

CLOSE ON Enrik.

                               ENRIK
                            (worried)
    How many days has it been now?

CUT TO:

16 INT. PRISON - SULLIVAN'S CELL - LATER

LOW ANGLE ON Sullivan - an upturned tray of food scattered across the floor
before him. He is laying on the floor in a semi-fetal position. There is dried
blood around his mouth and beard from biting Murphy.

A SERIES OF INSERTS/CAMERA ANGLES - Sullivan changing position in the cell to
covey that time has been passing.

WIDE - walking back and fourth like a caged animal from wall to wall, shoving
himself back off of each when he reaches them.

OVER HEAD - laying on his bed on his back staring up at the ceiling almost
expressionless.

LOW ANGLE CLOSE - in the corner of cell with his knees drawn up slowly rocking
himself back and forth.

MED - sitting on the edge of his bed staring out past the bars with hatred in
his eyes and clenched fists.

END SERIES OF SHOTS.

CLOSE ON Sullivan - laying on his side in bed with his eyes closed and breathing
deeply.

ECU ON Sullivan - suddenly his eyes snap open as if he hadn't even realized he
had gone to sleep.

Sullivan POV - the food has been mysteriously cleaned up from the floor of his
cell, but there is not a soul in sight.

WIDE LOW ANGLE - he sits up in bed confused. Stands, then slowly walks to the
bars, presses his face against them and searches everywhere for a sign of
someone else. Anyone.

                            SULLIVAN
                     (muttering to himself)
    What the hell is going on in here?
                         (pauses)
                         (yelling)
    Come on you fuckers, I know you're here!
    Stop fucking around with me.

16A INT. PRISON - WALKWAY - SAME

ANGLE ON Sullivan's hand mirror going through bars of cell. Reflection of empty walkway.

ANGLE ON mirror - Sullivan's reflection.

> SULLIVAN
> *(muttering to himself)*
> Where the hell did they all go?
> *(pauses to look around)*
> I'm so fucking hungry I could actually eat
> that piss-food right now...

16B INT. PRISON - SULLIVAN'S CELL - SAME

WIDE ANGLE from head of bed with walkway in background - Sullivan steps to his bed and lies down on his back, covers his face with his hands. RACK FOCUS to the cell across from him. Standing in the cell is an UNKNOWN WOMAN in her forties. She looks aged from abusing drugs and alcohol. Her hair is dry and unbrushed with streaks of early grey in it. She speaks with a rough voice from smoking too many cigarettes.

> UNKNOWN WOMAN
> Listen to you over there, still crying
> like a little bitch.

Sullivan jerks his head up and looks around to see where the voice is coming from.

Sullivan POV CLOSER ON Unknown Woman - standing in the middle of Sammy's old cell in a dated looking prison gown and a ratty old sweater. She looks vaguely familiar, but he can't figure out why.

> UNKNOWN WOMAN
> What the fuck are you gawking at?

She brings a half-full bottle of whiskey up to her lips and takes a long drink without flinching, and then lowers the bottle back to her side.

CLOSE ON Sullivan - licks his lips longingly, thinking about how great some whiskey would be right now and grows jealous.

> SULLIVAN
> Where the hell did you get that from?

Sullivan POV - Unknown Woman.

> UNKNOWN WOMAN
> Guards gave it to me, showed 'em my tits.

She starts laughing with a gritty cackling sound, but then loses her breath and starts full body smoker's-coughing.

OVER SHOULDER Sullivan - he turns to CAMERA with an expression of disgust and slight fear.

> UNKNOWN WOMAN
> Oh, for fuck's sake get that high-and-mighty
> expression off your god-damned face...
> *(slowly and clearly)*
> child killer.
> *(laughs)*

16C INT. PRISON - SAMMY'S CELL - SAME

OVER SHOULDER Unknown Woman - Angered, Sullivan lunges forward, tightly grips the bars of his cell, pressing his face between them as much as he can.

SULLIVAN
(yelling)

What did you say!?

CLOSE ON Unknown Woman.

UNKNOWN WOMAN

Well there's the little bastard I know.
Angry....Violent....Aggressive.
(pauses)
and a coward.

SULLIVAN

Shut up, you don't fucking know me.

16D INT. PRISON - WALKWAY - SAME

WIDE ON Sullivan - he turns his back on her, but stops dead in his tracks. SLOW DOLLY IN as her words start to offend him.

UNKNOWN WOMAN

Yeah, you're right it takes a real man
to kill twelve children.
(sarcastically)
You're not a coward at all.

DOLLY STOPS CLOSE ON Sullivan - spins around and rushes the bars in a rage.

SULLIVAN
(yelling)

I didn't fucking do it!

OVER SHOULDER Sullivan - she laughs and slowly walks to and sits down on her bed, still facing him. Takes another drink of whiskey.

UNKNOWN WOMAN

So you never drove an ice cream truck...

Turning to CAMERA - Sullivan clutches his head as if he is trying to fight a memory that is trying to invade his consciousness. He fights to repress.

FLASH CUT - Sullivan in a pink ice cream truck, talking to a little boy standing on the sidewalk outside the truck, eating an ice cream cone. There is NO AUDIBLE DIALOG, just the SCREECH OF STATIC that Sullivan is hearing inside his head.

UNKNOWN WOMAN
(continued)

And you didn't enjoy lurking in the park, raping your
way through July?

ECU Sullivan - SOUND OF a woman screaming "No! Get off me!" fills Sullivan's head as he clamps his hands over his ears. He becomes much more agitated, as he fights truth from taking over his mind.

CLOSE ON Unknown Woman - grinning as she watches him lose control.

CLOSE ON Sullivan - CAMERA RISES UP...

                              SULLIVAN
                             (screams)
         Shut up! Shuuuut uuup!

...TO OVER HEAD ANGLE - as he falls to his knees, starts crying.

                              SULLIVAN
         I've never hurt anyone...I would never...

CUT TO:

17 INT. 1960S SUBURBAN FAMILY HOME - LIVING ROOM - NIGHT

WIDE ANGLE - a few days before Christmas. The tree is in the corner all lit up,
and Christmas music is playing on a record player.

Richard Sullivan, age four, is setting up green army men along the coffee table
while Enrik(Tommy) age nine, is sitting on the couch reading a comic book.

Everything seems perfect and peaceful.

OFF CAMERA - SCREAMING is heard from the kitchen, as a man and a woman argue.

                            MOTHER(O.S.)
                             (drunk)
         Go then, go visit your whores instead
         of being home with your family.

                            FATHER(O.S.)
                             (angry)
         For the hundredth fucking time, I'm going to work!
         Someone has to!

CAMERA PUSHES TO TWO SHOT - Sullivan stops playing, looks scared, climbs up onto
the couch with Tommy.

Tommy puts down his comic book, puts an arm around his little brother to comfort
him.

                            MOTHER(O.S.)
                             (drunk)
         Oh fuck you, what's that supposed to mean?
         I never wanted any of this
         "house in the suburbs" bullshit,
         this was your dream...
                          (starts crying)
         not mine.

CLOSE ON Sullivan - he cringes as she yells and buries his face into his
brother's shoulder.

CLOSE ON Tommy - looks toward kitchen, listening closely to the fight.

Tommy POV - Father and Mother seen in the doorway of the kitchen facing off.

                              FATHER

So I guess I'm some kind of an asshole for not
wanting our children to grow up in the ghetto!

                    MOTHER
Oh please...you've never stepped foot in a ghetto...
                (laughs coldly)
just go, just get the fuck out of here already.
Your whore is waiting.

17B INT. SULLIVAN HOUSE - KITCHEN - SAME

TWO SHOT ON Father and Mother - with Tommy and Sullivan in BACKGROND. Sensing
that the fight is escalating, Tommy escorts Sullivan from the couch and they
start walking towards the stairway.

                    FATHER
I am going
                    (louder)
TO WORK!
                    (pause)
Believe whatever the fuck you want!

17C INT. SULLIVAN HOUSE - STAIRWAY - SAME

HIGH ANGLE ON Tommy and Sullivan - they're about halfway to the steps when the
sound of a liquor bottle being SMASHED across the kitchen counter makes them
both jump and hurry their steps.

                    MOTHER (O.S.)
                    (screaming)
I said get the fuck out!

TWO SHOT THROUGH bars of bannister on Tommy and Sullivan - as cling to the
rails at the foot of the steps.

                    ENRIK(TOMMY)
                (whispers to Sullivan)
Go upstairs and hide...

Sullivan clings to Enrik(Tommy), not wanting to go without him.

                    SULLIVAN
                    (crying)
Come with me!

                    ENRIK(TOMMY)
                    (whispering)
I'll be right behind you, now go!

Tommy remains at the bottom of the stairs to hear the fighting continuing in the
kitchen.

HIGH ANGLE top of stairs - reluctantly, Sullivan inches up the stairs.

OFF SCREEN SOUND - the backdoor opens and slams closed.

OFF SCREEN SOUND - Mother crying hysterically.

LOW ANGLE ON Tommy - knowing that she will come looking for him and Sullivan
next, he starts creeping quietly up the stairs.

                    MOTHER (O.S.)

(screaming)
Bastard! Stupid bastard!
(cries hysterically)

Tommy reaches the top of the stairs. SOUND OF Mother crying stops.

MOTHER(O.S.)
(yelling)
Tommy, Richie, Mommy needs you boys...

HIGE ANGLE top of stairs - as Tommy disappears from view into their shared bedroom, Mother comes around the corner into the living room. She is disheveled looking and carrying the top part of the vodka bottle she had smashed in the kitchen.

OVER SHOULDER Mother - she scans the room looking for them.

MOTHER

Tommy? Richie?

INSERT: record player - it reaches the end of the record and starts SCREECHING.

HANDHELD ON Mother - she WAILS and grabs the record off the player roughly and throws it against the framed family photo on the wall.

OVER SHOULDER Mother – as the record SHATTERS, but the picture is still intact, this enrages her even more and she smashes the framed photo with the remnants of the vodka bottle in her hand. Glass flies against her slightly bloody hand.

LOW ANGLE ON Mother - she realizes they have to be upstairs and starts heading in that direction. On her way she steps on some of Sullivan's army men and stumbles slightly.

MOTHER
(to herself)
Little fuckers...
(louder)

Get the fuck down here!

Silence.

HIGH ANGLE - top of stairs looking down on Mother.

MOTHER
(yelling)
I'm counting to three, your little asses better be in front of me...
(to herself)
because you don't want me hunting you down up there...
(yelling)
One...two...three...

Silence.

CUT TO:

18 INT. SULLIVAN HOUSE - UPSTAIRS BEDROOM - INSIDE THE CLOSET - MOMENTS LATER

ANGLE ON Tommy and Sullivan - huddled together in the corner of the small space. Tommy has a protective arm around Sullivan.

                         SULLIVAN
                        (whispering)
          She's coming up the stairs.

                         ENRIK(TOMMY)
                        (whispering)
          Shh, she'll pass out in her room
          before she ever finds us.

OFF SCREEN SOUND OF Mother stomping up the stairs.

                         MOTHER(O.S.)
          You two are really in for it this time!
          This is all your fault!
          Everything was perfect before you little shit
          stains came along...

                         MOTHER(O.S.)
                        (hushed muttering)
          Slayeth the evil that lives inside you...

                         ENRIK(TOMMY)
          Shh, I'll protect you.
          I'll always be right here to protect you.

                         MOTHER
                        (hushed muttering)
          Where they are walking the Devil walks too.

CLOSE ON Sullivan - he buries his face into his brother's chest.

CLOSE ON Tommy - holding back tears, he hugs him protectively.

CUT TO:

19 INT. PRISON - WARDEN'S OFFICE - REALITY - DAY

This is the first time we are seeing reality as it truly is, instead of the way
Sullivan has been filtering through his twisted mind.

WIDE ANGLE ON office - it appears like an average office with filing cabinets,
certificates on the wall, a coffee maker, and windows.

CLOSE ON Enrik - with sad tired eyes, he sits behind his desk with a cup before
him. He is holding a photograph and staring at it with a broken hearted
expression. We can only see the back of the photo at this point.

INSERT: cup of coffee with a film on it, like it has been sitting there for a
while.

Phone rings.

OVER HEAD ANGLE ON Enrik - as he places the photograph down and picks up the
telephone.

                         ENRIK
                        (into phone)
          Hello Governor Adams, thank you for getting back
          to me so soon. So have you considered my
          application?
                        (pause)

I see.
                    (pause)
I understand.

                    (pause)

                    ENRIK
                (continued)
No, I know you have to do what you feel is right.
                    (pause)
Well, thank you for your time.
                    (pause)
Thank you, all the best to your family as well.

CLOSE ON Enrik - hangs up phone.

Lifts cup of coffee to drink, but puts it down right next to the photograph he was looking at.

OVER SHOULDER Enrik - on photo from the 1960s of Father, Mother, 4 year old Richard Sullivan and older brother, TOMMY. Everyone looks very happy. He picks up some paperwork.

CLOSE ON paperwork - an application for a stay of execution for Richard Sullivan.

LOW ANGLE CLOSE ON Enrik - with tears in his eyes, he picks up a rubber stamp and stamps it down on the paperwork. "DENIED" in red.

CUT TO:

20 INT. PRISON - SULLIVAN'S CELL - REALITY - LATER

WIDE ANGLE ON Sullivan - curled on his side asleep in his bed. The cell looks entirely different now because we are seeing it how it REALLY is, and not how Sullivan is imagining it to look.

20A INT. PRISON - WALKWAY - SAME

The door at the end of the walkway is no longer ominous looking, but looks just like a regular prison door. It opens and Enrik steps through, his head hung low.

Enrik IN PROFILE MED DOLLY as he walks toward Sullivan's cell.

Stopping at Sullivan's cell. He stands there for a moment, unlocks cell door and opens it.

PAN OVER WITH Enrik - as he enters the cell, closes door behind.

Enrik goes up to Sullivan's sleeping form, puts a hand gently on his shoulder.

20B INT. PRISON - SULLIVAN'S CELL - SAME

OVER SHOULDER Enrik - on Sullivan.

                    ENRIK(TOMMY)
                (gently)
Wake up Richie.

Startled, Sullivan jolts upright in bed.

Sullivan POV - in an instant everything shifts back to Sullivan's IMAGINED
REALITY. The prison looks more ominous and Enrik is creepy looking like he was
earlier.

                         ENRIK(TOMMY)
        Wakey wakey, Mr. Sullivan!

CLOSE ON Sullivan - wipes the sleep from his eyes.

                         SULLIVAN
        Who..who's there?

Sullivan POV - Enrik leans in close.

                         ENRIK(TOMMY)
                         (mockingly)
        You wound me!
        Surely you remember all of the great times we've had!

OVER SHOULDER Sullivan - gripped in terror, he turns his back to Enrik. With his
face now in CAMERA we can see Enrik over his shoulder. Sullivan eyes closed
tight.

Enrik acknowledges the emotion.

                         ENRIK(TOMMY)
        Ah, that's better! I know it can be so hard to say
        goodbye, but --

Opening his eyes, Sullivan cuts him off.

                         SULLIVAN
        Goodbye??

Enrik continues.

                         ENRIK(TOMMY)
        Why, of course. This is your last day!

HIGH ANGLE WIDE - Sullivan jumps from the bed, falls to his knees with his hands
clasped in front of him and begs for his life.

                         SULLIVAN
                         (pleading)
        No! Please! I know I'm innocent, I can prove it!
        Please! You can't do this.

OVER SHOULDER Sullivan - on Enrik looming over.

                         ENRIK(TOMMY)
        Oh poor deluded Mr. Sullivan, there's no need to beg.
        Surely an innocent man like yourself must have
        some shred of dignity left.
        Besides, I'm not the one responsible for your
        sentence.
                         (pause)
        You were just living life as you always have, right?
                         (pause)
        Perhaps you should take a real close look at
        yourself, and focus on what really brought
        you here. Or maybe you already have, and you just
        don't like what you see.

Enrik turns to leave the cell.

HIGH ANGLE WIDE - Sullivan whimpering on the floor.

                    ENRIK(TOMMY)
                     (shrugs)
     Either way, I'm only the messenger.

Enrik leaves the cell and it SLAMS shut behind him.

LOW ANGLE CLOSE ON Sullivan - shakes at the sound of the cell slamming. In the background OUT OF FOCUS Enrik begins to walk down the walkway.

                    ENRIK(TOMMY)
     Enjoy the next thirty-six hours, Mr. Sullivan.
                     (pause)
     They will be your last.

20C INT. PRISON - WALKWAY - SAME

WIDE ANGLE ON Sullivan's cell - he lurches towards the bars, still on his knees. He grips them tightly, pressing his face into them as he calls out.

                    SULLIVAN
     Wait! Come back!
     I'm talking to you!
     Get me out of here, you can't do this!

Enrik in far corner of FRAME ignores Sullivan as he exits through the metal door. It closes behind him. SLAM!

CUT TO:

21 INT. PRISON - WARDEN'S OFFICE - REALITY - LATER

WIDE ANGLE - Enrik(Tommy) is sitting at his desk, upset.

Murphy enters, stands before desk.

                    MURPHY
     You wanted to see me?

                    ENRIK(TOMMY)
     Yes. Sullivan hasn't been eating. Why?

CLOSE ON Murphy.

                    MURPHY
     That is true sir, he keeps knocking his tray
     on the ground muttering that someone peed or
     spit in it. I don't know what he's thinking.

CLOSE ON Enrik.

                    ENRIK(TOMMY)
     Well, he has to be moved tomorrow morning, and it's
     too dangerous of a job with him fully conscious.

DIRTY OVER SHOULDER Enrik - on Murphy.

> MURPHY
> What about an injection?

> ENRIK(TOMMY)
> *(annoyed)*
> Well, he bit you earlier, so you of all people should
> know that he isn't going to allow anyone near
> him with a syringe. Just make sure he eats tonight.
> Do whatever you have to.

MED ON Murphy - turns INTO CAMERA to leave his back to Enrik. He mutters under
his breath.

> MURPHY
> It's not my job to feed psychos...

Murphy EXITS FRAME - RACK FOCUS TO Enrik - as he leans back in his chair. A
pained expression across his face, as he softly responds to Murphy's words.

> ENRIK
> It is indeed your job, Mr. Murphy. And sometimes our   jobs can be
most unpleasant.

CUT TO:

22 INT. PRISON - SULLIVAN'S CELL - REALITY - LATER

CLOSE ON Sullivan - he sits up INTO CAMERA blinks a couple of times, moving
slowly like he is in pain.

WIDE ANGLE Murphy - approaches cell with a tray of food. He slides the food
through the space provided.

> MURPHY
> Dinner time.

Sullivan doesn't move or acknowledge Murphy in any way.

> MURPHY
> *(irritated)*
> *(louder)*
> Hey! Sullivan!
> Dinner time!

Still no response from Sullivan.

> MURPHY
> *(angry)*
> Would you just eat your God-damned dinner.
> I ain't getting fired over a piece of shit child-
> killer like you for not eating when you're supposed   to!

22A INT. PRISON - WALKWAY - SAME

OVER SHOULDER Murphy on Sullivan - he just keeps sitting on his bed, staring off
into space. Oblivious to Murphy.

> MURPHY
> *(loudly to himself)*

        For Christ's sake...
                            (yells out)
        Opening number three.

Unlocks cell, opens it.

WIDE ANGLE - Murphy picks up the food and brings it directly to Sullivan. It looks like a TV dinner. Nothing weird.

He places it on the bed next to him, then steps back about a foot away from Sullivan.

                            MURPHY
        Now, it's right there. . .
        Eat it!

Still no response from Sullivan.

Murphy goes to the door to the cell and looks up and down the walkway to make sure no one else is around. Slowly, closes cell door, takes out his club, and holds it in a threatening manner.

22B INT. PRISON - SULLIVAN'S CELL - SAME

OVER SHOULDER Sullivan on Murphy.

                            MURPHY
                            (yelling)
        Eat God Damn it!
                            (waits a second)
        Fine, you want to fuck around?
                            (lifts club to hit Sullivan)
        This is what you get when you fuck around!

Murphy SWINGS the club, and it is about to make impact with Sullivan's head, he grabs it with one hand, stopping it. In and instant, as he stands up, punches Murphy in the throat with his free hand.

Gagging, Murphy stumbles backwards trying to regain his breath.

CLOSE ON Murphy - SLOW MOTION - as he brings the club up across his face in a backhanded motion. Face filled with RAGE as he swings.

CLOSE ON Sullivan - SLOW MOTION - blood hungry twinkle in his eyes. As the club comes toward his head, he raises his right arm to BLOCK. THUD! As the club hits against his forearm, knocking out of Murphy's hand, it goes flying to the floor.

TWO SHOT - ducking low, Murphy throws and uppercut punch into Sullivan's ribs.

INSERT: Fist into ribs. CRACK!

CLOSE ON Sullivan - full of adrenaline, he doesn't react or feel it. He head butts Murphy in the face.

OVER SHOULDER Sullivan - on Murphy as Sullivan's forehead SMASHES into his nose. He reels aback into the wall, trying to regain his wits. With both hands Sullivan grabs Murphy by the throat, pushing him HARD up against the wall.

INSERT: Murphy's feet lift up about two inches off the floor.

CLOSE ON Sullivan - leans into Murphy's ear.

SULLIVAN
(menacing whisper)
Good...I love it when they fight back...

CUT TO:

23 INT. PRISON - WARDEN'S OFFICE - REALITY - MOMENTS LATER

WIDE ANGLE - Enrik sitting at his desk with his head in his hands. The prison ALARM sounds (the same sound heard during the opening scene).

Enrik looks up quickly.

OVER SHOULDER Enrik - as the door slams open and Simmons runs in, panicked.

SIMMONS
(out of breath)
It's Murphy! He's locked in Sullivan's cell!

CUT TO:

24 INT. PRISON - SULLIVAN'S CELL - REALITY

WIDE ANGLE - Sullivan in the center of his cell with Murphy in a headlock in front of him.

Struggling to breath, holding onto Sullivan's forearm just to keep on his feet, Murphy pleads for his life.

MURPHY
Please! Don't do this!

OVER SHOULDER Sullivan - as Enrik, Simmons and Alvarez frantically ENTER FRAME in front of Sullivan's cell. Simmons armed with a shotgun. Alvarez with a tranquilizer dart gun. They aim almost in unison, but with Murphy being used as a human shield, neither guard is able to take a shot.

CLOSE ON Alvarez.

ALVAREZ
(nervous and yelling, visibly shaking)
Don't even THINK about moving!

CLOSE ON Sullivan - he eyes him the way a cat would eye a mouse, as if he is amused and wants to see what he is going to do next.

CLOSE ON Murphy.

MURPHY
Guys! (cough) Get me the fuck out of here...

Sullivan's forearm tightens into his windpipe.

OVER SHOULDER Sullivan.

SIMMONS
(gesturing with the shotgun)

Drop him and put your hands against the wall!

> ENRIK(TOMMY)
> Richie, stop this, let him go...

24A INT. PRISON - WALKWAY - REALITY - SAME

OVER SHOULDER Enrik on Sullivan/Murphy - Enrik calling him Richie catches him off guard for a moment. Calming him into an almost trance-like state.

He releases Murphy, who drops to his knees too weak to move. He gasps for breath.

ANGLE ON Enrik, Simmons and Alvarez as they start to relax slightly, as the situation comes under control.

> ENRIK(TOMMY)
> That's it. Just let him go...

OVER SHOULDER Enrik on Sullivan - hearing Enrik's voice again makes Sullivan snap out of his temporary trance. The expression on his face, switches to that of a rabid dog.

With both hands he grabs the sides of Murphy's head and twists it completely around SNAP! CRACKLE! POP! as the back Murphy's head now faces Enrik and the guards.

> ENRIK(TOMMY)
> NO!

ABOVE ANGLE as Murphy falls forward dead. His SHOCKED eyes staring down at his own back.

CLOSE ON ALVAREZ - he fires a tranquilizer dart.

INSERT: Sullivan's upper arm as the dart hits.

DOGGIE CAM ON Sullivan - suddenly light-headed, he drops to his knees and smiles creepily.

> SULLIVAN
> (slurred)
> Plenty m-more...where...that came...from...

He falls over onto his side, still smiling eerily and drooling INTO CAMERA.

CUT TO:

25 EXT. STREET - SUBURBAN NEIGHBORHOOD - DAY

LOW WIDE ANGLE ON pink ice cream truck - parked next to the sidewalk. A LITTLE BOY, about eight years old, is standing at the ice cream window, eating an ice cream cone. His bike laying on it's side behind him in the green grass.

> LITTLE BOY
> Mmm, strawberry is my favorite! What's your name?

Sullivan is inside the truck.

                         SULLIVAN
                  (off camera - friendly)
      My friends call me Sammy.

                        LITTLE BOY

      Am I your friend?

                         SULLIVAN
                      (off camera)
      Of course, I gave you that ice cream cone didn't I?
      And for free...

                        LITTLE BOY
                      (smiling)
      Yep!

START SLOW ZOOM as Sullivan steps into view.

                         SULLIVAN
      You can have as much as you want, too.
      I wont tell your mommy and daddy.
      It'll be our little secret. . .

                        LITTLE BOY
      Thanks mister! You know, you're nicer than my daddy,
      he never lets me have ice cream. He's always yelling
      at me to finish all my homework and get my chores
      done. I sure wish you were my daddy, you seem nice!

As the little boy is telling his story and going on and on about his parents and
his seemingly awful home life, Sullivan starts to zone out in a weird
gaze/stare.

The boy's dialogue becomes inaudible as the SOUND BLENDS INTO Sullivan's
parents' fighting. END ZOOM MED ON Sullivan and Boy.

Little boy notices that Sullivan isn't listening, so he taps on the side of the
truck.

                        LITTLE BOY
      Uh, mister? Mister are you okay?

CLOSE ON Sullivan - he snaps out of his fog and is all smiles again.

                         SULLIVAN
      Uh yeah. . . sure, kid.
      Hey, like I was saying, I have even more in here,
      would you like to see?

OVER SHOULDER Sullivan - on Boy.

                        LITTLE BOY
      I don't know, mommy said never to get in a
      stranger's car.

Sullivan looks over to the back of his truck.

                         SULLIVAN
      But it's all going to melt, and I need someone to

help me eat it. Plus, I thought we were friends now?

Little Boy has a puzzled look on his face, trying to figure out if he should go inside.

                         LITTLE BOY
     Okay, I'll help you!

                          SULLIVAN
     Great...
     go down the end so I can let you in...

WIDE ANGLE - still eating the ice cream cone, he walks to the end of the truck.

LOW ANGLE ON back of truck - Boy enters FRAME as the doors swing open to Sullivan wearing street clothes and a paper ice cream man hat. He reaches down a hand to help him up, and he takes it, steps up into the truck. Smiling, Sullivan pulls the doors closed.

CUT TO:

26 INT. PRISON - WARDEN'S OFFICE - REALITY - DAY

WIDE ANGLE - Enrik is sitting back at his desk with his elbows on the desk and his head in his hands.

Simmons is pacing around the room like a wild animal.

Alvarez sits in a chair in front of the desk still gripping the gun tightly, obviously shaken up by what just happened, seeing his partner get killed and failing to act fast enough.

                          SIMMONS
                          (angry)
     We should have just killed him,
     I had the damn shotgun, I should have just
     pulled the trigger!
                        ENRIK(TOMMY)
                        (looks up)
     You never had a clear shot, there wasn't anything you
     could've done. Murphy -

CLOSE ON Simmons.

                          SIMMONS
                        (cuts off)
     --is dead! Sullivan fucking killed him anyway!
     It didn't make a damn difference what we did or
     didn't do!

CLOSE ON Enrik.

                        ENRIK(TOMMY)
                      (face in his hands)
                    (muttering to himself)
     I knew he would become a problem, I should have
     been more careful, more honest.

WIDE ANGLE - Simmons and Alvarez exchange confused glances.

                        ENRIK(TOMMY)

                    (slams his fists on the desk)
                           (yells)
Damn it! I never wanted it to be like this...

                         SIMMONS
What's with all that "Richie" bullshit anyways?

                         ALVAREZ
Yeah, back in the cell.

CLOSE ON Enrik - he keeps rambling as if Alvarez and Simmons aren't even there.

                      ENRIK(TOMMY)
                  (rubbing his hands on his face)
After all he's done...after all he's put me through.
I can't do it...I still can't do it!

Enrik rests his head on his arms on his desk.

WIDE ANGLE - Simmons and Alvarez keep looking at each other and then back at
Enrik not knowing what is going on.

Simmons walks over to Enrik and insincerely puts a comforting hand on his
shoulder.

                        SIMMONS
   Enrik, what is it you're not telling us?

Enrik is paralyzed with emotion as he remembers the past.

CUT TO:

27 INT. 1960S SUBURBAN HOUSE - KITCHEN - AFTERNOON

HANDHELD ON ten year old, RICHIE - he runs into the kitchen and hides
underneath the sink cabinet, terrified, with a black eye, bloody lip, and
looking generally neglected. He pulls the cabinet door closed softly behind him.

OFF SCREEN - his drunken mother is yelling for him.

                       MOTHER
                      (yelling)
   Richie, Richard Sullivan!
   Get your ass out here!

CLOSE ON Richie - he closes his eyes tightly and tries to stay still.

                       MOTHER
                      (yelling)
   Richard!

WIDE ANGLE - Mother enters the kitchen, stumbling over her own feet as she
walks. She is wearing a faded cotton nightgown, a dirty sweater and dirty
slippers. Her hair has not been brushed in days and she looks older than her
forty years.

CLOSE ON Richie in cabinet - he cringes when he hears her feet on the linoleum
and tries to stay still with his eyes closed.

HANDHELD CLOSE ON Mother - as she fumbles about the room.

                    MOTHER
                    (yelling)
    Where the fuck are you?
    You can't hide from me forever!
    It's your fault your father left, and your
    brother stays out
    all the time with those fucking sluts,
    but not you Richard, I will
                    (louder)
    never let you go! Never!

CLOSE ON Richie - he clamps his hands tightly over his ears and is forcing himself not to start crying.

LOW ANGLE ON cabinet - Mother walks right his hiding spot, and stumbles into the counter, knocking a dish strainer half full of dishes over and they CRASH loudly onto the floor.

Plates and cups SHATTER and a large carving knife falls right outside the cabinet door with a METAL CLANG.

CLOSE ON Mother - she collects herself and keeps moving through the kitchen searching for her son.

                    MOTHER
                    (yelling)
    Do you fucking hear me?
    I will never let you leave me!
    You're my boy! Mine!

WIDE ANGLE - she exits the kitchen through the second doorway.

LOW ANGLE ON cabinet - Richie hearing that she is gone, opens the door a crack sees the knife at BOTTOM OF FRAME, the glimmer of the kitchen light off of it mesmerizes him. PUSH IN CLOSE ON Richie - he stops looking like a scared child as he reaches down for it.

27A INT. 1960S SUBURBAN HOUSE - LIVING ROOM - MOMENTS LATER

WIDE ANGLE ON Mother - shuffling her way through the living room now on her way to the stairs. She stops at the very bottom of the stairs looking up them.

FROM top of stairs ANGLE DOWN ON Mother.

                    MOTHER
    Richard!
                    (pause)
    Come down here you little shit!
                    (long pause)

                    (muttering quietly)
    Slayeth the evil that lives inside you...
    Where they are walking, the Devil walks --
                    (cuts off abruptly)

A pained look comes across her face. SLOW ZOOM - she becomes very still for a second and then pitches forwards and then back, but is still standing.

Blood starts to leak from her open mouth, as she collapses forward onto the steps. END ZOOM ON Richie - standing behind her with bloody knife in hand.

LOW ANGLE ON Richie - his dead eyed, expressionless face staring at her body at the bottom of FRAME.

Suddenly, he screams, leaping onto her body stabbing her over and over.

CUT TO:

28 EXT. 1960s SUBURBAN FAMILY HOME - NIGHT

WIDE ANGLE ON house - as TOMMY walks toward the front door.

28A INT. 1960s SUBURBAN FAMILY HOME - FRONT DOOR - MOMENTS LATER

MED ON Tommy - enters dress in fast-food uniform. He looks exhausted, like he has the weight of the world on his shoulders. Closes door. PULL BACK as he walks forward. PAN INTO POV ON stairway - *covered in blood, but the body is no longer there.*

CLOSE ON Tommy - he reacts in terror to this and assuming there is an intruder, looks around for a weapon and finds a baseball bat laying against the wall.

HANDHELD ON Tommy - he arms himself with the bat, slowly walks into the living room. There is a trail of blood as if a body had been dragged through, and items have been knocked over in it's path.

He proceeds cautiously, ready to swing the bat if needed.

He hears strange noises coming from the kitchen, and freezes. There is a metal CLANGING of pots and pans and a CHOPPING sound, then the garbage disposal kicks on, but GRINDS LOUDLY like it is clogged or broken.

Cautiously, he steps toward the kitchen doorway and peeks around the corner.

Tommy POV - blood is everywhere, the floor, the table, the walls. Wearing his mother's apron, Richie is standing on a stool doing something over the kitchen sink.

> TOMMY
> *(shaky)*
> Richie, what, what are you doing?

> RICHIE
> *(in a normal tone)*
> Cleaning up.

ANGLE ON Riche with Tommy approaching in BACKGROUND.

> TOMMY
> *(scared)*
> Cleaning up... *what?*

COMES INTO FOCUS - as he asks this he peers over Richie's shoulders and into the sink.

Tommy POV - a bloody hand is sticking up out of the garbage disposal and spinning in circles.

TWO SHOT - Richie continues jabbing at it with a wooden spoon to make it go down. Aghast, Tommy stumbles back.

LOW ANGLE Tommy - falls to the floor. Looks over to see the cause of his fall, Mother's blood covered, severed leg at his feet.

Tommy POV - looks around frantically, chopped up bits and pieces of her spread out all over the kitchen.

ABOVE ANGLE WIDE - Tommy tries to get up, but there is so much blood on the floor his hands and feet keep slipping.

> TOMMY
> *(horrified)*
> Richie, what did you do...what the fuck did you do!?

OVER SHOULDER Tommy - on Richie.

> RICHIE
> *(with his back to his brother)*
> She said I'd never ever get to leave. Never.

> TOMMY
> In a year I'll be eighteen, you could have come
> with me, we could have left together!

INSERT: *garbage disposal - the hand finally goes down the disposal with a* GRINDING *sound.*

OVER SHOULDER Tommy - Richie steps down off his stool to get another piece of the mother's body. He has a normal kid look on his face, like none of this is wrong or weird.

> RICHIE
> Well, now we don't have to wait, Tommy.

CLOSE ON Tommy.

DISOLVE TO:

29 INT. PRISON - WARDEN'S OFFICE - REALITY - DAY

CLOSE ON Enrik(Tommy) - sitting at his desk with his head in his hands. He is pale with dark circles under his eyes. Lifts his head and looks lazily at Simmons.

> ENRIK(TOMMY)
> Simmons, do you believe in fate?

OVER SHOULDER Enrik - on Simmons, standing near the door, looks at him oddly.

> SIMMONS
> No sir. . .

CLOSE ON Enrik - as he turns INTO CAMERA with Simmons in the BACKGROUND.

> ENRIK(TOMMY)
> I've spent my entire adult life trying to
> keep bad people behind bars, you know,
> trying to make the world a better place as they say.
> *(pause)*

> ENRIK(TOMMY)

(continued)
Moved to another state, went in
the total opposite direction in every
possible way. Hell, I even changed my name. . .

Simmons steps over in front of the desk, grabs Enrik by the lapels, pulls him to his feet.

TWO SHOT.

                    SIMMONS
          What the hell are you saying, Enrik?

                    ENRIK(TOMMY)
          And yet, here I am, and here he is.

                    SIMMONS
                (annoyed and angry)
          Enrik, what the fuck is going on!

                    ENRIK(TOMMY)
                (snaps at Simmons)
          He's my god-damn brother!

LOW ANGLE/OVER SHOULDER Enrik - on Simmons as pushes Enrik back into his chair.

                    SIMMONS
                (in complete disbelief)
          Your brother?? That psycho killed over thirty
          people! Half of them were children! He killed Johnny!
          He killed Murphy! He--

                    ENRIK(TOMMY)
                (cuts Simmons off)
          And he's still my brother.

Simmons looks completely floored, just astonished.

ANGLE ON phone with Enrik in FOCUS IN BACKGROUND - shakes his head sadly, looks down at his desk.

Phone RINGS.

Enrik(Tommy) gestures to Simmons to leave the office.

CUT TO:

30 INT. PRISON - WARDEN'S OFFICE - OUTER HALL - MOMENTS LATER

MED ON Simmons - steps out of Enrik's office, justas he answers the phone in BACKGROUNND. Simmons CLOSES DOOR.

WIDE ANGLE - frustrated and confused, Simmons walks into another office, looks around to make sure no one sees him and shuts the door behind him.

30A INT. PRISON - OUTER OFFICE - MOMENTS LATER

LOW ANGLE FROM desk - he walks and picks up the phone, dials Governor Adams' number.

                    SIMMONS

                         (into phone)
        Governor Adams please.
                         (pause)
        Sorry to bother you sir, but this is John Simmons,
                         (pauses listening)
        No, we have never met, I am a guard at the state
        prison,
                         (pauses listening)

        Well sir, I have some information
        that might be of interest to you...

CUT TO:

31 INT. PRISON - SULLIVAN'S CELL - REALITY - LATER

WIDE ON Sullivan - laying on his bed with his eyes closed.

OFF SCREEN SOUND - the door leading to the Warden's office opens and closes.

Sullivan doesn't flinch.

OFF SCREEN SOUND - heavy FOOTSTEPS approach, they stop in front of Sullivan's
cell.

Simmons appears in the far edge of FRAME.

                         SIMMONS
        Enrik might be having a hard time
        sending you off, but I sure as Hell don't...

Sullivan appears to be asleep.

Running his club along the bars, Simmons continues down walk way. CLICK! CLACK!
CLICK!

PUSH CLOSE ON Sullivan - his eyes open and stare menacingly at Simmons as he
walks away.

CUT TO:

32 INT. PRISON - THE WARDEN'S OFFICE - REALITY - LATER

Phone RINGS.

CLOSE ON Enrik - answers the phone on first ring.

                         ENRIK(TOMMY)
        Warden's office.
                         (pause)
        Hello Governor Adams -

On the other end of the phone Governor Adams cuts him off abruptly.

                         ENRIK(TOMMY)
                         (pause)
        - yes, yes I understand.

                              (pause)
          No, I wont let my personal feelings
          interfere with what needs to be done...

Hangs up the phone. Looks straight ahead, brokenhearted.

CUT TO:

33 INT. PRISON - BREAK ROOM - REALITY - LATER

WIDE ANGLE

SIMMONS is on his phone, texting, browsing, etc.

ALVAREZ is at the counter, looking for a drink but all he finds is coffee.

The mood in the room is tense and eerily quiet.

                         ALVAREZ
                      (to Simmons)
          Is there anything *stronger* than coffee around
          here?

                         SIMMONS
                       (deadpan)
          Hah... this place? Good luck.

   BOWEN enters the room.

                         BOWEN
                       (serious)
          Hey. . .
          Enrik wants to see us,
          all of us.

                         ALVAREZ
          What the hell is going on now?

                         BOWEN
          Not sure, but he just got
          off the phone with the Governor.

Simmons looks down, guilty.

CUT TO:

34 INT. PRISON - THE WARDEN'S OFFICE - REALITY - LATER

HAND HELD FOLLOWING Simmons, Bowen, and Alvarez as they burst through the door.
Enrik is sitting at his desk with his head in his hands.

                      ENRIK(TOMMY)
          I know this isn't normally how things are done,
          but in light of recent events, the Governor doesn't
          want me present during Richard Sullivan's execution.

CLOSE ON Enrik - he eyes Simmons coldly because he knows that he must have
informed Governor Adams.

CLOSE ON Simmons - he meets his gaze.

WIDE ANGLE.

                    ENRIK(TOMMY)
          Simmons, you're in charge now.
          I expect the rest of you to listen to
          him as if he were me.

                    SIMMONS
                  (clears his throat)
          Thanks Enrik, I appreciate you giving me this chance
          to prove myself. I wont let you or the Governor down.

Enrik coldly nods his head, stands, walks to the door, grabs his coat off the
hook and exits the office silently.

Before the other guards can start asking questions, Simmons begins commanding
them.

                    SIMMONS
          You all know what needs to be done.
          Do not let your guard down, you saw what happened
            to Johnny and Murphy...
          None of us are safe until he's dead.

Bowen and Alvarez nod in agreement, but still look a bit confused as to why
Enrik has been replaced by Simmons.

                    SIMMONS
          Okay.
                  (pause)
          Let's go.

CUT TO:

35 INT. PRISON - WALKWAY - REALITY - LATER

WIDE ANGLE ON Sullivan's cell - Enrik approaches wearing his coat, all ready to
go home. He stops in front of the cell, his back to CAMERA.

CLOSE ON Enrik - he stares at Sullivan and can't help but remember him as a
child, and his eyes start to water.

OVER SHOULDER Enrik on Sullivan - he's laying on his side facing the wall,
seemingly asleep.

                    ENRIK(TOMMY)
          Hey Richie, are you awake?

Sullivan rolls over onto his back, using his arm to block out the light.

35A INT. PRISON - SULLIVAN'S CELL - REALITY - SAME

CLOSE ON Sullivan - because of the medication he had earlier he is seeing
everything as it really is. He finally recognizes Enrik as his brother Tommy.

                    SULLIVAN
          Yeah...what'd you want?

PULL BACK WIDE/TWO SHOT.

                    ENRIK(TOMMY)
I just wanted to say goodbye...

                    SULLIVAN
Running away again, figures, you always were
the weak one.

                    ENRIK(TOMMY)
Look Richie, I know I haven't been
a perfect brother, but you brought all of
this upon yourself, you've got to see that.

Sullivan sits up and stares accusingly at Enrik.

                    SULLIVAN
Oh don't play big brother now, *Warden*,
you were always pretty good with your little
disappearing act whenever the shit hit the fan,
weren't you?

Enrik takes a step back, not expecting him to be so coherent.

                    ENRIK(TOMMY)
What are you talking about? I always -

Sullivan puts both feet on the floor and eyes Enrik like a wild animal.

CLOSE ON Sullivan.

                    SULLIVAN
- always what!?
                    (pause)
Always ignored my screams when she beat me,
when she tortured me! And when she was dead, what'd
you do? Convinced your "little problem" to join the
army! I bet you prayed that I'd die in there!

CLOSE ON Enrik.

                    ENRIK(TOMMY)
I tried my best Richie, I did everything I could
to protect you. . . from all of *this*.
But here you are.
Here *we are*.

CLOSE ON Sullivan.

                    SULLIVAN
I was the only one with enough balls
to give that bitch what she deserved.

OVER SHOULDER Enrik on Sullivan.

                    ENRIK(TOMMY)
You can't make excuses for the path you went down,
you weren't the only one that lived with her!
And I didn't end up killing people because of it!

                    SULLIVAN
                    (laughs and looks down)
You really are amazing, you know that?
You and your little guards saying that

I don't live in reality?

WIDE ANGLE Sullivan - he stands up and starts walking slowly towards Enrik.

> SULLIVAN
> I guess you don't remember helping me
> cram our mother down the garbage disposal and then
> *burning* what was left of her?

Enrik looks guilty and torn.

OVER SHOULDER Enrik - he jumps back startled, as Sullivan grabs the bars and starts yelling.

> SULLIVAN
> *(yelling)*
> Just because the government PAYS you to
> execute people doesn't mean you ain't a
> cold blooded killer!

Enrik looks down.

> SULLIVAN
> *(yelling)*
> You think you're soooo different than me,
> you think you're some kinda 'keeper of the peace',
> protector of the innocent?
> Ha, more like some self-righteous prick
> doing penance for letting his baby brother
> kill all those 'innocent' people.

Sullivan in a rage sticks his right arm as far through the bars as it can reach trying to grasp at Enrik.

CLOSE ON Enrik - he stares at what has become of his brother with tears in his eyes and the look of heartbreak on his face.

OVER SHOULDER Enrik on Sullivan - he's getting so worked up that REALITY STARTS TO SHIFT IN HIS MIND, and although he still sees Enrik as he truly is, he starts believing again that he tortured and killed all the other inmates he imagined.

> SULLIVAN
> *(yelling)*
> I've been rotting in this cell watching you and your
> guards torture and kill everyone here, what the
> hell do you call that if not cold-blooded murder!?

CLOSE ON Enrik - he looks down, exasperated and finally realizing that there is no hope for his brother. Sullivan needs to die to protect society.

> ENRIK(TOMMY)
> *(softly)*
> Oh Richie, you are so far gone...

35B INT. PRISON - WALKWAY - REALITY - SAME

WIDE ANGLE ON Sullivan's cell- knowing that there is no hope left of saving Sullivan, Enrik turns and walks down the walkway towards the exit. SLIGHT PAN WITH Enrik/down walkway - Sullivan IN EDGE OF FRAME.

> SULLIVAN

They should strap you into that chair right next to me!

Right before he reaches the door he stops and looks at Sullivan.

                    ENRIK(TOMMY)
                    (sadly)
        I pity you Richie, years and years of trying to help
        you, and what has come of it?
                    (pause)
        As far as I'm concerned,
        my brother died a long time ago.

He puts his hand on the doorknob and starts to exit.
Sullivan clamps both hands tightly around the cell bars.

                    SULLIVAN
                    (screaming)
        Get back here Tommy!
        You change your name and think that don't make us
        brothers anymore?
                    (pause)
        Get back here you son of a bitch!

Enrik walks through the door closing it behind him.

FADE OUT:

FADE IN:

36 INT. PRISON - SULLIVAN'S CELL - REALITY - LATER

WIDE LOW ANGLE ON Sullivan - he is sitting on the edge of his bed, with his feet
shackled.

SOUND OF the door opening at end of walkway.

EDGE OF FRAME - Simmons, Bowen, Alvarez and FATHER ALEXANDER, a priest, arrive
at his cell.

                    BOWEN
                    (to Sullivan)
        Father Alexander is here to read your last rites.
            (pause)
            (to Father Alexander)
        Just. . . (pause)
        Be careful.

                    SIMMONS
        Open it.

Bowen opens the cell door.

Father Alexander steps through. He carries a Bible with him. Cell door closes.

                    FATHER ALEXANDER
        Hello, Richard.

Sullivan is unresponsive.

WIDE ANGLE - Father Alexander starts to walk towards Sullivan and he puts a hand
on his shoulder.

FATHER ALEXANDER
(understanding and sympathetic)
The Lord is here for you, my son, if you're willing
to seek forgiveness.

Upon hearing these words, Sullivan quickly snaps and aggressively shrugs off
Father Alexander's hand.

SULLIVAN
(angry and mocking)
The Lord?

Father Alexander starts to back off, fearing Sullivan's reaction.

OVER SHOULDER Father ON Sullivan - he starts to rise as he continues, slowly
taking steps towards Father Alexander as he mocks him every time he says the
word "Father".

SULLIVAN
(angrily and rhetorically mocking)
You ever *kill* someone, *Father?*
See them in their death throes as they struggle to
breathe their last breath, clinging to the life
you're taking away with your own hands?
You ever wonder what that feels like, Father?
To play GOD.

WIDE ANGLE - Sullivan closes in on Father Alexander and if it weren't for the
shackles at his feet, he'd be much closer to him.

CLOSE ON Father Alexander - he is horrified, as if he's seeing the devil
himself. His face pressed against the bars, he panics and starts to call for the
guards.

FATHER ALEXANDER
Guards!

Standing behind him, Sullivan starts laughing, amused at Father Alexander's
distress. Bowen opens the cell door as Father Alexander rushes out.

SULLIVAN
(mocking as the Father bolts out the door past Bowen)
Where's your God now?

36A INT. PRISON - WALKWAY - REALITY - CONTINUOUS

HANDHELD - Father passes Alvarez on the way out of the metal door.

Alvarez
Are you all right, Father?

Father Alexander looks back at the cell area from where he came, thankful to be
out of there.

FATHER ALEXANDER
(panicked)
He's in God's hands now. . .

Father Alexander continues to rush and exits through the door.

ANGLE ON - the guards standing outside of Sullivan's cell. Alvarez ENTERS FRAME
joining them.

                              SIMMONS
                    (quietly to Bowen and Alvarez)
           Okay boys, remember. . . be ready for anything.
                           (to Sullivan)
           Put your back against the wall and extend your hands   out.

OVER SHOULDER Simmons - on Sullivan as he does as he is told.

CLOSE ON the guards - they exchange suspicious glances, as if this is just going
too easily.

WIDE ANGLE - the three guards enter the cell.

HAND HELD - Bowen puts hand cuffs on Sullivan, runs chain through waist belt -
PAN DOWN - as Alvarez connects the chain to the leg shackles.

Sullivan doesn't even try to resist.

WIDE - Bowen and Alvarez stand on either side of him and guide him out of the
cell.

                              SIMMONS
                            (mockingly)
           Dead man walking! Dead man walking!

DOLLY BACK as they start to walk Sullivan down the walkway. He begins to look
nervous, like a trapped animal.

OVER SHOULDER Sullivan - as they arrive at the door that leads to the electric
chair.

LOW ANGLE ON Sullivan - he falls to his knees weeping.

                              BOWEN
           Sullivan?

Sullivan gets into a praying position, crying.

                              SULLIVAN
           Please don't do this! I'm not like all the others.
           I'm not like Sammy and Tudley,
           I've never done anything wrong in my life!
           Oh my God, you can't do this to me!

HIGH ANGLE/OVER SHOULDER Simmons - looking down on Sullivan.

                              SIMMONS
           Get your ass up Sullivan, you ain't fooling anybody.

                              SULLIVAN
           No, no, I beg you, please...!

The door opens. The intense light from the room cascades over Sullivan.

OVER SHOULDER Sullivan - on Enrik standing in the doorway.

CLOSE ON Simmons - no one knew he was still in the building, and Simmons glares at him angrily.

                SIMMONS
               (to Enrik)
What the hell are you still doing here?

CLOSE ON Enrik.

              ENRIK(TOMMY)
I'll take care of this, you tried your best.

OVER SHOULDER Simmons - on Enrik.

                SIMMONS
Like hell you will!
Governor Adams gave me strict orders -

              (cuts off)

              ENRIK(TOMMY)
I don't care what the Governor wants,
this is my problem, and I need to be the
one who ends it.
             (to Sullivan)
Come on Richie, get up, it's time to go.

WIDE ANGLE - proudly, Enrik walks forward, places his hand onto Sullivan's shoulder.

Still on his knees pleading, Sullivan looks up at his brother.

In a huff, Simmons takes off down the hallway to phone the Governor.

TWO SHOT ON Sullivan and Enrik.

               SULLIVAN
Please! Please don't do this!

              ENRIK(TOMMY)
              (coldly)
Richie, don't make me have these men drag you away...

               SULLIVAN
But I'm innocent, don't do this Tommy!

WIDE ANGLE - Enrik nods to the Guards and they both grab an arm of Sullivan. DOLLY BACK as they start dragging him through the doorway and into the room where the electric chair is.

36B INT. PRISON - EXECUTION CHAMBER - REALITY - SAME

Terrified, Sullivan enters the STARK WHITE room. His eyes drawn instantly to THE ELECTRIC CHAIR in the center. He freezes, as the smell of the hundreds of men that have fired in this room hits him. RILEY is in the room already, preparing the chair.

               SULLIVAN
            (whispering)
Oh God...

OVER SHOULDER Sullivan - on the electric chair. Built around 1920 it's a fairly simple machine of wood, leather straps and copper wires.

DOGGIE CAM ON Sullivan - he falls to his knees.

RILEY
(to Sullivan)

    All right, all set...

ECU ON Sullivan - he stares at the floor trembling.

ECU ON Enrik - looks concerned.

LOW WIDE ANGLE - Bowen pulls on Sullivan's arm.

BOWEN

    Come on Sullivan, I said get up!

Suddenly, Simmons enters the room, pushes Bowen to the side.

SIMMONS

    He said get up, Sullivan.

Slowly, Sullivan looks up at Simmons, notices that he is carrying a handgun. With a menacing/wild look in his eyes, Sullivan smiles.

CAMERA RISES WITH Sullivan - as all 6ft 5 of him stands.

Simmons, scared, takes a cautious step backwards.

SIMMONS

    Hey...what the...?

In one quick motion Sullivan grabs the gun out Simmons' holster almost ripping it off the belt.

LOW ANGLE/OVER SHOULDER Simmons - as he falls over backwards, the rest of the guards jump towards Sullivan to try and restrain him.

OVER SHOULDER Sullivan - still handcuffed, he aims the gun right in Alvarez's face and pulls the trigger. BOOM! The bullet rips directly into his forehead.

SLOW MOTION - Alvarez falls straight back onto the floor next to Simmons.

LOW ANGLE ON Alvarez - blood spattered across his face, his DEAD eyes wide open. RACK FOCUS to Simmons looking on in FROZEN HORROR.

SIMMONS

    Alvarez!

Sullivan looks down at Simmons as everyone else starts backing up towards the exterior walls.

SULLIVAN

    Wrong move.

OVER HEAD WIDE ANGLE - everyone backs away as Sullivan aims the gun.

PUSH CLOSE ON Enrik - frozen against the wall in shock.

PUSH CLOSE ON Simmons - as he starts to stand, in an attempt to defuse the situation.

SIMMONS

Sullivan, just keep calm --

PUSH CLOSE ON Sullivan - aims gun. FIRES.

CLOSE ON Simmons - before he finishes the word "calm", Sullivan shoots him right in the chest. Gasping for air, Simmons stares at Sullivan in shock.

OVER SHOULDER Sullivan - on Simmons as he SLUMPS forward. DEAD.

MED ON Enrik - he points to the opposite corner of the room.

> ENRIK
> *(yelling)*
> Sound the alarm!

Sullivan POV - Riley makes a run to sound the alarm, but Sullivan shoots him in the back.

MED ON Riley - as the bullet EXPLODES out chest. He CRASHES into the wall, slides down dead.

OVER SHOULDER Sullivan - aims at Bowen, who quickly raises his hands out.

> BOWEN
> WAIT!

Sullivan lowers the gun. BOOM! Bowen's right knee EXPLODES. Screaming in agony, he topples to the floor like a house of cards.

LOW ANGLE ON Bowen - Sullivan in background walks over RACK FOCUS PAN UP as he stands over, aims, and shoots Bowen in head.

CAMERA RISES HEAD ON CLOSE ON Sullivan as he looks forward.
RACK FOCUS TO Enrik standing against the wall behind Sullivan. The only two left alive.

TWO SHOT - Sullivan turns around, aims the gun at his brother.

> SULLIVAN
> You son of a bitch! You were going to put me down
> like a dog...your own brother!

> ENRIK(TOMMY)
> What choice did I have! Look at what you've done!
> This is all you've ever done!

> SULLIVAN
> Shut up! Spare me your bullshit!

> ENRIK(TOMMY)
> If you kill me there will be no one
> left to fight for you. I can protect you!
> I can make things right!

> SULLIVAN
> *(dryly)*
> HA! And you've done a great job so far!
> You've been out of my life for over twenty
> years, think I can get used to you being
> gone--
> permanently.

CLOSE ON Sullivan - fires the gun into CAMERA BANG! THUD!

FADE TO BLACK:

FADE IN:

37 INT. OFFICE MR. BATES OFFICE - RECEPTIONIST OUTER OFFICE - MORNING

Early 2000's.

MED ANGLE ON the receptionist, MS. PRINCE - she is sitting at a desk outside of Mr. Bates, office. Sullivan is standing before her with his back to CAMERA.

> SULLIVAN
> I need to speak to Mr. Bates.

> MS. PRINCE
> *(doing computer work and not looking directly at Sullivan)*
> I'm sorry sir, but Mr. Bates is busy right now and -

> SULLIVAN
> - Fine.

Sullivan cuts her off and bursts into Mr. Bates' office.

> MS. PRINCE
> Sir? SIR!

Sullivan SLAMS the office door closed behind him.

MS. Prince picks up the phone and presses a button.

> MS. PRINCE
> *(terrified)*
> Security, you need to get up here right away!

CUT TO:

38 INT. OFFICE BUILDING - MR.BATES OFFICE - MORNING

Sullivan's POV - Mr. Bates is sitting at a desk. There is a computer on his desk which he keeps looking at as he is talking on the phone.

> MR.BATES
> *(into phone)*
> Yeah, like I told you already I got the email,
> but I still don't understand what is the
> hold-up with the merger.

As the CAMERA MOVES CLOSER on Mr.Bates, he remains fixated on his conversation and doesn't look up.

> SULLIVAN
> *(off screen)*
> *(politely)*
> Excuse me Mr. Bates.

Still fixated on his computer screen and the phone call, Mr. Bates doesn't look up but holds up his pointer finger to signal, 'one second'.

> MR.BATES

                              (to person on phone-annoyed)
          You keep talking in circles, look, if you
          can't give me a straight answer, then get me
          someone that can.

                              SULLIVAN
                              (off screen)
                              (politely)
          Mr.Bates, I need to talk to you, it's important.

Mr.Bates still doesn't look up. He puts the phone against his shoulder and head
to hold it in place while he starts typing with both hands.

                              MR.BATES
                              (to person on phone)
          What attachment? There is no attach -
                              (cuts off)
Mr. Bates doesn't finish his sentence because a large bloody kitchen knife
slides across the desk towards him, leaving blood all over his paperwork.

He looks up and the phone falls from his shoulder and hits the ground with a
CLANK.

                         VOICE ON OTHER END OF PHONE
          Hello? Mr. Bates? Helllloooo?

PUSH IN CLOSE ON Mr. Bates - staring at Sullivan frozen in terror.

As Sullivan talks, the CAMERA PANS INTO Mr. Bates POV ON Sullivan standing in
front of his desk wearing a greyish blue janitor's uniform/coveralls. He is
covered in blood spatter, begins talking as if nothing odd is going on at all.

                              SULLIVAN
          Sorry to bother you Mr. Bates, I hope
          that phone call wasn't too important.

OVER SHOULDER Sullivan on Mr. Bates - he folds his hands in front of him on the
desk, sees that he just put his hands on the bloody papers, and moves his hands
quickly into his lap.

He looks up at Sullivan trying his best to play along and remain calm.

                              MR.BATES
                              (nervously)
          No, no, not important at all if
          one of my employees needs to talk to me.

OVER SHOULDER Mr. Bates on Sullivan.

                              SULLIVAN
          Excellent. I wanted to talk to you about
          taking an early retirement, you see-
                              (cuts off)
Sullivan is cut off by the office door slamming open.

Two armed police officers along with the security guard enter. The security
guard gestures towards Sullivan and the two officers move in, OFFICER CHRIS BELL
and OFFICER #2. Officer Chris Bell speaks as he slowly steps towards Sullivan,
one hand on his gun and the other hand in a cautionary gesture. Officer #2
trails behind by a few feet.

                         SECURITY GUARD
          That's him.

OFFICER CHRIS BELL
Richard Sullivan?

Sullivan looks over his shoulder at the cop and then back at Mr. Bates with a confused expression, like he has no idea he is covered in blood, etc.

SULLIVAN
Umm, yes?

OFFICER CHRIS BELL
(yelling)
Please place your hands flat on the desk and do NOT   make a move!

IMPROVISED FIGHT SCENE - Sullivan resists arrest.

CUT TO:

39 INT. PRISON - EXECUTION CHAMBER - LATER

CLOSE ON Enrik's face only. He is unconscious from a bullet graze wound across his forehead. PULL BACK WIDE to reveal him strapped into the electric chair with Sullivan standing before him.

OVER SHOULDER Sullivan on Enrik - as he checks all of the straps on and then makes sure that the electric cap is firmly on his head.

Sullivan slaps him in the face to wake him up.

Enrik doesn't move. He has lost alot of blood from being shot, but Sullivan had intentionally just wounded and not killed him with the bullet.

CLOSE ON Sullivan - he slaps him again.

SULLIVAN
(mockingly)
Wakey, wakey Mr. Sullivan. HAH!

CLOSE ON Enrik - he slowly opens his eyes and when he tries to move he looks down and sees that he is in the electric chair.

ENRIK(TOMMY)
Huh? Richie?
What are you doing?

TWO SHOT.

SULLIVAN
You can change your name a hundred times
but you'll always be just plain old
Tommy Sullivan to me...

ENRIK(TOMMY)
(yelling and squirming)
Help! Help! Somebody please!

SULLIVAN
(yelling mockingly)

Help! Help!
                              (laughs)
Who do you think is going to hear you?

                    ENRIK(TOMMY)
                     (panicked)
Please Richie, don't do this.

                    SULLIVAN
Don't do what? Can't you see I'm helping you?
Obviously, you're not very good at your job.
                    (pauses, thinking)
Actually, you've never been very good at anything.
You failed to save me from becoming what I am,
you failed to save all those people I killed, and
now you've even failed to save yourself.

                    ENRIK(TOMMY)
Even if you kill me, you'll never escape!
There'll be cops surrounding the entire place!
They'll get you. They'll chase you down.

WIDE ANGLE - Sullivan walks over to the switch on the wall, continuing as if he
didn't even hear anything Enrik just said.

                    SULLIVAN
I'm not as stupid as you, big brother.
I know I'm a dead man either way.
                     (pauses)
But, just between you and me...
this was never about escape.

OVER SHOULDER Enrik on Sullivan - as he puts the gun against his temple, and
puts his free hand on the electric chair switch. Grips it tightly.

                    SULLIVAN
I've got one bullet left in this gun...
but it's not for you.

CLOSE ON Enrik - suddenly, he realizes what Sullivan is planning to do, and
frantically tries to wriggle out of the chair.

                    ENRIK(TOMMY)
                 (panicked screams)
Richie, no! Don't do this! No!

SLOW MOTION - CLOSE ON Sullivan - he pulls the trigger, shooting himself through
the head, blood and brains spatter across the white wall, as his body begins to
slide and the electric chair switch is pulled down.

MED ON Enrik - as the electricity surges through his body. PUSH IN CLOSE ON
Enrik - as blood pours from his eyes, mouth, nose, ears. Finally, his eyes
EXPLODE as the surge of electricity continues.

CUT TO:

40 INT. 1960s SUBURBAN FAMILY HOME - UPSTAIRS BEDROOM - AFTERNOON

WIDE ANGLE - the room appears empty. SLOW PUSH ON closet door.

41 INT. 1960s SUBURBAN FAMILY HOME - UPSTAIRS BEDROOM - CLOSET - SAME

LOW ANGLE TWO SHOT - Richie and Tommy huddled together in the corner.

                          SULLIVAN
        I'm scared Tommy.

                          MOTHER
                    (screaming off screen)
        Where the fuck are you kids!?

                          ENRIK(TOMMY)
        Just keep quiet Richie. Whatever happens I wont
        let her hurt you, I wont let anyone hurt you. . .

CUT TO:

42 INT. PRISON - EXECUTION CHAMBER - LATER

WIDE ABOVE ANGLE ON both Enrik(Tommy) and Sullivan dead in the execution room.
Smoke billows out from Enrik's eye sockets as Sullivan lay in a massive pool of
his own blood. The lights begin to flicker as the massive amount of electricity
expended begins to blow the breakers.

FADE TO BLACK:

The final line OFF SCREEN by young Enrik(Tommy).

                          ENRIK(TOMMY)
                    (off screen - continued)
        . . .ever again.

                       -THE END-

pencils

by

Kevin CHRISTENSEN

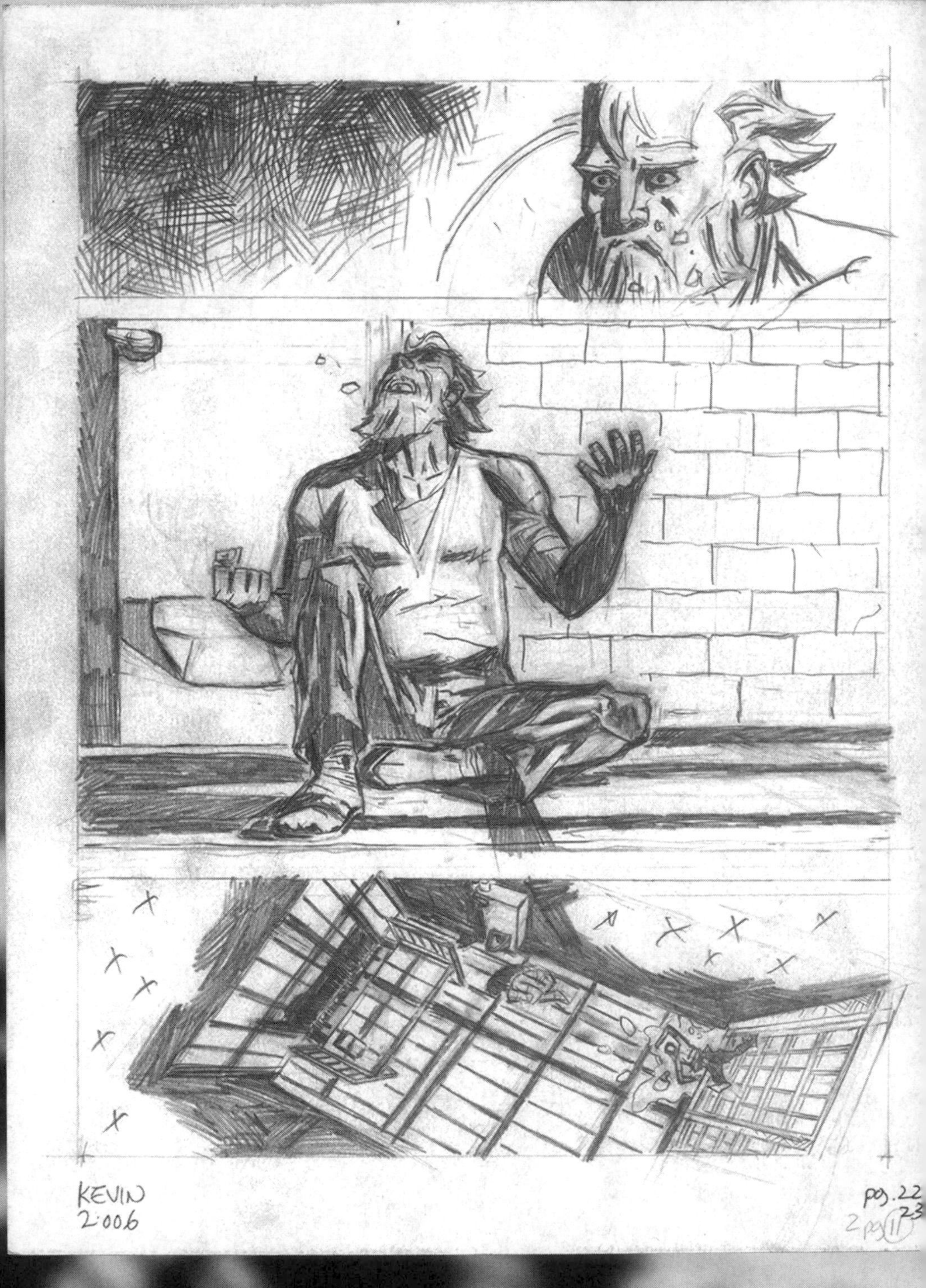
KEVIN
2006
pg. 22
23
2 pg 11

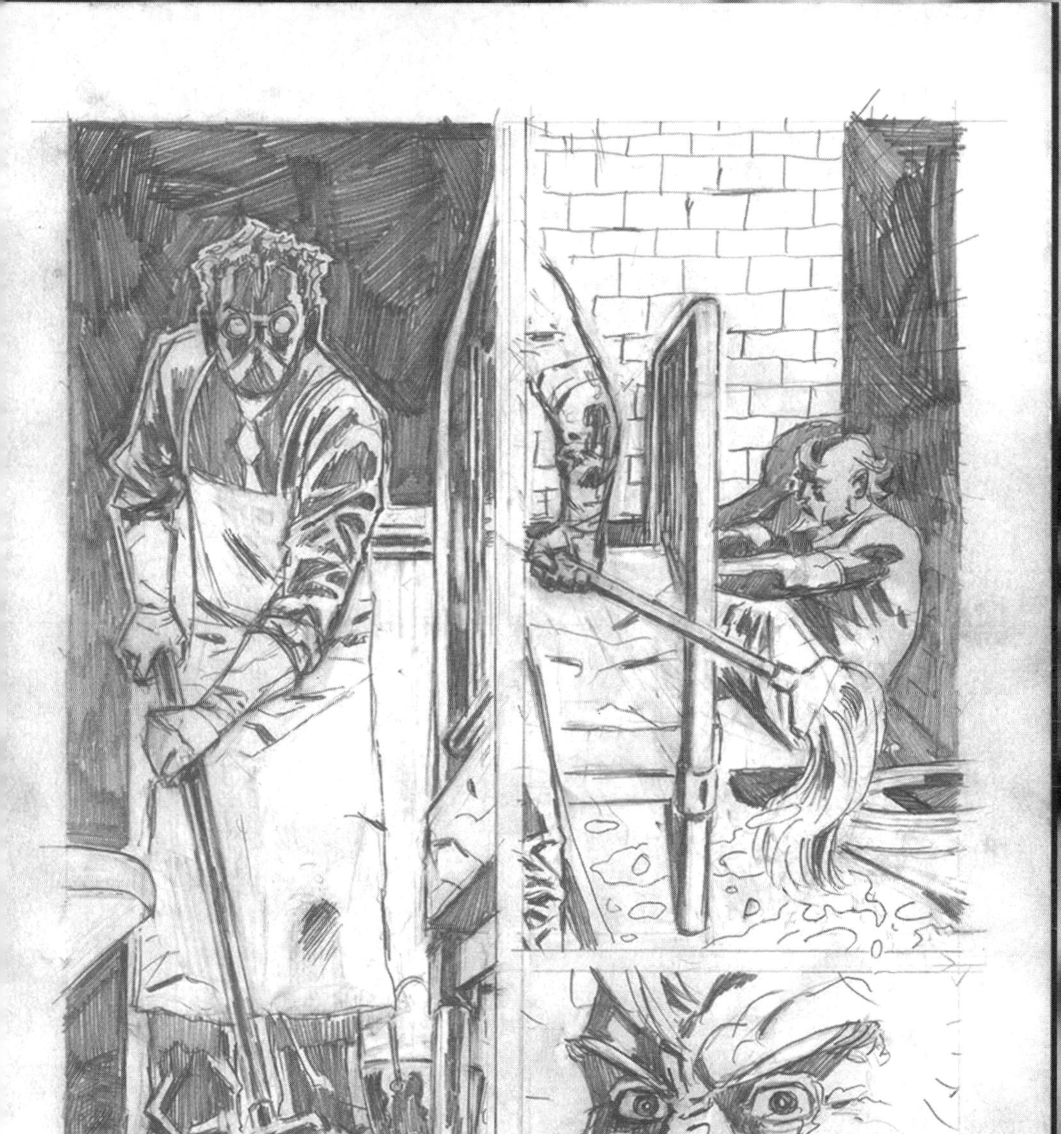
KEVIN
2006
pg.24
2 pg 12

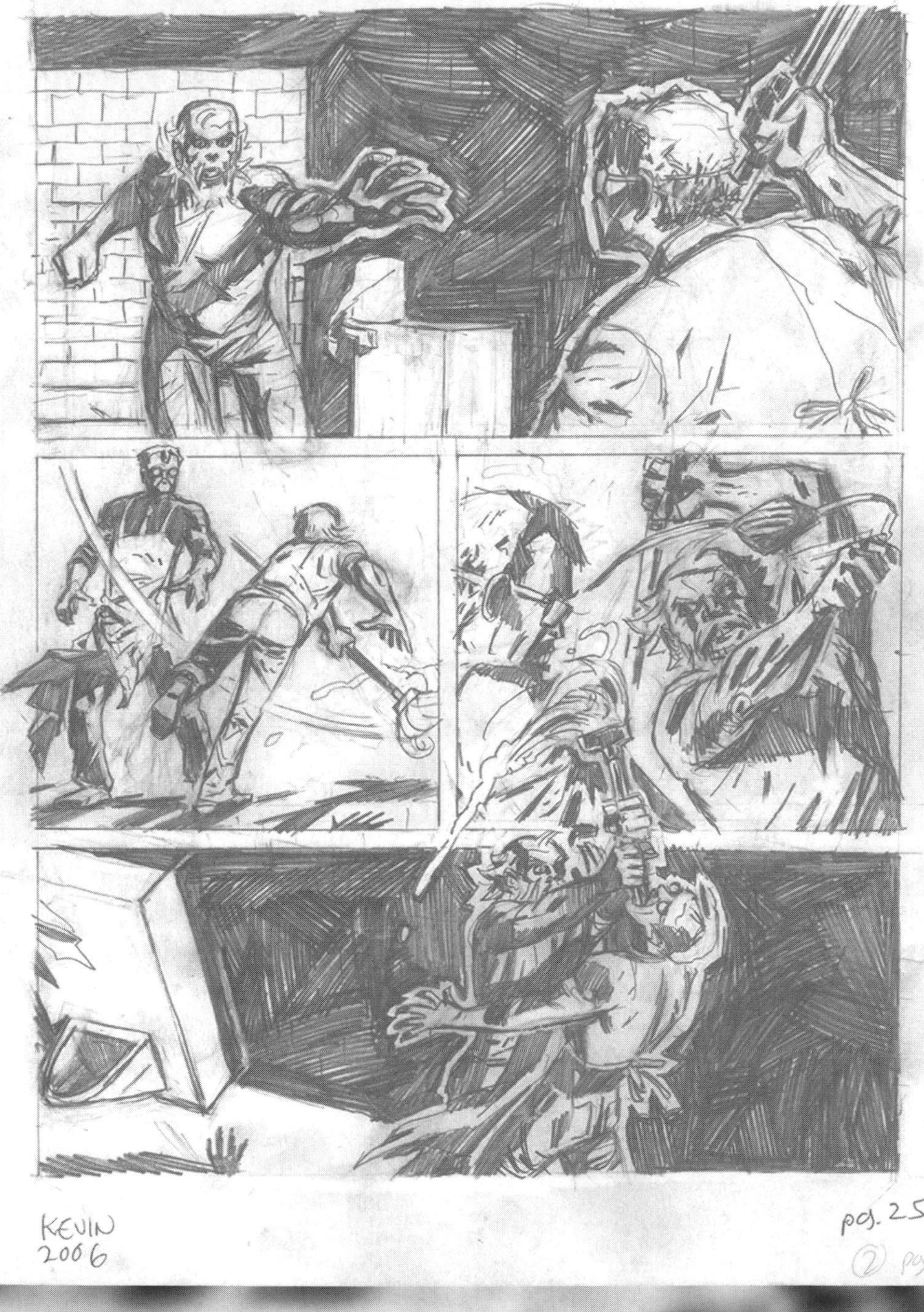

KEVIN
2006

pg. 25

(2) pg13

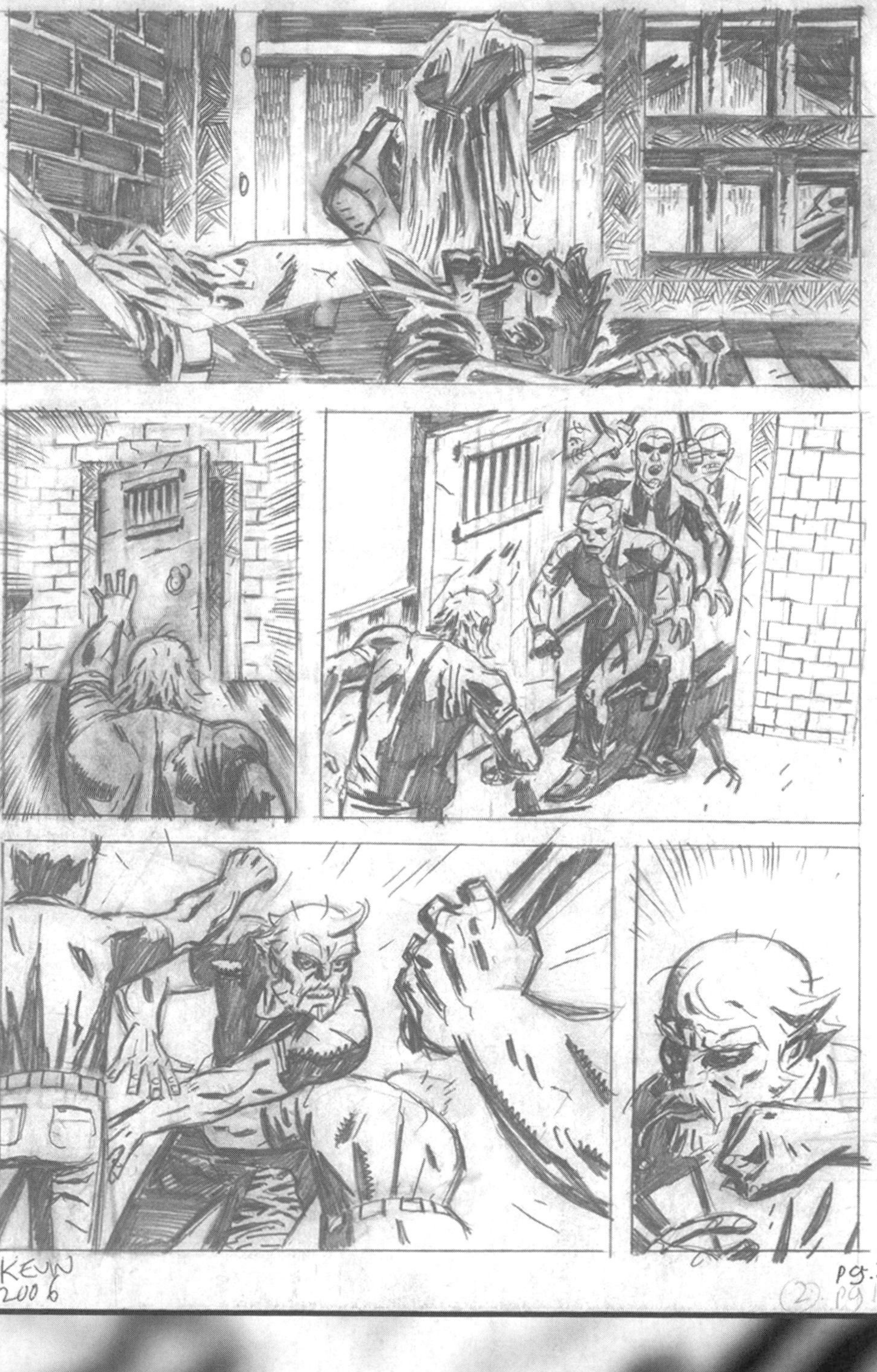

KEVIN
2006

pg.26
(2) pg 14

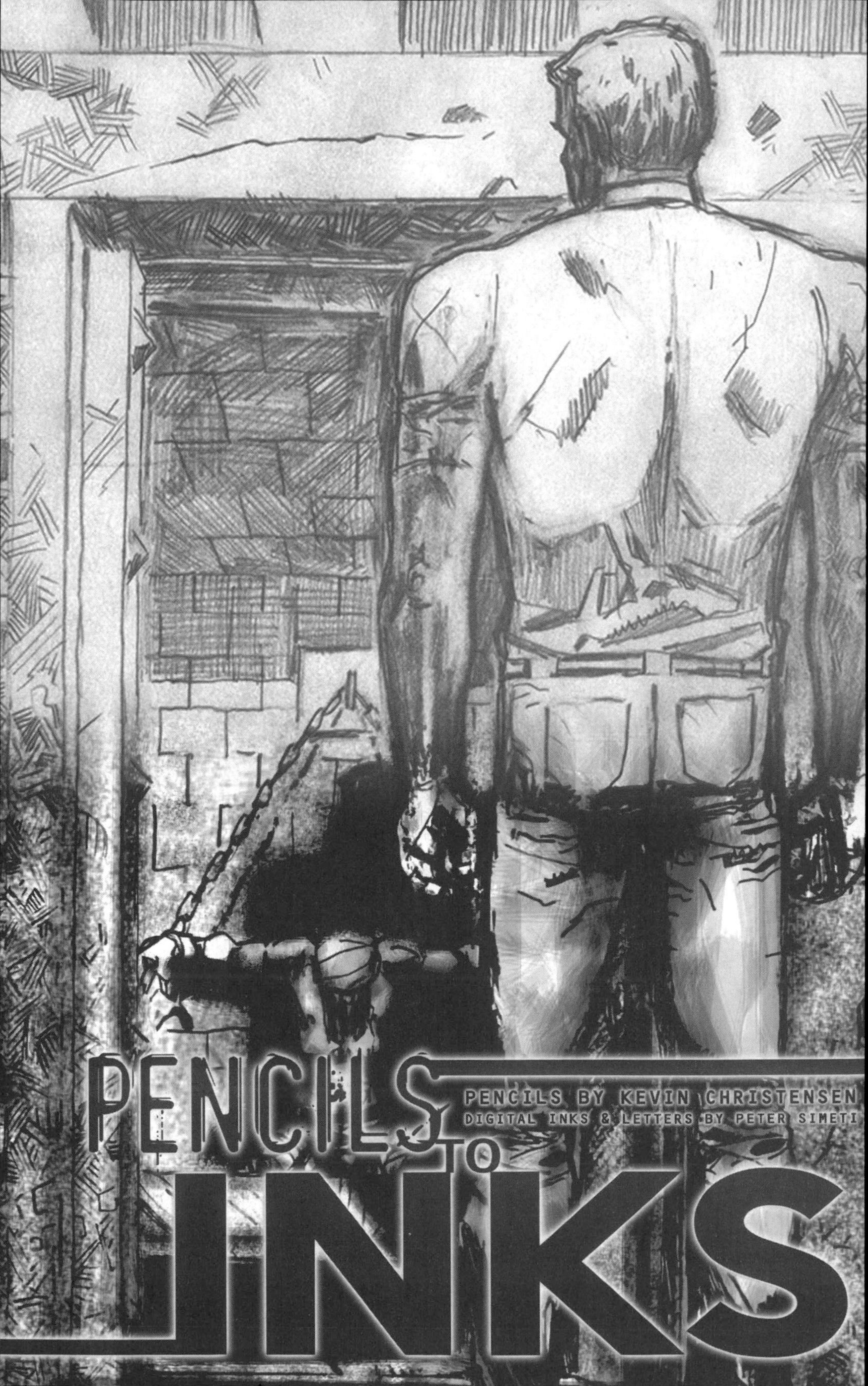
PENCILS TO INKS
PENCILS BY KEVIN CHRISTENSEN
DIGITAL INKS & LETTERS BY PETER SIMETI

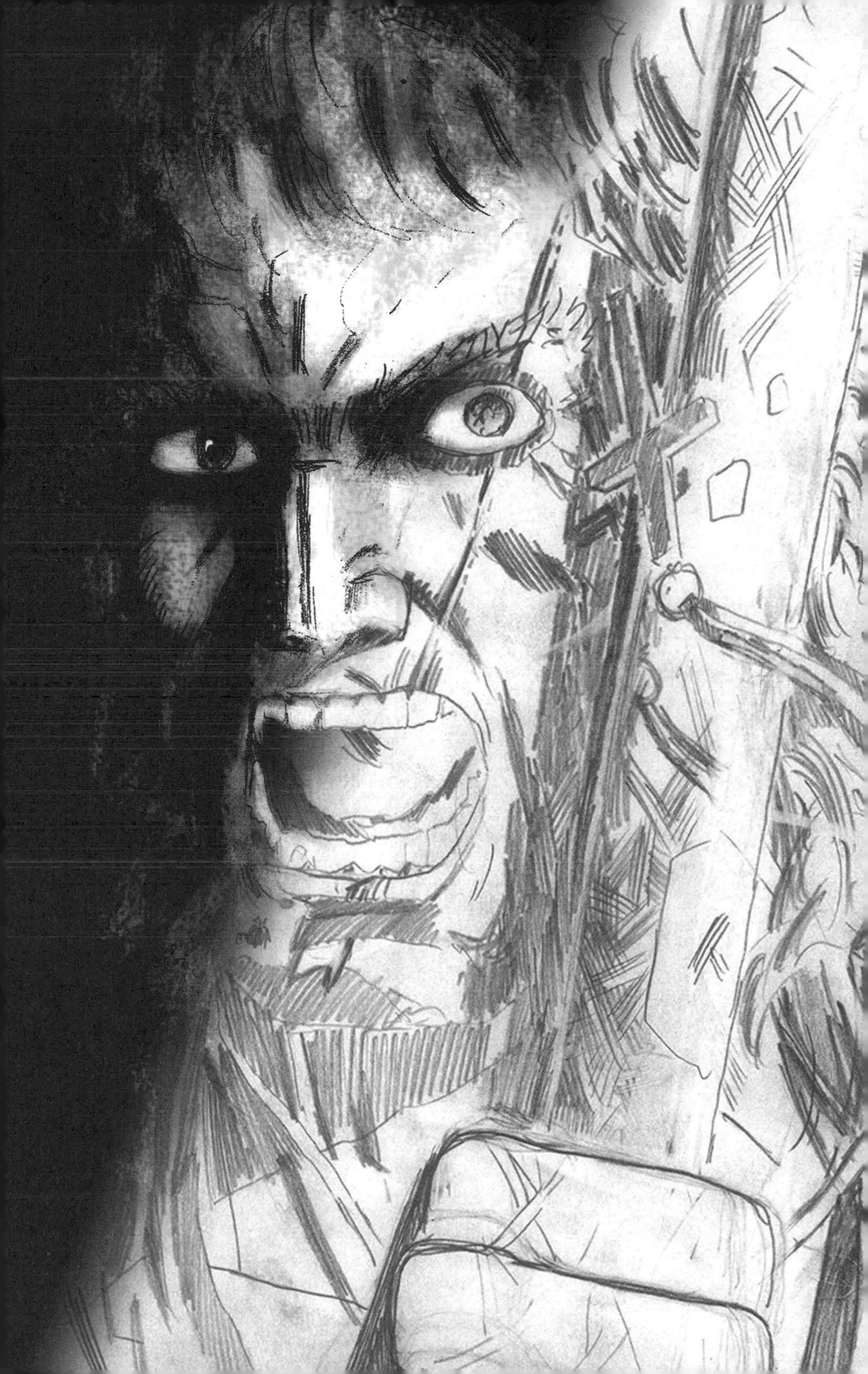

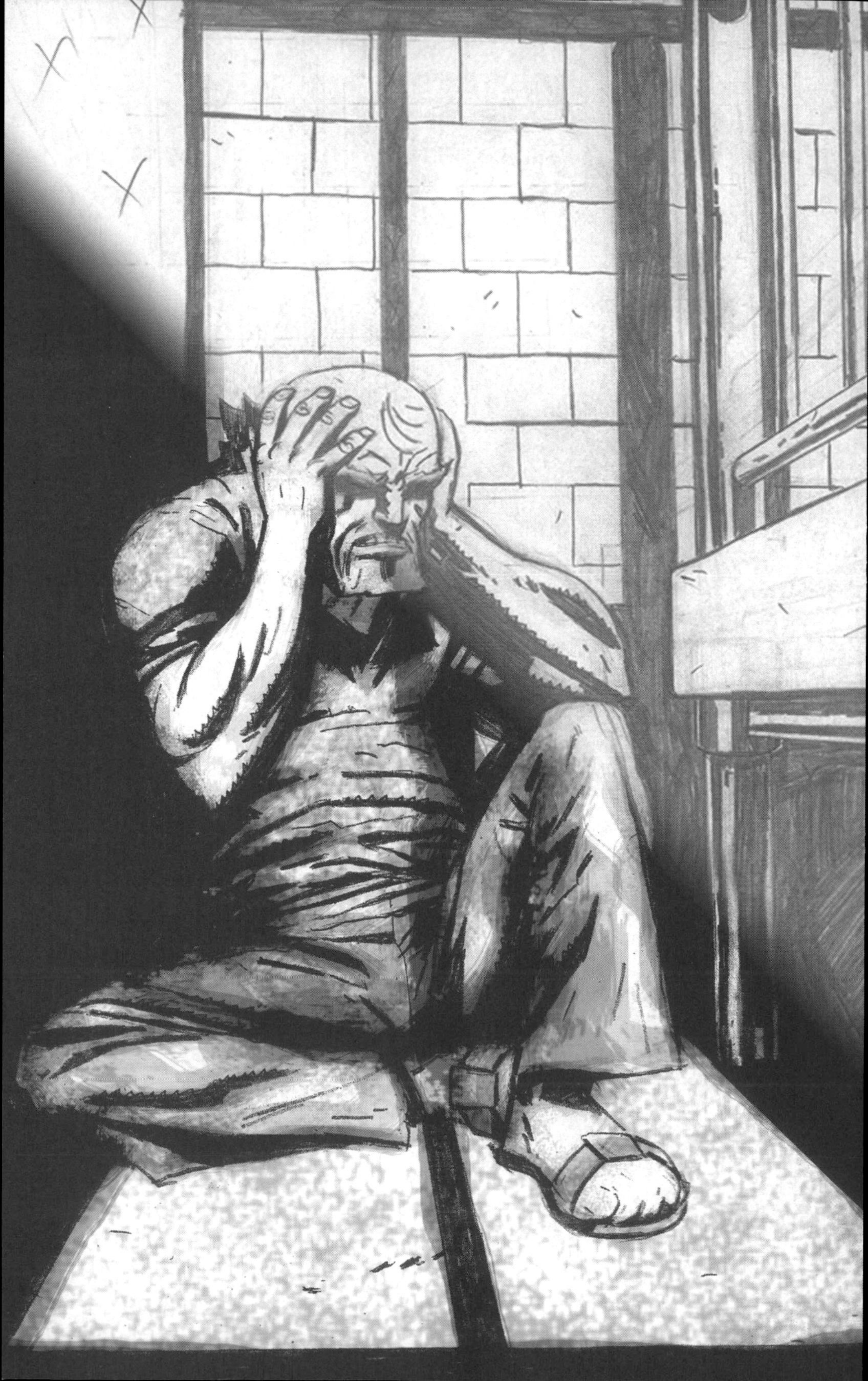

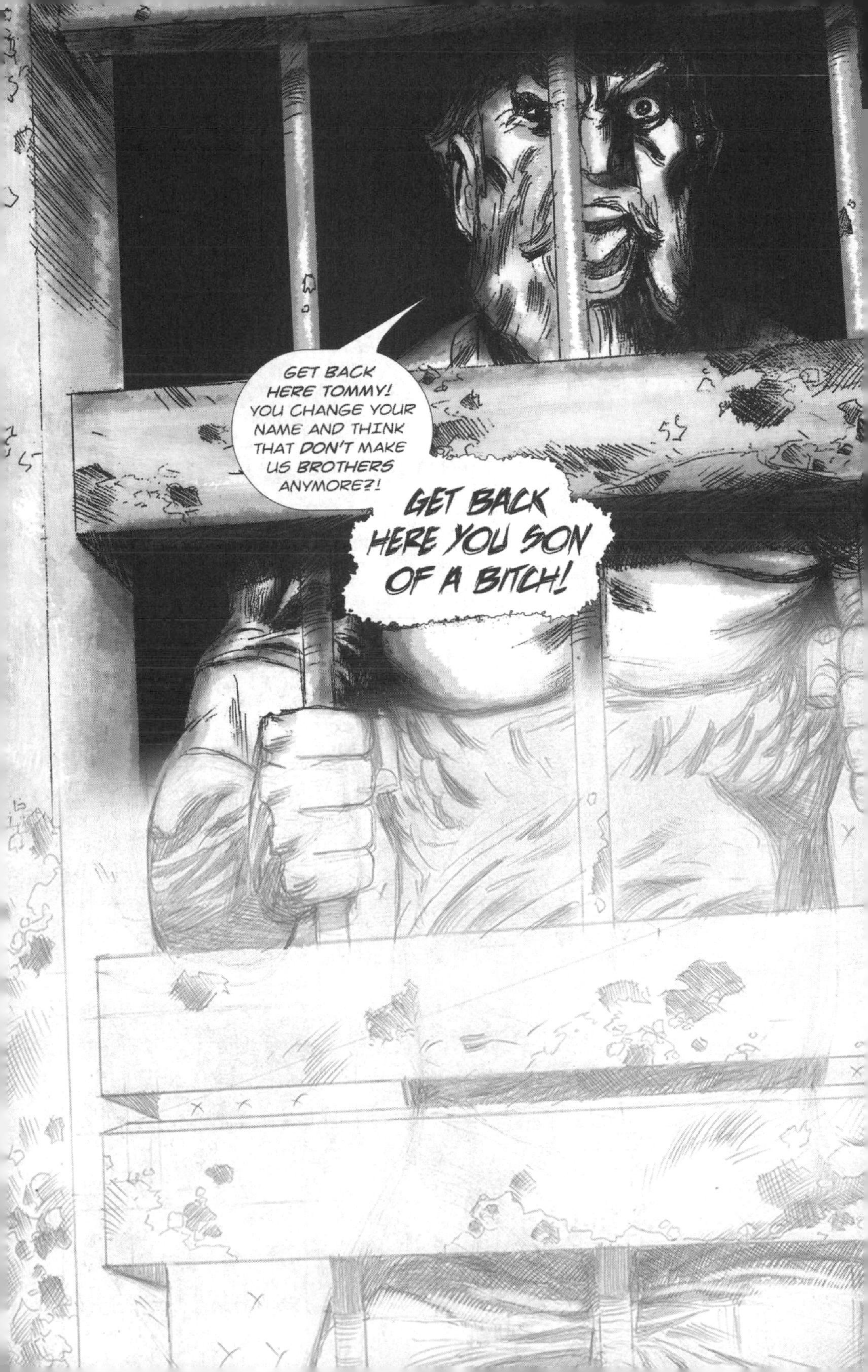
GET BACK HERE TOMMY! YOU CHANGE YOUR NAME AND THINK THAT DON'T MAKE US BROTHERS ANYMORE?!
GET BACK HERE YOU SON OF A BITCH!

BEHIND THE SCENES ON THE CHAIR

THE MAKING OF DEATH ROW

FILM FACT:

The death row set was made of plywood slats, PVC pipes, stucco, and a lot of skill and talent from the film's set designers and art departments.

photos by Kyle Hester

BEHIND THE SCENES ON THE CHAIR

THE MAKING OF DEATH ROW

FILM FACT:

The set was constructed two weeks prior to the start of filming.

photos by Kyle Hester

BEHIND THE SCENES ON THE CHAIR

THE MAKING OF DEATH ROW

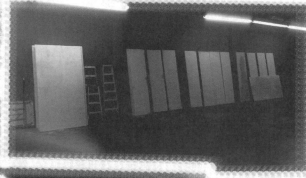

FILM FACT:

Once all of the set components were created, they were transported to Pollution Studios in Los Angeles, CA where the film's death row prison scenes were shot.

FILM FACT:

Due to the dramatic aging of the prison as seen through the eyes of Sullivan, The CHAIR was shot in reverse order with reality being filmed first and Sullivan's deluded reality being filmed afterwards.

top two photos by Kyle Hester, bottom photo by Birdie Thompson

BEHIND THE SCENES ON THE CHAIR

THE MAKING OF DEATH ROW

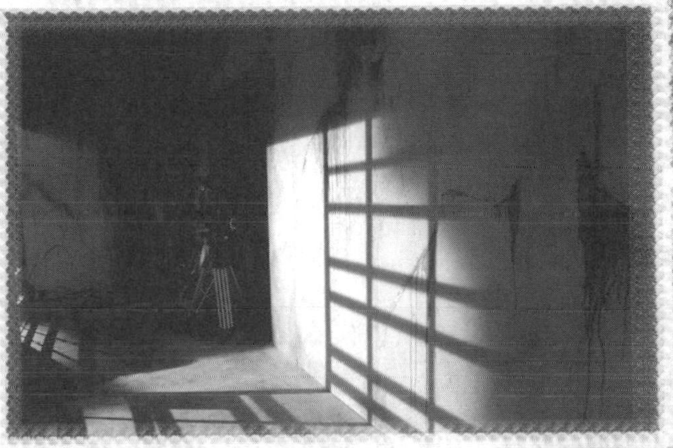

FILM FACT:

The walls and cells were aged and damaged to augment the hellish conditions of the prison. The lighting layout in the film also helped to create sinister shadows and a creepy atmosphere.

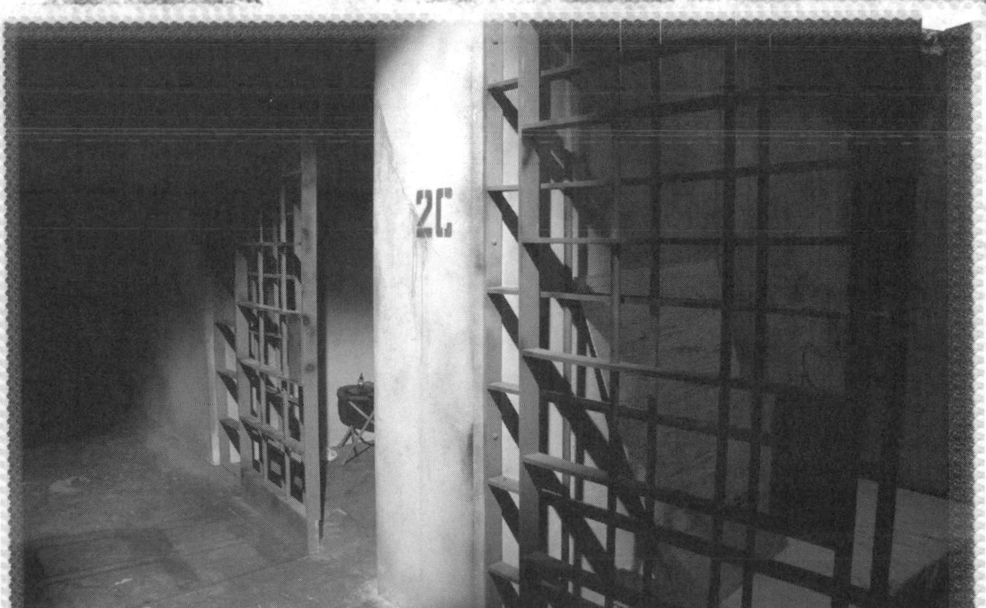
2C

photos by Birdie Thompson

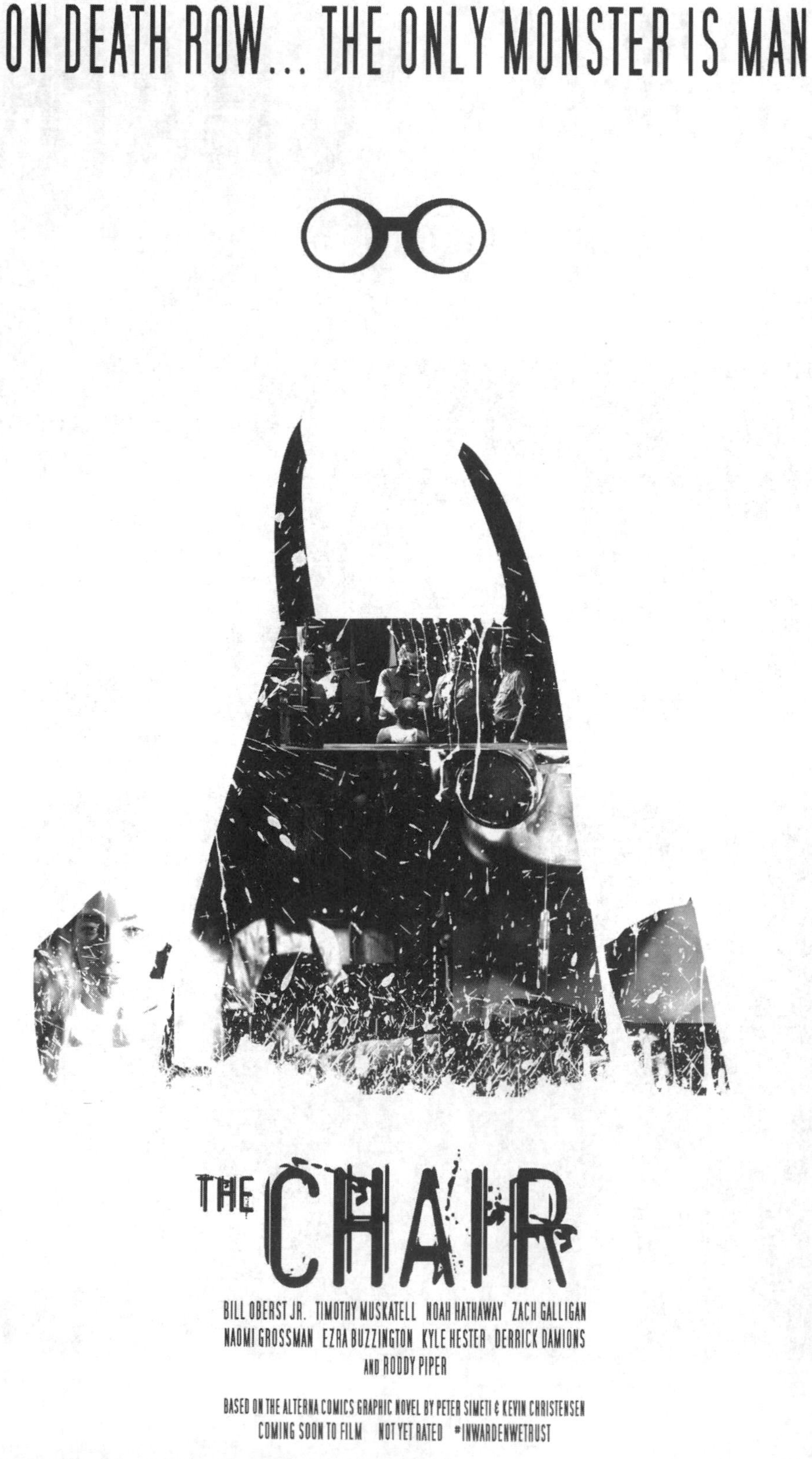
ON DEATH ROW... THE ONLY MONSTER IS MAN
THE CHAIR
BILL OBERST JR. TIMOTHY MUSKATELL NOAH HATHAWAY ZACH GALLIGAN
NAOMI GROSSMAN EZRA BUZZINGTON KYLE HESTER DERRICK DAMIONS
AND RODDY PIPER
BASED ON THE ALTERNA COMICS GRAPHIC NOVEL BY PETER SIMETI & KEVIN CHRISTENSEN
COMING SOON TO FILM NOT YET RATED #INWARDENWETRUST

CHARACTER PROFILES

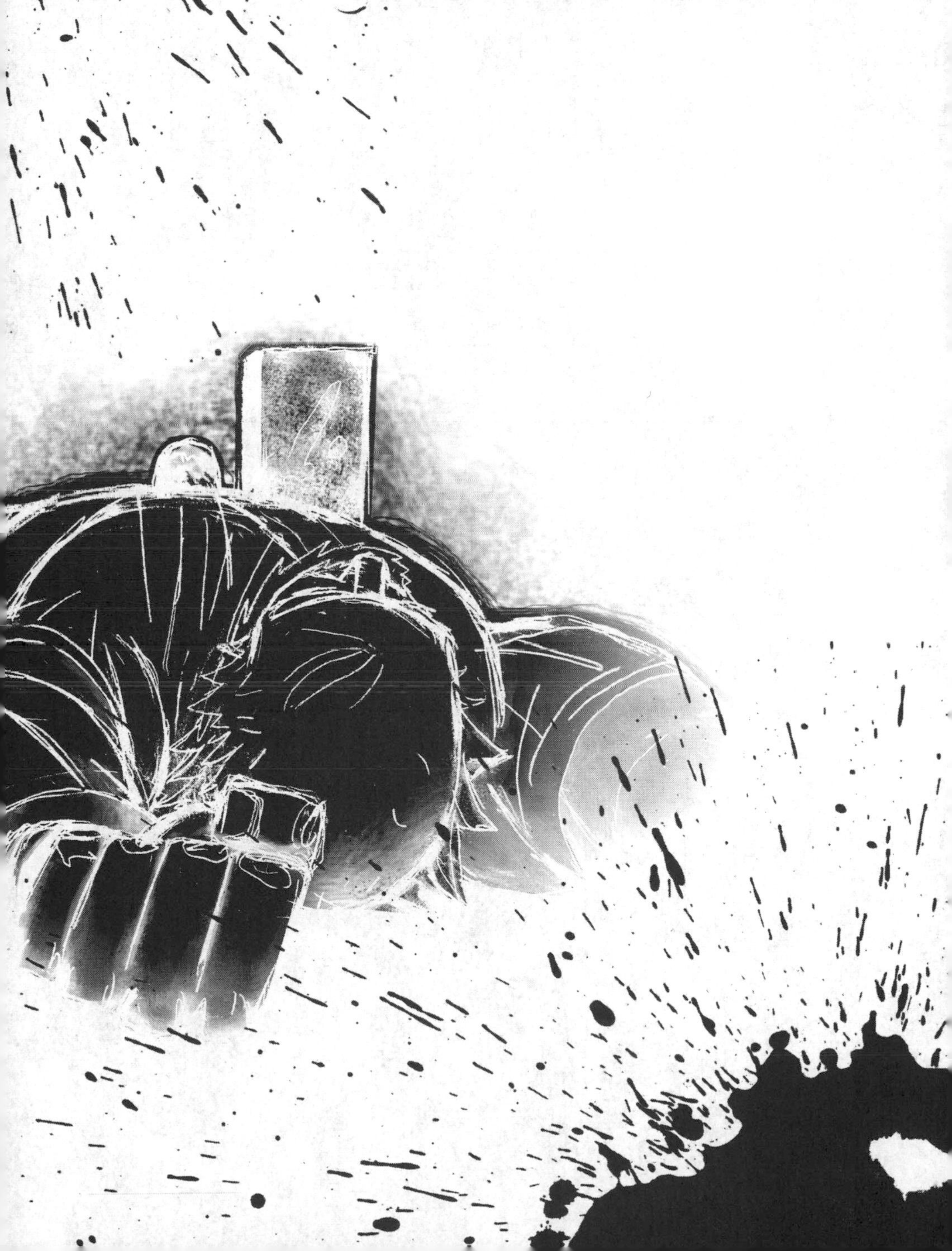

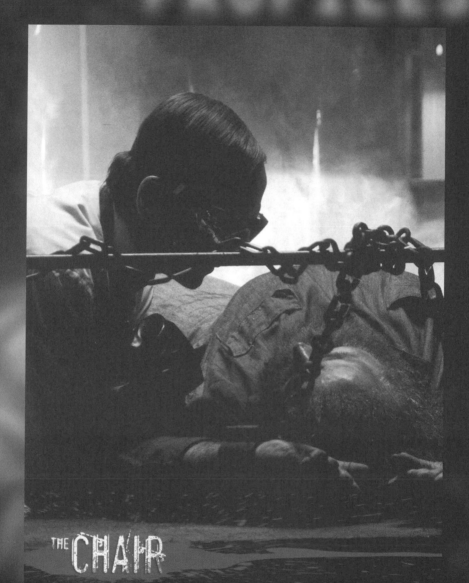

THE CHAIR

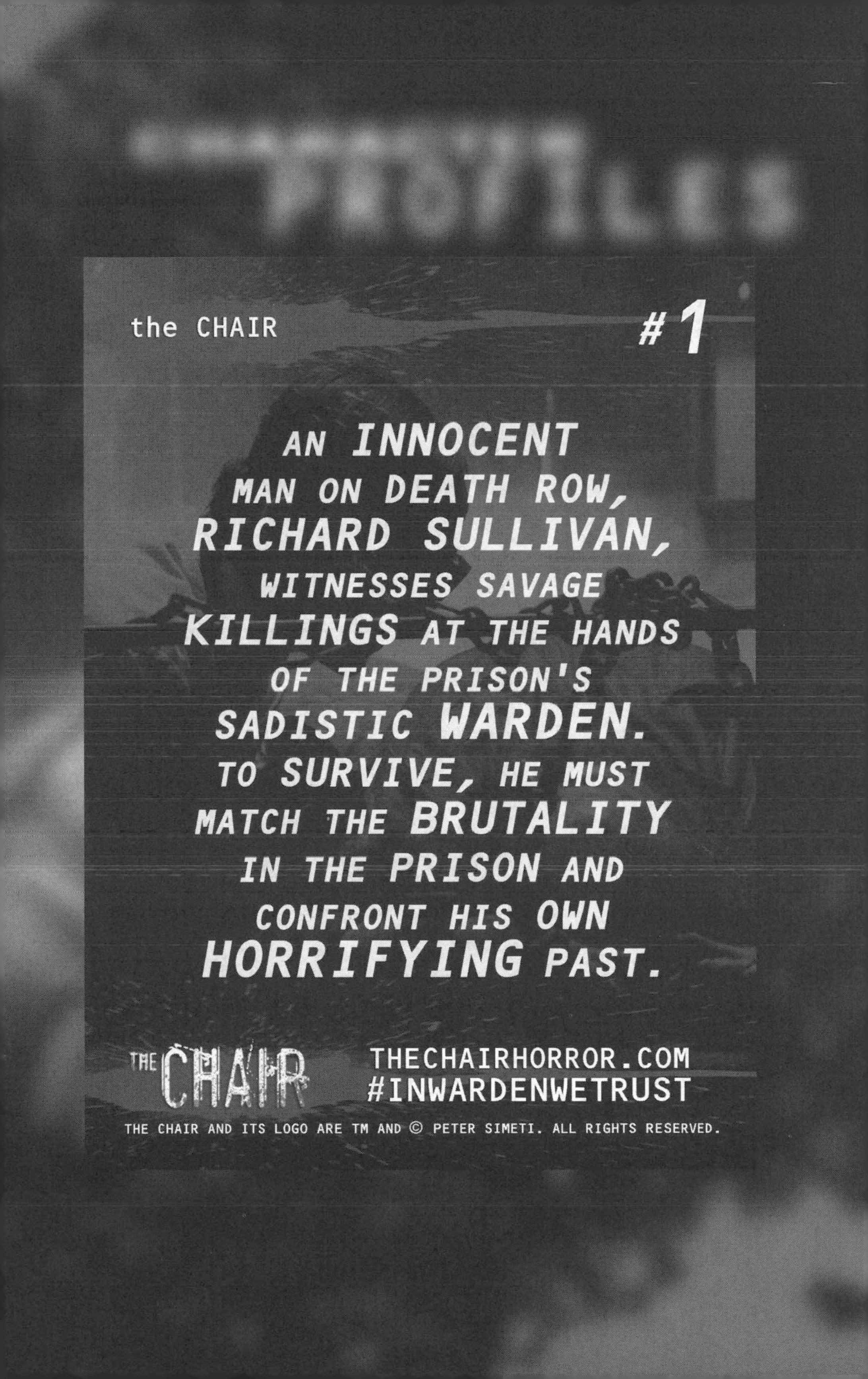
the CHAIR
#1
AN INNOCENT MAN ON DEATH ROW, RICHARD SULLIVAN, WITNESSES SAVAGE KILLINGS AT THE HANDS OF THE PRISON'S SADISTIC WARDEN. TO SURVIVE, HE MUST MATCH THE BRUTALITY IN THE PRISON AND CONFRONT HIS OWN HORRIFYING PAST.
THE CHAIR
THECHAIRHORROR.COM
#INWARDENWETRUST
THE CHAIR AND ITS LOGO ARE TM AND © PETER SIMETI. ALL RIGHTS RESERVED.

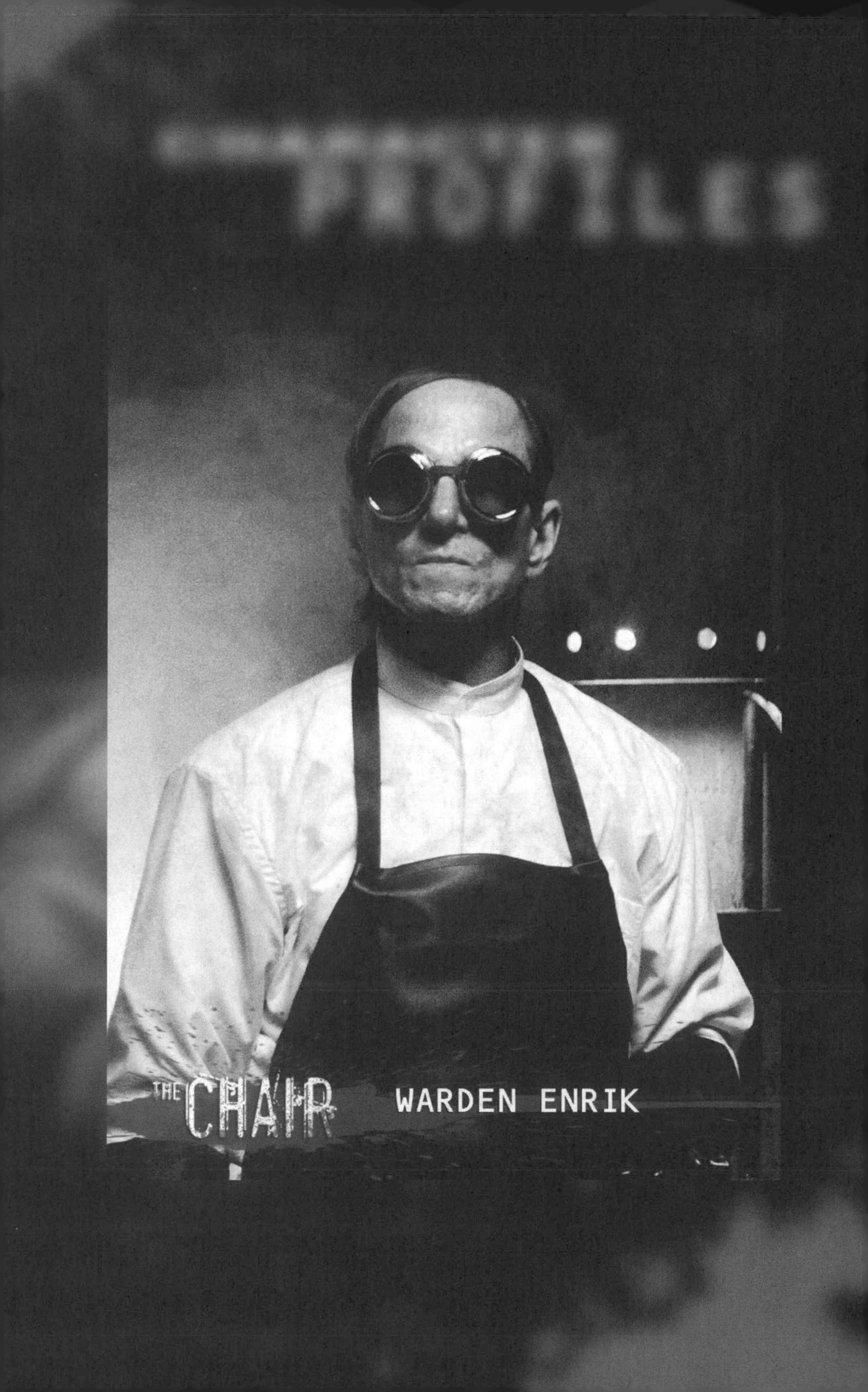
THE CHAIR
WARDEN ENRIK

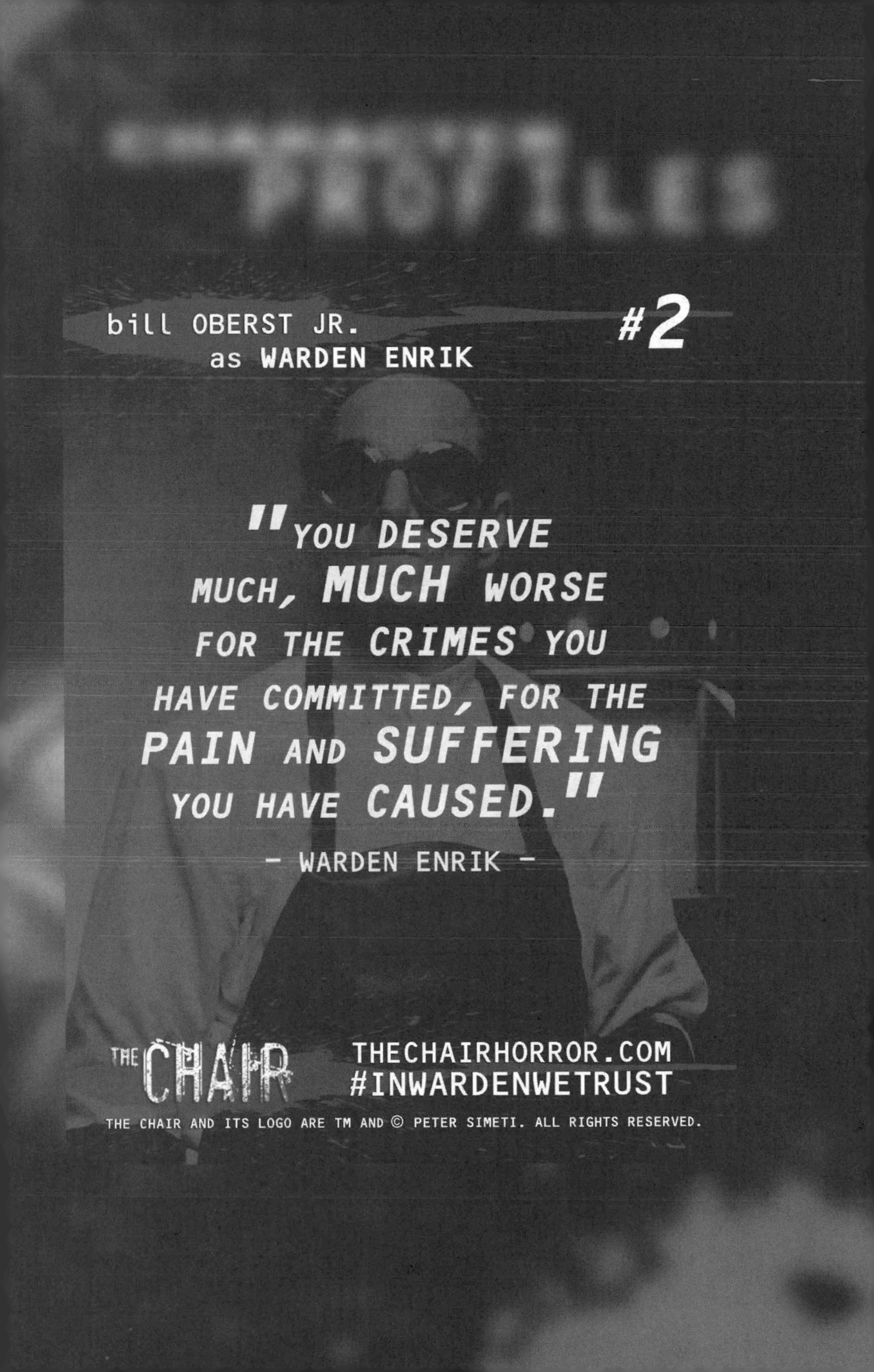
bill OBERST JR.
as WARDEN ENRIK
#2
"YOU DESERVE MUCH, MUCH WORSE FOR THE CRIMES YOU HAVE COMMITTED, FOR THE PAIN AND SUFFERING YOU HAVE CAUSED."
- WARDEN ENRIK -
THE CHAIR
THECHAIRHORROR.COM
#INWARDENWETRUST
THE CHAIR AND ITS LOGO ARE TM AND © PETER SIMETI. ALL RIGHTS RESERVED.

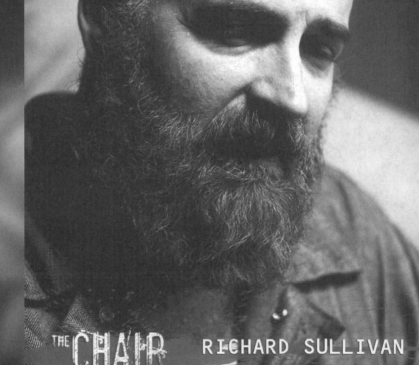

THE CHAIR   RICHARD SULLIVAN

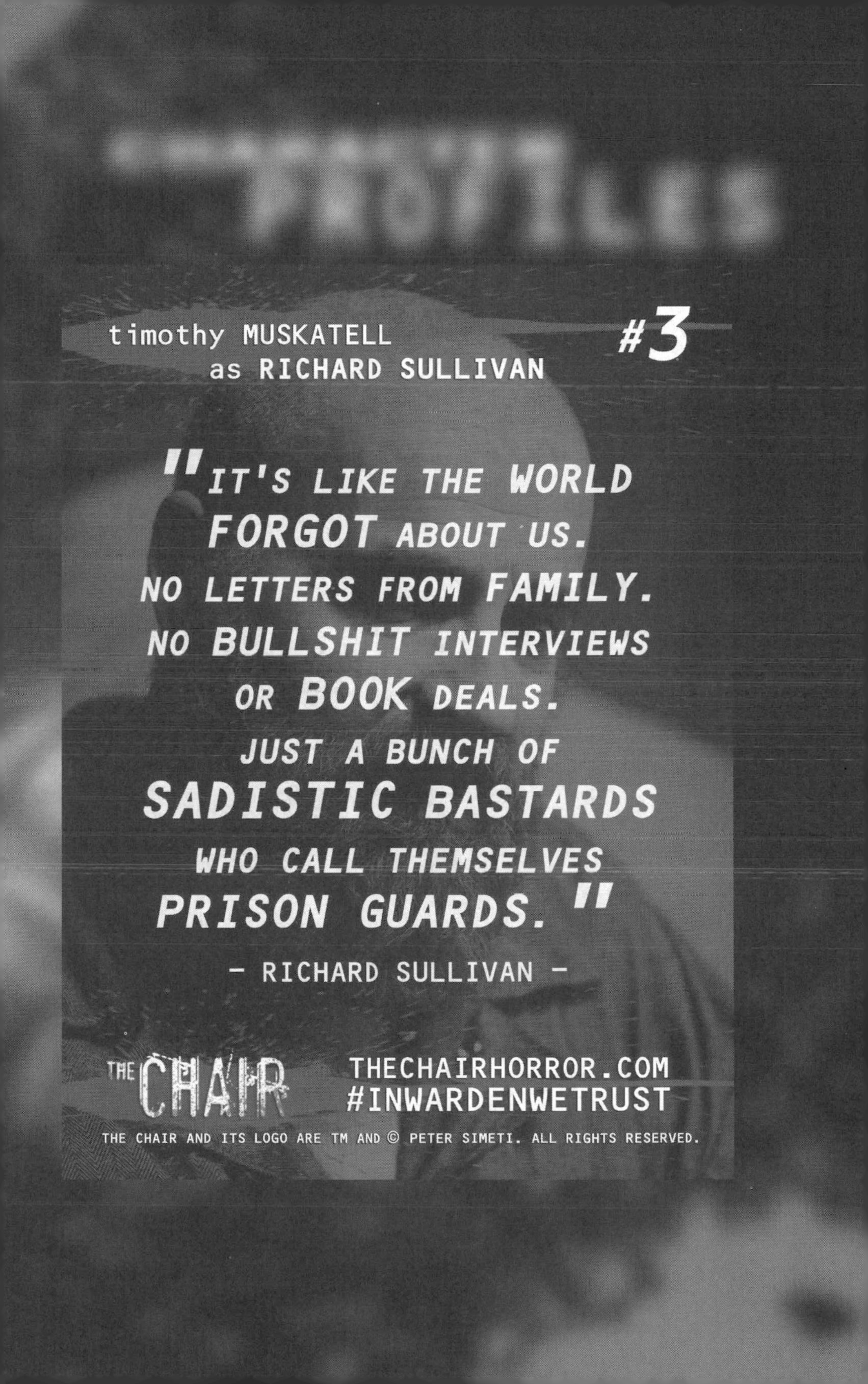
timothy MUSKATELL
as RICHARD SULLIVAN
#3
"IT'S LIKE THE WORLD FORGOT ABOUT US. NO LETTERS FROM FAMILY. NO BULLSHIT INTERVIEWS OR BOOK DEALS. JUST A BUNCH OF SADISTIC BASTARDS WHO CALL THEMSELVES PRISON GUARDS."
- RICHARD SULLIVAN -
THE CHAIR
THECHAIRHORROR.COM
#INWARDENWETRUST
THE CHAIR AND ITS LOGO ARE TM AND © PETER SIMETI. ALL RIGHTS RESERVED.

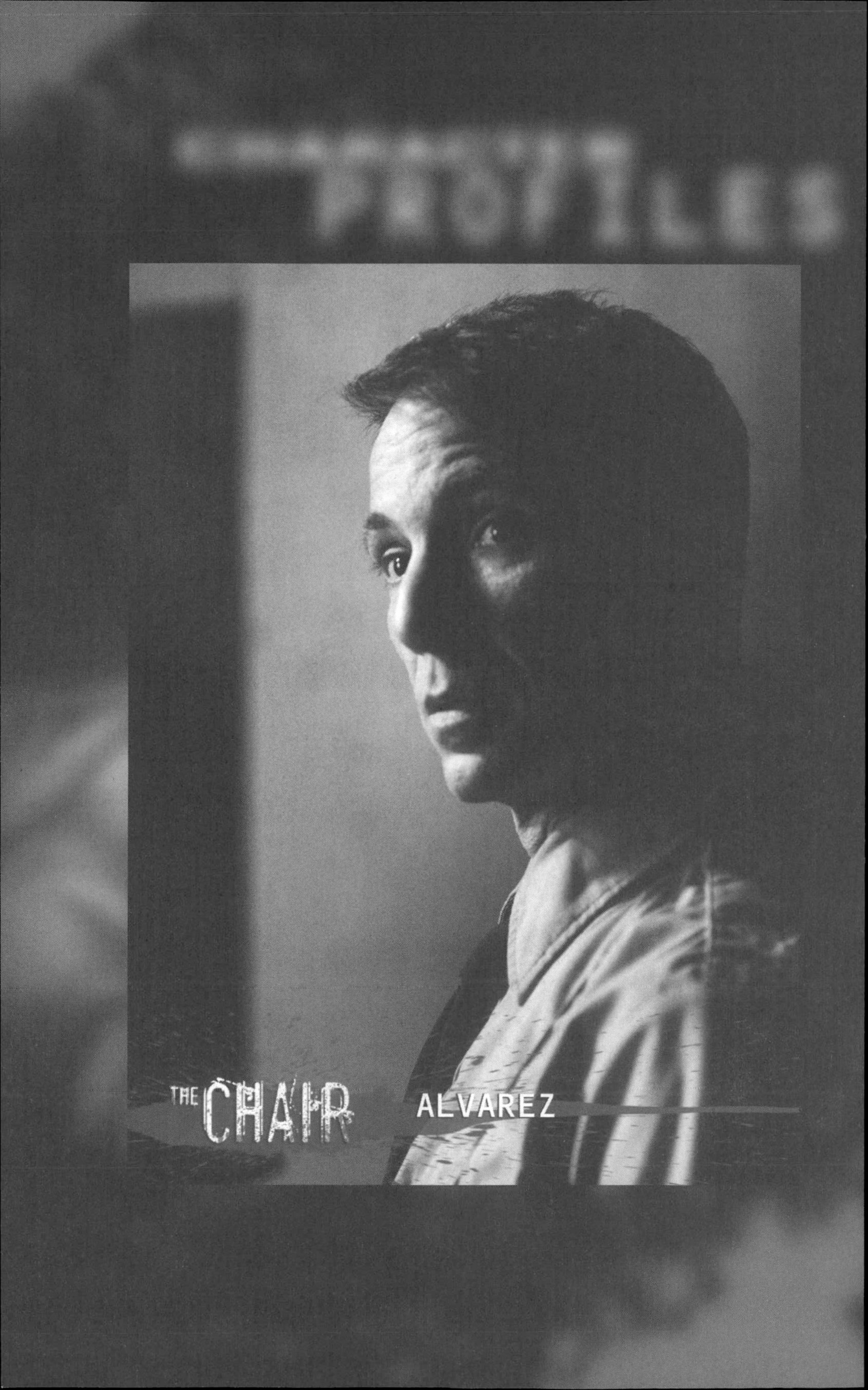
THE CHAIR
ALVAREZ

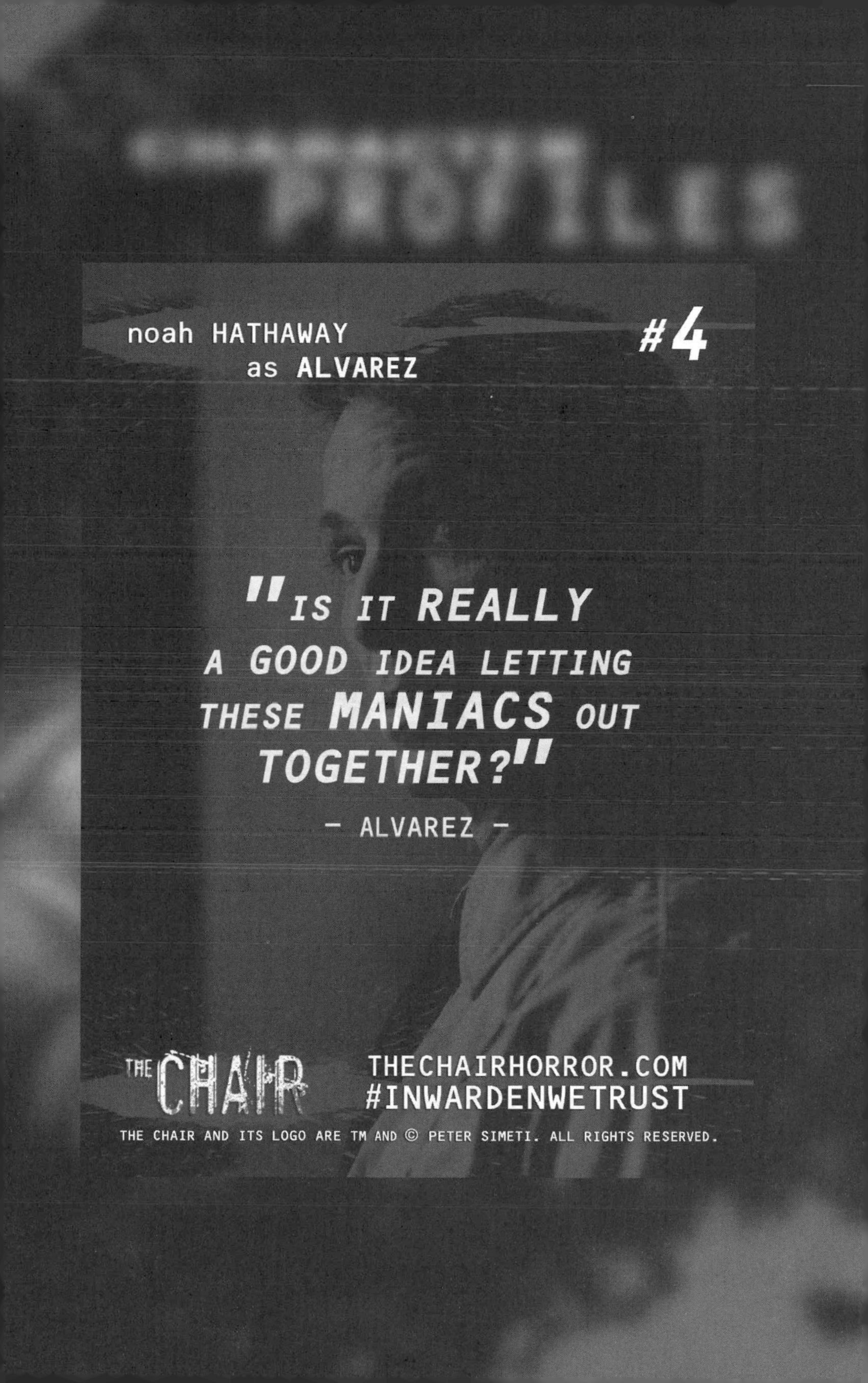
noah HATHAWAY
as ALVAREZ
#4
"IS IT REALLY A GOOD IDEA LETTING THESE MANIACS OUT TOGETHER?"
- ALVAREZ -
THE CHAIR
THECHAIRHORROR.COM
#INWARDENWETRUST
THE CHAIR AND ITS LOGO ARE TM AND © PETER SIMETI. ALL RIGHTS RESERVED.

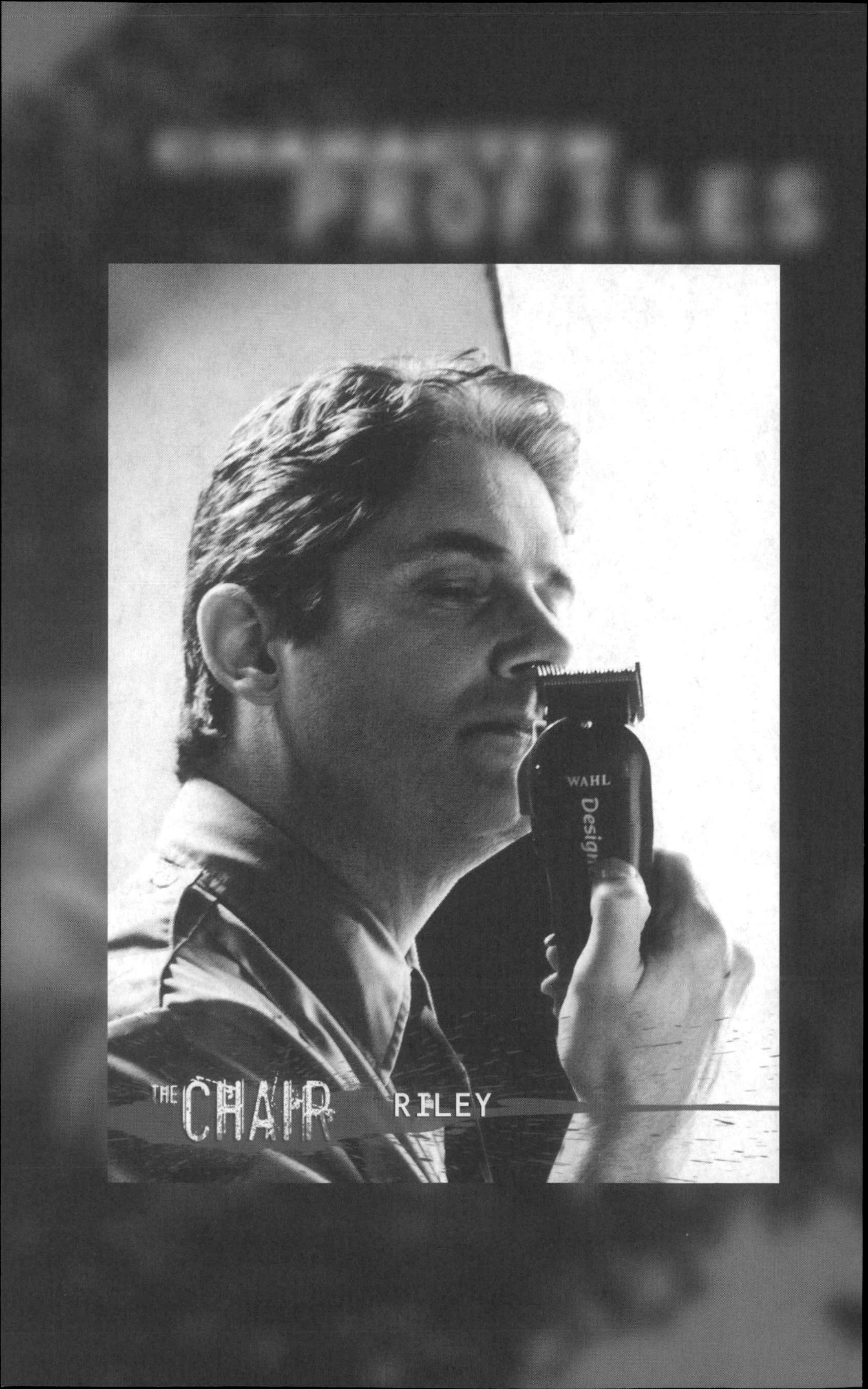
THE CHAIR
RILEY

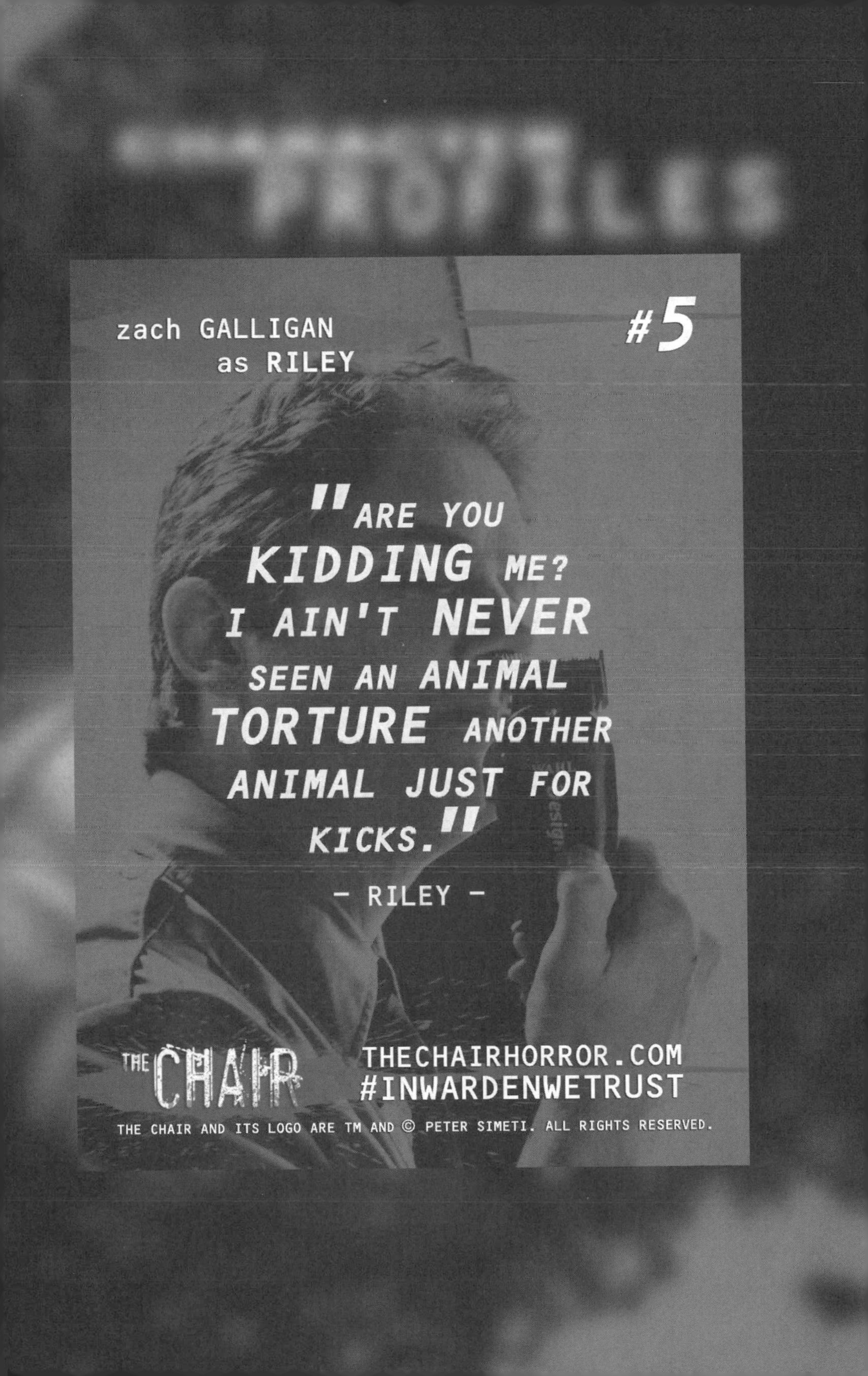
zach GALLIGAN
as RILEY
#5
"ARE YOU KIDDING ME? I AIN'T NEVER SEEN AN ANIMAL TORTURE ANOTHER ANIMAL JUST FOR KICKS."
- RILEY -
THE CHAIR
THECHAIRHORROR.COM
#INWARDENWETRUST
THE CHAIR AND ITS LOGO ARE TM AND © PETER SIMETI. ALL RIGHTS RESERVED.

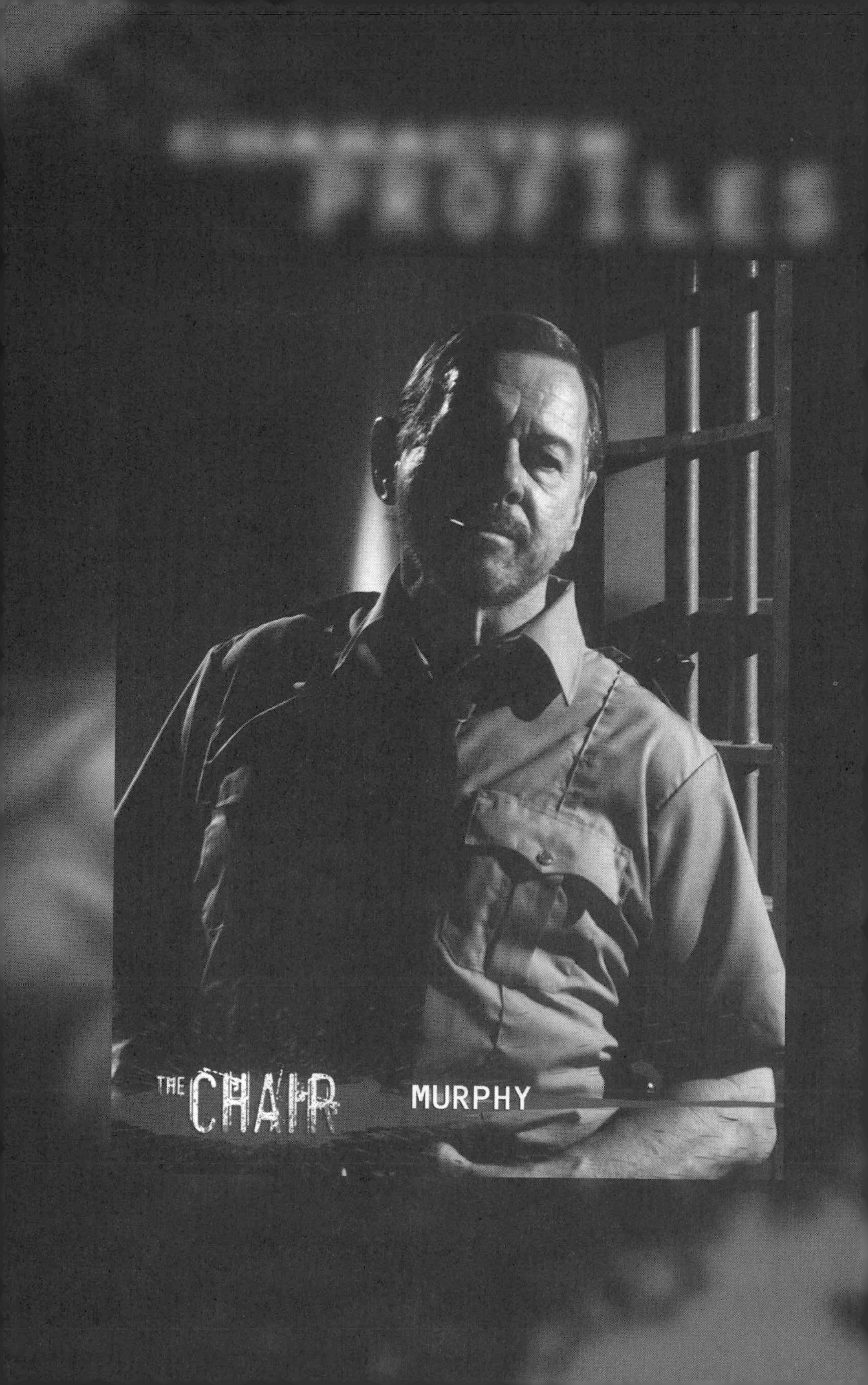
THE CHAIR
MURPHY

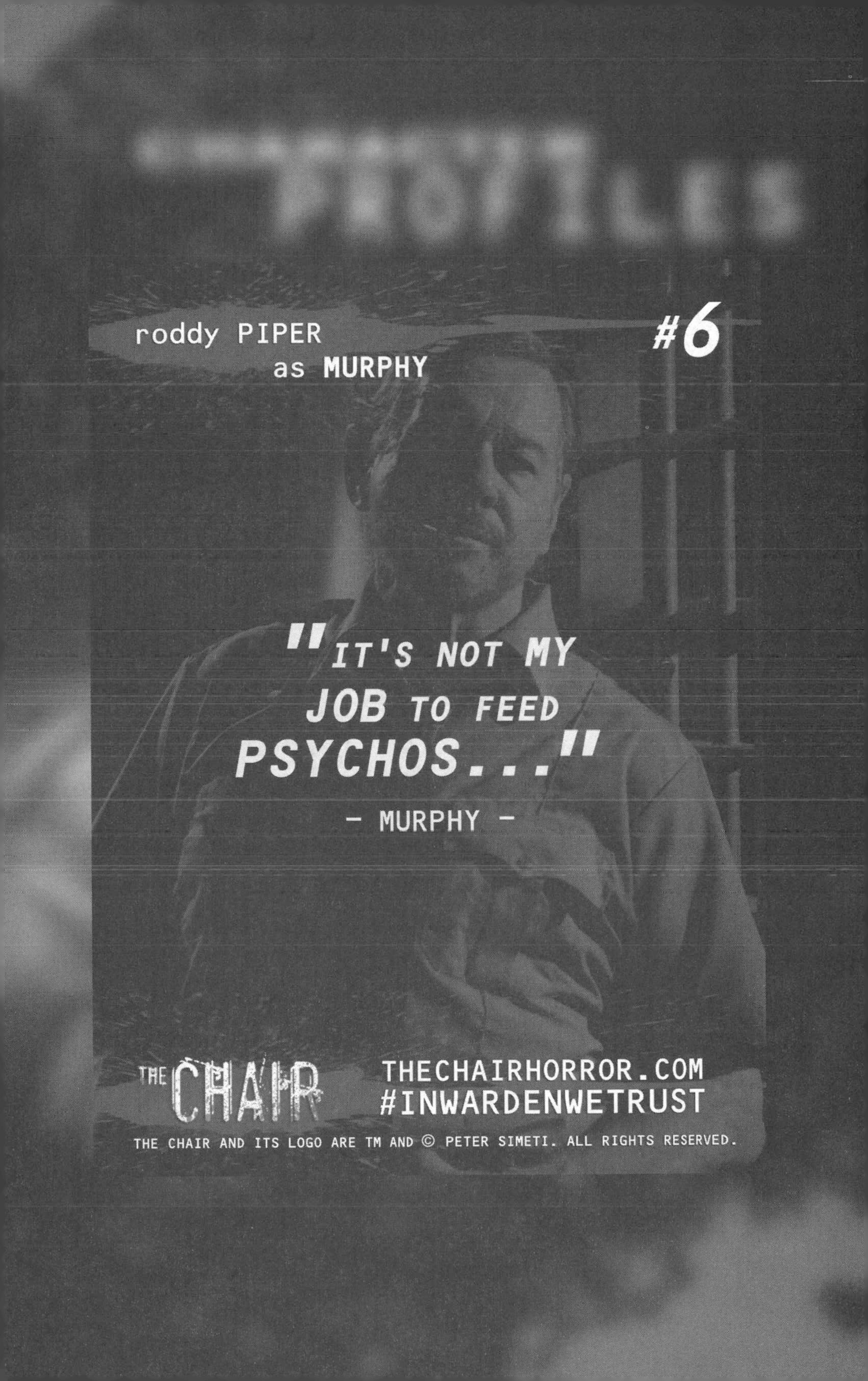
roddy PIPER
as MURPHY
#6
"IT'S NOT MY JOB TO FEED PSYCHOS..."
- MURPHY -
THE CHAIR
THECHAIRHORROR.COM
#INWARDENWETRUST
THE CHAIR AND ITS LOGO ARE TM AND © PETER SIMETI. ALL RIGHTS RESERVED.

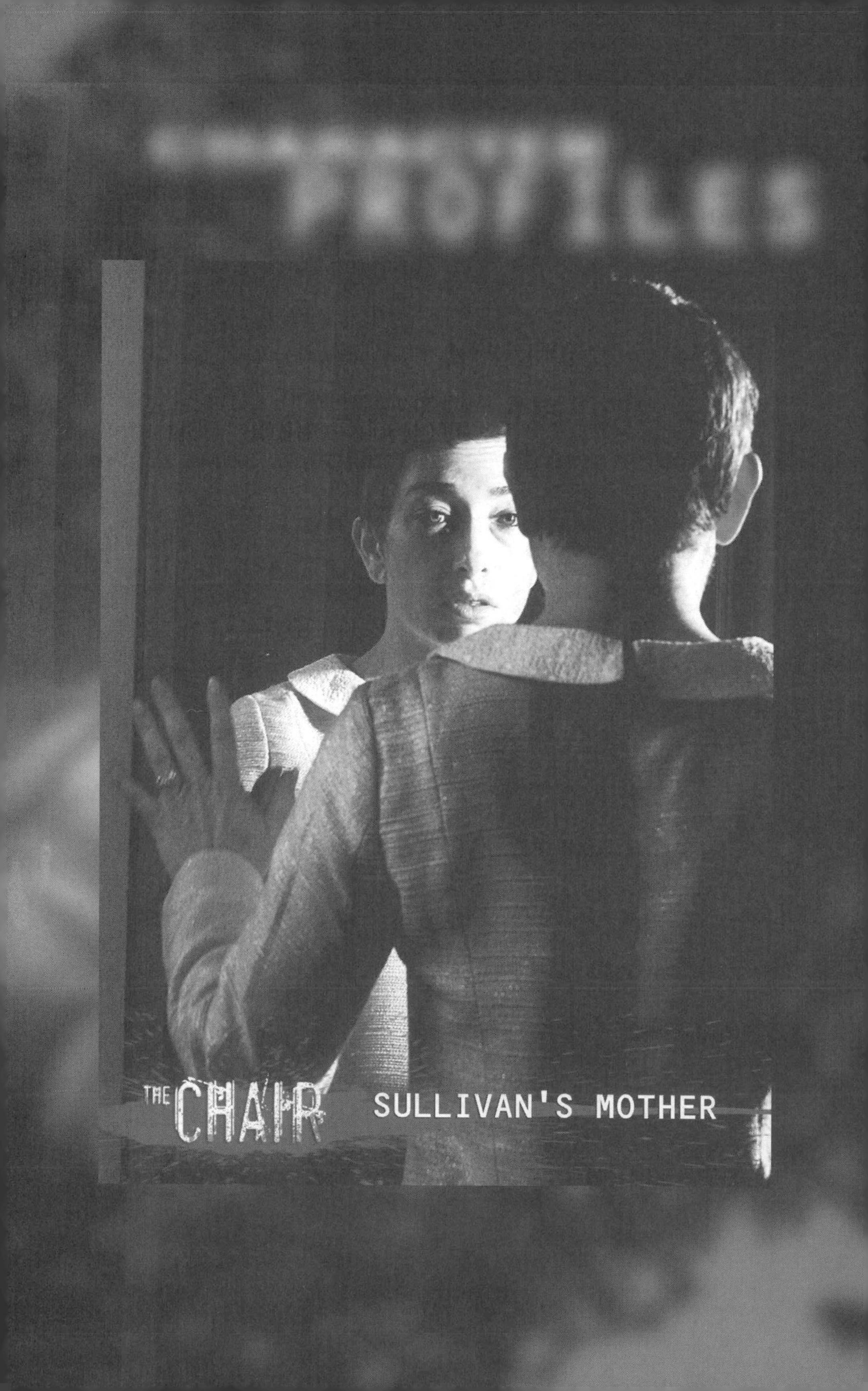
THE CHAIR
SULLIVAN'S MOTHER

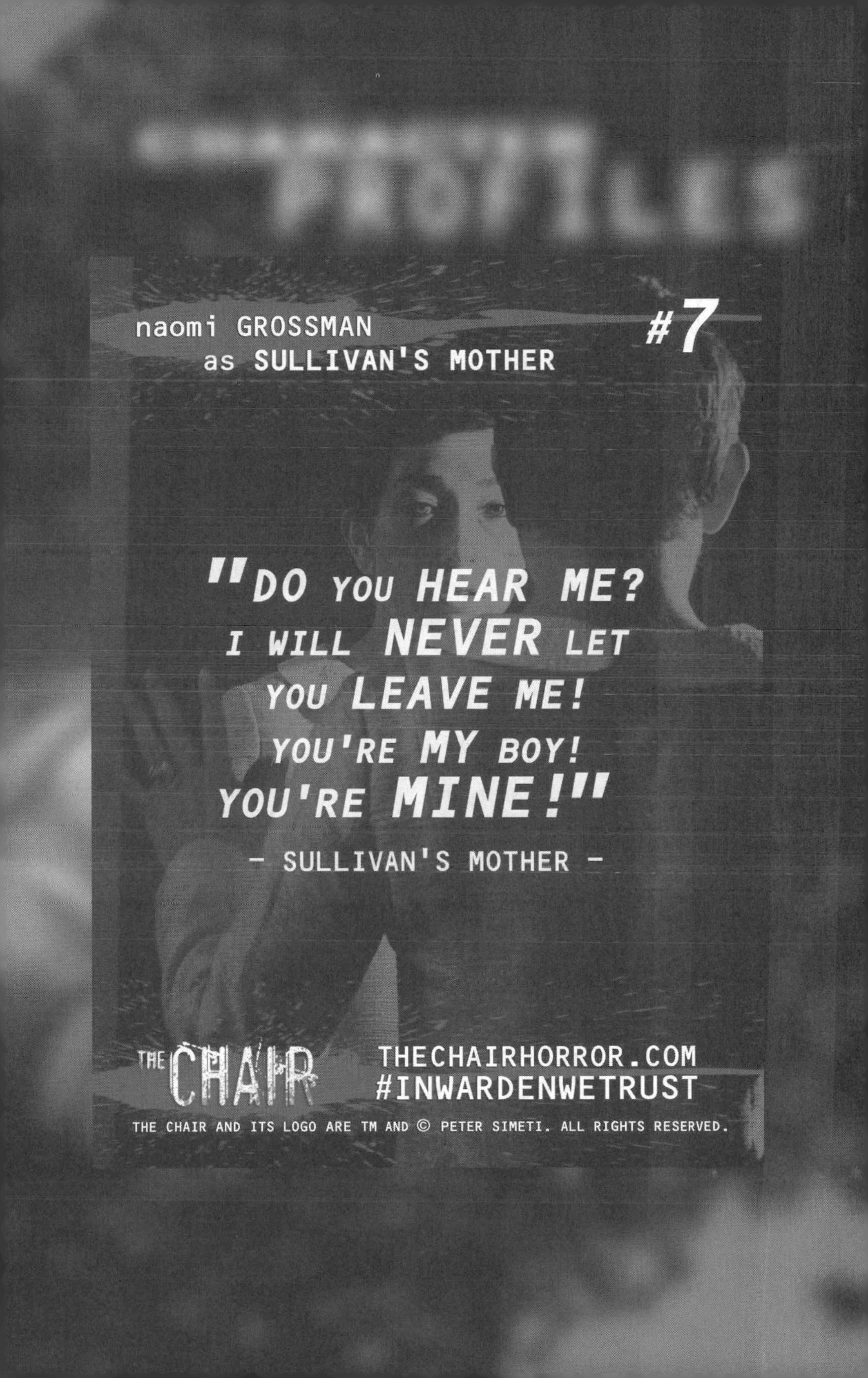

naomi GROSSMAN
as SULLIVAN'S MOTHER

#7

**"DO YOU HEAR ME?
I WILL NEVER LET
YOU LEAVE ME!
YOU'RE MY BOY!
YOU'RE MINE!"**

— SULLIVAN'S MOTHER —

THE CHAIR

THECHAIRHORROR.COM
#INWARDENWETRUST

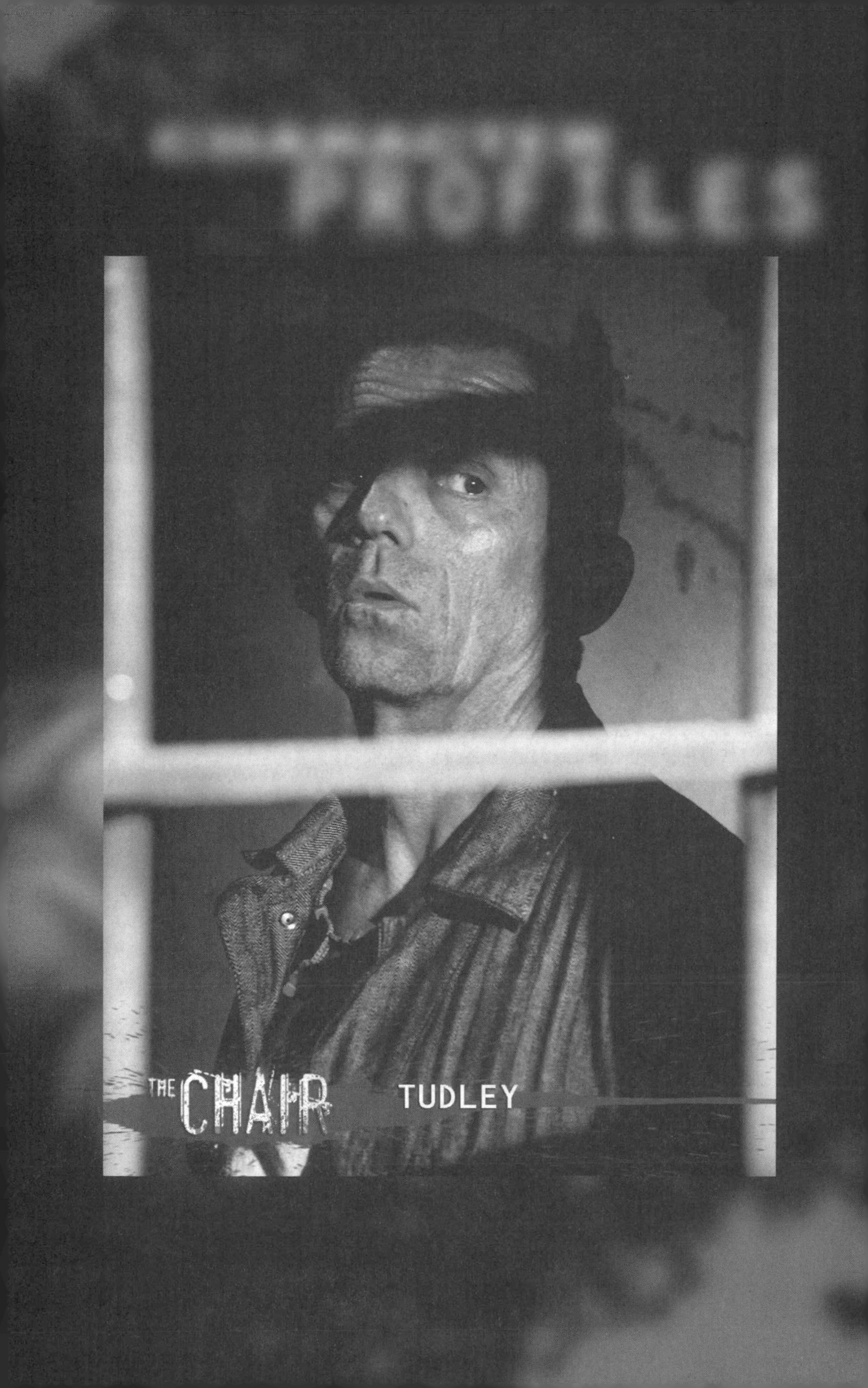
THE CHAIR
TUDLEY

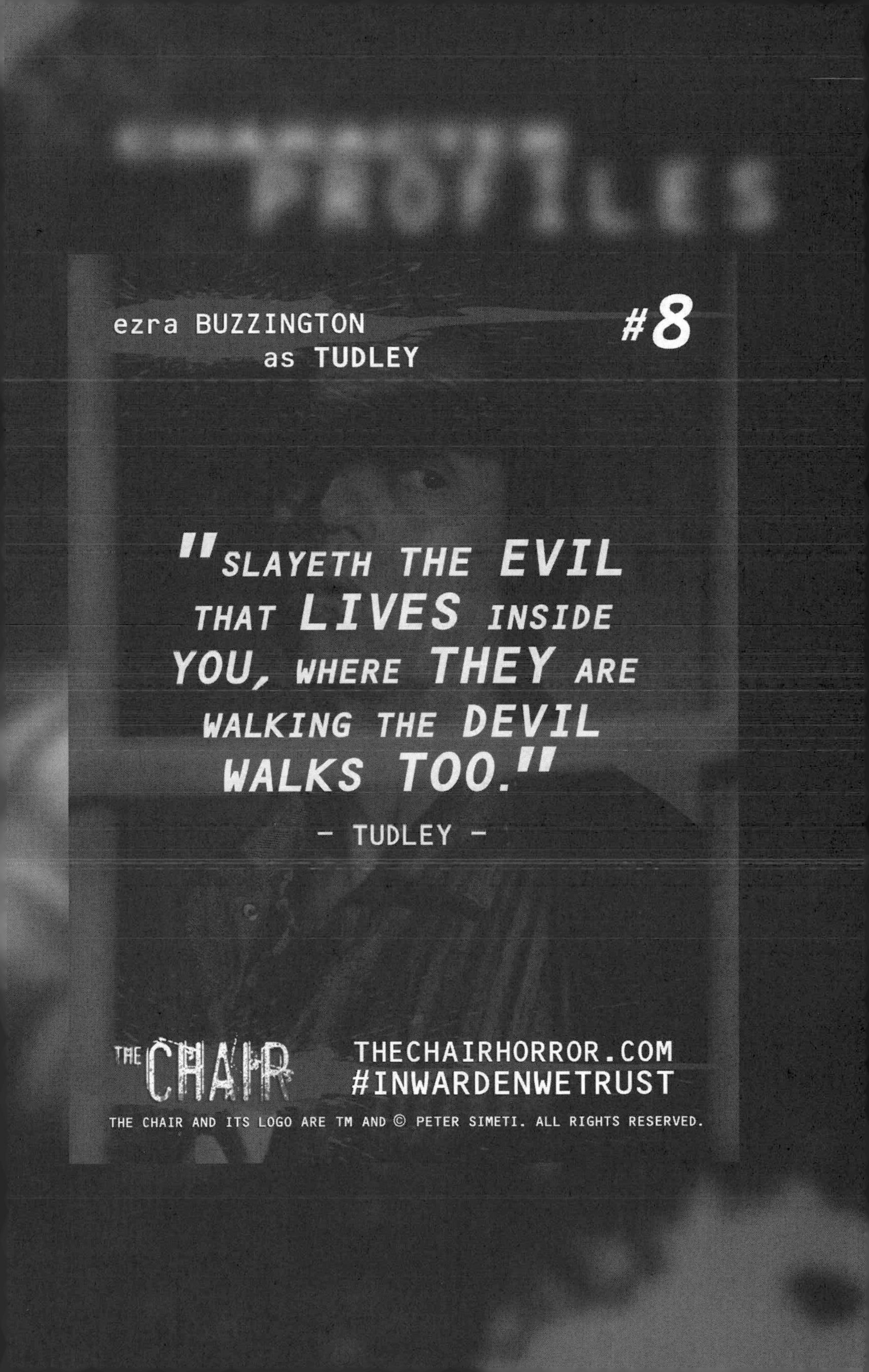
ezra BUZZINGTON
as TUDLEY
#8
"SLAYETH THE EVIL THAT LIVES INSIDE YOU, WHERE THEY ARE WALKING THE DEVIL WALKS TOO."
- TUDLEY -
THE CHAIR
THECHAIRHORROR.COM
#INWARDENWETRUST
THE CHAIR AND ITS LOGO ARE TM AND © PETER SIMETI. ALL RIGHTS RESERVED.

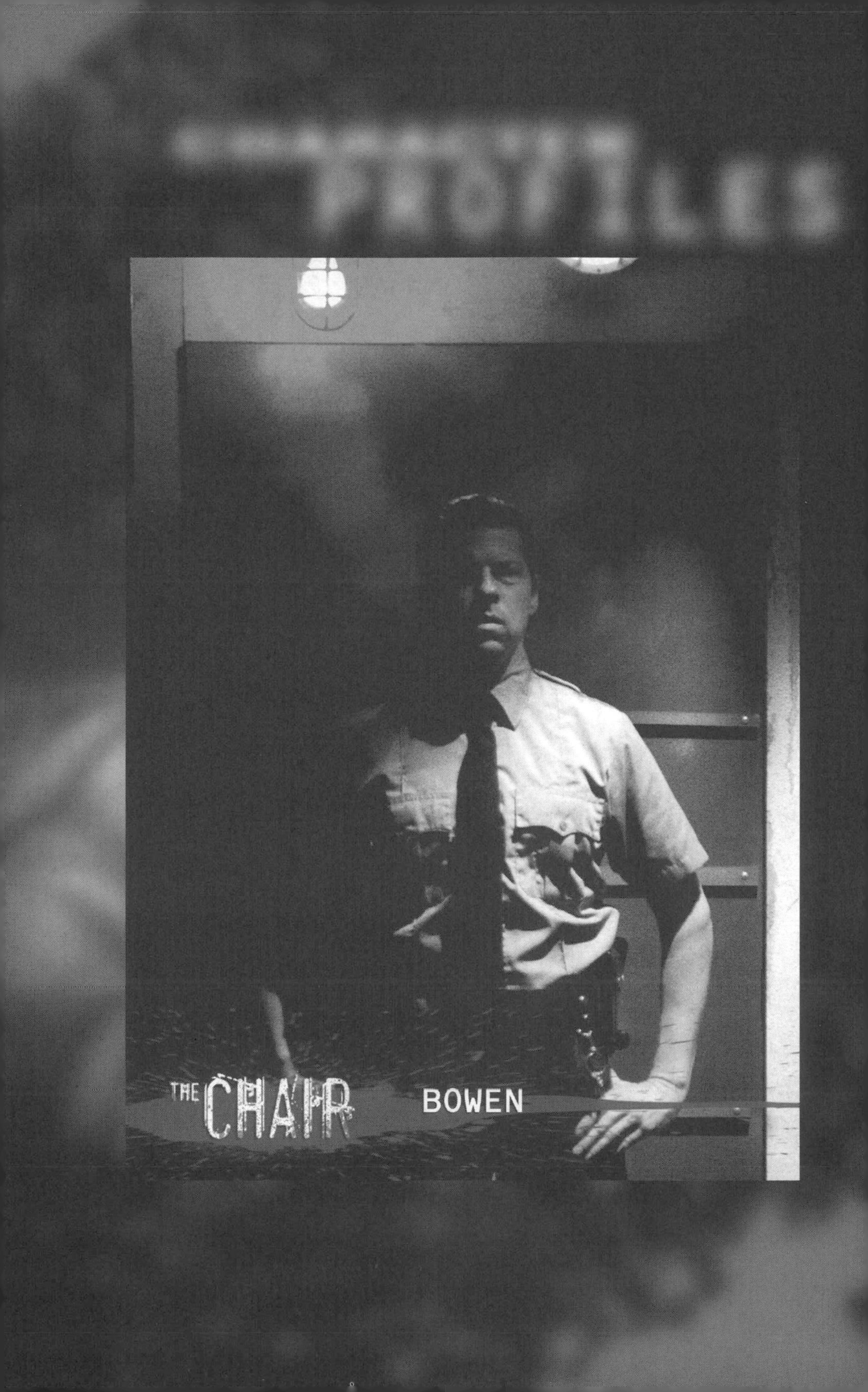
THE CHAIR
BOWEN

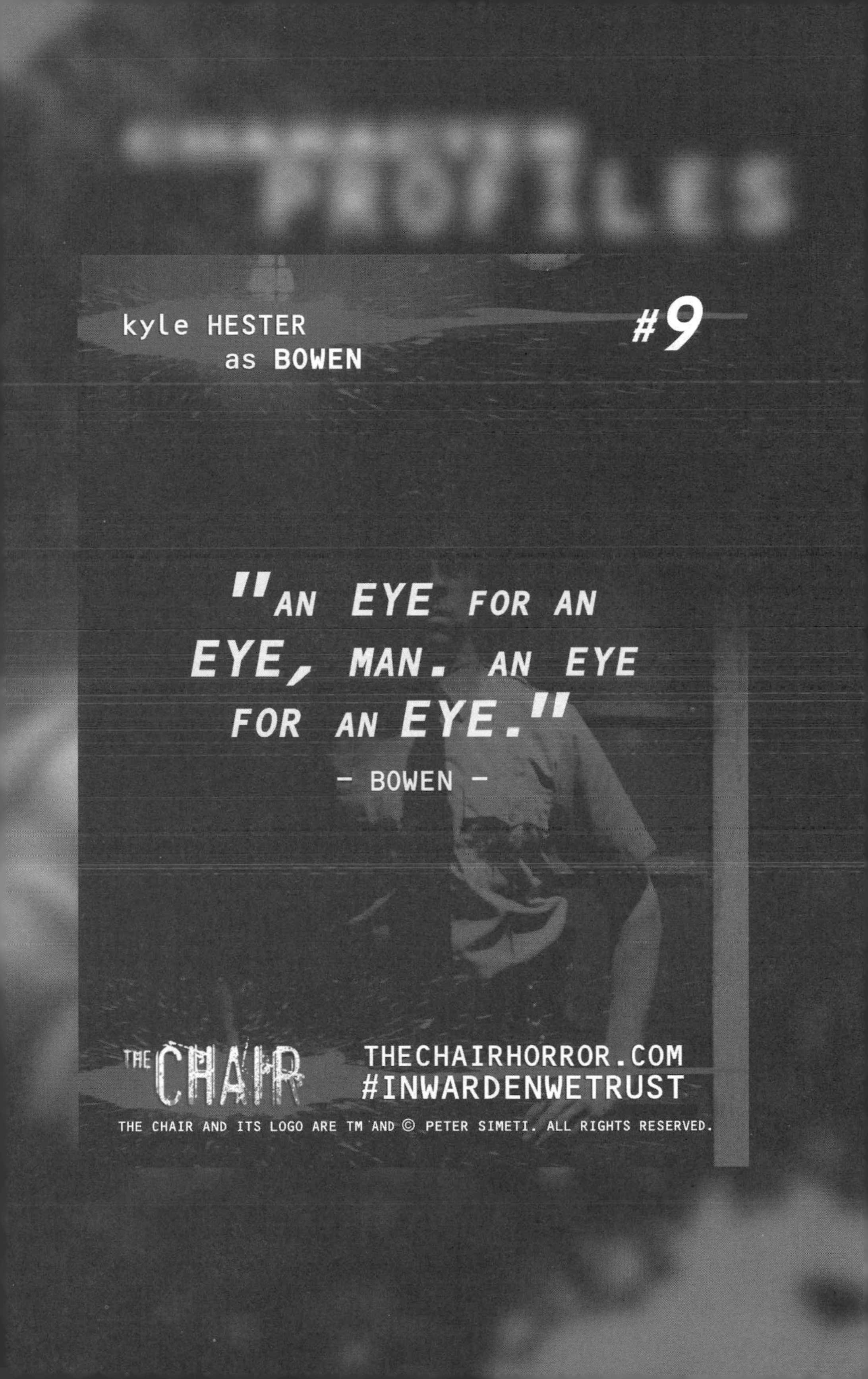
kyle HESTER
as BOWEN
#9
"AN EYE FOR AN EYE, MAN. AN EYE FOR AN EYE."
- BOWEN -
THE CHAIR
THECHAIRHORROR.COM
#INWARDENWETRUST
THE CHAIR AND ITS LOGO ARE TM AND © PETER SIMETI. ALL RIGHTS RESERVED.

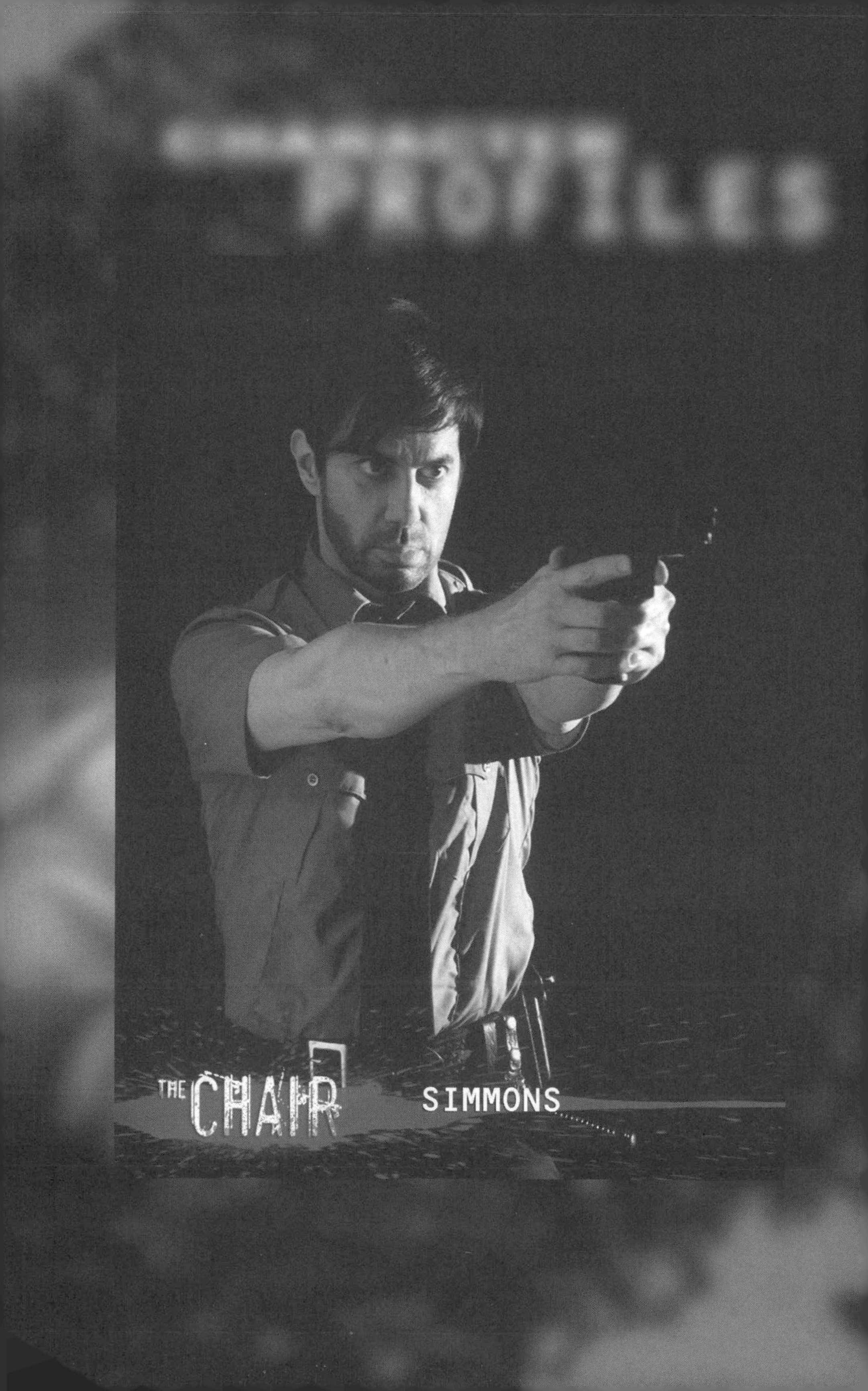
THE CHAIR
SIMMONS

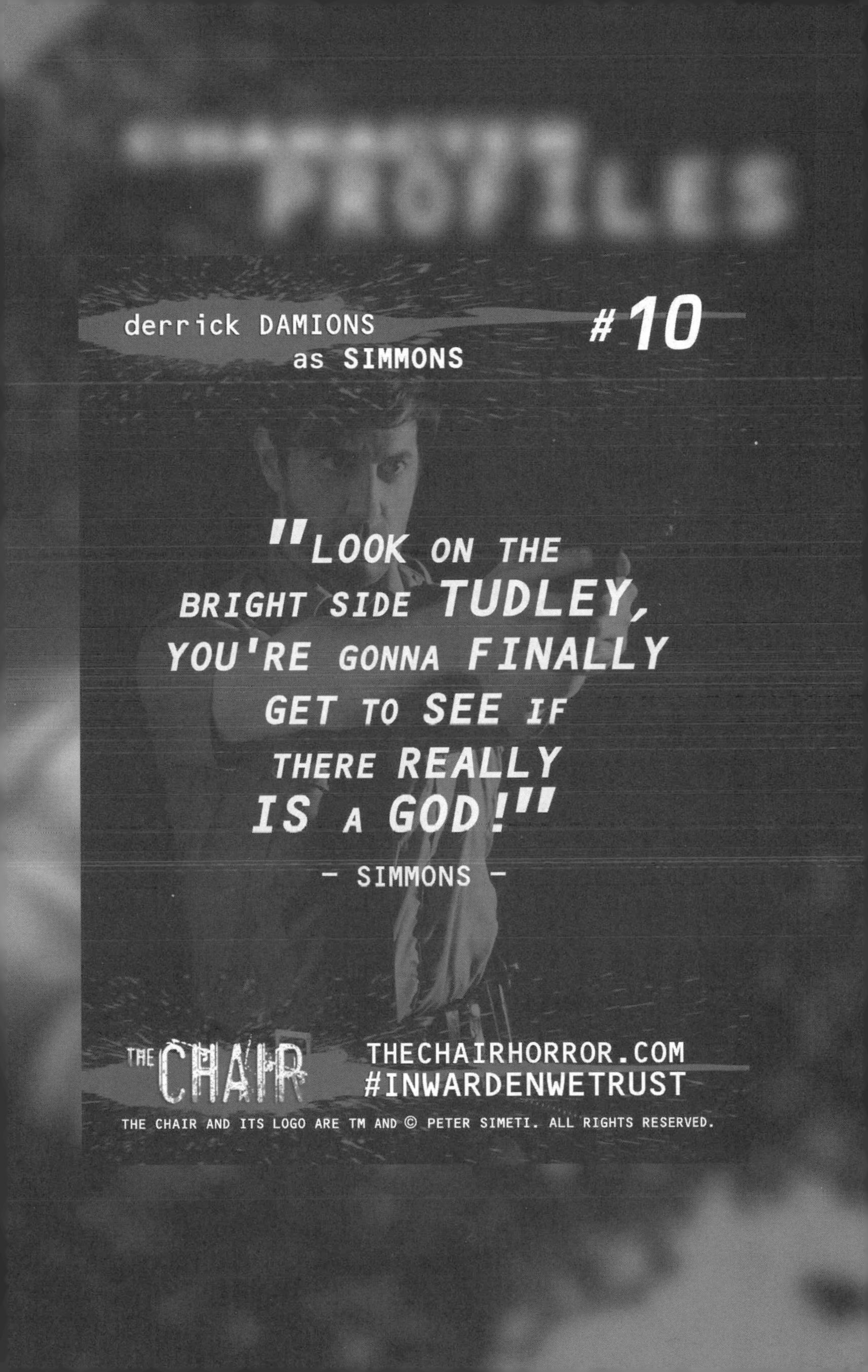
derrick DAMIONS
as SIMMONS
#10
"LOOK ON THE BRIGHT SIDE TUDLEY, YOU'RE GONNA FINALLY GET TO SEE IF THERE REALLY IS A GOD!"
- SIMMONS -
THE CHAIR
THECHAIRHORROR.COM
#INWARDENWETRUST
THE CHAIR AND ITS LOGO ARE TM AND © PETER SIMETI. ALL RIGHTS RESERVED.

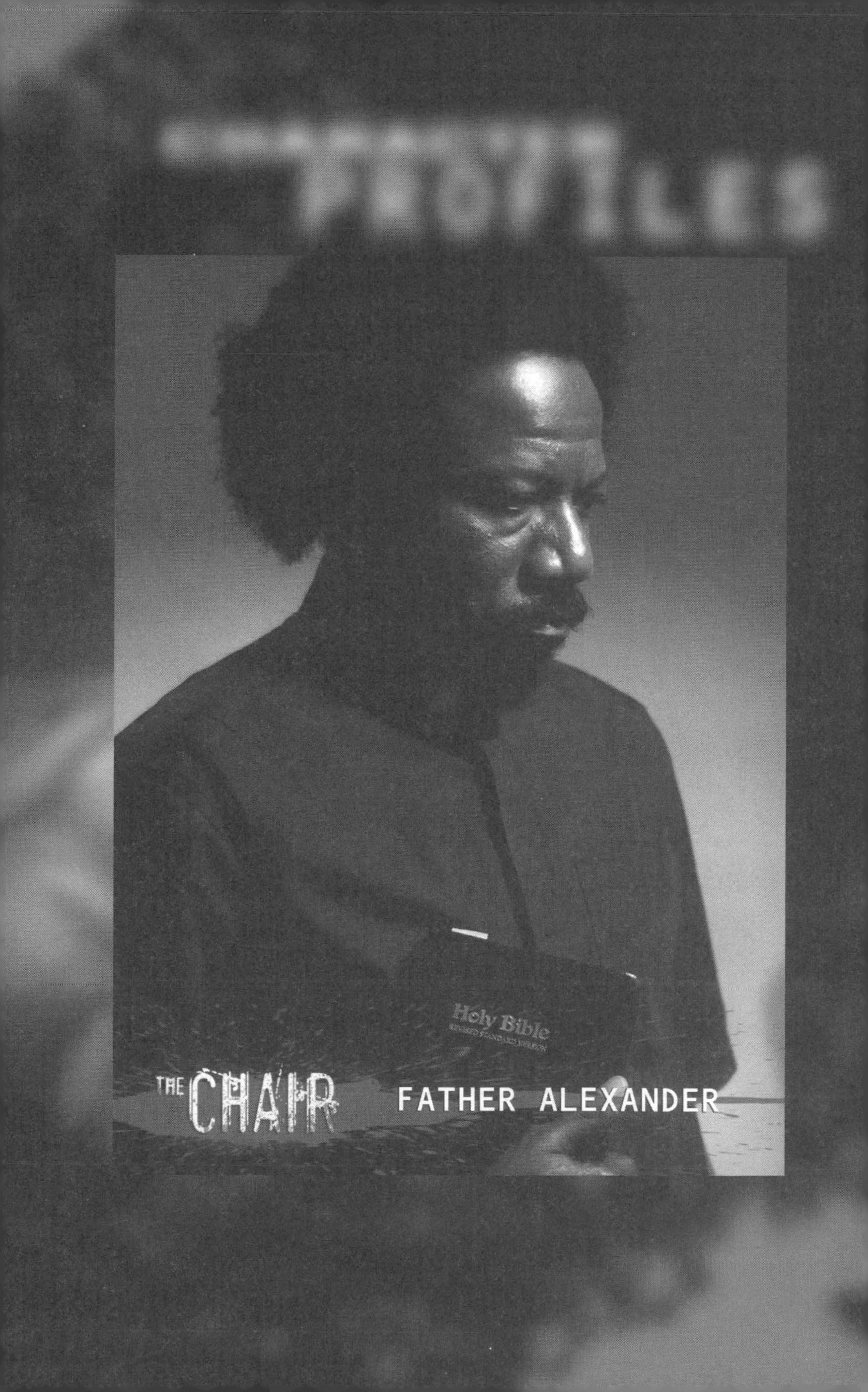
Holy Bible
THE CHAIR
FATHER ALEXANDER

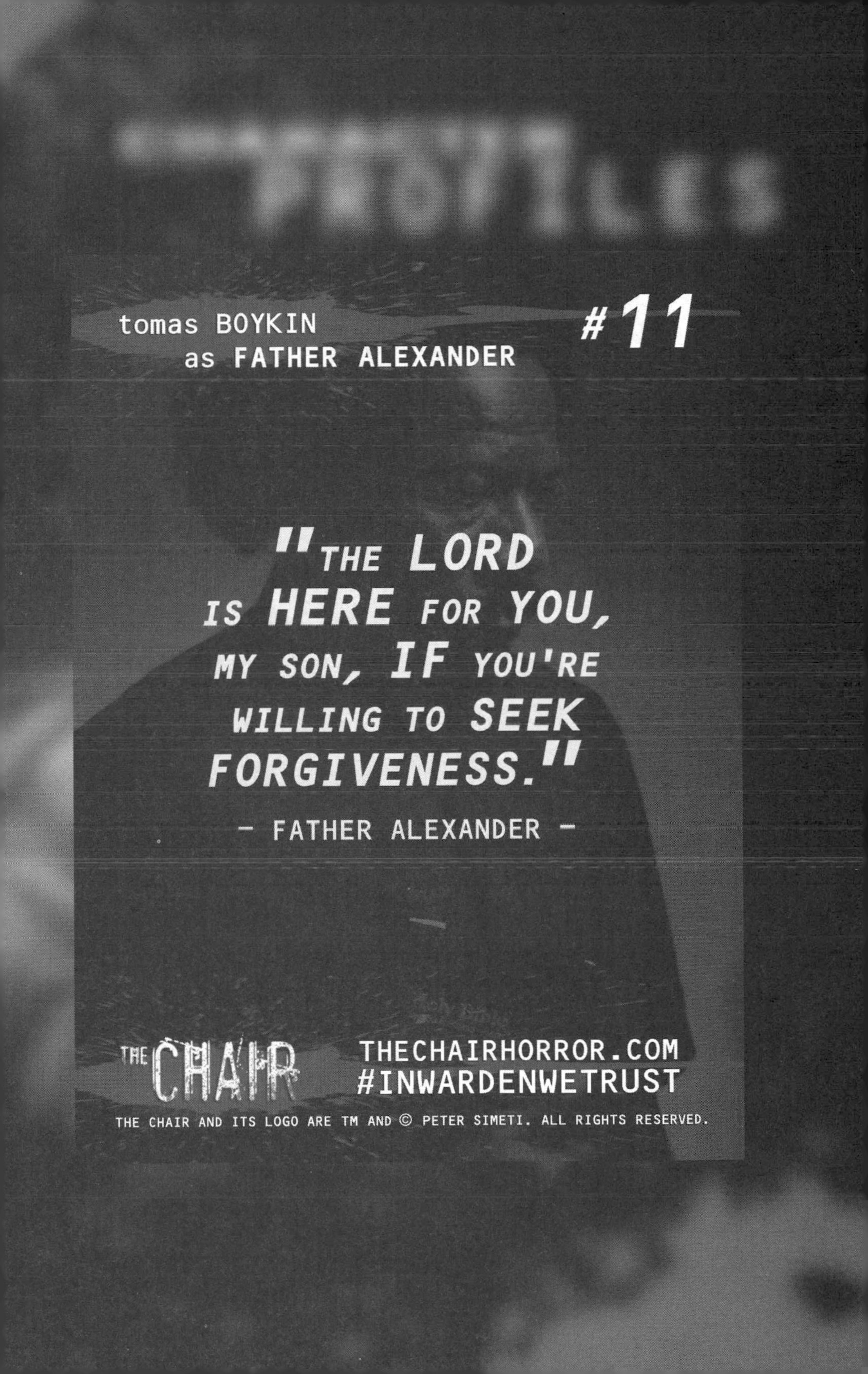
tomas BOYKIN
as FATHER ALEXANDER
#11
"THE LORD IS HERE FOR YOU, MY SON, IF YOU'RE WILLING TO SEEK FORGIVENESS."
- FATHER ALEXANDER -
THE CHAIR
THECHAIRHORROR.COM
#INWARDENWETRUST
THE CHAIR AND ITS LOGO ARE TM AND © PETER SIMETI. ALL RIGHTS RESERVED.

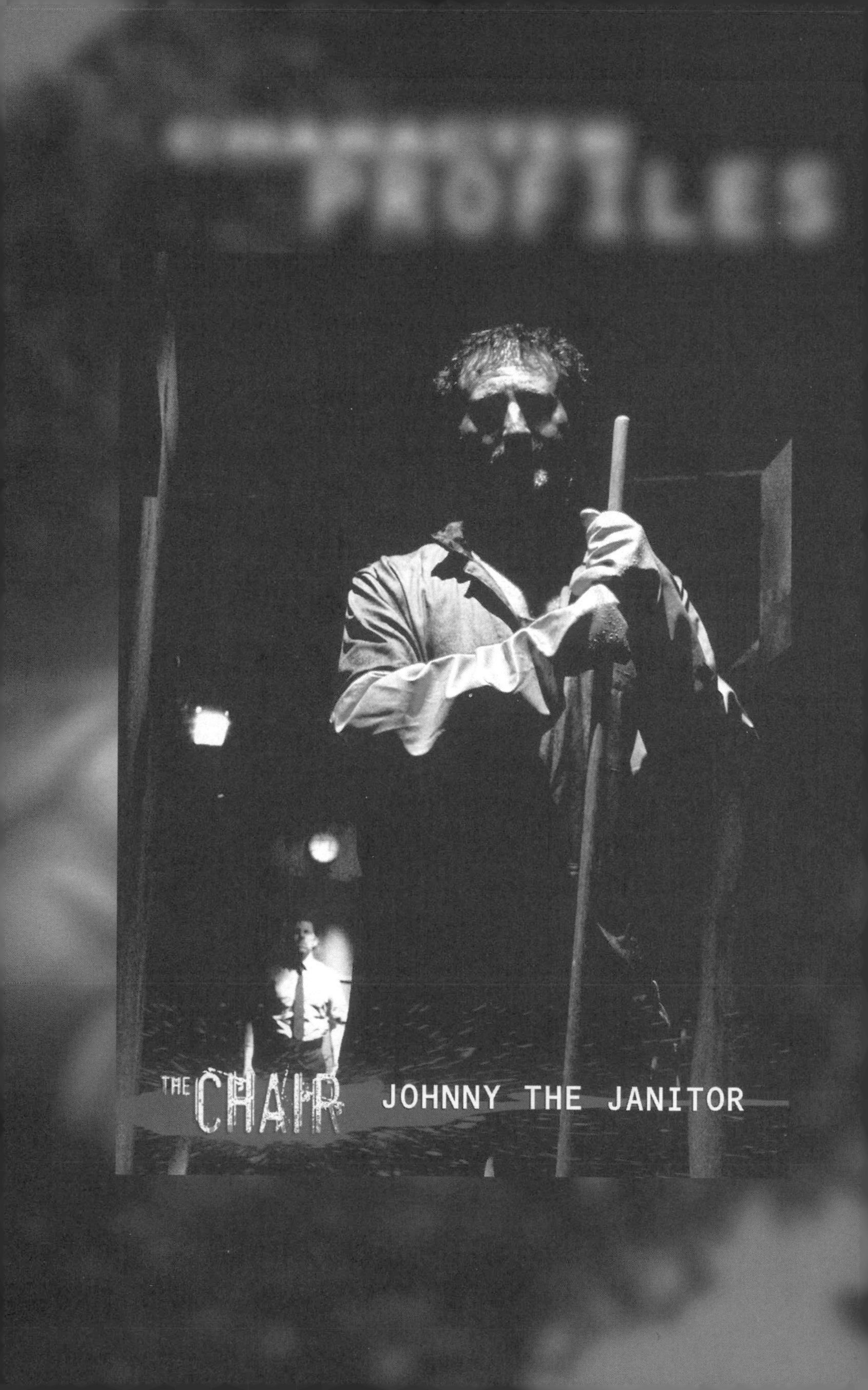
THE CHAIR
JOHNNY THE JANITOR

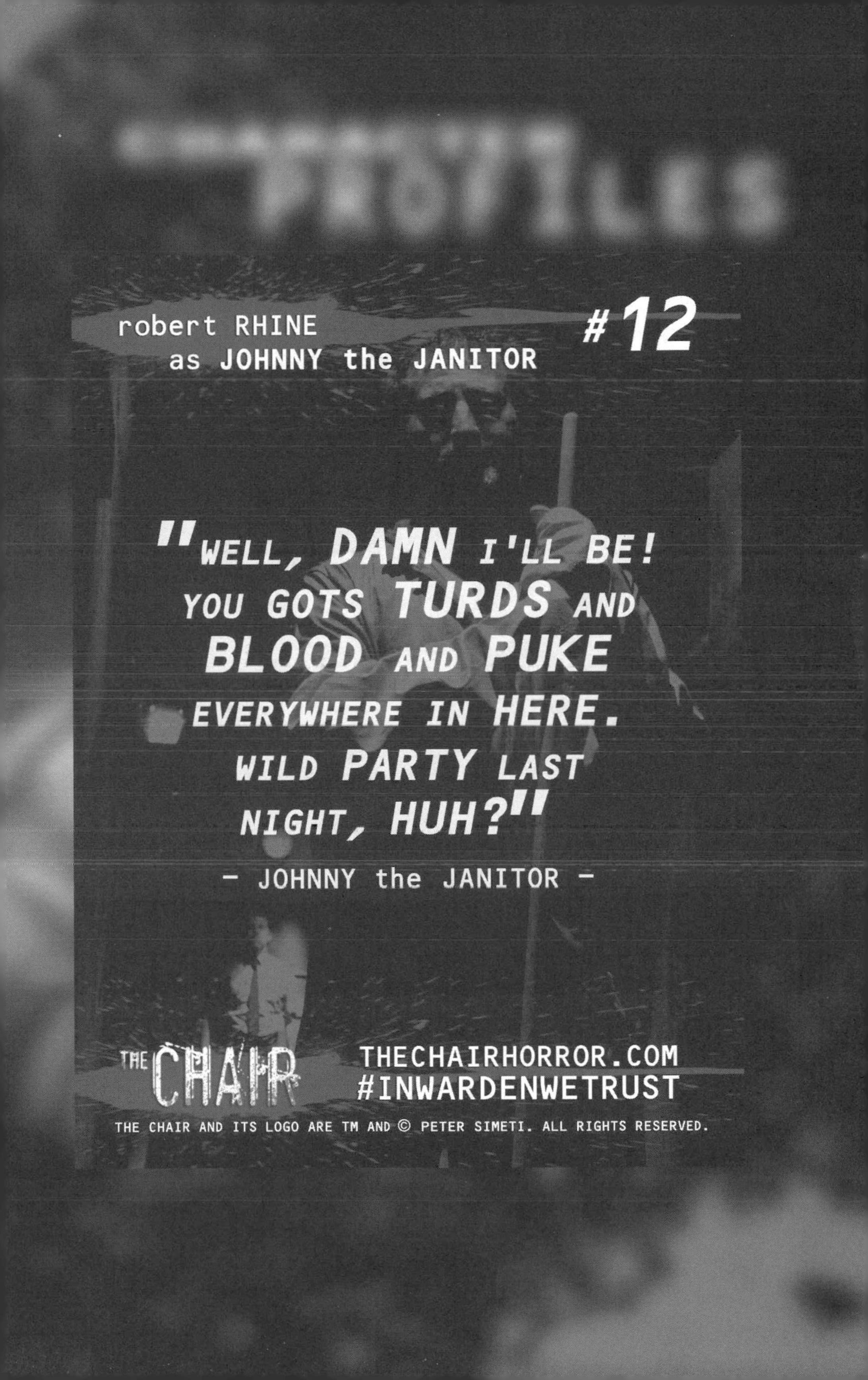
robert RHINE
as JOHNNY the JANITOR
#12
"WELL, DAMN I'LL BE! YOU GOTS TURDS AND BLOOD AND PUKE EVERYWHERE IN HERE. WILD PARTY LAST NIGHT, HUH?"
- JOHNNY the JANITOR -
THE CHAIR
THECHAIRHORROR.COM
#INWARDENWETRUST
THE CHAIR AND ITS LOGO ARE TM AND © PETER SIMETI. ALL RIGHTS RESERVED.

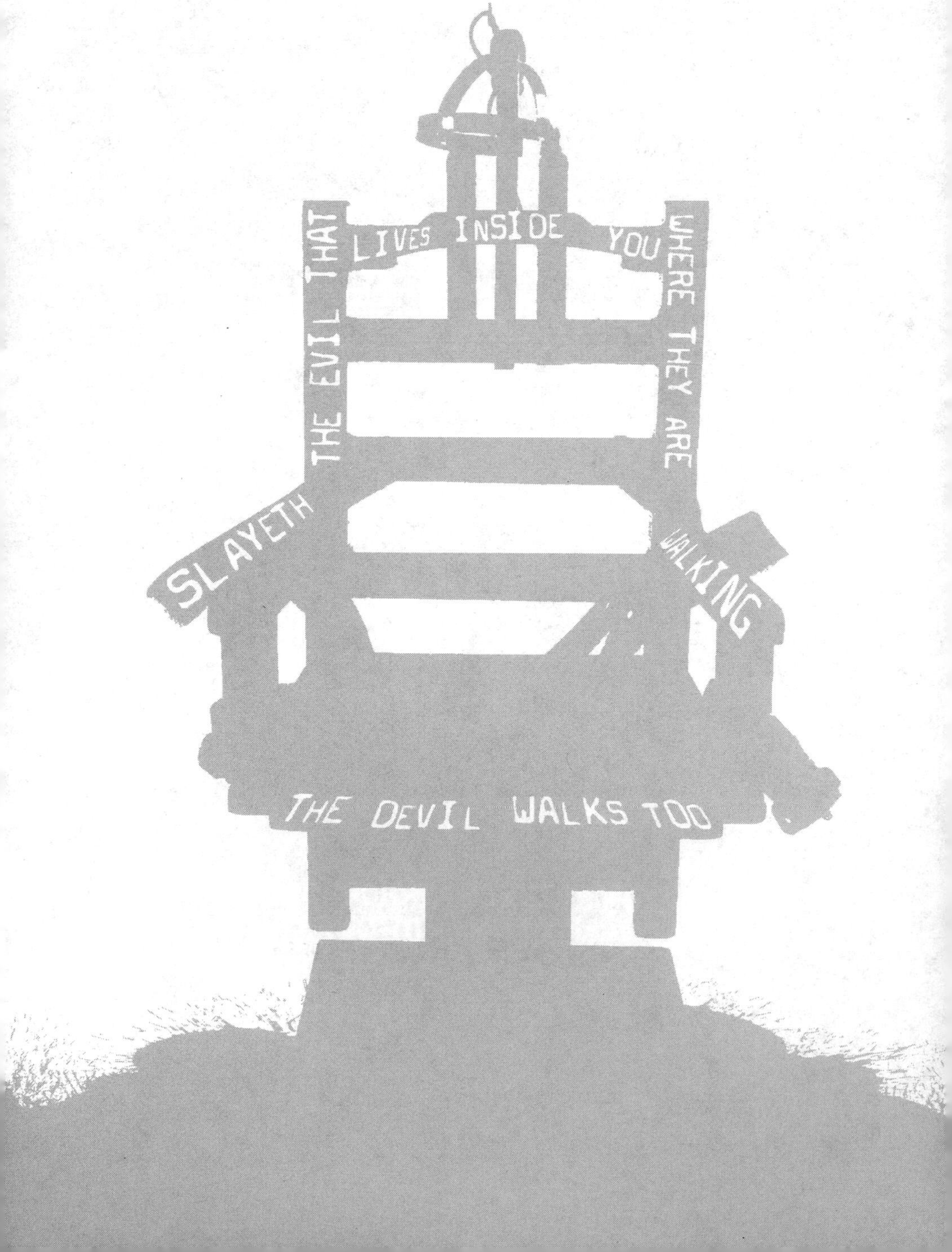
SLAYETH
THE EVIL THAT
LIVES INSIDE
YOU
WHERE THEY ARE
WALKING
THE DEVIL WALKS TOO